The Islamic World

Past and Present

The Islamic World

Past and Present

VOLUME 2

John L. Esposito, *Editor in Chief*

Associate Editors

Abdulaziz Sachedina

Tamara Sonn

John O. Voll

OXFORD UNIVERSITY PRESS
2004

Oxford University Press

Oxford New York

Auckland Bangkok Buenos Aires Cape Town Chennai Dar es Salaam
Delhi Hong Kong Istanbul Karachi Kolkata Kuala Lumpur Madrid Melbourne
Mexico City Mumbai Nairobi São Paulo Shanghai Taipei Tokyo Toronto

Published by Oxford University Press, Inc.
198 Madison Avenue, New York, 10016
http://www.oup.com

Developed for Oxford University Press by Visual Education Corporation, Princeton, NJ

For Oxford
PUBLISHER: Karen Day
EDITORIAL DEVELOPMENT DIRECTOR: Timothy DeWerff
EDITOR: Meera Vaidyanathan
EDITORIAL, DESIGN, AND PRODUCTION DIRECTOR: John Sollami
PROJECT EDITOR: Erica Pirrung
INTERIOR DESIGN: Maxson Crandall
COVER DESIGN: Mary Belibasakis

For Visual Education Corporation
PROJECT DIRECTORS: Jewel Moulthrop, Darryl Kestler
EDITORS: Carol Ciaston, Lauren Hauptman, Doriann Markey
ASSOCIATE EDITOR: Sarah Miller
WRITERS: Jean M. Brainard, John Haley, Kent M. Krause, Elizabeth Shostak
COPYEDITORS: Helen Castro, Maureen Pancza
ELECTRONIC PREPARATION: Fiona Shapiro
PHOTO RESEARCH: Susan Buschhorn
MAPS: Patti Isaacs, Parrot Graphics

Library of Congress Cataloging-in-Publication Data
The Islamic world : past and present / John L. Esposito, editor in chief ;
associate editors, Abdulaziz Sachedina . . . [et al.].
     p. cm.
Includes bibliographical references and index.
   ISBN 0-19-516520-9 (Hardcover 3 vol. set: alk. paper).—ISBN 0-19-517592-1
   (vol. 1 : alk. paper).—ISBN 0-19-517593-x (vol. 2 : alk. paper).—
   ISBN 0-19-517594-8 (vol. 3 : alk. paper).
 1. Islamic countries—Encyclopedias. 2. Islam—Encyclopedias.
I. Esposito, John L. II. Sachedina, Abdulaziz Abdulhussein, 1942-
   DS35.53 .I86 2004
   909'.097671'003—dc22

                              2003019665

Chronology of the Islamic World

Chronology of the Islamic World

747–750	*Abbasid family leads revolt against Umayyad dynasty*
750–1258	*Abbasid caliphate*
756	*Abd al-Rahman I ibn Mu'awiyah overthrows government of Andalusia and establishes amirate of Córdoba in Spain*
762	*Baghdad founded as capital of the Abbasid caliphate*
767	*Abu Hanifah, founder of Hanafi school of Islamic law, dies*
786–809	*Harun al-Rashid reigns as caliph; Abbasid power and cultural achievements reach peak*
795	*Malik ibn Anas, founder of Maliki school of Islamic law, dies*
801	*Rabiah al-Adawiyah, Sufi poet, dies*
813–833	*Al-Mamun reigns as caliph, encourages the development of Arabic science and literature*
820	*Muhammad al-Shafi'i, founder of Shafi'i school of Islamic law, dies*
836–892	*Abbasid capital moved from Baghdad to Samarra (Iraq)*
855	*Ahmad ibn Hanbal, founder of Hanbali school of Islamic law, dies*
859	*Islamic mosque-university, Qarawiyin, founded in Fez, Morocco*
874	*Abu al-Qasim Muhammad, son of the eleventh Shi'i imam, goes into hiding; becomes known as the Hidden Imam*
909	*Fatimid dynasty rises to power in Tunisia*
929	*Abd al-Rahman III establishes caliphate in Córdoba, Spain*
969–1171	*Fatimid dynasty conquers Nile Valley, eventually gaining control over Egypt and North Africa, Sicily, Syria, and Iraq; rivals the Abbasid caliphate*
970	*Al-Azhar University founded in Cairo*
977–1186	*Ghaznavid dynasty controls most of Afghanistan, Iran, and the Indus and Ganges Valleys*
1037	*Philosopher Ibn Sina, known in the West as Avicenna, dies*
1038–1194	*Seljuk dynasty rules Iraq, Iran, Syria, and parts of Central Asia; establishes a sultanate in Turkey*
1095	*Pope Urban II calls for a Crusade to take the Holy Land from the Muslims*
1099	*Christian crusaders occupy Jerusalem and establish Latin Kingdom*
1111	*Abu Hamid al-Ghazali, prominent theologian and legal scholar, dies*

1130–1269   *Almohad dynasty conquers North Africa and part of Spain*

1171–1250   *Ayyubid dynasty rules Egypt and Syria*

1187   *Saladin, leader of Ayyubids, defeats crusaders at Battle of Hittin and reconquers Jerusalem*

1198   *Philosopher Ibn Rushd, known as Averröes, dies*

1218   *Mongol ruler Genghis Khan sweeps across Central Asia into Iran*

1250–1517   *Mamluks, former slave soldiers in the Ayyubid army, establish dynasty in Egypt; extend control to Syria and western Arabia*

1258   *Mongols capture and destroy Baghdad, the Abbasid capital*

1273   *Jalal al-Din Rumi, poet and Sufi mystic, dies*

ca. 1300   *Osman I founds Ottoman Empire*

1334–1353   *The Alhambra is built in Granada, Spain*

1369–1405   *Mongol leader Tamerlane (Timur Lang) seizes power and reclaims former Mongol territories*

1406   *Historian Ibn Khaldun dies*

1453   *Ottoman sultan Mehmed II captures Constantinople*

1492   *Spanish monarchs Ferdinand and Isabella conquer Granada, driving Muslims from Spain*

1501   *Shah Ismail establishes Safavid empire in Iran*

1516–1517   *Ottomans conquer Egypt, Syria, and Islamic holy cities of Mecca and Medina*

1520   *Suleyman takes over as Ottoman sultan and brings the empire to peak of power and prosperity*

1526   *Battle of Mohacs brings Hungary under Ottoman control*

1526   *Mughal ruler Babur captures Delhi and establishes Mughal Empire in India*

1529   *Ottomans lay siege to Vienna, Austria*

1556–1605   *Mughal Empire in India reaches its height under the rule of Akbar I*

1571   *European victory at Battle of Lepanto off the coast of Greece stops Ottoman advance*

1588–1629   *Shah Abbas I rules Safavid Empire of Iran*

ca. 1645   *Mughal Shah Jahan completes Taj Mahal at Agra, India*

1658–1707   *Aurangzeb expands Mughal Empire through conquests; costs of military campaigns weaken the state*

Chronology of the Islamic World

1699	Ottoman Empire surrenders control of Hungary to Austria
1722	Afghan rebels capture the Safavid capital of Isfahan, bringing Safavid rule to an end
1750	Religious reformer Muhammad ibn Abd al-Wahhab joins forces with tribal chief Muhammad ibn Saud; the resulting Wahhabi movement conquers and unites tribes of Arabia
1798–1801	French armies led by Napoleon Bonaparte occupy Egypt
1803	British East India Company controls Delhi, seat of the Mughal Empire
1805	Muhammad Ali becomes Ottoman governor of Egypt and attempts to turn Egypt into a modern state
1809	Muslim reformer Usman Dan Fodio defeats Hausa rulers in Nigeria; establishes caliphate of Sokoto
1816	Dutch regain control of Indonesia from British
1821	Ottoman Empire takes control of Sudan
1830	French forces invade Algeria
1836	Ahmad ibn Idris, founder of Idrisi movement, dies
1857	Hindus and Muslims rebel against British rule in India; British depose last Mughal emperor
1869	Suez Canal opened in Egypt
1881	French troops invade and gain control of Tunisia
1882	British occupy Egypt
1885	In Sudan, forces of the Mahdi conquer Khartoum; establish Mahdist state
1898	Anglo-Egyptian invasion brings an end to Mahdist state in Sudan
1908	Young Turks overthrow sultan and restore constitutional government in Ottoman Empire
1914–1918	World War I
1919–1922	Ottoman Empire collapses
1921	Reza Khan seizes power in Iran; becomes Reza Shah Pahlavi in 1925
1922	British grant independence to Egypt but maintain control of foreign affairs
1923	Mustafa Kemal (later called Atatürk) establishes Turkish Republic
1928	Hasan al-Banna establishes Muslim Brotherhood in Egypt

1932 *The territories of Abd al-Aziz ibn Saud proclaimed the Kingdom of Saudi Arabia*

1935 *Persia renamed Iran*

1938 *Political writer Muhammad Iqbal, who led campaign in the Indian subcontinent for a separate Muslim state (Pakistan), dies*

1939–1945 *World War II*

1941 *Muhammad Reza Shah Pahlavi replaces Reza Shah in Iran*

1945 *The Arab League formed*

1947 *Pakistan is founded as a homeland for Indian Muslims*

1948 *The Jewish state of Israel is established*

1952 *Officers under the leadership of Gamal Abdel Nasser seize power in Egypt*

1954 *National Liberation Front (FLN) formed in Algeria and begins war against French rule*

1962 *Algerians win independence*

1964 *Founding of Palestine Liberation Organization (PLO)*

1965 *Malcolm X assassinated*

1966 *Sayyid Qutb, religious thinker and militant Islamic leader of the Muslim Brotherhood, is executed by Egyptian government*

1967 *Israeli victory in Six-Day War between Israel and Egypt, Syria, and Jordan*

1973 *October (Yom Kippur/Ramadan) War between Israel and Egypt and Syria*

1978 *Egyptian president Anwar el-Sadat and Israeli prime minister Menachem Begin sign peace agreement known as the Camp David Accords; peace treaty follows in 1979*

Coup in Afghanistan brings communist government to power; former Soviet Union occupies the country in 1979

1979 *Ayatollah Ruhollah Khomeini leads coalition of groups in Iranian Revolution, which overthrows the Pahlavi government and drives the shah of Iran into exile*

Iranians hold a group of Americans hostage at the United States embassy in Tehran

1980 *Hizbullah founded in Lebanon*

1980–1988 *Iran-Iraq War*

1981 *Muslim extremists assassinate Egyptian president Anwar el-Sadat*

Chronology of the Islamic World

1987 *Palestinians launch intifadah (uprising) in protest against Israeli occupation of the West Bank and Gaza*

1988 *Benazir Bhutto becomes prime minister of Pakistan; first female head of state elected in Muslim world*

1989 *Ayatollah Ruhollah Khomeini, head of Islamic Republic of Iran, dies*

1990–1991 *Iraq invades Kuwait, setting off the Persian Gulf War; United States and allies launch Operation Desert Storm against Iraq*

1992 *Resistance fighters (the Mujahidin) in Afghanistan defeat the country's communist government after 10 years of war and begin a battle for control of the country*

1993 *World Trade Center in New York City bombed; Shaykh Umar Abd al-Rahman charged with the attack*

1994 *Taliban fundamentalists take control in Afghanistan*

In West Bank city of Hebron, Jewish settler (Baruch Goldstein) kills worshippers at Friday prayer in Mosque of the Patriarch, provoking suicide bombings by military wing of Hamas

1997 *Election of Muhammad Khatami as president of Iran opens door to greater liberalization and contact with the West*

1998 *Increasing violence in Kosovo leads to international sanctions against the Yugoslavian (Serbian) government*

2001 *September 11: Members of al-Qaeda terrorist network hijack four American airliners and attack the World Trade Center in New York City and the Pentagon in Washington, D.C., killing about 3,000 people*

2001 *United States heads a military campaign against Afghanistan to destroy the al-Qaeda network and oust the Taliban*

2003 *Charging Iraq with failure to remove weapons of mass destruction, United States leads an invasion of the country and ends Saddam Hussein's regime*

Hizbullah

The term *hizb Allah* comes from the Qur'an and refers to the "soldiers of God" among Muslim believers, who form the "party of God" that will triumph over the Devil's party. Shi'is in Iran use the term *Hizbullah* to refer to their "Party of God," which they claim follows the teachings of Ayatollah Ruhollah al-Musavi Khomeini. The Hizbullah slogan states its philosophy as follows: "Only one party, the Party of Allah; only one leader, Ruhollah." Hizbullah (also spelled Hezbollah) groups have been most active in Iran and Lebanon since the 1980s.

Support for Iran's Revolution. Islamic activism in Iran dates back to the 1940s and 1950s, when scattered extremist organizations resisted injustices under the shah's autocratic rule and opposed his efforts to modernize society. They feared that modernization was just an excuse to "westernize" society, undermining traditional Islam and replacing it with nonreligious or anti-Islamic norms. This fear was heightened when they were denied the right to express their views. Some, including the Hizbullah, resorted to violence. In 1978 and 1979, members of Iran's Hizbullah played a central role in the organization of demonstrations and strikes that led to the downfall of Reza Shah Pahlavi's regime. Following the victory of the revolution, they served as unofficial watchdogs for the Islamic Republican party. Often recruited from poor city neighborhoods, members of Iran's Hizbullah used clubs, chains, knives, and guns to disrupt the rallies of opposing parties. They beat members of the opposition and ransacked their offices. The violent actions of Hizbullah led to the closing of universities, enforcement of veiling, suppression of the press, and intimidation of the people into silence. In addition, Iran's Hizbullah provided a steady supply of fighters eager to enlist in the war against Iraq in the 1980s. Although the Iranian Hizbullah has never achieved formal party status, it remains very active informally. Some Hizbullah squads have become private militias* for powerful clerics, and some are reported to have links to international terrorist organizations.

See map in Middle East (vol. 2).

* **militia** group of citizens organized for military service

Hizbullah groups have been very active in Iran and Lebanon since the 1980s. Here, Hizbullah soldiers rally in a southern Lebanese village to mourn the death of their leader by Israeli forces.

Attacks on the West. Lebanon's Hizbullah arose among Shi'is after the Iranian revolution and became a major political force during the 1980s. The organization gained international attention for its attacks against Israeli forces occupying southern Lebanon, its attacks against French and American troops in Lebanon, and its taking of Western hostages. Hizbullah has become the major rival of the established Amal movement in Lebanon, and it has as its stated goal the transformation of Lebanon into an Islamic state. The party has used both violence and parliamentary elections to further its goal.

In 1985 Lebanon's Hizbullah issued an "open letter" to the world stating that they "are proceeding toward a battle with vice at its very roots, and the first root of vice is America." The letter identified four goals—the termination of all American and French influence in Lebanon; Israel's complete departure from Lebanon as a "prelude to [Israel's] final obliteration;" submission of the Lebanese Phalangists (a Christian political party and militia sympathetic to Israel) to "just rule" and trial for their "crimes"; and allowance for people to choose their own system of government. Lebanon's Hizbullah has used both open and clandestine actions to carry out its program. It created a secret branch called Organization of the Islamic Jihad* to operate against Western targets. Islamic Jihad members conducted assassinations and bombing campaigns, and they implemented the policy of using suicide attackers in the struggle. Suicide attacks destroyed the command facilities of Israeli forces in 1982 and 1983; the Beirut barracks of American and French peacekeeping troops in 1983; and the U.S. Embassy and its annex in two separate attacks in Lebanon in 1983 and 1984. Hundreds of people died in these assaults, the worst of which killed 241 American marines in their barracks. Hizbullah has also conducted kidnappings and airline hijackings to free members imprisoned in Europe and the Middle East.

Lebanon's Hizbullah faced political change when a Syrian-backed government came to power in 1989. In Beirut and parts of the south, Hizbullah laid down its arms and turned over positions to the newly reconstructed Lebanese army. Islamic Jihad, however, remained exempt from this general disarming and continued to wage guerrilla* war against Israel in the south. Hizbullah gained credit for forcing the withdrawal of Israeli forces from Lebanon in 2000. Although Hizbullah did not accept the specifics of the Ta'if Accord that brought an end to the Lebanese civil war in 1989, it actively participated in the political system created by the agreement. In the 1992 parliamentary elections, it won the largest single bloc of seats—eight—and since that time, has been the leading opposition force to the Syrian-dominated governments of the late 1990s and early 2000s. (*See also* **Iran; Lebanon.**)

An International Dispute

The Canadian government's official position on Hizbullah has proven controversial. Although Canada banned the organization's militant wing in 2001, it recognized that Hizbullah's political wing supports humanitarian causes, such as schools and hospitals. Canadian leaders refused to add the group to its list of terrorist organizations that are banned from raising funds or recruiting new members in Canada. Hizbullah includes many supporters among Lebanese Muslims in Montreal, Toronto, and Vancouver.

In 2002 when Hizbullah leader Hassan Nasrallah urged Palestinians, in a live television broadcast from Lebanon, to "take suicide bombings worldwide," Jewish groups pressured Canada to reconsider its position. Later that year, Canada changed its policy and placed a total ban on Hizbullah and its activities.

* **jihad** literally "striving"; war in defense of Islam

* **guerrilla** unconventional warfare

Homosexuality

Recognizing the sexual nature of human beings, Islam teaches that sexuality provides an important balance in a person's life. Like Christianity and Judaism, Islam holds that sexual fulfillment should occur within the boundaries of marriage. Muslims view sex as an integral part of the relationship between a husband and a wife.

Islam teaches, however, that sex between members of the same sex violates God's natural order. Most Muslims view homosexual behavior as abnormal. The Qur'an* contains several passages suggesting that Allah does not approve of sexual activity between men. The book includes examples of wrath and destruction visited on those who engage in homosexual behavior. For example, it cites the nation of Lut, which God destroyed because the people practiced homosexuality. As with the story of Lot in the Old Testament, God allows the Prophet Lut and his family to escape, sparing all but his wife.

Some Islamic governments are especially opposed to homosexual activity. In Saudi Arabia, for example, gay men and women have no civil rights. Those convicted of homosexual activity may receive the death penalty. Iran takes a similar position on same-sex activity. Since that country's Islamic revolution in 1979, the government there has executed more than 4,000 homosexuals.

Other Muslim governments prosecute homosexuals for their "abuse of religion." In May 2001, the Egyptian government instituted a crackdown against openly gay activity. That month, the police rounded up more than 50 suspected homosexuals. An Emergency State Security Court prosecuted the cases. Those convicted, 23 in all, received sentences ranging from one to five years of hard labor. One suspect, a 16-year-old boy, received a three-year prison sentence. After his conviction, the youth stated that the police confined and beat him in order to extract a confession. Citing several civil rights violations, the international Human Rights Watch asked Egypt to overturn the boy's conviction.

Despite persecution, homosexuality continues to exist in the Muslim world, perhaps even encouraged by a system that seeks to segregate the sexes. Indeed, some parts of the Islamic world display tolerance toward gay men and women, viewing homosexuals as a "third sex." (*See also* **Sexuality**.)

* **Qur'an** book of the holy scriptures of Islam

Honor

In Islam, honor is culturally understood to be a sign of God's pleasure, and as such it is considered part of one's Muslim identity. Honor can be displayed in many ways including through ownership of land, social interactions, family solidarity, the chastity of women, and the personal characteristics of courage, generosity, hospitality, wisdom, honesty, and self-control.

The opposite of honor is shame. More specifically, shame comes as a result of dishonorable dealings and social failures, which may be self-inflicted or caused by another person. Honor and shame have long been part of various Islamic cultures. For centuries, Arab tribes in the early Muslim world valued bravery, independence, generosity, and self-control. They also considered honor a function of how well one could control interactions with others. Religious devotion, or piety, is perhaps the most important expression of honor, while the understanding of shame in the Islamic world centers on the absence, lapse, or loss of control.

Behavior guided by reason is considered honorable. Those dictated by emotions and uncontrolled appetites are thought of as shameful. Although negative, shame can motivate a person to declare a personal jihad, a striving for deeper religions devotion. Recognition of the significance of shame should keep people from shaming others. In fact, much of the ritual politeness displayed in Muslim society has to do with avoiding shame, shaming others, or calling attention to their shame.

Another type of honor has to do with a family's reputation. Hundreds, perhaps even thousands, of women in countries throughout the world are killed each year by their families in the name of honor. (As with other cultural practices, honor killings in the Islamic world exist in both Muslim and non-Muslim communities, such as among Arab Christians.) Exact numbers of honor killings are difficult to obtain because the vast majority are never reported. A woman can be killed by a male member of her family for a wide variety of offenses. Marital infidelity, divorce, and even rape can all be perceived as bringing shame and dishonor to a family. Nothing in the Qur'an permits or condones honor killings; pre-Islamic tribal norms are the source of this practice. Nonetheless, in many parts of the Muslim world, honor killings continue to be a problem. Several Islamic human rights organizations have emerged in recent years to end the practice. (*See also* **Human Rights; Women in the Qur'an.**)

Hostages

Hostages are people who are captured and held by a group in an effort to force a third party to comply with the group's demands. Hostage taking usually involves serious threats to the safety of the captives.

The Arabic term for hostages, *raha'in*, means persons held as security. Classical Islamic law, which developed from the 700s to the 1100s, permitted a Muslim country to exchange hostages with a non-Muslim state to ensure that the terms of a treaty were being upheld. Muslims were prohibited from killing the captives for any reason, even if the other party violated the agreement. If war broke out, Muslim forces were commanded to safely return the hostages to their country of origin. Furthermore, Islamic law prohibited the use of civilians as human shields to prevent attack in an armed conflict.

Islamic scholars also developed criteria for the treatment of non-Muslim civilians whose governments had no peace treaty with a Muslim country. During a war, these individuals could be detained, but they could not be used in negotiations with the enemy power. In other words, no captive could be considered a hostage.

After Islamic nations gained their independence from colonial rule in the mid-1900s, most of them formally approved the Geneva Conventions, a series of international treaties governing the treatment of soldiers and civilians during wartime. These agreements prohibit the taking of hostages.

Despite the requirements of Islamic and international law, hostage taking remains an issue in the Middle East. One of the most notorious cases occurred in Iran in 1979. After the American-supported regime of Reza Shah Pahlavi collapsed, Islamic revolutionaries seized control of the government. The Ayatollah Khomeini, Iran's political and religious leader, was bitterly

See map in Middle East (vol. 2).

opposed to the West and encouraged Iranians to engage in anti-American activities. In November 1979, Iranian students attacked the U.S. Embassy in Tehran and took 70 American hostages. Iran kept the captives for more than 400 days.

Members of guerrilla* groups or national liberation movements have justified the taking of hostages as a means of fulfilling their political goals. On June 14, 1985, Lebanese Shi'i* Muslims hijacked a TWA jet on its way from Athens to Rome. The terrorists, who were members of the Hizbullah organization, held 39 passengers captive in Lebanon and demanded the release of Lebanese prisoners being held in Kuwait, Israel, and Spain. In January 2002, Islamic terrorists in Pakistan kidnapped *Wall Street Journal* reporter Daniel Pearl. They killed Pearl when the United States did not respond to their demands for the release of Pakistanis held at the U.S. Naval Station at Guantanamo Bay, Cuba, in connection with the terrorist attacks of September 11, 2001. Although some Muslims have claimed that hostage taking is a practical necessity, most view it as un-Islamic and illegal. (*See also* **Khomeini, Ruhollah al-Musavi; September 11, 2001; Terrorism.**)

One of the most infamous hostage situations in the Middle East occurred in Iran in 1979. Angered by American support for Muhammad Reza Shah Pahlavi's regime, Iranian students attacked the U.S. Embassy in Tehran, taking 70 Americans hostage. In this 1981 photo, three of the former captives arrive in Germany after more than 400 days in captivity.

* **guerrilla** member of a group of fighters, outside the regular army, who engages in unconventional warfare

* **Shi'i** refers to Muslims who believe that Muhammad chose Ali ibn Abi Talib and his descendants as the spiritual-political leaders of the Muslim community

See *Capital Punishment.*

Hudud

Hukumah

See *Government*.

Human Rights

According to the standards of international law, men and women are equally entitled to certain rights and freedoms, regardless of race, religion, or nationality. Although all Muslim countries have adopted constitutions containing some or all of these principles, governments and individuals throughout the Islamic world take many different positions on human rights. At times, specific religious considerations dominate policy and practice.

Guiding Principles. A number of sources shape the individual and collective lives of Muslims. These include the Qur'an*, the sunnah*, hadiths*, *fiqh* (jurisprudence, a system or body of law), *madhhab* (schools of law), and the *shari'ah**. The Qur'an, however, is the foundation of Islamic faith and morality. According to its teachings, God gave human beings certain fundamental rights, including life, respect, justice, freedom, sustenance, work, and privacy. Because God granted these rights, no earthly government has the authority to amend them in any way, and every Muslim has the duty to uphold them.

For most of Islamic history, the concept of human rights was assumed under the fulfillment of obligations. Protection of the rights of humans involved the community of believers as a whole and the duties of all, including rulers, were defined in the relationship to God. Rulers were to govern in accordance with *shari'ah*, and subjects were to obey such rulers. In this context, Muslims did not separate the responsibilities and obligations involved in human rights from other aspects of faith and practice.

When Muslims began to define human rights in more modern terms in the 1800s, they adopted European concepts of government. Many officials,

* **Qur'an** book of the holy scriptures of Islam

* **sunnah** literally "the trodden path;" Islamic customs based on the exemplary behavior of Muhammad

* **hadith** reports of the words and deeds of Muhammad (not in the Qur'an, but accepted as guides for Muslim behavior)

* **shari'ah** Islamic law as established in the Qur'an and sunnah, the exemplary behavior of the Prophet Muhammad

Bosnian Muslims who had lost family members in the fighting of the early 1990s marched in Sarajevo in 2001. Demanding to know what happened to their loved ones, the demonstrators shown here carry a sign with the names and photos of the missing.

diplomats, and writers from Muslim countries spread the idea of constitutionalism—the idea that a government should operate according to established principles and laws and guarantee certain rights to the people under its rule. Some Muslims, such as Egyptian scholar Shaykh Rifaah Rafi al-Tahtawi and Persian diplomat Malkom Khan, argued that such concepts were in agreement with Islamic principles.

Guaranteed Rights. European powers also pressured the leaders of Muslim countries to incorporate human rights into the law. They sought to ensure equal legal protection for non-Muslims living in Islamic regions. In 1861 Tunisia became the first Muslim country to adopt a constitution. The document guaranteed equality for all citizens, regardless of religion, race, or nationality. Non-Muslims and Muslims would pay the same taxes.

Reformers compelled the government of the Ottoman Empire to approve a constitution in 1876. It mandated equal treatment for all, regardless of religion, and also included a provision for the freedom of the press. The constitution secured protections against unlawful arrests and property seizures.

The movement for human rights continued to spread in the early 1900s. Concern about the religious legitimacy of a constitution and its guaranteed rights led some governments to modify Western legal concepts. Persia's first constitution gave the country's inhabitants equal rights before the law. Shi'i* religious leaders, however, qualified some of the document's provisions to ensure that it did not conflict with Islam. For example, the constitution guaranteed freedom of the press, excluding publications considered heretical*. Islamic and Western concepts were also combined in the constitution of Afghanistan, which was adopted in the early 1920s. This document declared all residents to be equal regardless of religion. Nevertheless, the Afghan government forced Hindus and Jews to pay a special poll tax and to wear distinctive emblems on their clothing.

Despite these advances, the human rights movement faced significant barriers. Ironically, Europeans sometimes provided the opposition. For example, the French colonial government suspended Tunisia's constitution in 1881. In the 1920s, Turkey's secular* government repressed various Islamic groups. The communist* rulers of the Soviet Union restricted the religious freedoms of the Muslims of Central Asia. Marxist* regimes in Albania (1945–1991) and Afghanistan (1978–1992) also opposed the practice of Islam.

Variations on International Law. After World War II ended in 1945, international support for human rights increased. Muslim countries were among the founding members of the United Nations, whose charter called for fundamental freedoms and respect for human rights. In 1948 the United Nations issued a Universal Declaration of Human Rights. Despite some objections, every Muslim country, except Saudi Arabia, ratified the declaration.

Subsequent U.N. agreements generated considerable debate in the Muslim world. Opponents held that the United Nations based its human rights policies on Western or Judeo-Christian values. The organization's call for religious freedom was especially controversial. Many Muslims did not want to accept a person's right to convert from Islam to another religion. Others disliked provisions calling for full equality regardless of sex or religion.

In 1990 the Organization of the Islamic Conference (OIC)—an international organization founded in 1973 that includes most Muslim nations—

* **Shi'i** refers to Muslims who believe that Muhammad chose Ali ibn Abi Talib and his descendants as the spiritual-political leaders of the Muslim community

* **heretical** characterized by a belief that is contrary to established religious doctrine

* **secular** separate from religion in human life and society; connected to everyday life

* **communist** refers to communism, a political and economic system based on the concept of shared ownership of all property

* **Marxist** refers to a political philosophy that rejects capitalism and advocates a classless society

Cruel and Unusual Punishment?

Classical Islamic law divides the punishment for crimes into two categories: *hudud* are mandatory punishments established by God, and *tazir* are punishments at the discretion of a judge. The *hudud* punishments, which cover sexual activity outside of marriage, renunciation of faith, drinking alcoholic beverages, and theft, are severe. Human rights activists in the West have publicized and criticized the amputations of the limbs of thieves in Afghanistan, Saudi Arabia, Iran, Sudan, and Nigeria. Several justifications are offered for these penalties. Muslims believe that adultery, theft, and other crimes classified as *hudud* threaten the morality of the Muslim community and therefore must be severely punished. They also argue that *hudud* sentences deter others from committing the same crime, thus reducing crime rates.

* **polygyny** practice of having more than one wife at the same time

issued its own standards on human rights. The Cairo Declaration of Human Rights in Islam combined elements of international and Islamic law. All the freedoms described in the declaration were subject to the *shari'ah.* Notably absent were provisions calling for the observance of democratic principles in political systems and guarantees of freedom of religion, freedom of association, freedom of the press, and equal protection of the law.

Muslim nations vary in their commitment to the basic freedoms supported by the United Nations. Some regimes that claim to govern in the name of Islam are harsh and repressive, and groups that promote human rights in these nations risk persecution. Muslims continue to debate the relationship between Islamic law and international standards of human rights.

Women's Rights Debated. In the Muslim world, the issue of women's rights has been particularly divisive. Conservative Muslims maintain that the concept of full equality for women violates Islamic teachings. Liberals disagree, arguing that a society in which men are considered superior to women is un-Islamic. They hold that an inadequate study of the Qur'an and other religious guidelines has led to discrimination against women.

Liberal Muslims first addressed women's issues in the late 1800s. Egyptian writer Qasim Amin believed that the inferior status of women in the Middle East was not a product of Islam but a product of non-Muslim social customs and influences. He linked the fight for women's freedom to larger human rights issues. In 1930 Tunisian scholar al-Tahir al-Haddad advanced the idea that Islam mandates full equality for women, and he advocated the reform of Islamic law. Conservative Muslims denounced him as a heretic.

The most dramatic reform in the Arab world was the Tunisian Law of Personal Status of 1956. Presented as an Islamic law, the code improved the status of women by abolishing polygyny* and establishing equal rights for men and women in divorce.

Today most Muslim nations continue to deny full civil and political rights to women, despite constitutional provisions that guarantee the equality of all citizens. Many Muslim leaders have held that Islamic law justifies preserving gender inequality. (*See also* **Democracy; International Law and Diplomacy; Minorities; Modernism; Women and Reform.**)

Husayn ibn Ali

626–680
Shi'i Muslim leader

* **caliph** religious and political leader of an Islamic state

* **imam** spiritual-political leader in Shi'i Islam, one who is regarded to be directly descended from Muhammad; also, one who leads prayers

* **Shi'i** refers to Muslims who believe that Muhammad chose Ali ibn Abi Talib and his descendants as the political-spiritual leaders of the Muslim community

Husayn ibn Ali was Muhammad's grandson and son of Fatimah, the Prophet's daughter. His father was Ali ibn Abi Talib, Muhammad's cousin and devoted follower, who became the fourth Muslim caliph* and the first imam* of the Shi'i* branch of Islam. The Shi'i revere Husayn as their third imam and as a martyr.

After Ali's assassination in 661, Husayn's older brother, Hasan, became caliph and second imam. Hasan soon abdicated, however, in favor of Mu'awiyah, a powerful clan leader and political rival who established the Umayyad caliphate. While Husayn reluctantly recognized Mu'awiyah's rule, he refused to pledge allegiance to him. Husayn believed that, as direct descendants of Muhammad, Ali's sons were the rightful heirs to the caliphate.

When Mu'awiyah died in 680, the caliphate passed to Yazid, Mu'awiyah's son and chosen successor. Husayn refused to recognize the legitimacy of Yazid's rule and again withheld his allegiance to the Umayyads. Yazid, however, threatened to kill anyone not loyal to him, prompting Husayn to flee to Mecca seeking sanctuary.

Shi'i Muslims in Kufa, a city in Iraq, asked Husayn to lead them in a revolt against Yazid and to claim his rightful position as caliph. Husayn's cousin, Muslim ibn Aqil, verified that he had strong support in Iraq. Husayn then set out for Kufa with family members and followers. The governor of Iraq, a supporter of Yazid, sent 4,000 men to intercept the caravan. At Karbala, this force trapped Husayn's small band, which numbered less than 100. He refused to surrender, however, and led his men out into battle, where they were massacred. The Iraqi governor displayed the heads of Husayn and his followers in Kufa as a warning to other Umayyad enemies.

Husayn's martyrdom is considered a defining event in Shi'i Islam. Few personalities in Muslim history have had as enduring an influence on Islamic thought and piety as Husayn. His death provided his followers with a new passion. Shi'i Islam gained in strength, ensuring the continuance of Husayn's legacy. Shi'i Muslims still consider a pilgrimage to his tomb in Karbala second in importance only to the hajj*. Modern Muslim political groups draw inspiration from Husayn as a symbol of resistance against tyranny. (*See also* **Ali ibn Abi Talib; Karbala and Najaf; Shi'i Islam; Umayyad Caliphate.**)

* **hajj** pilgrimage to Mecca that Muslims are required to make once in their lifetime

Ibn al-Arabi

1165–1240
Sufi mystic and writer

* **shaykh** tribal elder; also, title of honor given to those who are considered especially learned and pious
* **Sufi** refers to Sufism, which seeks to discipline the mind and body in order to experience directly the presence of God

Muhyi al-Din ibn al-Arabi, known as "the greatest shaykh*," was a mystic spiritual guide and poet who many believe created a systematic Sufi* philosophy. His ideas sparked much debate during his lifetime and still provoke controversy in the Muslim world.

Ibn al-Arabi was born in Murcia, Spain, to a prominent family that included a number of Sufis. He studied with numerous masters, including one who was so impressed with the boy that he turned pale and began trembling after their first meeting. At the age of 33, Ibn al-Arabi had a vision that inspired him to leave Spain and travel east. He visited the holy city of Mecca, where he received a divine commandment to begin his most important work, *The Meccan Revelations*. This huge book (560 chapters) discusses the mystical sciences of Islam, as Ibn al-Arabi understood them, and reveals much about the author's inner spiritual life.

While in Mecca, Ibn al-Arabi also met a young, beautiful girl whom he viewed as the embodiment of eternal wisdom. He wrote a book of love poems, *The Interpreter of Desires*, adding his own commentary to the verses. In later life, Ibn al-Arabi composed what many consider a leading work in mystical philosophy, the *Bezels* of Wisdom.

In his writings, Ibn al-Arabi emphasized the "oneness of being." He claimed that the only true reality is God, who, according to Muhammad, is a hidden treasure desiring to be known. The universe serves as a mirror for God with each aspect manifesting one of God's names. In each age, one per-

* **bezel** rim around an transparent disk, as of a watch; facet of a gem

son appears who contains all of these names. This person serves both as a microcosm of God and as God's most perfect mirror. Ibn al-Arabi believed that such a person could worship God in any form—through the Qur'an*, the Hebrew Torah*, or any other system of belief. He further contended that God is the source of all love and beauty and that any appreciation of love and beauty is really an appreciation of God. A man's admiration of a woman serves as the most perfect example.

Critics have denounced Ibn al-Arabi's teachings as pantheistic* and have accused him of worshipping Muhammad as a god, idolizing women, and making all religions appear equal. Ibn al-Arabi's interpretations of the Qur'an are viewed by many as dangerous, and his version of Sufism is widely considered extreme. During his lifetime, some Egyptian scholars wanted him executed as a heretic*, and Egyptian groups still attempt to ban his works. Ibn al-Arabi's writings, however, continue to influence Sufi orders, which distribute them in a simplified and popular form. (*See also* **Sufism.**)

* **Qur'an** book of the holy scriptures of Islam

* **Torah** first five books of the old Testament, constituting the holy scripture of Judaism

* **pantheism** belief that divinity is inherent in all creation

* **heretic** person whose belief or practice is contrary to established religious doctrine

Ibn Hanbal

780–855
Muslim jurist and theologian

* **Sunni** refers to the largest branch of the Muslim community; the name derives from sunnah, the exemplary behavior of the Prophet Muhammad

* **doctrine** principle, theory, or belief that is taught or presented for acceptance

* **Qur'an** book of the holy scriptures of Islam

* **caliph** religious and political leader of an Islamic state

Ahmad ibn Hanbal was a leading scholar of hadith, the reported words and deeds of the Prophet Muhammad. His most important work is the *Musnad*, a major collection of hadith traditions. Ibn Hanbal's followers later founded the Hanbali school of legal thought, one of the major Sunni* schools of law.

Ibn Hanbal began studying hadith at age 15 and traveled widely to learn from the leading Islamic scholars of his time. His austere life of self-denial, strict discipline, and devotion to his faith won him many admirers. Ibn Hanbal became most famous for his stand against the doctrine* that the Qur'an* was created. According to this view, God chose to reveal His will to humanity in a specific context—through the person of Muhammad. The Prophet put God's revealed will into words that human beings could understand. Some caliphs* supported this position, arguing that they, therefore, had the right to interpret the text.

Ibn Hanbal, however, rejected this idea and defended the view that the Qur'an was uncreated and that the word of God is eternal and unchangeable. Only its expression by the Prophet Muhammad and its recording by human beings had occurred in history. Ibn Hanbal believed that, for this reason, only religious scholars could interpret the Qur'an. The caliph's role was to carry out the laws and customs of the Islamic community, not to serve as the source of Islamic beliefs. Ibn Hanbal even suggested that the law should not be written at all and that scholars should answer legal questions based solely on their reading of religious texts.

Ibn Hanbal's beliefs brought him into conflict with the caliph al-Mamun. In 833 al-Mamun required all Muslims to adopt the doctrine that the Qur'an was created. Ibn Hanbal refused to do so, a move that challenged the authority of the caliph, and for which he was beaten and imprisoned. Ibn Hanbal was greatly admired by conservative* Muslims for refusing to abandon his beliefs. The next caliph, al-Wathiq, continued to suppress Ibn Hanbal's teachings. Ibn Hanbal's popularity, however, kept the new caliph from

* **conservative** generally opposed to change, especially in existing political and social institutions

harming him. The campaign against Ibn Hanbal ended in 848, during the reign of caliph al-Mutawakkil, who returned the caliphate* to the view that the Qur'an was uncreated. (*See also* **Law.**)

* **caliphate** office and government of the caliph, the religious and political head of an Islamic state

Ibn Khaldun

1332–1406
Historian and philosopher

* **sociology** study of society and social institutions

The Islamic thinker Abd al-Rahman ibn Khaldun is best known for his historical writings and his theories about political development in the Arab world. Because he was one of the first scholars to carefully examine human social organization, some people consider him the father of sociology*. Many historians also see him as a pioneer in the study of history as a science.

Ibn Khaldun was born in the North African city of Tunis at a time when that part of the Arab Muslim empire was in decline. He held several government positions, including secretary of state and ambassador, before moving to Cairo in 1382, where he taught and served as a judge. Driven to discover the reason for the political turmoil of his day, Ibn Khaldun began to apply the principles of philosophy to history. Before this time, philosophers had ignored the study of history because it dealt with only passing events, not eternal truths. Ibn Khaldun, however, believed that human society was governed by universal laws and that one could uncover them through study. He took a scientific approach to history, formulating theories based on his careful observations.

Ibn Khaldun argued that *asabiyah*, or social solidarity, enables a group to acquire power and to survive. It also leads the group to conquer others and establish its own state. The luxury and leisure of urban life, he believed, weakens the group and leads to its decline. This allows a stronger group to conquer the old one, thus starting the cycle of rise and decline over again. Ibn Khaldun's ideas emphasized the differences between nomadic and settled societies, as well as his belief that nomadic societies had a superior sense of solidarity.

Ibn Khaldun also wrote about tyranny, observing that it usually leads to egotism* in rulers. He stressed the need for social control of human activities. Some modern scholars believe that Ibn Khaldun's ideas apply only to the age in which he lived. Others compare his teachings with those of Machiavelli and other European scholars. Ibn Khaldun produced two major works—*Autobiography*, a frank evaluation of his career, and a large work of history. In the introduction, or *Muqaddimah*, to this work, he makes his most important observations concerning the rise and fall of civilizations. (*See also* **Historians.**)

* **egotism** exaggerated sense of one's own importance

Ibn Rushd

1126–1198
Physician, judge, and philosopher

Ibn Rushd, known in the West as Averroës, was a physician and religious judge in Muslim Spain. He was also one of the greatest thinkers of the Muslim world and a follower of the Greek philosopher Aristotle. Ibn Rushd became well known for his writings on Aristotle, earning him the name of "The Commentator."

Ibn Rushd

A physician and religious judge, Ibn Rushd is a revered figure in the history of Islamic philosophy. This memorial statue of him resides in his birthplace of Córdoba, Spain.

* **theology** study of the nature and qualities of God and the understanding of His will

* **Qur'an** book of the holy scriptures of Islam

* **theologian** study of the nature and qualities of God and the understanding of His will

* **mystic** one who seeks to experience spiritual enlightenment through various physical and spiritual disciplines

* **treatise** long, detailed essay on a particular subject

Ibn Rushd was born in the Spanish city of Córdoba to a well-educated and cultured family. Both his father and grandfather served as judges in that city. Ibn Rushd devoted most of his time to scholarly pursuits, studying mathematics, medicine, Islamic law, and theology*. He later became a physician and chief judge at the royal court in Muslim Spain.

In his philosophical commentaries, Ibn Rushd tried to harmonize the teachings of the Qur'an* with those of Aristotle. He believed that religion and philosophy had the same goal—to help people live according to the truth so they could achieve salvation after death. He thought that religion was for everybody but that philosophy should be reserved for the most intelligent members of society. He argued that a philosopher-king, who could establish order and provide laws to guide the masses toward proper action, ruled in an ideal society.

Ibn Rushd's best known philosophical study is *The Incoherence of the Incoherence.* This was written in response to an earlier attack on philosophy, *The Incoherence of the Philosophers*, by Muslim theologian* and mystic* Abu Hamid al-Ghazali (died 1111). In addition to his philosophical works, Ibn Rushd produced commentaries on medicine, law, music, astronomy, and logic. His important medical treatise*, known in Latin as *Colliget*, sheds light on the prevention, diagnosis, and cure of many diseases.

Ironically, Ibn Rushd's writings became better known in the West than in the Islamic world. For many medieval* Europeans, his commentaries on Aristotle were their only source of knowledge about ancient Greek philosophy. His work influenced Jewish and Christian philosophers, including Maimonides and Thomas Aquinas. Some Islamic religious scholars, on the other hand, condemned Ibn Rushd's work as unorthodox*, even though he was a devout Muslim. (*See also* **Ghazali, Abu Hamid al-; Philosophy.**)

* **medieval** refers to the Middle Ages, a period roughly between A.D. 500 and 1500

* **unorthodox** contrary to accepted beliefs and practices

Ibn Sina

980–1037
Persian physician and philosopher

Also known by his Latin name, Avicenna, Ibn Sina was a famous and influential philosopher in the Islamic world. Trained as a physician and scientist, he worked as a doctor by day and wrote about philosophy, science, and medicine at night. *Canon of Medicine*, one of the most highly regarded books in the history of medicine, includes information on herbs, organ diseases, fevers, surgery, and other subjects. Ibn Sina based the *Canon of Medicine* on the writings of ancient Greek physicians as well as his own experiences as a doctor. His most noted philosophical work, the *Book of Healing*, is a vast encyclopedia of science, mathematics, psychology, music, logic, and other subjects. It is probably the largest work of its kind written by a single author. Scholars translated both books into Latin in the 1100s, spreading Ibn Sina's knowledge and ideas throughout the West.

Born in Bukhara, a city in present-day Iran, Ibn Sina grew up in an intellectual household where his father held gatherings with leading scholars. By the age of 10, he memorized the Qur'an* and a large amount of Arabic poetry. Teaching himself after he had surpassed his masters, Ibn Sina became proficient in law, medicine, the sciences, and many other branches of learning. He was recognized as an outstanding physician at the age of 16 and was in great demand by the time he was 21.

Turkish invasions, however, swept through Persia and forced Ibn Sina to leave his home, a pattern that continued throughout his life. Ibn Sina spent some time in prison and in hiding to avoid his enemies. Despite these setbacks, he continued to study, write, and practice medicine. Ibn Sina wrote nearly 200 treatises on various subjects. He became a court physician and vizier* and held discussions with students in the evening. These sessions often continued until late in the night, involving musical performances and boisterous parties. Ibn Sina's strong physical constitution enabled him to carry on such a lifestyle, but he died at 57 of a stomach ailment and exhaustion while accompanying a Persian ruler on a battle campaign.

A follower of the ancient Greek philosophers, Ibn Sina tried to reconcile the writings of Aristotle and Plato with the teachings of the Qur'an. To that end, he developed his own system of religious philosophy. It rested on the concept of God as the original being, whose self-contemplation brings forth the universe and all other entities. Like his mentor Abu Nasr al-Farabi, Ibn Sina believed that prophets learn divine truths through intuition and insight rather than through logical processes. They have the most perfect understanding of God and communicate their knowledge through images and symbols.

* **Qur'an** book of the holy scriptures of Islam

* **vizier** Muslim minister of state

Ibn Sina's writings influenced Sufi* scholars, such as Ibn al-Arabi, as well as other Muslim philosophers. Many of his ideas, however, run contrary to traditional Islamic views. Ibn Sina's belief that the world was created from the thoughts of God contradicts the orthodox* Islamic view that it emerged from nothing. Nonetheless, his works continue to inspire philosophers, physicians, and scientists from all over the world. (*See also* **Farabi, Abu Nasr al-; Ibn al-Arabi; Medicine; Philosophy; Sufism.**)

Ibn Taymiyah

1263–1328
Thinker and political figure

Taqi al-Din Ahmad ibn Tamiyah was a controversial thinker and prominent political figure who was persecuted for his unorthodox* ideas. As a young boy, he fled with his family from a Mongol invasion and settled in the Syrian city of Damascus. Descended from a long line of Sunni* scholars, Ibn Tamiyah studied religion and became the head of a local mosque* and a professor of the Hanbali school of law by his mid-twenties.

Ibn Tamiyah attacked many of the religious movements, such as Shi'ism* and Sufism* that arose after the Prophet Muhammad and his first four successors. His essential argument was that the Qur'an*, the sunnah*, and the practices of early Muslims were the supreme and authoritative sources of Islam. He criticized the veneration* of saints, a popular practice in the Muslim world, as sinful. Ibn Tamiyah also rejected the practice of relying on established judgments with regard to Islamic law. Ibn Tamiyah believed that Muslim legal experts should combine careful reasoning with a thorough reading of sacred texts to find solutions to legal issues.

These ideas outraged many of the *ulama* (religious scholars), who viewed such teachings as a threat to their authority. Ibn Tamiyah was persecuted and jailed in Egypt and Syria, where he eventually died. Ibn Tamiyah influenced later thinkers, such as Hasan al-Banna and Sayyid Qutb, and his ideas are important in the Wahhabi movement. Some Islamic groups have even used Ibn Tamiyah's teachings to justify revolution against their governments. (*See also* **Ijtihad; Muslim Brotherhood; Qutb, Sayyid; Wahhabi.**)

Iconography

See *Art*.

Idrisi

The term *Idrisi* refers to a Sufi* spiritual tradition based on the writings and teachings of Moroccan scholar Ahmad ibn Idris (ca. 1749–1837). His followers later established Muslim brotherhoods and schools to spread the tradition. Idrisi also refers to a specific religious order that was founded by Ahmad ibn Idris's son some 40 years after Ibn Idris's death.

Ibn Idris was a teacher who wrote numerous prayers and recitations*. In his writings, he attacked authority and emphasized the individual's duty to seek union with God. He opposed schools of Islamic law and philosophers who considered themselves to be higher authorities than the average Muslim. He believed that God alone grants each Muslim an understanding of the Qur'an* and sunnah*.

Through his students, Ahmad ibn Idris's teachings spread throughout the Islamic world. The Idrisi tradition reached not only the rest of North Africa and the Middle East, but also India, Sudan, and the East African coast. It eventually spread to Malaysia, Thailand, and Indonesia, most likely carried there by pilgrims returning from Mecca and other holy cities.

In the mid-1800s, one of Ibn Idris's younger sons, Abd al-Al (1830/31–1878), worked actively to continue his father's religious traditions by establishing the Idrisi order. The order remained small and localized in Egypt and Sudan, and it avoided involvement in politics until the early 1900s. Ibn Idris's great-grandson, commonly known as "The Idrisi" (1876–1923), led a successful revolt against the Ottoman Empire and Yemen in 1907 in the Arabian province of Asir and established an Idrisi state there. Between 1908 and 1932, Asir played an important role in Arabian politics. After the Idrisi died, however, Asir rapidly declined and was eventually absorbed into Saudi Arabia. (*See also* **Muslim Brotherhood; Sufism.**)

* **recitation** verbal passage meant to be read or spoken aloud

* **Qur'an** book of the holy scriptures of Islam

* **sunnah** literally "the trodden path"; Islamic customs based on the exemplary behavior of Muhammad

Ijtihad

The Arabic term *ijtihad* means "the utmost effort an individual can put forth in an activity." In a legal sense, it refers to independent reasoning, a scholar's careful and complete use of mental abilities to find a solution to a legal problem.

During the early years of Islamic society, when religious law was being formulated, qualified jurists practiced a type of *ijtihad*, known as *ra'y*. In cases where the Qur'an* and sunnah* did not provide clear guidelines for a decision, jurists used *ra'y* to render legal decisions that were intended to serve the interests of the Muslim community.

As religious law developed, *ra'y* came to be considered insufficiently rigorous to ensure that legal judgments were in keeping with the Qur'an and sunnah. At the same time, the meaning and scope of *ijtihad* became more clearly defined. *Ijtihad* was limited to a systematic method of interpreting the law on the basis of authoritative texts (the Qur'an and sunnah). According to this method, the ruling of the Qur'an and sunnah may be extended to a new problem as long as the precedent* and the new situation share the same cause.

The practice of *ijtihad* became a religious duty and a *mujtahid* (one qualified to practice *ijtihad*) who failed to use it was thought to have sinned. According to Islamic legal theory and practice, a jurist must meet certain requirements to become a *mujtahid*. The individual must have a thorough knowledge of Arabic, the Qur'an, and the sunnah, as well as of legal theory and precedent.

* **Qur'an** book of the holy scriptures of Islam

* **sunnah** literally "the trodden path;" Islamic customs based on the exemplary behavior of Muhammad

* **precedent** prior example that serves as a model

By the beginning of the 900s, the Sunni* jurists believed that all major matters of religious law had been addressed. Following established legal precedents and traditions, or *taqlid*, became more important than *ijtihad*. Unlike the Sunnis, however, Shi'i Muslims* continued to emphasize the importance of *ijtihad*. Although both branches of Islam accept the Qur'an as the primary source of law, they rely on different sets of prophetic traditions. While the Sunnis believe in consensus as the source of truth after the time of the Prophet, Twelver Shi'is consider the sayings and writings of the twelve imams* to be infallible. Accordingly, Twelvers acknowledge human reasoning and intellect as a legal source that supplements the Qur'an and other revealed texts.

During the 1600s, Sunni reformers began to criticize *taqlid* and called for greater practice of *ijtihad* in legal matters. They argued that jurists should not rely on the practices developed by generations of religious scholars. Instead, they should establish doctrine and rules of behavior by interpreting the original and sacred sources of Islam—the Qur'an and the sunnah.

In recent years, Muslim reformers have advocated the replacement of *taqlid* with *ijtihad* as a way to confront legal issues raised by contact with modern Western society. In practice, Islamic jurists have typically revised the law in response to specific issues, making virtually no attempt to build a new legal philosophy on which to base necessary changes to existing Islamic law. As a result, some scholars question whether their efforts can even be considered *ijtihad*. (*See also* **Law; Shafi'i.**)

Imam

The Arabic term *imam*, literally "one who stands in front," generally refers to the religious and political leader of a Muslim community. The specific meaning of the word differs for Sunnis* and Shi'is* and also depends on the context in which it is used.

In Sunni Islam, the title *imam* is typically given to the person chosen by the Muslim community to lead the congregation in prayers in a mosque*. Although this individual usually has training in religious studies, any respected Muslim may lead the prayers. Sunni Muslims also apply the title to caliphs* and prominent jurists (experts in Islamic law).

Shi'i Muslims believe that the Prophet Muhammad chose his son-in-law, Ali ibn Abi Talib, and Ali's descendants as the imams of the Muslim community. Divinely appointed and protected from sin, the imams were infallible and, therefore, had supreme authority in all religious and legal matters. Although the last of the twelve imams disappeared in 872, Shi'i Muslims preserve their memories by reciting the prayers some of the imams composed and by making pilgrimages* to their shrines* and the tombs of their descendants. They also anticipate the return of the twelfth imam at a time when God will establish justice throughout the world.

In 1979 Shi'i religious leader Ayatollah Ruhollah Khomeini led a successful Islamic revolution in Iran. He was given the title of imam, which led some to say that the use of this designation was intended to suggest the approach of the time of the return of the twelfth imam. Most Iranians, however, viewed the title as recognition of his role as leader of the country. To prevent confusion, one conservative group referred to Khomeini as the deputy of the twelfth imam. (*See also* **Ali ibn Abi Talib; Shi'i Islam; Sunni Islam.**)

Iman

The word *iman* is an Arabic term meaning "faith" or "belief." It refers specifically to faith in the religion of Islam. The presence of *iman* is said to distinguish Muslims from non-Muslims. It is, therefore, the basis for Muslim solidarity.

Several specific beliefs are associated with *iman*, including belief in a single god who is referred to as Allah, as well as the belief in angels, prophets, and the afterlife. In Islam, adopting these beliefs is considered to be a matter of free choice. God does not compel anyone to believe, so *iman* is based on individual choice. God does, however, give support to those who believe and may harden the hearts of those who have become evil so they may not believe until the Day of Judgment, when they will be punished.

The Qur'an* establishes a close connection between *iman* and *amal*, or between "belief" and "action." True faith shows itself in appropriate conduct. In fact, true faith and good behavior are considered to be inseparable—faith without good deeds is without value, and good deeds without faith are not possible. Good conduct includes obeying Allah, the Prophet Muhammad, and various other authorities; fulfilling one's commitments; being truthful; performing ritual prayers; working and giving money to help the poor; avoiding drinking, gambling, and unfair business practices; and treating people with respect. (*See also* **Afterlife; Allah; Muslim Brotherhood.**)

* Qur'an book of the holy scriptures of Islam

Imperialism

See *Colonialism.*

India

Islam has been a presence on the Indian subcontinent for over 1,000 years. Today, Indian Muslims comprise one of the largest Muslim populations in the world. About 12 percent, or 120 million, of India's residents are Muslims.

Mughal Rulers of India. Arab invaders first brought Islam to India in the 700s. Although India had a Hindu majority, Muslims gained widespread control over the region after the rise of the Mughal Empire in the 1500s. The empire's founder, Babur, claimed to be a descendant of Mongol conqueror Genghis Khan. Babur's successors extended Muslim rule over nearly the entire subcontinent.

India

The Mughal Empire emerged in India in the early 1500s, spreading Islam over most of the subcontinent. In the late 1600s, the Hindu and Sikh populations rose in opposition to Muslim rule. The empire fell into decline after the death of the emperor Aurangzeb in 1707.

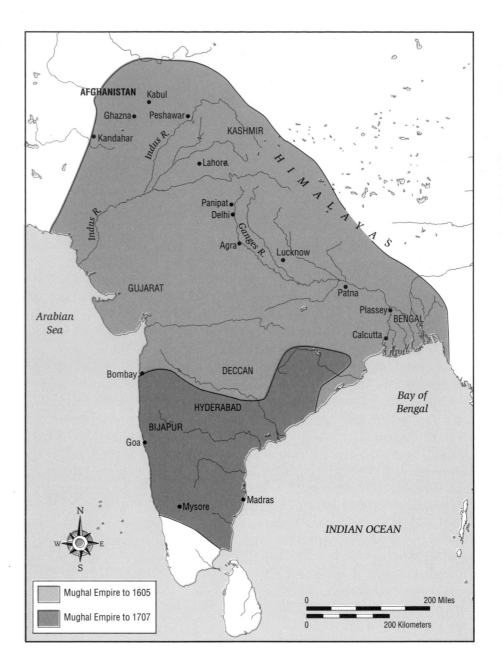

See color plate 14, vol. 2.

*Sikh refers to Sikhism, a branch of Hinduism that rejects caste and idolatry

The most famous Mughal emperor, Akbar, reigned for half a century, until 1605. He promoted religious tolerance, banning the tax on non-Muslims and allowing Hindus, Muslims, and Christians to live according to their faith. Akbar employed Hindus at all levels of government and even married Hindu princesses. Education and the arts flourished under Akbar's rule, as did trade relations with Britain.

Islamic civilization thrived in India until the late 1600s, when Hindu and Sikh* groups rose in opposition to the imperial rule. Despite the protests, the emperor Aurangzeb reinstated the tax on non-Muslims and replaced Hindus and Christians in the government with those of Islamic faith. The empire fell into decline after Aurangzeb's death in 1707. By the mid-1700s, attacks by Persian and Afghan invaders, along with those from the Marathas of central India, had weakened the Mughal grip on the region.

Hoping to reverse the empire's decline, court scholar Shah Wali Allah (1703–1762) urged religious reform and promoted a deeper devotion to the hadith*. He believed that a broad interpretation of Islamic law could restore political order, and he sought to serve as a guide to the princes. Although the Mughal decline continued, Shah Wali Allah's movement led to the publication of an influential collection of fatwas* and to the advancement of Urdu, a regional language, as the court language (replacing Persian).

British Influence in India. In the 1700s, Great Britain extended its power to India. The British initially sought economic rather than military conquest and battled with the French over trading centers in the region. By 1803, however, Britain's East India Company had taken over Delhi, the seat of the Mughal Empire. The Mughal Empire continued as a British protectorate* but had little true power. Social rank became important to Muslims as they lost political control, and they developed the concept of the *ashraf* (a privileged or well-born class). Members of the *ashraf* were fluent in Urdu and claimed to be descendants of important historical figures. They took such titles as *sayyid* (descendant of the Prophet), *shaykh* (descendant of Muhammad's companions), and Pathan (descendant of Afghan leaders). They typically owned land and worked as government officials or as religious figures.

Noting the declining power of the Muslims, scholar Sayyid Ahmad Barelwi (1780–1831) sought to rebuild a strong Muslim state. He became the first Indian Muslim to widely circulate printed material in order to spread religious teachings. Barelwi believed that false beliefs had divided and weakened Islam in India. He called for Muslims to reject certain Sufi* and Shi'i* practices, and he promoted social reforms to bring practice into conformity with Islamic norms. For example, he opposed the practice of preventing widows from remarrying as un-Islamic. In 1826 he urged Muslims to unite in a jihad* against a Sikh kingdom. The campaign failed in large part because of internal divisions, and Barelwi's movement declined after his death in 1831.

To the east in Bengal, Hajji Shari'atullah led a separate Muslim reform campaign in the 1820s. His Faraizi movement emphasized reform of individual religious practice in the context of British rule. Supporters printed pamphlets to spread his teachings, and his son Dudhu Miyan led an uprising of Muslim peasants against their Hindu landlords. The British, seeking to maintain order, helped suppress the revolt.

Although Hindus and Muslims often clashed, they found a common enemy in the British. Tensions boiled over in 1857, when both groups united against Great Britain. After savage fighting, the British crushed the revolt, established formal political rule over India, and sent the last Mughal emperor into exile. Although Hindus as well as Muslims had participated in the revolt, British leaders placed greater blame on the Muslims because of their status as former rulers. Some members of the Muslim elite moved to Arabia (now Saudi Arabia) and communicated with their followers through publications and meetings in Mecca.

Following the rebellion, the British sought "natural leaders" to help govern India. They wanted to build a loyal force that would not rebel against them. The British found candidates among the *ashraf* class and promoted them to leadership positions. These aristocrats supported Islamic learning, music, and medicine and encouraged the acceptance of English education and values.

* **hadith** reports of the words and deeds of Muhammad (not in the Qur'an, but accepted as guides for Muslim behavior)

* **fatwa** opinion issued by an Islamic legal scholar in response to a question posed by an individual or a court of law

* **protectorate** country under the protection and control of a stronger nation

* **Sufi** Islamic mysticism, which seeks to develop spirituality through discipline of the mind and body

* **Shi'i** refers to Muslims who believe that Muhammad chose Ali ibn Abi Talib and his descendants as the spiritual-political leaders of the Muslim community

* **jihad** literally "striving"; war in defense of Islam

Efforts Toward Reform and Independence. In the 1870s, Islamic scholar Sayyid Ahmad Khan emerged as a strong voice calling for reform. To overcome lingering British mistrust, he argued that the Muslims were not disloyal and that the British should promote them to high positions because of their past experience as rulers in the region. He also urged Muslims to face the reality of British rule. In 1875 Ahmad Khan founded the Mohammedan Anglo-Oriental College (later Aligarh Muslim University) to provide Muslims with a British education. He modeled the school after the famous English universities Cambridge and Oxford. Ahmad Khan hoped that its graduates would adopt British culture and emerge as leaders in the colony. Queen Victoria recognized his loyalty to Britain by knighting him as Sir Sayyid.

As part of his call for reform, Ahmad Khan tried to show that Islam could exist harmoniously with modern science. He encouraged the *ulama** to depart from centuries-old interpretations of the Qur'an* and directed Muslims to accept Western education practices and modernism. Ahmad Khan discouraged literal readings of religious texts. For example, he held that scholars should interpret the miracles in the Qur'an as metaphors (likenesses), stating that the Qur'an itself rejects the possibility of events that violate nature.

Ahmad Khan gained many followers, but his acceptance of British rule undermined his popularity among some Muslims. The *ulama* denounced Ahmad Khan's reforms as un-Islamic. They set up the Dar al-Ulum at Deoband, a school that promoted hadith study and traditional religious learning. The Deoband scholars avoided politics, believing that devoted teachers and prayer leaders held the key to reshaping society.

While Islamic scholars debated the best way to adjust to British rule, Hindus and Muslims continued to compete for power. Hindus wanted to establish democratic elections, but Muslims opposed this idea, fearing the domination of the Hindu majority. They stressed their higher levels of education and greater leadership experience in promoting greater influence for themselves. The British outraged some Muslims in 1900 when they advanced Hindi as an official language along with Urdu.

Activists of both faiths continued to seek the end of British rule. In 1885 the Indian National Congress was formed to promote this goal. Some Muslims joined the Congress party, which pressed for a modern secular* nation state. Others believed that Islam could not survive in a region with a Hindu majority. Muslims favoring a separate Islamic state formed the All-Indian Muslim League in 1906.

The issue of independence overlapped with that of religious reform. The poet and philosopher Muhammad Iqbal (died 1938) became an important advocate for a modern Islam. Iqbal viewed India's Muslim community as corrupt and backward, in contrast to the creative, dynamic nature of God's law. Iqbal taught that God's law is inseparable from all aspects of life and that an Islamic state would acknowledge God's presence. Similar to Ahmad Khan, Iqbal faulted the *ulama* for adhering to a reactionary viewpoint. He believed that they should reinterpret and reapply Islamic law according to the current situation.

After World War I (1914–1918), Muslim-Hindu tensions increased. Riots broke out in many communities. In this atmosphere of hostility, Muslim religious leaders sought new ways to promote their faith. In the 1920s, the

* ***ulama*** religious scholars

* **Qur'an** book of the holy scriptures of Islam

* **secular** separate from religion in human life and society; connected to everyday life

Tablighi Jama'at movement sought to provide Muslims with guidance. Leaders of the movement revived the teaching of Islamic principles, and encouraged all Muslims to spread these teachings. The Jamaat-i Islami movement, founded in 1941, looked to change society by rejecting the decadence of the West.

Muslims remained divided over the issue of whether they should partition themselves off into a separate state. In the 1930s, Mohammad Ali Jinnah assumed the presidency of the Muslim League. Under his leadership, the league's popularity increased. Jinnah portrayed the Congress as pro-Hindu and hostile to Islam and pushed for the creation of a separate state. Scholars are uncertain about whether Jinnah actually wanted a Muslim state, or whether he used this demand as a bargaining tool. By the 1940s, however, most Muslims supported his cause.

Partitioning the Country. Britain's grip on India had begun to loosen in the early 1900s. To gain Indian support during World War I, the British promised to grant more freedoms to Hindus and Muslims. Afterward, however, Britain enacted only limited governmental reforms. Muslims took further offense when Britain helped to break up the Ottoman Empire after the war.

World War II (1938–1945) had drained much of Britain's power. Faced with an Indian independence movement led by Mohandas Gandhi in the 1940s, it could not retain its hold on the colony. In August 1947, Britain partitioned India into two independent states the predominantly Hindu India and Muslim Pakistan, of which Jinnah served as the first governor-general.

The Muslim state of Pakistan included the northwestern section of the former British colony. It also included the province of Bengal in the north, which became the independent state of Bangladesh in 1971. Ten million Indian Muslims left their homes in India to move to Pakistan, some against their will. Hindus also had to leave the newly created Muslim nations. Muslim-Hindu tensions remained high during this transitional period. Fighting broke out, claiming the lives of nearly one million people.

Bitter relations between Pakistan and India continued through the following decades. The two countries fought twice over Kashmir, a province claimed by both sides, in 1947 and in 1965. During the partition, Kashmir had a choice of whether to join India or Pakistan. The Muslims, accounting for 80 percent of the population, wanted to join Pakistan, but the Hindu Kashmiri ruler consented to go with India in 1948. Since then, more than 30,000 Kashmiris have died fighting for their independence.

Hindu-Muslim Tensions Continue. India's Muslims are spread unevenly throughout the country. In the north central plain, once the Mughal heartland, Muslims make up less than 15 percent of the population. In Malabar in the southwest, Muslims account for 25 percent of the population.

India's Muslims are also a diverse population. They exist at all income levels and speak at least seven major languages. Muslims tend to marry locally, within their original status group, and remain in the region of their birth. Illiteracy and poverty are common in some Muslim communities, especially after many educated and wealthy Muslims moved to Pakistan.

The majority of India's Muslims are Sunni*, and about 10 percent are Shi'i. Anti-Muslim attitudes have increased among the Hindus since the 1980s. Many Hindus blame the Muslims for past wrongs and current problems in

Minority Within a Minority

Muslim women in India have suffered persecution for both their gender and their faith. In the late 1900s, some women successfully challenged oppressive religious laws and customs. In one case, a Muslim woman received a fatwa preventing fundamentalists from trying to take over her secular school. In another case, an Indian high court banned the Muslim custom that allowed a man to divorce his wife by merely saying "I divorce you" three times. This ruling protects women from being cast aside with no financial support, a cause of poverty for Muslim women of all classes. Groups such as the Muslim Women's Forum continue to campaign for women's rights in India, looking to Turkey and other Muslim countries for examples of equality laws.

* **Sunni** refers to the largest branch of the Muslim community; the name derives from sunnah, the exemplary behavior of the Prophet Muhammad

21

*assimilate to adapt socially and culturally to the larger population

India and demand that they either assimilate* or leave the country. Hindu activists have also sought to end the separate Muslim civil code in India. Although all Indians must abide by the same criminal laws, Hindus and Muslims have separate regulations governing marriage, inheritance, divorce, and other civil proceedings. This issue erupted in 1985 in the case of Shah Banu, an elderly Muslim woman who sued her estranged husband for support—a provision not required in Islamic law. Although the Supreme Court decided in favor of Shah Banu, Prime Minister Rajiv Gandhi reasserted the Muslim code.

Hindu-Muslim tensions have often led to violence. For over a decade, the two groups have argued over a mosque in the town of Ayodhya. Hindu activists claim that Mughal leaders built the mosque on the birthplace of Rama after destroying a temple honoring the god. Muslims deny this claim and seek to preserve the mosque as an Islamic place of worship. In December 1992, a Hindu mob tore down the building. (*See also* **Ahmad Khan, Sayyid; Colonialism; Iqbal, Muhammad; Kashmir; Mughal Empire; Pakistan.**)

Indonesia

*archipelago large group of islands

Indonesia is the world's largest archipelago*, consisting of some 17,000 islands (6,000 inhabited) between the Indian Ocean and the Pacific Ocean in Southeast Asia. Home to more than 231 million people, it is the fourth most populous country in the world, behind China, India, and the United States. Almost 90 percent of its inhabitants are Muslim—the largest Muslim population in any country. Indonesia's history and culture have produced a unique form of Islam that includes elements of Hinduism, Buddhism, and local animist* religions.

*animist refers to the belief that natural phenomena and objects have souls

Strategic Location Key to Islam

Indonesia's location between mainland Asia and Australia is responsible for its complex cultural and religious history. Location also provided Indonesia with an important role in the development of the region.

A Land of Many Wonders. Indonesia's many islands extend over more than 733,000 square miles between Australia and Southeast Asia. Most of its islands are small and low-lying, and many are heavily forested. The largest islands, including Borneo, Sumatra, Java, and Sulawesi, have interior mountain ranges. Indonesia's strategic location along major sea lanes between the Indian and Pacific Oceans has had a profound effect on its history and social structures, due in large part to contact with foreign cultures.

Indonesia's many natural resources, including petroleum, tin, natural gas, timber, coal, gold, and silver, have made it a prime destination for traders and merchants for centuries. Islam first came to the Indonesian islands in the 1200s with the arrival of Muslim traders from India. Spices drew Europeans to the islands in the early 1500s. Indonesia's rich reserves of oil, natural gas, timber, and rubber also made it valuable to the Japanese army

Indonesia has the largest Muslim population of any country. Here, worshippers gather at Jakarta in the main hall of the Istiqlal Mosque, one of the largest mosques in Southeast Asia.

during World War II (1939–1945). These same resources are still among the most abundant in Indonesia.

A Historical Overview. Before the arrival of the Europeans, various Hindu-Buddhist kingdoms held power over Indonesia. Indian merchants brought Islamic culture to the islands in the 1200s and several powerful Muslim states arose in Indonesia after 1400. By 1509 the Portuguese had established coastal trading posts, but the Dutch had the most significant European influence on Indonesia's history.

In the early 1600s, the Dutch East India Company took control of what they called the East Indies. The East India Company controlled the region with the cooperation of local leaders until the late 1790s, when France conquered the Netherlands. Indonesia became a part of the French empire in 1810, but a year later the British occupied Java and quickly forced the surrender of French forces.

In 1816 Britain returned the islands to the Dutch, who remained in power until Indonesia won its independence in 1949. President Sukarno, the country's first chief executive, was elected in 1945 and reelected in 1955. Two years later, he declared martial law* and ruled under a military dictatorship until 1965. President Suharto replaced Sukarno as head of the government in 1965 after an attempted coup* by the communist party triggered massive uprisings in east and central Java. Suharto continued military rule until severe economic troubles prompted his resignation in 1998.

Today Indonesia is a republic headed by a president who makes the law with the help of an appointed cabinet*. A national assembly meets every five years to elect a new president, to review government policies, and to consider changes to the constitution. During elections for the assembly, citizens vote for parties rather than for individual candidates. Each party receives a number of seats in the assembly based on its percentage of the total votes cast. The winning parties then decide which of their members will serve in the assembly.

* **martial law** rules imposed by the military

* **coup** sudden, and often violent, overthrow of a ruler or government

* **cabinet** individuals appointed by a head of state to supervise departments of government and to act as official advisers

Islamic Practices Restricted

Although the spread of Islam in Indonesia was largely peaceful, conflict between Muslims and non-Muslims was common on the central island of Java. The ruling Javanese culture was based on a caste system that placed people in fixed and unequal social classes. The coastal people, who later accepted Islam, were at the bottom of the social order. Islam offered them a community where social rank was not a factor and in which all believers had an equal chance of success. As coastal kingdoms grew wealthy from trade in the 1500s, they tried to expand and bring Islam to the interior of the island by force. Their efforts failed, and in the 1600s the interior kingdom of Mataram conquered the coastal people. Until the late 1800s, the rulers of Java exercised strict control over the practice of Islam on the island.

Islam's Role in Indonesia

Indonesia's first large-scale contact with outsiders was with Hindu and Buddhist cultures from India. The customs and beliefs of those civilizations were well established in the archipelago by the time Islam was introduced in Indonesia in the 1200s. Indonesian rulers were tolerant of different religions and cultures, enabling Islam to spread throughout the islands. Islam would eventually grow to dominate Indonesian culture, but it would be an Islam quite different from that which is practiced in the Middle East.

Indonesia's Islamic Culture. Two factors influenced the practice of Islam in Indonesia. The first was Islam's interaction with Buddhism, Hinduism, and local Indonesian religions. Instead of abandoning their traditional beliefs in favor of Islam, Indonesians adapted their practices to fit Islamic observances. A form of Islam known as *abangan*, a blend of Muslim and non-Muslim elements, resulted. Unlike traditional Islam, *abangan* places less importance on religious law and rituals. Instead, it combines Muslim beliefs with belief in spirits, ritual feasting, and traditional medicine.

Sufism, a branch of Islam characterized by mystical beliefs and practices, was another important influence on the development of Islamic practices in Indonesia. By the 1500s, many of the islands' leading Muslim scholars practiced Sufism. Tolerance toward local religious traditions made Sufism very appealing to Indonesians. In addition, Indonesia's limited cultural contact with the rest of the Muslim world enabled Indonesia's Islamic traditions to develop their own unique practices.

As long-distance travel became easier in the early 1900s, Indonesia's Muslims became less isolated. Before the twentieth century, only a small number of Indonesians made the annual pilgrimage to Mecca. By the mid-1920s, however, more than 120,000 people had begun to make the journey from the islands each year. At the same time, the number of Indonesian students in Middle Eastern universities grew substantially. Those who returned to Indonesia brought a new commitment to traditional Islam. They criticized Indonesia's blended form of Islam and called for the adoption of a purer form of the faith.

Those who support a purer form of Islam are called *santri*. They reject the acceptance of legal and religious traditions created by Islamic judges over time. The *santri* believe that the law should be based on the Qur'an, but they also support the use of independent reasoning in interpreting the law. Traditional Islamic practices, such as attendance at Friday prayer services and veiling of women, have increased in recent years. Popular Islamic culture, however, is still strongly influenced by non-Mulsim traditions.

Islam's Role in Indonesian Politics. Because Indonesia is home to so many diverse ethnic groups, Islam has provided a common identity for many who live there. Under Dutch rule, Islam played only a limited role in Indonesian politics. The first large-scale Muslim organization, Muhammadiyah, was formed in 1911 as a movement for modernist reform. Sarekat Islam, established in 1912, emerged after World War I as a more nationalist movement.

The Dutch saw Islam as a danger to established peace and order so they followed a policy known as the Reception Theory, by which local customs and laws would be followed in most places on the islands. Islamic law would be enforced only if it agreed with local laws. The Dutch eventually established separate religious courts to oversee matters of marriage, divorce, and inheritance.

In the years before World War II, secular* organizations such as the communist party became more important in domestic politics than Islamic groups. In 1926 Nahdatul Ulama, a traditional Muslim party, replaced Sarekat Islam as the most influential Muslim party. Secular parties, however, continued to lead the drive for independence.

By the time Indonesia gained legal independence from the Dutch in 1949, Islamic political power was divided among three groups. Nahdatul Ulama supported traditional views, while Masjumi represented those who supported a modern Islamic socialist* party. Both competed for the support of Indonesians who wanted a government based on Muslim values and who were opposed to communist influences. The third group in Indonesian politics consisted of radical Muslim military units, such as Darul Islam, that violently opposed the secular government. Conflict among these groups lasted throughout the 1950s. Although S.M. Kartowuwirjo, leader of Darul Islam, was captured and imprisoned in 1962, other militant Islamic groups continued to fight the government.

Islam's Influence on Indonesia's Government. During the early years of Indonesia's independence, Muslim leaders pushed to make Islam a part of the national constitution. The original agreement, drawn up in 1945, subjected all Muslims to Islamic law and required that Indonesia's head of state be a Muslim. Concern about the rights of other religious groups led to President Sukarno's declaration of a new ideology* called the Pancasila, or Five Principles. This doctrine stated that Indonesians should believe in God; to do otherwise would call attention to one's communist tendencies. Muslim groups initially opposed this state policy, fearing that by accepting Pancasila, they would be betraying their faith. They also feared that Pancasila would become the official religion of Indonesia. President Sukarno promised this would not happen.

The attempted coup in 1965 by the communist party briefly united the government and elements of the Muslim community. After learning that the Indonesian communist party had played a role in the failed takeover, groups of Muslim young people attacked and killed many communists. When President Suharto came to power after the coup attempt, some segments of the military wanted Islam to become the unifying spiritual connection for members of the armed forces. Muslim political organizations hoped this connection would bring closer cooperation with the military. President Suharto, however, reduced Muslim control over education and marriage and strongly supported the Pancasila.

In other moves to limit Muslim political influence, Suharto outlawed the Masjumi party and would not allow members to regroup. In 1973 Suharto forced all Muslim parties to unite into a single party known as the United Development Party (PPP). His tactics led to the rise of small radical Muslim groups opposed to the Suharto regime. During the 1970s and 1980s, youth groups such as Kommando Jihad and the Islamic Youth Movement carried out kidnappings, hijackings, and bombings to protest government policies.

President Suharto demanded that all organizations accept the Pancasila as their guiding ideology. Many who expressed public opposition to it were

* **secular** separate from religion in human life and society; connected to everyday life

* **socialist** refers to socialism, the economic system in which the government owns and operates the means of production and the distribution of goods

* **ideology** system of ideas or beliefs

Indonesia

This chart shows the percentage of Muslims living in countries throughout the world. Muslims populations in the United States, Canada, Central America, South America, and most portions of Europe are currently less than 5%.

Percentage of Muslim Population	Country		
86–100	Afghanistan	Iraq	Somalia
	Algeria	Jordan	Syria
	Azerbaijan	Libya	Tunisia
	Bahrain	Mali	Turkey
	Bangladesh	Mauritania	Turkmenistan
	Comoros	Morocco	United Arab Emirates
	Djibouti	Pakistan	Uzbekistan
	Egypt	Qatar	Western Sahara
	Gambia	Saudi Arabia	Yemen
	Indonesia	Senegal	
	Iran		
66–85	Albania	Niger	
	Guinea	Oman	
	Kuwait	Sudan	
	Kyrgyzstan	Tajikistan	
	Lebanon		
36–65	Bosnia and Herzegovina	Ivory Coast	
	Brunei	Kazakhstan	
	Burkina Faso	Malaysia	
	Chad	Nigeria	
	Ethiopia	Sierra Leone	
	Guinea-Bisseau		
16–35	Cyprus	Mauritius	
	Eritrea	Mozambique	
	Ghana	Suriname	
	Liberia	Tanzania	
	Macedonia	Uganda	
	Malawi	Yugoslavia	
	Maldives		
5–15	Benin	India	
	Bulgaria	Israel	
	Cameroon	Kenya	
	Central African Republic	Madagascar	
	Congo	Philippines	
	Georgia	Sri Lanka	
	Ghana	Togo	
	Guyana		

imprisoned. Nahdatul Ulama and the PPP eventually accepted the Pancasila. In return, Suharto granted more of their requests, such as greater control over religious education. With the Pancasila as the official government policy, many Muslim groups abandoned politics, concentrating instead on local issues such as economic development and education.

Suharto's resignation in 1998 weakened Indonesia's central government as well as the power of the Pancasila. Separatist groups calling for local independence sprang up in many of the outer islands. A succession of government leaders did little to stabilize the situation. East Timor, a country occupying the eastern portion of the island of Timor, won independence from Portugal in 1999 and was recognized as a sovereign state three years later. At the same time, Muslim militant groups attacked symbols of non-Muslim influence, and organizations such as the Star Moon Party called for the government to give Muslims special rights over foreigners, such as the Chinese. Religious violence between Christians and Muslims has also increased in recent years. As of 2003, President Megawati Sukarnoputri led the nation, but with growing concern over terrorist attacks, Western governments increased pressure on Sukarnoputri to keep tighter control over militant Muslim organizations. (*See also* **Modernism; Southeast Asia.**)

Inheritance

The Qur'an* contains more specific guidelines on inheritance than on any other subject. For this reason, customs have remained largely unchanged for centuries. Inheritance is, however, one of the topics on which Sunni* and Shi'i* law sharply disagree.

Prior to the founding of Islam, Arabs followed a patriarchal, or male-dominated, system of inheritance. A deceased person's property passed to the nearest male relative on the father's side of the family. The Qur'an introduced important changes. Female relatives, including wives, daughters, sisters, and grandmothers of the deceased, received a fixed share of the inheritance. The remaining property then passed to the senior male in the family. The Qur'an did not, however, eliminate inequality between men and women with regard to inheritance rights. In most cases, a woman was entitled to only one-half of the share of a man inheriting from the same family member. Furthermore, some women were intimidated when they tried to pursue their inheritance rights, and in some cases, women did not receive their share of an estate because they were ignorant of the law.

According to Sunnis, the Qur'anic verses on inheritance only modified the existing system of dividing an estate. Consequently, Sunni legal experts have developed a complex set of rules that reconcile the requirements of both pre-Islamic and Islamic traditions. Shi'is, by contrast, believe that the Islamic law of inheritance supersedes the pre-Islamic system. In practice, Shi'is keep most of the inheritance in the immediate family and often place the daughter(s) of the deceased in a more favorable position than under Sunni law.

Islamic law places limits on wills. A Muslim may include no more than one-third of his or her property in a will so that the majority of the estate will

* **Qur'an** book of the holy scriptures of Islam

* **Sunni** refers to the largest branch of the Muslim community; the name derives from sunnah, the exemplary behavior of the Prophet Muhammad

* **Shi'i** refers to Muslims who believe that Muhammad chose Ali ibn Abi Talib and his descendents as the spiritual-political leaders of the Muslim community

be preserved for the heirs mandated by the Qur'an. Sunni law further prevents an individual from giving property to relatives who are already due to receive a share. Moreover, a Muslim who is ill and nearing death may not give away any property and thus diminish the portions prescribed by the Qur'an.

Typically, an estate will have a large number of rightful heirs. Because the requirements of the law would divide the property into small unusable shares, Muslims sometimes set aside land in a *waqf*. This is the practice of reserving property and the income it generates for charitable purposes. (*See also* **Charity**.)

International Law and Diplomacy

* **Qur'an** book of the holy scriptures of Islam

* **sunnah** literally "the trodden path;" Islamic customs based on the exemplary behavior of Muhammad

In the Muslim tradition, the primary sources for all law, including international law, are the Qur'an* and the sunnah*. Additional sources include the consensus (*ijma*) of legal scholars and analytical reasoning (*qiyas*). While modern international law recognizes the existence of many self-governing states, traditional Islamic law is based on the theory of one universal state— defined by adherence to Muslim traditions, rather than by geographical boundaries. By the end of the 1900s, the Islamic legal system and Western international law had moved closer together, but the concept of Islamic solidarity is still a guiding principle in Islamic international law.

Guiding Principles of Islamic Law

* **secular** separate from religion in human life and society; connected to everyday life

Similar to secular* law, Islamic law provides rules that govern social relations among people. Islamic law also seeks to define the relationship between human beings and God, assumed to be a special connection that influences the interactions between Muslims and non-Muslims.

Religious Beliefs and Islamic Law. Despite general agreement on the two main sources of Islamic law, there are several distinct schools of legal thought. These variations developed at different times and in different parts of the Islamic world. The close relationship between religion and law has had a profound effect on international relations between Muslims and non-Muslims, as well as interactions among people within the Islamic world.

Distinct Realms of Islamic Law. Traditional Islamic law divides the world into three distinct groups: the realm of Islam (*dar al-Islam*), where peace prevails because people are protected and guided by Islamic law; the realm of treaty (*dar al-sulh*), where Muslims and their allies are protected because the rulers have agreed to respect one another's rights and pay tribute to the Muslim ruler; and the realm of war (*dar al-harb*), where people are subjected to chaos and the whims of rulers who do not respect Islam. In classical Islamic theory, *dar al-harb* is temporary. The question of how the rest of the world should conform to the teachings or values of Islam is a source of much debate.

According to Islamic law, *dar al-Islam* is engaged in a struggle with *dar al-harb* that can only end with the eventual victory of *dar al-Islam*. Islamic tradition justifies this struggle with the concept of jihad, meaning "effort" or "struggle." Jihad is sometimes used to mean "holy war," or active aggression against nonbelievers. Jihad, however, refers more specifically to the collective duty to expand *dar al-Islam* to the entire world. Historically, jihad has often involved waging war, but it also includes teaching and setting good examples. Furthermore, the Qur'an draws distinctions between just and unjust wars and also portrays jihad as a means of defending Islam.

In practice, *dar al-Islam* consists of the many different nations that accept Islamic law. In theory, however, these many nations are united as a single Islamic community or nation under the power of God. While traditional Islamic law does not formally recognize the existence of separate Muslim states, Muslim legal scholars generally accept the fact that current political conditions have created distinct Muslim nations.

See color plate 4, vol. 3.

Islamic Law and International Relations

From the early days of the Qur'an, there existed laws for governing non-Muslims, especially People of the Book, referring to Christians, Jews, and other protected minorities. The early expansion of Islam through territorial conquests occurred so rapidly that Muslim leaders spent little time thinking about how best to interact with foreigners. When it became clear that Muslims could not convert the entire world, Islamic leaders adjusted the way they dealt with non-Muslims. As political and religious divisions occurred within Islam, Muslim leaders also changed their views regarding *dar al-Islam*.

Interacting With Non-Muslims. Some people believe that jihad assumes a state of war that prevents any sort of real peace between Muslims and non-Muslims. Indeed, the Qur'an refers to fighting nonbelievers when they are aggressors. In practice, however, Islamic law makes distinctions between different types of nonbelievers. Those who believe in many gods are especially disapproved, because in the Qur'an, people who do not believe in God are incapable of living virtuous lives. Those who believe in a single God and follow written scriptures*—such as Christians and Jews—are to be fought only if they attack first and until they are "humbled" and made to pay a special tax.

* **scripture** sacred writings that contain revelations from God

Political reality has been as important as Islamic law in establishing the nature of relations between Muslim and non-Muslim states. Muhammad himself offered the example of making a truce with nonbelievers, and later caliphs* often made peace with one enemy to enable them to fight others. Christian and Muslim states exchanged ambassadors and signed formal treaties, even during the Crusades*. Muslim rulers could point to chapters in the Qur'an to defend their treaties with nonbelievers.

* **caliph** religious and political leader of an Islamic state

* **Crusades** during the Middle Ages, the holy wars declared by the pope against non-Christians, mostly Muslims

Can Islam and Nationalism Coexist? The concept of *dar al-Islam* as a universal Muslim nation stands in contrast to the idea of self-governing nation-states, one of the main forms of modern political organization. Some verses in the Qur'an suggest, however, that such state-like divisions are natural. For example, the Qur'an says that God purposely separated humans into nations and tribes and states: "If God had so willed, He would have made them one community."

Dar al-Islam assumes the unity of the Muslim world, but after the first few centuries of Islam, political divisions began to develop. As early as the

The Ummah and the *Dhimmis*

The concept of *dar al-Islam* is connected to another important idea known as *ummah*—the community of faithful Muslims. According to traditional Islam, it is religion that determines membership, not birthplace or parental status. Membership in the *ummah* assures that a Muslim is eligible to fill any post or political office in a Muslim land, even one far from his homeland. In contrast to the *ummah* are the *dhimmis*, protected non-Muslim minorities who live in Muslim lands. In some Muslim countries, *dhimmis* are required to pay a special tax and they are not granted full civil rights. For example, non-Muslims are not allowed to openly display their own religious symbols in Saudi Arabia. This law applied to Western military forces stationed there during the Gulf War in 1991. Although *dhimmis* are not allowed to carry weapons, this aspect of the law was not enforced during the Gulf War.

700s the first Arab empire was breaking up into different provinces and regions that had their own culture and language. This process to revive ethnic identities gained momentum during the early days of the Abbasid rule in the 800s. The Muslim world eventually split into various states based in Spain, North Africa (the Maghrib), Egypt, the Mashriq (eastern Arab lands), Persia, and India. Muslim states drew up treaties to formalize their boundaries. Muslim leaders, however, still referred to the unity of the Islamic world and tried to present themselves as defenders of Islam rather than as rulers of specific territories. At the same time, Islamic scholars accepted political divisions and began to discuss Islamic unity in terms of moral and social solidarity.

Colonial expansion by Europeans during the 1800s helped to introduce Western legal practices to the Muslim world. Much of the Islamic world fell under European domination during this time as Europeans ruled Islamic lands according to their own concepts of state, law, and sovereignty. Later, decolonization and the realization that individual states had rights to their own natural resources contributed to the idea of truly independent Muslim states.

Acceptance of the concepts of international law and national sovereignty by Muslim nations forced significant changes in the Islamic theory of international law. Most Islamic states now reject the idea of a state of war expressed by jihad. Most Muslim leaders respect national boundaries and recognize the sovereignty of foreign states. Yet there are forces still pushing for greater unity among Muslims.

In recent years, militant Muslims have become more active in state politics in the Islamic world. From 1966 until early 2002, the fundamentalist Islamic group known as the Taliban ruled Afghanistan. These groups have consistently ignored international laws regarding human rights and the safety of diplomats and other foreigners in their country. They have also attempted to export the Islamic revolution to secular Muslim states. These countries are, however, the exceptions. While many Muslims still hope for a day when they will all be united in a universal *dar al-Islam*, most have no desire to overturn the modern nation-state system. (*See also* **Arab-Israeli Conflict; Arab League; Colonialism; Fundamentalism; International Meetings and Organizations; Islamic State; Jihad; Law; Nationalism; Terrorism.**)

International Meetings and Organizations

* **imperialism** extension of power and influence over another country or region

Muslim intellectuals first proposed the idea of holding international Islamic congresses during late 1800s. They were looking for a way to unite Muslims in the fight against Western imperialism*. Throughout the 1900s, Muslim leaders and activists convened meetings in an effort to obtain Islamic consensus for particular causes. Some of these congresses led to the formation of permanent international Islamic organizations that promoted interaction among Muslim peoples and states.

Vying for Support. The Muslim reformist movement and its leading journal, *Al-manar*, began promoting an international congress in the late 1890s. Leaders of the Ottoman Empire* opposed the idea, however, and prevented

* **Ottoman Empire** large Turkish state existing from the early 1300s to the early 1900s

The Organization of the Islamic Conference was established in 1971 as a way to promote unity among Muslim nations. Here members attend the opening session of the organization's 2003 meeting in Iran.

the meeting from taking place. The Ottoman sultan* feared that such a large gathering of Muslims would undermine his own religious authority and lead to political unrest.

After World War I ended in 1918 and the Ottoman Empire collapsed, a number of Muslim leaders and activists called for Islamic congresses. Some sought wider Muslim support against non-Muslim enemies. Others desired the title of caliph*, which they hoped to secure through the approval of a Muslim assembly. Among the topics of discussion at meetings during the 1920s and 1930s were the problems associated with the abolition of the caliphate* by Turkey, the Arab struggle against British rule, and Zionism (the movement to create a Jewish state in Palestine).

Each of the early congresses resolved to create a permanent organization and to convene additional meetings. Their resolutions failed, however, as a result of disagreements among competing Muslim groups or intervention by European powers. During the 1940s and 1950s, Saudi Arabia and the Muslim regions of India led attempts to establish an international Islamic organization, but they faced severe opposition from the secular* governments of Egypt, Turkey, and Iran. Egyptian president Gamal Abdel Nasser led a popular movement for Arab nationalism* aimed at the political reunification of all Arab-speaking states from the Persian Gulf to the Atlantic Ocean. In the name of this movement, the Egyptian government suppressed the Muslim Brotherhood, a popular Islamic fundamentalist* organization. Egyptian authorities also launched a propaganda campaign that attacked Saudi Arabia's system of government.

In response to these events, Saudi Arabia organized a Pan-Islamic* movement and sponsored the establishment of the Muslim World League in 1962. The league, which was based in Mecca, assembled numerous congresses of Muslim activists and religious scholars from abroad, especially from among the Muslim Brotherhood. Not to be outdone, Egypt organized similar meetings in Cairo. The actions inspired a series of "dueling" congresses in Mecca

* **sultan** political and military ruler of a Muslim dynasty or state

* **caliph** religious and political leader of an Islamic state

* **caliphate** office and government of the caliph, the religious and political head of an Islamic state

* **secular** separate from religion in human life and society; connected to everyday life

* **nationalism** feeling of loyalty and devotion to one's country and a commitment to its independence

* **fundamentalist** generally refers to the movement that promotes a literal interpretation of scripture; in Islam, a movement that promotes politicization of religion to create an alternative public order

* **Pan-Islamic** refers to the movement to unify all Islamic peoples

Global Links

and Cairo, each claiming the right to define Islam in a way that supported their country's policies.

Islamic Solidarity. After Israeli forces defeated the armies of Egypt, Syria, and Jordan and occupied large Arab territories in 1967, the movement for Arab nationalism lost support. Instead, Muslim countries united to defend their shared interests. Toward that end, the first Islamic summit was held in Morocco in 1969. In May 1971, the participating states established a permanent association, the Organization of the Islamic Conference (OIC).

The organization's activities fall into three broad categories. First, the organization provides moral support to Muslim states and movements engaged in conflicts with non-Muslims. For example, it has endorsed Muslim resistance movements in Afghanistan and the Philippines. Second, the organization mediates disputes between its own members, although it lacks military forces for peacekeeping. Finally, the OIC sponsors a variety of institutions that promote political, economic, and cultural cooperation among Muslims worldwide. The most influential of these institutions is the Islamic Development Bank. Funded by the wealthier OIC states, it finances development projects in poor Muslim countries.

United or Divided? As a major financial contributor of the OIC, Saudi Arabia has wielded considerable influence in the organization. For this reason, the OIC has not had unanimous support throughout the Muslim world. During the 1980s, for example, Iran virtually ignored the OIC and convened frequent congresses of its own, including the International Conference to Support the Islamic Revolution of the People of Palestine.

During the 1990s, a growing number of Islamic movements acquired legitimacy and power. Consequently, they launched their own congresses, such as the World Islamic Popular Gathering, which was held in Jordan in 1990. The large number of organizations that convened Islamic conferences during the 1990s reflected the high degree of competition for authority among Islamic nations. All of these competing organizations and their congresses help to unite the Muslim world. It remains uncertain, however, whether they will bridge the differences among Muslims or serve only to widen them. (*See also* **Muslim Brotherhood; Nationalism; Youth Organizations.**)

Intifadah

In December 1987, Palestinians living in the Israeli occupied territories of the West Bank and Gaza Strip launched an uprising, or *intifadah*. The Israeli government had controlled these lands following its victory in the Six-Day War in 1967. After 20 years of discrimination, the imprisonment of tens of thousands of Palestinian men and women, and the building of Jewish settlements in the heart of Arab towns and cities, Palestinians decided to fight for control of the territories.

The Palestinians attacked Israeli troops and Jewish settlers with knives and stones. In general, however, their methods of protest were nonviolent. They staged labor strikes, boycotts of businesses, and other demonstrations.

Palestinians of all classes supported the uprising, which even drew sympathy from some Israeli Arabs. The Israelis attempted to contain the movement with swift and harsh retaliation. Authorities closed universities and schools, destroyed homes, and imposed curfews in the territories. The Israeli army fought with Palestinians on a daily basis. During the first year of the *intifadah*, Palestinian casualties included more than 300 dead and 11,500 wounded. More than one-half of the wounded were under the age of 15. By 1990 the Israeli government had imprisoned more than 16,000 Palestinians.

Soon after the *intifadah* began, it came under the leadership of the Unified National Command of the Uprising. The group eventually joined forces with the Palestine Liberation Organization (PLO), the official representative of the Palestinian people. Despite its original goals, the costs of the *intifadah*—in terms of lives lost or disrupted and economic decline—soon became intolerable. The leaders of the Unified Command urged PLO chairman Yasir Arafat to abandon the armed struggle and recognize Israel's right to exist. They believed that Israelis and Palestinians could reach a compromise based on a two-state solution. Rejecting this concept, a militant Muslim group known as Hamas sought to gain control of the *intifadah*.

In 1988 the PLO expressed interest in compromising with Israel, and in 1993, the two sides signed a Declaration of Principles as a first step to resolving the conflict. According to the agreement, Israel would gradually cede control of the West Bank and Gaza Strip to the Palestinians. In May 1994, Israel withdrew from the Gaza Strip and the West Bank town of Jericho.

Despite this agreement, issues remain unresolved. The two sides continue to disagree over the boundaries of a Palestinian state, the right of Palestinian refugees to return to their property or be compensated for it, the status of Jerusalem, and control over water resources. Jewish settlers living in the occupied territories and militant Palestinian groups such as Hamas and Islamic Jihad have tried to sabotage the agreement by committing acts of violence. In September 2000, a second *intifadah* erupted. During this intensified campaign, Palestinians have increasingly used suicide bombers to attack Israeli targets. A peaceful solution to the Arab-Israeli conflict remains elusive. (*See also* **Arab-Israeli Conflict; Hamas; Palestine; Palestine Liberation Organization.**)

See map in Israel (vol. 2).

Iqbal, Muhammad

1877–1938
Poet and political writer

Muhammad Iqbal was born in Sialkot, India (now a part of Pakistan), and raised in a devout Muslim family. After completing high school, he attended Scotch Mission College for two years. Iqbal then went to Government College in Lahore, where he graduated with honors. He remained at the school to earn a master's degree in philosophy. After teaching for a few years in Lahore, he traveled to Europe to continue his education. He studied at Cambridge University and Munich University, where he received a doctorate in philosophy.

Iqbal's extensive schooling enabled him to develop an expertise in many areas. He was fluent in several languages, including Urdu, Arabic, Persian,

English, and German. At Government College, he gained a deep understanding of Western philosophy, Islamic culture, and Arabic literature. His advanced studies in Europe included law and Islamic mysticism*. Returning to India in 1908, Iqbal pursued a career as an attorney and a college professor. It was his poetry, however, that made him famous.

Iqbal wrote his best-known poems in Persian and Urdu. Muslims across the Indian subcontinent recited his verse. Even the illiterate became familiar with his poetry. Reynold Nicholson, a tutor at Cambridge University, translated his classic poem *Secrets of the Self* (1915) into English. Several themes emerge from Iqbal's poetry. Disturbed by what he perceived as the moral decline of Muslim culture, many of his poems call for greater obedience to the law of Islam. Although Iqbal is critical of nationalism*, much of his verse promotes Muslim unity.

Iqbal used prose to elaborate on his philosophical approach to religion. Influenced by Indian writer and political activist Sayyid Ahmad Khan (1817–1898), Iqbal believed the modernization of Islam held the key to Muslim advancement. In *The Reconstruction of Religious Thought in Islam*, he wrote that Muslims could achieve economic gains by embracing science and technology. Furthermore, he called for a reinterpretation of the Qur'an* and the sunnah* as a way to create new social and political institutions. His thinking helped to shape modernist Islam in the broader Muslim world.

Although Iqbal was uncomfortable with politics, his ideas influenced several important political figures. He even served in the Punjab Legislative Assembly from 1926 to 1930. By that time, he had become concerned about the political future of Muslims in India.

In 1930 Iqbal gave a speech rejecting the idea that India's Hindus and Muslims could live together in a single nation. He became a leading spokesperson for a separate Muslim state in northwestern India. According to Iqbal, this state should be based on the principles of Islam and it could then function as part of a larger community (*ummah*) of Muslim countries.

Iqbal's vision had a lasting political impact. The All-India Muslim League vigorously promoted Iqbal's ideas. This campaign gained strength in the late 1930s and 1940s. In 1947 Great Britain partitioned India into two independent states—the predominantly Hindu India and the Muslim state of Pakistan. Iqbal died in 1938 and did not live to see the realization of his goal. Nonetheless, he remains one of Pakistan's national heroes. (*See also* **Ahmad Khan, Sayyid; India; Pakistan.**)

* **mysticism** belief that spiritual enlightenment and truth can be attained through various physical and spiritual disciplines

* **nationalism** feelings of loyalty and devotion to one's country and a commitment to its independence

* **Qur'an** book of the holy scriptures of Islam

* **sunnah** literally "the trodden path;" Islamic customs based on the exemplary behavior of Muhammad

Iran

Iran is an Islamic country in the Middle East. Once called Persia by outsiders, its inhabitants have always called it Iran, meaning Land of the Aryans, or "noble people." In 1935 the government formally requested that the world community adopt the name Iran. The region has one of the world's oldest civilizations, dating back to 2700 B.C.E.*

Iran borders the Caspian Sea, Gulf of Oman, Persian Gulf, and Strait of Hormuz. The latter two serve as vital water routes for the transport of oil.

* **B.C.E.** before the Common Era, which refers to the same time period as B.C.

Iran shares boundaries with several countries, including Turkey, Iraq, Pakistan, and Afghanistan. The country has a mostly dry climate. The terrain consists of a rugged mountainous rim, high central plateau, and small plains along the coasts. Only about 10 percent of the land is suitable for farming. Crops include grains, fruits, sugar beets, and cotton. Iran has rich reserves of petroleum, natural gas, and minerals and relies mostly on oil exports for its economy.

In 2002 the population of Iran numbered 67 million. Around 90 percent are Shi'i* Muslims, and most of the remaining Iranians are Sunni*. The national language is Farsi, an Indo-European language now written in Arabic script. The present government, established in 1979, is an Islamic republic, led by officials who are regarded as divinely guided. The capital is Tehran.

Early Dynasties

In 2700 B.C.E. the warlike Elamites dominated parts of present-day Iran. By 1300 B.C.E. Indo-Europeans from the west had gained control the region. Beginning in 559 B.C.E. and continuing for the next thousand years, a succession of three dynasties* ruled Iran and surrounding areas. They were the Archaemenids, Parthians, and Sassanians, and all of these civilizations contributed to the culture of present-day Iran.

Built in the early 1600s, the shimmering yellow mosque of Shaykh Lutfallah in Isfahan, Iran, was used solely by the ruler's family and associates. The mosque has no courtyard or minarets because it was not intended for public worship.

* **Shi'i** refers to Muslims who believe that Muhammad chose Ali ibn Abi Talib and his descendants as the spiritual-political leaders of the Muslim community

* **Sunni** refers to the largest branch of the Muslim community; the name derives from sunnah, the exemplary behavior of the Prophet Muhammad

* **dynasty** succession of rulers from the same family or group

Arabs Invade Iran. The year 637 C.E.*—the date of the Arab invasion—marks a turning point in Iran's history. Before the Arab conquest, people in Iran practiced Zoroastrianism, a religion centered around the idea of an unending struggle between the forces of good and evil. The Arabs brought Islam with them and influenced many Iranians to convert. The Iranian people, however, still kept many of their own traditions. They retained their language, although they added many Arabic words and the Arabic alphabet eventually replaced their own. For the next several centuries, Iran was governed as a territory of the caliphate*. The Iranians made contributions to Islamic civilization in literature, art, philosophy, medicine, and science.

Rise of the Safavids. Following the Arab conquest, many Iranians converted to Islam. When the Safavid dynasty gained control in 1501, it instituted Shi'i Islam, which has prevailed in the region ever since. The 1500s also witnessed the emergence of the *ulama* (Islamic religious scholars) as an important social force. These clerics struggled to gain power in Iran from that time onward, eventually succeeding in the 1970s. Safavid rule collapsed in the early 1700s, to be followed by the rule of a military commander, Nadir Shah, (ruled 1736–1747) and the short-lived Zand dynasty. The Qajar dynasty took over in the late 1700s.

Problems During Qajar Rule. Weak rulers, a failing economy, and foreign domination characterized the reign of the Qajar shahs*. Throughout the early 1800s, Iran lost territory to the Russians and suffered two defeats by the British when the Qajars attempted to take over parts of Afghanistan. Iran narrowly escaped partition by Russia and Britain in 1907 and conversion into a British protectorate* in 1919. The Qajar shahs allowed European companies to dominate Iran's transport, banking, mining, oil, and tobacco industries. Competition with foreign investors forced many Iranian businessmen into bankruptcy*.

Around 1900, large-scale protests erupted in opposition to Iran's submission to the Europeans and the incompetence of the shah. Merchants, fed up with the influx of foreign goods and the privileges granted to foreigners, rose to challenge the Qajar ruler. Members of the *ulama* also spoke out against the Qajar government, backing the protests with their moral authority. By the time World War I broke out in 1914, the Qajar dynasty faced constant challenges to its authority. In 1921 a military leader named Reza Khan seized power.

The Pahlavi Reign

In 1923 Reza Khan installed himself as prime minister of Iran. A few years later, he elevated himself to the throne as Reza Shah Pahlavi, thus beginning the Pahlavi dynasty. In 1941 his son, Muhammad Reza, succeeded him. Throughout their rule, the Pahlavi shahs stressed modernization, westernization, and secularism*. They resolved to eliminate traditional practices and beliefs and replace them with new ones from abroad. Ultimately, these policies led to the dynasty's overthrow and replacement by a religious regime controlled by the *ulama.*

Reza Shah's Reforms. The first Pahlavi ruler mounted military campaigns at the borders of Iran to strengthen his control over the territory.

---

* **c.e.** Common Era, which refers to the same time period as A.D.

* **caliphate** office and government of the caliph, the religious and political head of an Islamic state

* **shah** king (Persian); ruler of Iran

* **protectorate** country under the protection and control of a stronger nation

* **bankruptcy** state of financial ruin

* **secularism** belief that religion should be separate from other aspects of human life and society, especially politics

Within the country, he brutally suppressed unruly tribal groups, established a centralized state bureaucracy*, and formed a loyal standing army. Reza Shah based his central administration on a French model and replaced the Islamic legal system with European codes. He modeled many reforms on those of the Turkish ruler Mustafa Kemal Atatürk.

Hoping to invigorate the economy, the shah took over several major industries. He used the revenue to build roads and railroads and to pay for his growing army. His economic policies did not have much success, however, and private enterprise failed to flourish. Reza Shah also remained unable to gain control of the British-owned Anglo-Iranian Oil Company (AIOC), a major source of income for Great Britain.

Reza Shah Pahlavi's social reforms met with more success than his economic policies. The shah established state schools and training programs for teachers, as well as hospitals, clinics, laboratories for medicine and food testing, and vaccination programs for children. In 1934 Reza Shah opened Tehran University, the first institution in what would become a national university system. He also sponsored student trips to European universities to encourage the study of modern sciences and medicine. He had less success at implementing other reforms, such as abolishing the requirement that women wear veils, introducing Western-style dress, and reducing the influence of the *ulama*. In order to maintain his hold on the country, the shah exiled, jailed, tortured, and killed those who disagreed with him. One of the people he persecuted was Mohammad Mossadegh, future prime minister of Iran and leader of the Iranian nationalist movement.

As World War II (1939–1945) approached, Reza Shah allied himself with the Germans. He was not sympathetic to the Nazi cause, but he hoped to reduce British influence in his country by helping their enemies. His plan backfired. In 1941 British and Soviet forces invaded Iran and forced the shah from the throne.

Muhammad Reza Struggles With Dissent. Reza Khan's son, Muhammad Reza Pahlavi, took over in 1941. Inexperienced and unsure of himself, he served as little more than a figurehead controlled by the British. Gradually, however, he gained the support of the army. He also created an upper chamber of parliament that supported him against his critics. Through these means, he gradually assumed a position of power.

In 1949 Mohammad Mossadegh formed an organization called the National Front. The organization pushed for the nationalization* of the AIOC. Mossadegh gained widespread support, and public opinion forced the reluctant shah to appoint him prime minister. Mossadegh immediately acted to take control of the AIOC and became involved in a bitter dispute with the British. Highly popular among the people, Mossadegh engaged in some bizarre behaviors, such as wearing pajamas for public appearances, making speeches from his bed, and indulging in fits of weeping. Muhammad Reza attempted to unseat the minister in 1953, but mobs forced him to flee to Rome. A few days later, however, groups backed by the United States and Britain overthrew Mossadegh.

The shah returned to Iran and began to rule as an absolute dictator. The Kennedy administration urged him to gain support among his people by initiating reforms. Although Muhammad Reza did not want to do this, he felt

* **bureaucracy** agencies and officials that comprise a government

See map in Gulf States (vol. 1).

* **nationalization** process by which a government takes control of its industries

that he had no choice if he wanted to retain support from the United States. In the early 1960s, he launched a program called the White Revolution. The revolution introduced reforms in land ownership; construction of a centralized secular regime; and modernization of education and the economy along Western models. It also included a movement aimed at extending voting rights to women.

The clergy disapproved of the shah's policies, especially those involving land redistribution and women's rights. They joined with intellectuals and professionals who opposed the shah's autocratic* rule. In 1963 major clashes broke out at Tehran University between student protestors and the army. The term *gharbzadagi*, meaning "dazed by the West," became a powerful and widely used accusation against the Iranian government. A Shi'i religious leader, Ayatollah Ruhollah Khomeini, publicly denounced the shah. The government planned to execute Khomeini but sent him into exile instead. Khomeini spent 14 years abroad but continued to protest Iran's dependence on the United States, its tolerance of Israel, and the suppression of the *ulama*.

Despite political instability, the Iranian economy boomed in the 1970s. Oil prices were high, and the shah became extremely wealthy. He spent millions of dollars celebrating the 2,500th anniversary of the Iranian monarchy and buying expensive weapons and nuclear reactors. Critics became outraged by his neglect of the infrastructure*. In the late 1970s, Iran experienced a dramatic decline in income due to falling oil prices, and economic problems led to public unrest and frequent protests. From his exile in Iraq and then France, Ayatollah Khomeini also criticized the shah and his policies, adding fuel to the fire.

Islamic Republic of Iran

In 1979 Ayatollah Khomeini returned to Iran and led a coalition of clerics, intellectuals, students, and other anti-government groups in the Iranian Revolution. Thousands of urban poor joined in the struggle, angered by land reform policies that had driven them from the countryside. Together, these forces overthrew the Pahlavi government and drove the shah into exile. In place of the monarchy, Khomeini established the Islamic Republic of Iran.

Khomeini's New Government. The new Islamic government centered around the authority of Ayatollah Khomeini. He appointed a temporary government and designated himself as chief *faqih* (Islamic jurist), keeping the power in his own hands and those of the Revolutionary Council, made up of his supporters. He believed that clerics should rule the country and that Islamic law should be implemented in all aspects of Iranian life. Under Khomeini's leadership, the Islamic Republic undid many of the reforms of the Pahlavi dynasty.

Like the shahs before him, Khomeini set about eliminating rivals and critics. First, he went after intellectuals, liberals*, and guerrilla* fighters who had participated in the revolution, but who now threatened his regime with their own demands. When the main guerrilla group began to assassinate key clerics in the government to gain power for themselves, Khomeini unleashed a bloody reign of terror that lasted around four years. In addition to guer-

* **autocratic** characterized by unlimited authority

* **infrastructure** basic facilities and institutions that a country needs in order to function

* **liberal** person who supports greater participation in government for individuals; one who is not bound by tradition

* **guerrilla** member of an group of fighters, outside the regular army, who engages in unconventional warfare

rillas and intellectuals, he executed hundreds of officials from the former shah's government. By the time elections took place in 1980, no serious opposition existed to challenge Khomeini's candidates. Supporters of Khomeini took over the crucial institutions of the state and used their power to crush any remaining critics.

War With Iraq. Almost immediately after the Iranian Revolution, Iraq attacked, marking the beginning of the Iran-Iraq War. Iraq claimed that it needed to defend itself against Iran's revolutionary threats and regain its portion of the Shatt al-Arab waterway that it had been forced to give up under the shah's regime. The attack set off a bloody and expensive war between Iran and Iraq that lasted for eight years.

During the war, Iraq drew worldwide outrage by using chemical weapons. Nevertheless, the United States supported Iraq in this war with Iran, and U.S. companies sold them weapons. Iran, lacking modern equipment and tactics, enlisted countless numbers of its young men to fight the Iraqis, leading to some of the deadliest battles of the century. The conflict greatly affected the world economy and shipping in the Persian Gulf, leading to food shortages and economic hardship in Iran. Iran and Iraq finally accepted a United Nations peace plan, and fighting ceased in 1988. Ayatollah Khomeini, who had once said that he had not engaged in the revolution to ensure material well-being, described the ceasefire as more bitter for him than a poisoned drink.

Iran at the Turn of the Century. In 1989 Ayatollah Ruhollah Khomeini died. A month later, the Iranian government amended the constitution to eliminate the position of prime minister and to give more power to the president and other nonreligious government officials. Religious leaders, however, retained control of key institutions, such as the military.

During the 1990s, Iran maintained a wary relationship with most of its neighbors. Some surrounding countries accused Iran of training radical Muslims to overthrow their governments and replace them with Islamic theocracies*. Iran and the West remained unfriendly. In 1991, when the United States and its allies fought Iraq in the Gulf War, Iran remained neutral despite its former hostilities with Iraq.

In 1997 Muhammad Khatami was elected president of Iran. He showed more tolerance of Western practices and beliefs than did his predecessors, and his election highlighted the growth of cultural, economic, and scholarly communication between Iran and the West. In 2000 the Iranians elected a liberal majority to parliament, and in 2001, Iranians re-elected Khatami as president.

During this time, the position of women in society improved. Women became active in professional capacities and as elected representatives, appointed government officials, and judges. In 2003 the Nobel Committee awarded its prestigious Peace Prize to human rights lawyer and former judge Shirin Ebadi, for her efforts on behalf of women and children. Although reaction to the award was mixed in Iran—conservatives trying to ignore it and liberals hailing the committee's decision—the country is seen as one of the more progressive Muslim nations with respect to women's rights. (*See also* **Atatürk, Mustafa Kemal; Great Britain; Gulf States; Iraq; Khomeini, Ruhollah al-Musavi; Safavid Dynasty.**)

Students Hold Americans Hostage

When Khomeini overthrew Muhammad Reza in 1979, the shah fled the country. Dying of cancer, he pleaded with President Jimmy Carter to allow him to come to the United States for treatment. Despite warnings from the American embassy in Tehran, Carter permitted the shah to enter the country. Many Iranians believed that the United States intended to restore the shah to the throne. In protest, Iranian students raided the American embassy in November of 1979, holding most of the diplomats hostage. Although Khomeini had not ordered the seizure of the embassy, he supported the takeover. The students kept the hostages until January of 1981—444 days after their capture—and released them on the day of Ronald Reagan's presidential inauguration.

* **theocracy** government headed by religious leaders and believed to be divinely guided

Iraq

* **caliph** religious and political leader of an Islamic state

* **Shi'i** refers to Muslims who believe that Muhammad chose Ali ibn Abi Talib and his descendants as the spiritual-political leaders of the Muslim community

* **Sunni** refers to the largest branch of the Muslim community; the name derives from sunnah, the exemplary behavior of the Prophet Muhammad

* **caliphate** office and government of the caliph, the religious and political head of an Islamic state

* **sultan** political and military ruler of a Muslim dynasty or state

Iraq has been a part of the Islamic world since the 600s. Powerful caliphs* once ruled vast empires from Baghdad, the capital of present-day Iraq. At the beginning of the twenty-first century, 24 million people live in the country. Shi'i* Muslims make up 60 percent of the population, and Sunni* Muslims account for around 35 percent. The remaining 5 percent include Jews, Christians, and other minorities. Iraq has ethnic as well as religious minorities. Most Iraqis are Arabs, but 15 to 20 percent are Kurds who mainly live in northern areas. Conflict between different groups has created longstanding tensions in Iraq. The nation struggles to find stability in the face of internal dissent and threats from other countries.

Succession of Conquests

Arab armies first brought Islam to the Iraqi region in the mid-600s. The Umayyad caliphate* ruled the area until 750, when the Abbasid caliphate took over. The Abbasids created the city of Baghdad as their capital, and it became a powerful and thriving metropolis. In 1055 Seljuk Turks captured the city. The Abbasids regained much of the region in the early 1200s, but Mongol armies invaded the area in 1258. In 1535 the Ottomans seized Iraq and added it to their growing empire.

Iraq Under Ottoman Rule. The Ottoman sultans* made many reforms in Iraq. They reorganized the local government, increased trade, and improved living conditions. They also established Sunni Islam as the ruling faith in Baghdad. The Shi'i Muslims in the south identified more with Shi'is

After the fall of Iraqi president Saddam Hussein in 2003, Iraqi Shi'i Muslims take their ritual walk to the holy city of Karbala for the first time in many years. Shi'i Muslims were not allowed to make this pilgrimage under Saddam's regime.

in Iran than with the Ottoman administration. The tension between the Shi'i population and the dominant Sunnis led to many conflicts.

Ottoman influence in Iraq began to wane in the 1600s. The sultans in Istanbul relaxed their grip on Iraq, granting greater authority to local leaders. Iranian forces took the opportunity to invade Iraq, killing and enslaving thousands of Sunni Muslims. The Ottomans regained control and retaliated by executing much of Baghdad's Shi'i population. The Mamluks, a dynasty of slave soldiers who had gained power over the caliphs, took over parts of Iraq in the mid-1700s, suppressing conflicts and helping to stabilize the region. The Ottomans returned in 1831. After World War I (1914–1918), however, the Ottoman Empire collapsed. The League of Nations, an international peacekeeping organization, established the borders of present-day Iraq, adding portions of Kurdistan to traditional Iraqi lands along the Tigris and Euphrates Rivers. The League of Nations then gave Iraq to Great Britain as a mandate so that Britain would prepare the country for its eventual independence.

See map in Gulf States (vol. 1).

Britain and Independence. Great Britain remained a major presence in Iraq for nearly 40 years. In 1921 British leaders established Faysal I, an Arab leader who had been exiled from Arabia, as king of Iraq. During Faysal's reign, Iraqis increasingly sought to break away from Great Britain. British troops suppressed rebellions of Kurds in the north and Shi'is in the south. Many British officials also wanted to withdraw from the region. In 1932 Britain granted Iraq its independence, and the League of Nations accepted the nation as a new member. British troops, however, maintained bases in Iraq, and Iraqi officials remained subservient, agreeing to consult with Britain, especially on issues of foreign policy.

King Faysal died in 1933. The following year, three governments rose and fell with tribal uprisings. Military leaders and various factions vied for control of Iraq, and World War II (1939–1945) caused even more confusion. Iraqi leaders originally retained their loyalty to Britain, but supporters of a Pan-Arab alliance pushed to gain further independence. They formed military ties to Britain's enemies, Germany and Italy. British forces quickly defeated Iraqi troops and forced the nation to support Britain in its war effort.

Iraq experienced more political unrest after the war. Several governments formed and fell. Shi'i leaders in the south remained resentful of British influence, and Kurds in the north challenged Iraqi leaders. In 1958 a group of officers organized a military takeover of the government. Ranking officer Abd al-Karim Qasim declared Iraq a republic on July 14, and the new constitution affirmed Islam as the state religion and abolished the monarchy.

Triumph of the Ba'th Party

Soon after the revolution of 1958, Iraq once again plunged into political turmoil. Qasim's regime fell in 1963. The Ba'th Party, an Arab political group advocating socialism* and nationalism, emerged as a strong force. In 1968 the Ba'th Party gained the support of the army and took control of the government. Ahmad Hassan al-Bakr assumed the presidency with Saddam Hussein as his right-hand man.

The new government sought to expand the economy and to replace free enterprise with socialism. They also worked to free their industries from for-

* **socialism** economic system in which the government owns and operates the means of production and the distribution of goods

* **nationalize** to place an industry under government control

* **imam** spiritual-political leader in Shi'i Islam, one who is regarded as directly descended from Muhammad; also, one who leads prayers

* **shah** king (Persian); ruler of Iran

* **communist** follower of communism, a political and economic system based on the concept of shared ownership of all property

* **ayatollah** highest ranking legal scholar among some Shi'i Muslims

* **secular** separate from religion in human life and society; connected to everyday life

eign control. In the 1970s, Iraq nationalized* its oil production, leading to an increase in the nation's wealth. The new government also sponsored irrigation projects, agricultural reforms, and programs to improve living conditions for the peasants. Farming projects produced little success, however, and industrial production lagged as well. The Ba'th government eventually abandoned its socialist goals and allowed for private investment and private enterprises.

Clashes With Kurds and Shi'is. Ethnic and religious divisions posed a challenge for the Ba'th leaders, who were Arabs belonging to the Sunni faith. Shi'i groups in the south worked to free the cities of Najaf and Karbala from Ba'th control. These cities contain some of the most holy sites in the Islamic world, and believers from many countries make pilgrimages to visit the tombs of imams*. Najaf also served for a time as a refuge for future Iranian leader and Shi'i rebel Ruhollah Khomeini during his 14-year exile from Iran. The *marja'iyah*, a network of religious leaders, led uprisings against the Ba'th government to rid the cities of Sunni influence and gained international support for its struggles.

In the north, the Kurdish people sought to break away from Iraq and form a separate state. In 1968, with support from Iran, the Kurds engaged the Iraqi army in a civil war. In 1970 the Iraqi government agreed to recognize the Kurds as a separate group entitled to self-rule. War broke out again in 1974, after the government failed to honor certain agreements. Wishing to gain territories in northern Iraq, the shah* of Iran again provided aid to the Kurds. Iraqi leaders met with the shah, and the two parties reached an agreement regarding Iraqi borders. Iran withdrew its support for the Kurds, and the conflict died down.

In 1979 Ahmad Hassan al-Bakr retired from the presidency, and Saddam Hussein replaced him. The new leader quickly suppressed a plot against his rule, executing 22 conspirators. Hussein tolerated no opposition. He arrested dozens of communists*, forcing them to flee the country. Other opposition parties either disbanded or operated in secret.

Iraq at War. In 1979 a militant Shi'i group under the leadership of Ayatollah* Ruhollah al-Musavi Khomeini took control of the government of Iran. Khomeini denounced Hussein's regime as secular* and declared that he would establish an Islamic government in Iraq. Hussein sought to fend off Khomeini and also to regain access to the Shatt al-Arab waterway, which Iraq had been forced to cede to Iran during the 1970s. In September 1980, Iraqi forces invaded Iran, bombing strategic targets and beginning a war between the two nations that lasted for eight years.

In the early stages of the Iran-Iraq War, Iraqi forces advanced into Iran. The Iranian army grew in strength and numbers and invaded Iraq in 1982. Iraqi Kurds took the opportunity to rise up against Baghdad. Hussein fought back with poison gas and weapons acquired from France, the United States, and the Soviet Union. In order to stop Khomeini, the United States provided Saddam Hussein with intelligence information. Iraq pushed the Iranian troops back, and in 1988, Khomeini agreed to end the war.

Both Iran and Iraq suffered heavy losses during the war, and little territory changed hands. Iraq owed a debt of at least $80 billion to Saudi Arabia, Kuwait, and other countries in the region. Saddam Hussein believed that his debtors would release him from his obligations, and even help pay for the reconstruction of Iraq, out of sympathy for his struggle to prevent the spread of

Islamic fundamentalism*. The leaders of these countries, however, insisted that Iraq repay the debt, despite its war losses. They also increased their own oil production, leading to a drop in oil prices that reduced Iraq's income.

U.S. and British leaders became alarmed when Saddam Hussein decided to take revenge on Kuwait. For decades, Iraqi leaders had claimed that British and Ottoman leaders had unjustly separated Kuwait from Iraq. Kuwait had also played a role in driving down oil prices. In August 1990, Iraq invaded the country, beginning the Persian Gulf War.

The United Nations condemned the attack and imposed economic sanctions on Iraq, preventing the import of such goods as food and medicine. U.S. President George Bush feared a threat to his nation's economic interests in Kuwait. Following his lead, several nations, including a few Muslim countries, formed an alliance against Saddam Hussein and attacked Iraqi targets in January 1991. By April, ground troops had routed the Iraqi army and driven it out of Kuwait.

Iraq suffered heavy economic losses during both wars. Bombs and missiles had damaged several cities, and the Iraqi armed forces had been seriously weakened. In 1991, encouraged by the United States, both Kurds and Shi'is rebelled against the central government. Saddam Hussein, however, had just enough military strength to crush these rebellions. His forces were especially brutal in their campaign against the Kurds. Thousands died from hunger and disease, and others fled to Turkey.

End of the Regime. The Baghdad regime continued to face threats from the Shi'is in the south and the Kurds in the north. Saddam Hussein survived uprisings in part because his enemies lacked unified strategies. In 1992, however, several groups opposed to the Ba'th party met in Vienna to form the Iraqi National Congress, an organization with the goal of toppling Hussein.

The Iraqi leader faced economic problems as well as frequent uprisings. After the Gulf War, the United Nations demanded that Iraq give up its missiles and weapons of mass destruction. When Iraq failed to comply, the U.N. imposed trade sanctions*. Iraq's economy and population suffered greatly. In 1996 the U.N. created an oil-for-food program, allowing Iraq to sell oil to other countries if it would agree to use the money to buy food and medicine for its people. Conditions improved slightly for the nation's citizens, but hunger, poverty, and poor health care remained widespread problems.

Saddam Hussein took steps to ensure that he remained in power. Aware that another uprising could devastate Iraq, he tried to increase his popularity with the Shi'is. He donated gold and silver to decorate the domes of Shi'i holy tombs and rewrote his family history to claim that he descended from Muhammad through the Shi'i line. Hussein also continued to use force to suppress dissent. After the 1991 uprising, for example, he had over 100 Shi'i clerics and religious scholars executed.

In early 2003, President George W. Bush of the United States claimed that Saddam Hussein had failed in his promise to the United Nations to remove all of his biological and chemical weapons. Bush openly declared his intention to have Hussein removed from power, and an American-led coalition invaded Iraq and succeeded in ending Saddam Hussein's regime. (*See also* **Abbasid Caliphate; Gulf States; Iran; Mamluk State; Seljuk Dynasty; Umayyad Caliphate.**)

* **fundamentalist** generally refers to the movement that promotes a literal interpretation of scripture; in Islam, a movement that promotes politicization of religion to create an alternative public order

* **sanction** economic or military measure taken against a nation that acts in violation of International law

Women's Rights in the New Iraq

In early May 2003, while thousands of Iraqis flocked to prayer services, women in a Baghdad beauty salon debated their own and their country's future. As enormous political changes swept the nation, these women wondered how the new government would affect women's rights.

A conservative Baghdad radio station called for women to wear the *hijab*, and attendance at religious services increased dramatically in the aftermath of Saddam Hussein's regime. Although a conservative government would be a serious setback—especially for older educated women who fought long and hard against veiling, arranged marriages, and other social constraints—only time will tell how the new Iraq will be governed.

Ishmail

See *Ismail.*

Islam: Overview

With more than one billion followers, Islam is the second-largest religion in the world. Muslims constitute a majority in 48 countries from North Africa to Southeast Asia and a significant minority in many others. Although the Arab world is often considered to be the heartland of Islam, it has spread to the traditionally Christian countries of Europe and North America, as well as throughout Asia and Africa.

For information on Islam in specific countries or regions of the world, see the following entries:

Albania	India	Pakistan
Algeria	Indonesia	Palestine
Bangladesh	Iran	Philippines
Bosnia	Iraq	Saudi Arabia
Brunei	Jordan	Somalia
Canada	Kashmir	South Asia
Caribbean	Kosovo	Southeast Asia
Caucasus	Latin America	Southern Africa
Central Africa	Lebanon	Sudan
Central Asia	Libya	Syria
China	Malawi	Tunisia
East Africa	Malaysia	Turkey
Egypt	Middle East	United States
Europe	Morocco	West Africa
Great Britain	Nigeria	Yemen
Gulf States	North Africa	

See color plate 2, vol. 1.

The Heart of the Message

The term *islam* comes from the Arabic root *s-l-m*, which means "submission" or "peace." Because Muslims surrender themselves to the will of God, they are at peace with themselves and with God. At the center and foundation of Islam is Allah (God, the Merciful, the Compassionate), who is the supreme ruler—all-powerful, all-knowing—and the creator and judge of the universe. Islam teaches that God revealed his will to humankind through a series of messengers, known as prophets. Muhammad received the last of these revelations, which were later collected and recorded in the Qur'an, Islam's sacred scripture.

Core Beliefs. The Qur'an states that God created two similar types of creatures: human beings from clay and *jinn*, a type of spirit, from fire. The scriptures provide few details about *jinn* but suggest that they possess intelligence and responsibility and sometimes make trouble for human beings. People are the noblest of God's creatures and are therefore superior to all of nature.

At the same time, however, the Qur'an notes that humans are frail, rebellious, and filled with pride, which causes them to forget their limitations and dependence on God. When human beings act in prideful ways, disobeying God, they commit the most serious of sins.

The duty of humans, according to the Qur'an, is to obey and serve God. Historically, Allah chose special messengers, or prophets, to communicate his commands and prohibitions to a particular community. At the end of time, the members of the community would receive rewards or punishments based on their adherence to these standards. Islam recognizes Adam (the first man), and several prophets, including Abraham, Noah, Moses, and Jesus. Muslims do not acknowledge Jesus as the Son of God, and they reject the concept of God as three persons—father, son, and Holy Spirit. The Qur'an asserts that all the prophets anticipated the coming of Muhammad as the final messenger who would confirm all that had been revealed to them.

See color plate 11, vol. 3.

Muhammad, a merchant and caravan leader, became Muhammad, the Prophet, during the month of Ramadan in 610. On the Night of Power and Excellence, the angel Gabriel brought to him the first of many divine revelations. Islamic tradition states that he fell into a trance while receiving the message and that he knew that it had come from God. The Qur'an, in fact, denies any earthly origins, noting that such a source would make it susceptible to "manifold doubts and oscillations [opposing beliefs]."

Although Allah has demonstrated mercy to human beings by sending them prophets to guide them, the Qur'an suggests that people tend to forget or reject these teachings. The scripture states that Satan (Iblis) deliberately tries to tempt people to sin. Satan was once a high-ranking *jinn*, but when God commanded the angels to honor Adam, he refused to comply, unwilling to acknowledge the superior status of humans. His disobedience angered God, who cast him out of heaven. While he awaits his punishment, to be delivered at the end of time, Satan attempts to lead people astray.

See map in Sunni Islam (vol. 3).

In the biblical story of Adam and Eve, Satan takes the form of a serpent and persuades them to eat the forbidden fruit of a certain tree in the Garden of Eden. Unlike the biblical account, the Qur'an does not regard this act as the original sin (the Christian belief that all humans are sinful as a result of Adam's fall). Instead, the Qur'an suggests that sinful behavior results when human beings willfully abuse the freedom that Allah has given to them. If a person commits a sin, feels remorse, and makes atonement for the evil deed, God forgives the sin. Moreover, genuine repentance is enough to restore a Muslim to a state of sinlessness.

Muslims believe that the world will end on the Last Day, and God will resurrect the dead and judge each person according to his or her deeds. Those who are saved will live forever in paradise, a place of physical and spiritual delights. Those who are condemned will go to hell, a place of eternal fire.

The Qur'an does not provide a clear answer to the theological* question of free will versus predestination. Some passages support the argument that human beings are truly free to choose their own actions, while others indicate that an all-knowing God predetermines all actions. Nevertheless, the scripture is clear about the absolute power of God, without whose permission or creative act nothing occurs. It is also clear that people are account-

* **theological** refers to the study of the nature, qualities, and will of God

able for their actions, despite the fact that they are dependent on God for the ability and power to act.

The Paths of Islam. Those who embrace Islam become members of a worldwide religious community, or *ummah*. Because Islam emphasizes practice more than belief, law rather than theology is the principal source of instruction for Muslims. Islamic law (*shari'ah*) developed over a period of several hundred years following the death of the Prophet Muhammad. *Shari'ah* dictates a Muslim's duties to God and to society, incorporating regulations governing prayer and fasting as well as rules on family life, crime and punishment, and international politics. In general, the four recognized sources of law are the Qur'an, sunnah*, rules derived from the Qur'an and sunnah by analogy (*qiyas*), and consensus of the scholars (*ijma*).

The *aqidah*, or five articles of Islamic faith, are belief in the oneness of God, angels, prophets, revealed books, and the afterlife. All Muslims are required to practice the five Pillars of Islam: the profession of faith, which acknowledges that "There is no god but Allah, and Muhammad is His messenger"; prayer five times each day and community prayer in the mosque* on Fridays; *zakat*, setting aside a portion of one's wealth for the poor; fasting during the holy month of Ramadan; and pilgrimage to the holy city of Mecca for every Muslim who is able, physically and financially, at least once in a lifetime. Some scholars consider *jihad*, or striving to accomplish God's will, to be a sixth pillar.

As Islamic law developed during the 700s and 800s, some Muslims began to shift their focus from the external obligations of the faith to their inner spiritual life. The movement known as Sufism* emerged. It called on Muslims to detach themselves from the distractions of this world to concentrate on holiness and complete devotion to God. By the 1100s, the followers of Sufism, attracted to its ritual practices, had created a vast network of orders, or brotherhoods.

Social Interactions. Islam emphasizes the ideals of community, equality, and social justice. The Qur'an describes the *ummah* as "the best community evolved for mankind, enjoining what is right and forbidding what is wrong" so that "there is no mischief and corruption" on earth. Islam teaches that all people are "equal children of Adam," rejecting the concept of privilege based on social class or race. Consequently, prosperous Muslims must strive to help the poor. Hoarding wealth and ignoring the needs of the poor places a prosperous Muslim at risk of severe punishment in the hereafter.

Islamic tradition emphasizes order, stability, and harmony in society. It expects individuals to dress and behave modestly and to treat their bodies with dignity. This means that Muslims should eat only lawful foods (*halal*) and should avoid the use of alcohol, tobacco, and illegal drugs. Behaviors that threaten the social order—such as theft, drug abuse, adultery, and homosexual relationships—receive harsh punishments.

The family is the foundation of Islamic society. It shapes a person's identity, determining social class, political affiliations, and cultural practices. Islam encourages Muslims to marry and produce children. In a traditional Muslim family, the father expects obedience from his wife and children. In turn, he must support and protect his family.

* **sunnah** literally "the trodden path;" Islamic customs based on the exemplary behavior of Muhammad

* **mosque** Muslim place of worship

* **Sufism** Islamic mysticism, which seeks to develop spirituality through discipline of the mind and body

The Muslim Community in History

A variety of religious traditions, including ancient Egyptian and Mesopotamian religions, Zoroastrianism, Judaism, and Christianity, began in the Middle East. The founding of Islam in the early 600s, in the Arabian city of Mecca, launched a new religious movement and a new era in world history.

Gods, Goddesses, and Retaliation. The Bedouin* tribes of Arabia worshipped at the Kaaba, a religious shrine that housed the idols of hundreds of gods and goddesses. They also believed in Allah, a supreme god who created and sustained life but was uninvolved in day-to-day affairs. The members of this pre-Islamic society asserted that fate controlled everyday events. They had no concept of the hereafter and the belief that they would be held accountable for their actions on earth.

The people of Arabia lived in a culture that emphasized loyalty to the tribe and valued the characteristics of honor and bravery. In the absence of a central political or legal authority, threats to a family or to the tribe often met with group retaliation. The dry desert landscape forced people to compete for scarce resources, such as water and pasture, and as a result, conflicts and rivalries erupted frequently. At the same time, the trade routes in the region, which connected the Indian Ocean and the Mediterranean Sea, brought tremendous wealth to cities such as Mecca and Medina.

Unwelcome Message. Born around 570, Muhammad prospered as a merchant in the caravan trade of Mecca. At the age of 40, he received a calling to become a prophet of God. He began to preach against the polytheistic* practices of the people and against the inequality between the wealthy elite and the poverty-stricken masses. Muhammad's claim to be a prophet challenged the authority of the ruling class, and his emphasis on monotheism* threatened to wipe out the city's profits from religious pilgrimages to the Kaaba, which housed the various gods and goddesses of Arabia. As a result, the Meccans actively persecuted him and his followers. The situation became so difficult that Muhammad and his followers left Mecca for the city of Medina in 622. This migration, known as the Hijrah, marked a turning point in the history of the Islamic movement and the beginning of the Islamic calendar. The Muslim community became a religious-political entity with Muhammad as its leader.

Muhammad introduced a new moral order to Arabian society. Life no longer revolved around tribal or personal interests. Now the people were concerned about submitting to God's will. Belief in the Day of Judgment and the afterlife gave the community a dimension of human responsibility and accountability that had been absent from the pre-Islamic Arabian religion. A religious community governed by God's law replaced tribal affiliation and custom as the dominant features in society.

The Prophet's impact on Muslim life and history cannot be overestimated. His character and personality inspired confidence and commitment. Muhammad's example (sunnah) became the standard for community life, and reports of his words and deeds (hadith) were preserved and passed on in oral and written form.

Irreconcilable Differences. After the Prophet's death in 632, his followers disagreed about who should succeed him. One group believed that

* **Bedouin** nomadic Arab of the desert, especially in North Africa, Syria, and Arabia

* **polytheistic** believing in several gods

* **monotheism** belief that there is only one God

47

Islam: Overview

See color plate 2, vol. 3.

* **imam** spiritual-political leader in Shi'i Islam, one who is regarded as directly descended from Muhammad; also, one who leads prayers

* **caliph** religious and political leader of an Islamic state

* **missionary** person who works to convert nonbelievers to a particular faith

Muhammad died without designating a successor, and therefore, the elders of the community should select the next leader of the community. The other group believed that the Prophet had named his son-in-law, Ali ibn Abi Talib, as the imam* of the Muslim community. Divinely appointed and protected from sin, the imam was considered infallible, and therefore, had supreme authority in all religious and political matters. This dispute eventually led to the division of Muslims into two major groups—Sunni and Shi'i. Today Sunnis represent about 85 percent of the world's Muslims, and Shi'is constitute about 15 percent.

The majority of the Prophet's followers chose to follow Abu Bakr, Muhammad's companion who was chosen by the community elders to be the first caliph* after Muhammad. Several Arab tribes rejected Abu Bakr's leadership, believing that religion and politics are separate and that the death of Muhammad signified the end of their allegiance to the Muslim community. Abu Bakr believed that Muslims must remain politically as well as religiously united and so he forced the tribes to be loyal to him. He led the community until he was succeeded by Umar ibn al-Khattab in 634.

When Umar ibn al-Khattab died in 644, Uthman ibn Affan became the third caliph. Uthman's assassination in 656 threatened Muslim unity. Although Ali ibn Abi Talib was elected fourth caliph, he never had wide political support. Fatally wounded in 660, Ali was buried in Najaf, which became an important pilgrimage site for Shi'i Muslims.

Conquest and Expansion. With the growth of Islam, Muslims turned their attention to economic and political gain in lands beyond the Arabian Peninsula. Much of the Middle East was under the control of the Byzantine Empire. Muslim armies defeated the Byzantines and gained control of Jerusalem in 638. By 641 they had gained control of Syria, Palestine, and Egypt and had defeated the Persian Empire as well. Soon after, they swept across North Africa. The Muslims viewed their astonishing military success as a confirmation of the Qur'anic message that a society governed by God's laws would thrive.

As Muslim invaders reached new territories, they established Islamic rule in the conquered regions. Many conquered people voluntarily converted to Islam and gained full citizenship in the empire. In accordance with Islamic law, Muslim leaders extended legal protections to Jews and Christians living under their rule. Muslims considered these groups to be People of the Book, meaning that they were guided by scripture, sacred writings that contained revelations from God. As long as they obeyed the local Islamic ruler, they were permitted to practice their faith and to follow their religious leaders and law in personal matters. Muslim rulers did, however, require their non-Muslim subjects to pay special taxes. In areas where people worshipped pagan gods, especially in North Africa, Muslims forced the inhabitants to convert to Islam under threat of death. At times, the invaders fought against groups that rejected or resisted Muslim rule. Islam also spread through migration and settlement, as Muslims established new towns and cities throughout the empire. In addition, merchants, traders, and missionaries* brought Islam to new areas.

Rise and Fall of an Empire. Within a century after the Prophet's death, the sphere of Muslim influence extended from the Arabian Peninsula to Spain,

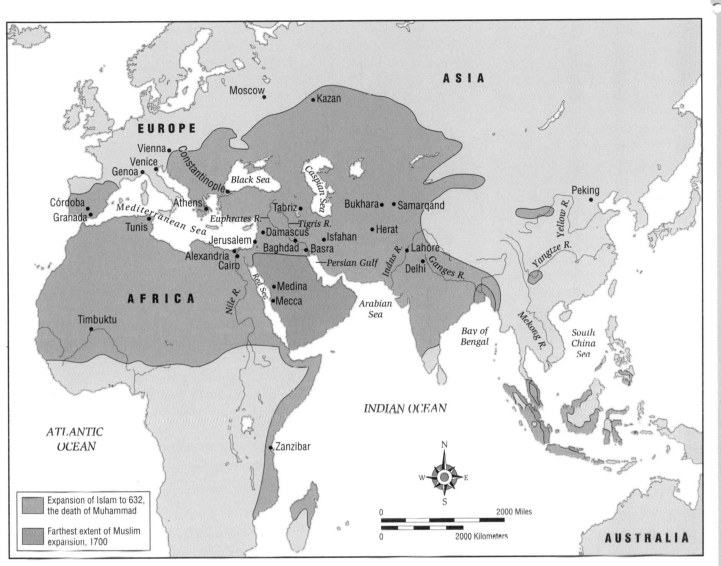

Expansion of Islam to 632, the death of Muhammad

Farthest extent of Muslim expansion, 1700

In the 600s, Islam spread from the Arabian Peninsula into Egypt and the Middle East. In the 700s, it moved west into North Africa and east into Afghanistan. By 1700, a millennium after its birth, Islam had expanded widely throughout Asia, Africa, and Europe. The map shows the farthest reaches of Islam from its beginnings to about 1700. However, by this time Spain was no longer part of the Islamic world.

* **caliphate** office and government of the caliph, the religious and political head of an Islamic state

* **sultanate** government of a sultan, the political and military ruler of a Muslim dynasty or state

Central Asia, and the Indian subcontinent. Under the leadership of two caliphates*, the Umayyad (661–750) in Damascus (Syria), and the Abbasid (750–1258) in Baghdad (Iraq), the Muslims consolidated their power. Islam became a mighty political force and Islamic civilization developed and flourished.

Muslim rulers established courts and instituted systems of government. They encouraged learning and supported the arts. They built magnificent cities that included palaces, mosques, aqueducts, libraries, schools, public baths, and gardens. Muslim physicians advanced the study and practice of medicine, and scholars wrote books on history, philosophy, and mathematics. At a time when many Europeans lived in relatively primitive conditions, Muslims enjoyed the luxuries of an advanced civilization.

In 1258 Mongols from the East destroyed the Abbasid caliphate. For the next 500 years, the Islamic world consisted of several local states or sultanates*. Among the most powerful of these were the Ottomans (which included Turkey, much of the Arab world, and Eastern Europe), the Safavids (in Persia), and the Mughals (on the Indian subcontinent).

* **protectorate** country under the protection and control of a stronger nation

* **imperialism** extension of power and influence over another country or region

* **communist** refers to communism, a political and economic system based on the concept of shared ownership of all property

* **liberal** supporting greater participation in government for individuals; not bound by tradition

* **secular** separate from religion in human life and society; connected to everyday life

* **autocrat** one who rules with unlimited authority

Against the Establishment

The early Sufis practiced strict self-denial as a way to develop spiritual discipline. They led lives of poverty, wore coarse woolen garments, and isolated themselves from the rest of society. Their beliefs contradicted established Islamic doctrine and practice, and as a result, they came under the attack of Islamic scholars and orthodox Muslims. For example, they emphasized mental prayer over ritual prayer (one of the Pillars of Islam), and claimed to be inspired by God, which appeared to be a challenge to Muhammad's unique role as His messenger. Over time, Sufis were accepted into mainstream Islam, and they developed a vast network of orders. Their practices varied—some engaged in silent meditation, and others used dance, music, and poetry in their rituals.

During the late 1700s and 1800s, European nations increased their power and influence in the Muslim world, establishing colonies in the Middle East, Africa, and India. When the Ottoman Empire collapsed after World War I ended in 1918, Great Britain and France divided most of the land between them, to be governed as protectorates*.

Resurgence. Muslims struggled with the impact of European imperialism* and the intellectual and moral challenges of a changing world. During the 1800s, a series of Islamic revivalist movements emerged. These various movements, including the Wahhabi in Arabia and the Mahdi in Sudan, shared a common concern about the decline of Muslim societies. They advocated a return to the teachings of the Qur'an and the sunnah, and they drew support from those who sought to establish new Islamic states.

Later, modernist movements attempted to bridge the gap between the growing influence of the West and traditional Islam. Men such as Jamal al-Din al-Afghani and Muhammad Abduh in the Middle East and Sayyid Ahmad Khan and Muhammad Iqbal in South Asia sought to restore the pride, identity, and strength of the Islamic community. They emphasized that Islam is compatible with reason, science, and technology but also argued for the need to reinterpret Islam in light of modern issues and concerns. This modernist movement appealed mainly to educated people. The majority were attracted to more traditional organizations, such as the Muslim Brotherhood. The brotherhood criticized Islamic modernists for attempting to emulate Western ideals and declared that Islam offers an alternative path. These reformers sought to implement an Islamic system of government through social and political action.

During the 1950s and 1960s, most of the Muslim world gained independence. Many of the new states, including Lebanon, Syria, Sudan, Jordan, Iraq, and Pakistan, were created by the colonial powers and drawn with artificial or arbitrary boundaries. European governments even appointed their rulers. As a result, issues of political legitimacy and national identity added to the problems of nation building.

Communist* movements, liberal* reformers, and Islamic revivalists competed for influence. In some cases, as in Egypt, secular* governments imprisoned activists who lobbied for a religious-based government. The majority of Muslim nations developed political, economic, legal, and educational systems based on Western models and did little to recognize the role of Islam in public life.

Islam reemerged as a powerful global force in Muslim politics during the 1970s and 1980s. The belief that existing political, economic, and social systems had failed led many Muslims to embrace religious revivalism. Authoritarian regimes—led by kings, military officers, or former military officers—ruled most Islamic nations. These autocrats* banned or restricted political parties and manipulated elections or cancelled them entirely. Economically, urban areas suffered from a growing tide of poverty and illiteracy. Some Muslims charged that the westernization of Muslim societies had contributed to the breakdown of the traditional family and the increase in spiritual complacency.

At the heart of revivalism is the belief that the Muslim world is in a state of decline because Muslims have departed from the straight path of Islam.

The remedy is a return to Islam in personal and public life that will ensure the restoration of Muslim identity, values, and power. Although revivalists condemn the westernization and secularization of society, they consider science and technology as compatible with Islam.

Today, Islamic revivalism is a widespread religious and social movement, present in virtually every Muslim country. Islamic organizations work in the fields of social services (hospitals, clinics, legal aid societies), economics (Islamic banks, investment firms), education (schools, childcare centers), and in religious publishing and broadcasting.

The history of the Islamic community has spanned more than 14 centuries. Islam continues to be a vibrant and dynamic religious tradition, expanding geographically and facing new challenges. Muslims have many different perspectives on such matters as the nature of the state, Islamic law, and the status of women and minorities in the Muslim community. As they grapple with these issues, Muslims demonstrate the unity, diversity, and endurance of Islam. (*See also* **Abbasid Caliphate; Afterlife; Allah; Christianity and Islam; Colonialism; Government; Hadith; Imam; Islamic State; Jihad; Judaism and Islam; Law; Mecca; Mughal Empire; Muhammad; Ottoman Empire; Qur'an; Shi'i Islam; Sufism; Sunnah; Sunni Islam; Umayyad Caliphate.**)

Islamic State

For most of the history of Islam, the "state" did not exist as an institution with legal authority. Nonetheless, since the days of Muhammad, Muslim scholars have theorized about the relationship between religion and government. During the 1900s, the modern Islamic state emerged. Although Islamic states may follow similar practices with regard to moral and social issues, their political features vary greatly.

The Art of Improvisation. The Qur'an* and hadith* offer little guidance on matters of government and the state. The Muslim community faced its first political crisis when the Prophet Muhammad died in 632. His followers disagreed about the proper way to select his successor, which eventually led to the division of Islam into various sects*. A majority, however, chose to follow Abu Bakr, who became the first caliph* after Muhammad. Several Arab tribes rejected Abu Bakr's leadership, arguing that religion and politics are separate and that the death of Muhammad signified the end of their allegiance to the Muslim community. Abu Bakr countered the opposition to his rule, asserting that religion provides legitimacy to a political system.

Specific information on the subject of politics is also notably absent from the Constitution of Medina, one of Islam's earliest political documents. Written in the 620s, it calls for Muslims and their allies (in this case, several Jewish tribes) to form one community (*ummah*) that unites to ensure social order, security, and defense. As Islamic sovereignty spread, Muslims combined various sources to create their political systems. These sources included *shari'ah**, Arabian tribal traditions, and the political customs of conquered peoples, especially the Persians and Byzantines.

* **Qur'an** book of the holy scriptures of Islam

* **hadith** reports of the words and deeds of Muhammad (not in the Qur'an, but accepted as guides for Muslim behavior)

* **sect** religious group adhering to distinctive beliefs

* **caliph** religious and political leader of an Islamic state

* **shari'ah** Islamic law as established in the Qur'an and sunnah, the exemplary behavior of the prophet

* **dynasty** succession of rulers from the same family or group

* **Sunni** refers to the largest branch of the Muslim community; the name derives from sunnah, the exemplary behavior of the Prophet Muhammad

* **theocracy** government headed by religious leaders and believed to be divinely guided

* **autocracy** government in which one person rules with unlimited authority

Building the Islamic State

Many Muslims believe that Egyptian jurist and legal scholar Abd al-Razzaq al-Sanhuri coined the phrase, *al-Islam din wa dawlah,* which means "Islam, religion and state." Sanhuri's work greatly advanced the development of the modern Islamic state. He devoted much of his career to modernizing Islamic law, combining *shari'ah* and Western principles. Egypt and Iraq were the first nations to adopt his civil codes. Other Muslim nations later followed suit. Sanhuri laid the foundation for modern legislation in the Arab world, and his work remains the standard reference for Islamic legal scholars.

The concept of the state in traditional Islamic political theory was closely tied to the concepts of community, justice, and leadership. Muslim jurists insisted that the primary task of any ruler is to ensure that Islamic law is implemented. Beyond that, they focused mainly on types of statesmanship, the problems associated with government, and the conduct of the ruler.

Of particular importance was the issue of legitimacy. Religion largely shaped the institutions in the governments of the first four caliphs, who ruled from 632 to 661. They based their right to rule on the principles of *shura* (inner consultation), *aqd* (a contract between the ruler and his subjects), and *bay'ah* (oath of allegiance). During the Umayyad (661–750) and Abbasid (750–1258) dynasties*, the question of legitimacy took on greater relevance, as caliphs came to power through heredity. At that time, Muslim scholars emphasized the authority of the ruler and the unity of the *ummah* as the basis for government.

By the 1100s, Muslim loyalties were divided among several leaders, and Muslim lands faced increased threats from invaders. In the absence of political and societal unity, jurists maintained that authority derived from *shari'ah*. A government established legitimacy through its ability to defend its domain from foreign powers.

Sunni* jurists described the ideal Islamic state as a community governed by God's law, rather than a theocracy* or an autocracy*. The state should provide security and order so that Muslims can attend to their religious duties—doing good and preventing evil. In the ideal state, the caliph serves as the guardian of the community and the faith; the religious scholars offer religious and legal advice; and the judges settle disputes according to Islamic law. The government's primary function is to promote Islam. In the 1400s, jurist and historian Ibn Khaldun said that all citizens are entitled to life, religion, education, family, and property. Over time, Muslims came to believe that this utopian community had actually existed. Contemporary militant movements have evoked the vision of the ideal state as a model for Muslim countries.

From Iranian culture, Islamic political theorists adopted the idea that the universe is arranged in a certain order. Each person has a place in this order. A caliph or king is at the top of the social pyramid, and he is the representative of God on earth. Opposing him and thereby dividing the community would be considered a sin. Muslim political theory thus came to emphasize obeying the ruler and avoiding civil strife.

Back to Basics. Prior to the 1800s, Muslims thought of politics in terms of the *ummah* and the caliph or sultan. Islam had served as the foundation for several great empires, and religion informed legal, political, educational, and social institutions. Colonial occupation by European countries during the 1800s brought new political realities. Many Muslims blamed Western influences and the subsequent straying from Islamic practices for the decline of their societies. They believed that a return to Islam as the basis for government would ensure political and spiritual revival.

The concept of the modern Islamic state emerged as a reaction to the abolition of the Muslim caliphate in Turkey in 1924. Alarmed by this event and the break up of Muslim communities by European colonial governments, some Muslims began to promote the idea that Islam is both a religion and a state. Noted jurist Abd al-Razzaq al-Sanhuri even called for a new caliphate to govern all Muslim countries and communities.

During the 1930s, Indian-Pakistani writer Sayyid Abu al-Ala Mawdudi advocated an Islamic state governed by true believers who use the Qur'an and sunnah as the basis for their rule. God alone would have total sovereignty in this state. Moreover, the government would enforce Islamic moral order in the state's legal, political, and economic affairs. Hasan al-Banna (1906–1949), founder of the Muslim Brotherhood, held similar views. To him, Islam was everything—a fatherland and a nationality, a religion and a state, spirituality and action. Fundamentalist* leader Sayyid Qutb (1906–1966) added that the Muslim community must be free from polluting influences, including non-Islamic ideas such as patriotism and nationalism*. He believed that the first priority for Muslims is to establish a pure Islamic order. Afterward, they can determine its laws and system of government. Several militant Islamic groups have embraced Qutb's antisecular position.

During the 1970s, Iranian Shi'i* leader Ayatollah Ruhollah Khomeini advanced new ideas about the modern Islamic state. He argued that the essence of such a state was the special quality of its leaders, not its compliance with religious law. An expert in Islamic law should be the guardian of the government, and any act that he deemed appropriate could be defined as Islamic. Khomeini thus shifted final religious authority from the *shari'ah* to the state's leadership.

Different Interpretations. Today Muslims continue to disagree about the precise relationship between religion and the state. The few political organizations that identify themselves as Islamic states may follow similar practices, such as applying mandatory punishment for certain crimes (*hudud*) or trying to enforce the Qur'an's ban on *riba* (interest). Nevertheless, they differ with regard to their political institutions and constitutional arrangements.

Saudi Arabia created the first Islamic state in the modern era (early 1930s). Its government is a monarchy, although the king exchanged the title of "his royal majesty" for the more Islamic "servant of the two sanctuaries" of Mecca and Medina. Using the Qur'an as its legal code, Saudi Arabia does not have a constitution, a parliament, or political parties. The state does, however, include a modern cabinet and a bureaucracy*. The *ulama** exert a powerful influence on the country's political and legal affairs.

Iran, by contrast, is a republic with a constitution, a president, a parliament, and political parties. Islamic clerics and jurists, however, dominate all levels of the government.

Historically, the majority of Pakistanis have differed from their political leaders with regard to the concept of an Islamic state. The authorities viewed Islam as a way to identify the community and the nation, but most of the people and religious leaders believed that Islamic law should inform all political institutions. Military regimes* have dominated the state since the late 1970s, and their leaders have used Islam as a way to legitimize their rule. (*See also* **Caliph; Caliphate; Government; Mawdudi, Sayyid Abu al-Ala; Iran; Pakistan; Saudi Arabia.**)

* **fundamentalist** generally refers to the movement that promotes a literal interpretation of scripture; in Islam, a movement that promotes politicization of religion to create an alternative public order

* **nationalism** feelings of loyalty and devotion to one's country and a commitment to its independence

* **Shi'i** refers to Muslims who believe that Muhammad chose Ali ibn Abi Talib and his descendants as the spiritual-political leaders of the Muslim community

* **bureaucracy** agencies and officials that comprise a government

* *ulama* religious scholars

* **regime** government in power

Ismail

Son of Abraham

* **Qur'an** book of the holy scriptures of Islam

* **scripture** sacred writings that contain revelations from God

* **shrine** place that is considered sacred because of its history or the relics contained there

* **polytheist** person who believes in more than one god

* **monotheistic** refers to the belief that there is only one God

* **covenant** solemn and binding agreement

* **pilgrimage** journey to a shrine or sacred place

Ismail was the firstborn son of Abraham, the patriarch (founding father) of Judaism and Islam according to both the Qur'an* and the Bible. Muslims trace their religious roots to Abraham through Ismail. Jews, in contrast, trace their spiritual lineage to Abraham through Ismail's younger half-brother Isaac.

The Qur'an and the Hebrew Bible agree about Ismail on several points. Both scriptures* describe Abraham and his wife Sarah as having been unable to conceive a child for many years. Although Sarah was very old, God had promised her a child. Sarah, nevertheless, persuaded Abraham to have a child with Hagar, her Egyptian maidservant. Hagar bore Abraham a son, Ismail. Several years later, Sarah became pregnant and gave birth to Isaac. Sarah then became jealous of Hagar and Ismail because, as Abraham's firstborn son, Ismail was heir to his father's inheritance. Sarah pressured her husband to send Hagar and Ismail away, which greatly distressed Abraham. At first he resisted Sarah's demands, but he finally gave in after God promised to make Ismail the father of a great nation. The Qur'an and the Old Testament both describe how Hagar and Ismail nearly died of thirst in the desert but were saved by God, who provided them with a spring of water that miraculously flowed from the sand.

The Qur'an differs from the Bible, however, on several other points concerning Ismail. In the Old Testament, God tests Abraham's faith by asking him to sacrifice Isaac. The Qur'an does not specify which son God asked Abraham to sacrifice, but Islamic scholars believe that the son in question was Ismail. Muslims believe that Abraham and Ismail demonstrated their faith by accepting God's command. Jews and Muslims agree that, in the end, God spared the life of Abraham's son.

Islamic scriptures also diverge from the Bible about Ismail's fate after he was sent into the desert. The Qur'an describes how Hagar and her son eventually settled near Mecca. Abraham later sought them out and was reunited with them. After hearing about their near death in the desert and how God had saved them, Abraham wanted honor their God. He and Ismail rebuilt the Kaaba, a holy shrine* in Mecca. Many Muslims believe that Adam had built the original Kaaba as the first temple of the one true God, but that a flood had destroyed it.

According to Islamic sources, polytheists* took over Mecca in the years following Ismail's death and filled the Kaaba with many idols. In the early 400s, Ismail's descendants, called the Quraysh, who were also polytheists, recaptured the city. In 630 Muhammad, who had emigrated from Mecca several years earlier, returned triumphantly from his exile and cleansed the Kaaba of its idols, finally restoring the monotheistic* religion of Abraham to Mecca.

Muslims today continue to remember Ismail in their worship practices. They consider the Kaaba he helped build as their most sacred site. They believe that Ismail and Abraham placed the Black Stone inside the cube-shaped structure as a symbol of God's covenant* with his people. Each day, Muslims around the world turn in the direction of the Kaaba to pray.

Ismail's experience is also an important part of Muslim pilgrimage* rites. As part of their journey to Mecca, pilgrims drink from the well of Zamzam, which they believe to be the water that God provided for Hagar and Ismail.

Pilgrims also visit the site where Abraham prepared to sacrifice his son. They throw stones at three pillars, symbolizing their rejection of the devil, who tried to tempt Abraham into disobeying God's command to sacrifice his son. (*See also* **Abraham; Kaaba.**)

Ismaili

The Shi'i* movement known as the Ismaili influenced Islamic intellectual and religious life from the 900s through the 1200s. The movement takes its name from Ismail, son of Jafar al-Sadiq, the sixth imam*. Jafar had named Ismail as his successor, but Ismail died before his father. After Jafar's death in 765, many of his followers still considered Ismail to be the seventh imam. As a result, Ismailis are often referred to as Seveners.

In the mid-800s, Ismaili movements formed in Iraq, Persia (present-day Iran), Yemen, and India. Directed from a central headquarters, they resisted the rule of Sunni* caliphs*. Ismailis believed that a "hidden" imam (one existing in spiritual form), the son of Ismail, would return to rule the world. In 899 Syrian leader Ubayd Allah al-Mahdi claimed to be this hidden imam. Most Ismailis in Iraq and Persia rejected al-Mahdi's claim, and over the centuries, the Ismailis experienced a number of splits within the movement over religious and political matters. One of these splits led Ubayd Allah al-Mahdi and his heirs to establish the Fatimid dynasty in Egypt and North Africa in the 900s.

After the overthrow of Fatimid caliph al-Mustansir, the movement split again. Ismailis in Egypt followed al-Mustansir's son, al-Mustali. Those in eastern lands were loyal to al-Mustali's older brother, Nizar. The Nizaris violently resisted Sunni Abbasid caliphs. Due, in part, to their violent tactics, the Nizaris were known as Assassins. Several years after Muslim military leader Saladin conquered Egypt and ended the Fatimid dynasty, Mongol armies captured the last Nizari stronghold in 1256. Ismailis from both groups scattered. One of the Nizari leaders fled to India where his followers became known as the Khojas and he took the title of Aga Khan, meaning chief commander. All Nizari Ismaili imams since then have held the title of Aga Khan.

Modern Aga Khans have been active in politics, education, and humanitarian causes. Mustali Ismailis also maintain a large community in India. Although followers of both sects live mainly in India, Ismaili communities also exist in Syria, Central Asia, Iran, Africa, North America and Europe. The total worldwide Ismaili population is about two million. (*See also* **Assassins; Fatimid Dynasty; Shi'i Islam; Titles, Honorific.**)

* **Shi'i** refers to Muslims who believe that Muhammad chose Ali ibn Abi Talib and his descendants as the spiritual-political leaders of the Muslim community

* **imam** spiritual leader in Shi'i Islam, one who is regarded as directly descended from Muhammad; also, one who leads prayers

* **Sunni** refers to the largest branch of the Muslim community; the name derives from sunnah, the exemplary behavior of the Prophet Muhammad

* **caliph** religious and political leader of an Islamic state

Israel

For most of its nearly six decades as a state, Israel has been a battleground between Jews, who consider the land to be theirs by virtue of God's will and historic rights, and Palestinians, who inhabited the territory for centuries. As a minority in this Jewish nation, Palestinians have struggled to preserve their identity and achieve equal rights. In recent years, some Israeli Muslims have turned to Islam for guidance on social and economic issues.

Ancient Kingdom to Modern State. Israel is the only Jewish nation in the modern world. Situated on the eastern edge of the Mediterranean Sea, it shares borders with Egypt, Lebanon, Syria, and Jordan. Israel covers 7,992 square miles, not including the territories that the country occupied after the 1967 Arab-Israeli war. These territories—the West Bank, Gaza Strip, Golan Heights, and East Jerusalem—are still in dispute. About 80 percent of Israelis describe themselves as Jewish in terms of their ethnicity and religion. The remaining 20 percent are largely Arab and Sunni Muslim. Christians account for a small minority of the population. The capital city of Jerusalem contains many sites sacred to Jews, Christians, and Muslims. Indeed, one of the most divisive issues in Jewish-Muslim relations is control of this city.

The region that is presently known as Israel has a long, rich history. Sometime during the Late Bronze Age (ca. 1500–1200 B.C.E.*), Semitic* people settled in the highlands of Canaan. They were called Hebrews and referred to themselves as the children of Israel, or Israelites, a reference to one of their ancestors. Around 1000 B.C.E., they established a kingdom to unite their various tribes. Within less than a century, the ancient kingdom of Israel split into a northern federation (known as the tribes of Israel) and a southern federation (known as the tribes of Judaea). The kingdoms fell under the control of their powerful neighbors, including the Assyrians, Babylonians, and Persians. In 63 B.C.E., the region became part of the Roman Empire. When the Jews rebelled against Roman rule, they were sent into exile and not allowed to return. This forced exile is referred to as the Diaspora. The Byzantines* later established their rule over the region.

During the 600s C.E.*, Muslim armies conquered the area. The Muslim rulers permitted Jews and Christians to make pilgrimages to holy sites in Jerusalem and elsewhere in the region. Between the late 1000s and the 1300s, Christian armies engaged in the Crusades, a series of bloody military expeditions in an attempt to gain control the region, then generally known as Palestine. They failed to dislodge the Islamic armies, except for brief periods, and the area remained under Muslim control until the early 1900s. In 1917 Great Britain issued the Balfour Declaration, stating its support for the creation of a Jewish national homeland in Palestine. After World War I ended in 1918 and the Ottoman Empire* collapsed, the League of Nations declared Palestine a mandate territory under British control.

The British authorities had to mediate the conflicting interests of the Jewish and Arab communities in Palestine. While the Jews immigrating mainly from Europe sought to increase the amount of land that they owned, the Arabs attempted to halt their progress. When the Nazis seized control of Germany in 1933, they began to persecute Jews throughout central and eastern Europe. Threatened with complete annihilation, thousands of Jews fled to Palestine. After World War II ended in 1945, those Jews who had survived in Europe urgently pressed for the creation of a homeland in Palestine. Faced with increasing violence and demands to end the protectorate*, Britain set May 14, 1948, as the deadline for its withdrawal from the region and asked the United Nations to help resolve the conflict. The U.N. attempted to partition the region into two states, but failed to create a plan acceptable to both the Arabs and the Jews.

* B.C.E. before the Common Era, which refers to the same time period as B.C.

* Semitic refers to subfamily of languages that includes Hebrew, Aramaic, Arabic, and Amharic

* Byzantine refers to the Eastern Christian empire that was based in Constantinople

* C.E. Common Era, which refers to the same time period as A.D.

* Ottoman Empire large Turkish state existing from the early 1300s to the early 1900s

* protectorate country under the protection and control of a stronger nation

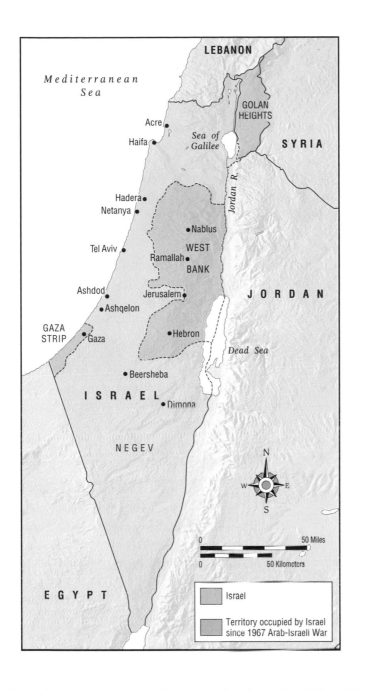

LEBANON

Mediterranean Sea

Acre

Haifa

Sea of Galilee

GOLAN HEIGHTS

SYRIA

Hadera

Netanya

Nablus

Tel Aviv

WEST

Ramallah

BANK

Jordan R.

Ashdod

Jerusalem

Ashqelon

JORDAN

GAZA STRIP

Gaza

Hebron

Dead Sea

Beersheba

ISRAEL

Dimona

NEGEV

N

W E

S

50 Miles

50 Kilometers

EGYPT

Israel

Territory occupied by Israel since 1967 Arab-Israeli War

Since the 1967 Arab-Israeli War, Israel has occupied the West Bank, the Golan Heights, and the Gaza Strip. During the war, Israeli forces also seized East Jerusalem, which had been under Arab control since 1948, and declared the newly reunited Jerusalem to be the capital of Israel.

Israel proclaimed its independence on the date of British withdrawal. Neighboring Arab countries, rejecting its claim to statehood, invaded the new Jewish nation. War lasted until the U.N. was able to broker a cease-fire agreement in July 1949. Under the terms of the agreement, Jordan occupied the West Bank, the section of Palestine west of the Jordan River. As a result of the war, about 600,000 Arabs living in the part of Palestine that had come under Israeli control fled their homes. They went to refugee camps under U.N. supervision in Gaza, the West Bank, southern Lebanon, and Syria. The Israeli government has refused to allow these refugees to return, and many have lived in the camps for decades.

Secular Versus Sacred. After the Arab-Israeli War (1948), the life of the Palestinian community in Israel changed dramatically. Many Christian offi-

shari'ah Islamic law as established in the Qur'an and sunnah, the exemplary behavior of the Prophet Muhammad

cials remained in Israel, but many members of the Muslim religious establishment fled, including religious court judges, prayer leaders, and other important officials. The Supreme Muslim Council ceased to exist when Jordan took over the West Bank. Muslim religious affairs, including the administration of the *waqf* (religious endowments), became the responsibility of the Israeli government. The authorities created the Muslim Department of the Ministry of Religious Affairs to oversee these matters.

It took years to reconstruct the *shari'ah** court system, mainly because few people were qualified to serve as judges. In May 1961, the Knesset (Israeli parliament) ratified the Qadis Law, which stated that a committee with a Muslim majority, appointed by the president of Israel, would select judges for the religious courts. The judges, however, were obliged to dispense justice in accordance with Israeli laws.

Israel granted Muslim religious courts full jurisdiction in cases pertaining to marriage, divorce, and inheritance but restricted their authority over certain matters. With the objective of thoroughly reforming the status of Muslim women, Israeli legislation prohibited the marriage of girls under age 17, outlawed polygyny*, and forbade a man from divorcing a woman against her will. The secular laws did not overrule *shari'ah*, but Muslims who failed to follow them were punished. In other matters, such as awarding child custody to mothers, Israeli law replaced Muslim law. With the 1965 Succession Law, the Knesset abolished the jurisdiction of the *shari'ah* courts over estates and wills, transferring this power to the state district courts. As a result of these measures, Muslims felt particularly persecuted, and a degree of tension developed between Christian and Muslim Palestinians.

polygyny practice of having more than one wife at the same time

A Balancing Act. Since the late 1970s, the Muslim community in Israel has been undergoing a process of Islamic revival. Renewed contact with the Palestinians of the West Bank and Gaza Strip after the 1967 Arab-Israeli War strengthened the religious identity of Israeli Muslims. When Israel occupied the West Bank and Gaza Strip, they regained access to holy sites in Jerusalem and Hebron. Through the efforts of the Muslim High Council in Jerusalem, which was reestablished after the war, Israeli Muslims were permitted to take part in the hajj*. The council also helped young Israeli Arabs enroll at Islamic colleges in the occupied territories.

hajj pilgrimage to Mecca that Muslims are required to make once in their lifetime

Socioeconomic changes also fueled a resurgence of Islam. Rapid modernization weakened the conservative family values and clan structure of Israeli Muslims. The threat to traditional social frameworks created doubts and confusion, prompting many to turn to Islam for moral guidance. At the same time, economic differences between the relatively wealthy Jewish population and the poorer Arabs produced resentment and tension. As these tensions worsened, and Israeli Arab political leaders failed to improve the situation, the Arab community sought to remedy the imbalance on their own. As in other parts of the Muslim world, the Islamic revivalist movement filled the void, stimulating both organized resistance and practical solutions to local problems.

Ayatollah Ruhollah Khomeini's rise to power in Iran in 1979 led to the formation of the first underground group of Islamic militants in Israel. Usrat al-Jihad (the Jihad Family) aimed to bring about the destruction of Israel. The group carried out acts of sabotage, including arson, and took steps to reverse secular trends among Israeli Muslims. Muslim militancy was dampened, however, when Israel arrested all 70 members of the organization and sentenced them to lengthy prison terms.

During the mid-1980s, activist Shaykh Abd Allah Nimr Darwish refocused Islamic efforts in Israel to nonviolent change. A former member of Usrat al-Jihad, he organized projects devoted to religious education and community work. His influence led to the formation of Islamic associations in several Arab areas. Mosque attendance increased steadily, and the number of mosques grew from 60 in 1967 to 240 by 1993. Darwish's movement achieved notable success in inspiring active, Islamically-oriented work in Muslim communities. Muslim volunteers built roads in Arab villages, constructed bus shelters, and established kindergartens, libraries, clinics, and drug treatment centers. The Islamic movement also promoted sports. Darwish's declaration, "If the state is not ready to help us, we shall help ourselves," became the movement's central motto.

Darwish's approach helped to promote political change among Israeli Muslims. Political participation increased. In municipal elections in 1989, Islamic representatives competed in 14 localities and won almost 30 percent of the total seats. In five villages and townships, Islamic candidates won mayoral elections. This trend continued in the 1993 elections.

The Islamic movement continues to face conflicts related to politics and religion. Activists are torn between religious revival, Palestinian nationalism*, which has traditionally focused on secular change, and the need to act within the bounds of Israeli law. These conflicts have caused disagreements about the purpose of Islamic activism and the best approach to sensitive issues, such as the solution of the Palestinian problem and the *intifadah* (Palestinian uprising). Israeli Muslims do not universally agree on the goal of destroying Israel. Some, like Darwish, support the creation of Islamic states in the region, but reject the notion that such a state should replace Israel. Others, however, embrace the more radical* views of militant groups such as Hamas. The continued activities of the Islamic movements in Israel will depend on the resolution of the conflict resulting from Israel's occupation of the West Bank and Gaza.

Differences of Opinion. Israel, a parliamentary democracy, guarantees all minorities equal citizenship. The law prohibits discrimination on the basis of race, religion, political beliefs, gender, sexual orientation, marital status, and age. Israeli Arabs, most of whom are Muslims, have full civil rights. Many Arabs participate in Israeli politics and serve as elected representatives. They are exempt from compulsory military service.

Despite these legal protections, many Israeli Arabs feel that they live under hostile occupation. Certain economic benefits, such as housing and access to mortgages, are reserved for military veterans and therefore are not available to Arab citizens. Furthermore, within Israel itself, the poverty rate among Arabs—about 30 percent—is almost twice that of the general population. The same pattern exists in the unemployment rate, which is 20 percent for Israeli Arabs—more than twice the national average. Few Arabs have been able to penetrate the ranks of large national employers, such as the airline industry and electricity and telephone companies. Arab municipalities have consistently received less government support than Jewish ones. (*See also* **Arab-Israeli Conflict; Great Britain; Hamas; Intifadah; Jerusalem; Jihad; Palestine.**)

Burdens on Women

Muslim women in Israel encounter particular hardships. Health care is scarce, and in some parts of the country, the infant mortality rate among Arab Bedouin women is three times that of Jewish women. Domestic violence is prevalent: 25 percent of Palestinian women experience physical abuse at least once in their lives. Only two of the country's 12 shelters for married women are available to Arabs, however, and police cite religious differences as a reason not to intervene in cases of domestic and sexual abuse. With only rare opportunities for employment, fewer than 20 percent of Arab women in Israel have jobs outside of the home. Those who do hold jobs earn only half of what Jewish women earn. The average wage for Arab women is less than the national minimum wage.

* **nationalism** feelings of loyalty and devotion to one's country and a commitment to its independence

* **radical** favoring extreme change or reform, especially in existing political and social institutions

Istanbul

See color plate 7, vol. 2.

* **B.C.E.** before the Common Era, which refers to the same time period as B.C.

* **C.E.** Common Era, which refers to the same time period as A.D.

* **minaret** tall, slender tower of a mosque from which the faithful are called to prayer

* **mosaic** art form in which small pieces of stone or glass are set into cement to form a picture or pattern

* **fresco** method of painting on freshly spread moist plaster which bonds with the color as it dries

* **secular** separate from religion in human life and society; connected to everyday life

Istanbul, the largest city in Turkey, has a long history marked by the influence of several different cultures. The city in northwestern Turkey was first known as Byzantium and became Constantinople when the emperor Constantine made it the capital of the Roman Empire. After 1453 it became known as Istanbul, the seat of the Ottoman Empire. The city served as the capital until 1923, when the government moved to Ankara. Istanbul remains Turkey's trade and cultural center.

Founded around 660 B.C.E.*, the ancient part of the city covered a triangular peninsula on the European side of the Sea of Marmara near the entrance to the Bosporus, a narrow strait that connects the Mediterranean Sea to the Black Sea. The Bosporus is an important shipping channel that separates Istanbul's European and Asian districts. In fact, Istanbul is the only major city in the world to straddle two continents. In 330 C.E.*, Roman emperor Constantine the Great moved the capital of the Roman Empire to Byzantium and renamed the city Constantinople. During his rule, Constantine, a Christian, ordered the construction of many beautiful buildings in the city. The emperor Justinian built the largest of the churches, the Hagia Sophia.

Turkish leader Mehmed II captured Constantinople in 1453 and renamed the city Istanbul. Ottoman rulers later transformed Hagia Sophia into a mosque by adding minarets* and a grand chandelier to the building's immense dome. In 1935 the mosque became a museum. The Kariye Mosque, near the Adrianople Gate, was also converted from an early Christian church. It is famous for its intricate mosaics*, marbles, and frescoes*. The Ottomans built many new mosques. In fact, art historians consider the mosques built between the mid-1400s and the mid-1500s to be the most magnificent of the Ottoman dynasty. The Mosque of Suleyman, designed by architect Mimar Koca Sinan and built from 1550 to 1557, remains one of Istanbul's artistic treasures and one of the world's great buildings. The Blue Mosque, which features six minarets instead of the usual four, is perhaps Istanbul's most popular mosque.

The Ottomans beautified their capital city in other ways as well. In 1462 Mehmed II ordered the construction of the Seraglio, a stately palace that served as the sultan's official residence until the early 1800s. The Ottomans also built about 400 fountains in Istanbul, many for public enjoyment. The most outstanding of these fountains flows from behind the apse, the semicircular room at one end of the Hagia Sophia. Istanbul's Great Bazaar, still operating and believed to be the largest covered bazaar in the Muslim world, is laid out in a gigantic grid. It includes some 4,000 shops and more than 90 interior streets. Each street specializes in a particular trade, such as the street of the shoemakers, the street of the tentmakers, or the street of the jewelers. The bazaar also includes mosques and fountains.

Modern Istanbul has grown dramatically. In the past 50 years, the city's population has soared from one million to more than nine million. Much of this growth has been fueled by migration from rural communities, where employment opportunities are scarce. Many newcomers to Istanbul are conservative Muslims whose traditional religious beliefs sometimes conflict with the more secular* views of the city dwellers of Istanbul. Since Turkey became a republic in 1923, it has strictly separated church and state. For example, it is illegal for Muslim women to wear traditional head coverings in public offices and schools. Such restrictions frustrate some religious conservatives and have contributed to renewed interest in political changes that favor more traditional Islamic practices. (*See also* **Ottoman Empire; Turkey.**)

Ithna Ashari

Following the death of the Prophet Muhammad in 632, Shi'i* Muslims split into factions over a disagreement about the number of true imams* who had descended from Muhammad. The Zaydis recognized five imams and thus are called Fivers; the Ismailis recognized seven imams and are known as Seveners; the Ithna Ashari recognized twelve imams and are called the Twelvers. The Ithna Ashari form the largest subgroup of Shi'i Muslims, comprising a majority in present-day Iran. They also exist in large numbers in Iraq, Lebanon, and Bahrain.

After the death of sixth imam Jafar al-Sadiq in 765, the Ismailis, who believe that Jafar's son Ismail was the seventh imam, broke away from the majority who recognized Ismail's younger brother (Musa al-Kazim) as the seventh imam. The twelfth imam in the Ithna Ashari line, Muhammad al-Muntazar al-Mahdi (Muhammad the "Awaited One" and "Divinely-Guided One") disappeared in 874 while he was still a child. Because he was too young to have fathered any children, his followers faced the problem of finding a successor. They established the doctrine of the Hidden Imam, which states that the twelfth imam never died but will remain in an unseen spiritual form, known as occultation, until the end of time. The Ithna Ashari, or Twelvers, believe that the Hidden Imam will return at the end of the world as the Mahdi, a divinely guided leader, who will restore justice and equality on earth.

Twelvers acknowledge *mujtahids* as deputies of the Hidden Imam, who interpret Islamic law using independent reasoning. The most respected of these leaders are the ayatollahs, a title that means "signs of God." The role of the ayatollahs is to provide guidance to the faithful while they await the coming of the Mahdi. (*See also* **Ismaili; Shi'i Islam; Titles, Honorific.**)

* **Shi'i** refers to Muslims who believe that Muhammad chose Ali ibn Abi Talib and his descendants as the spiritual-political leaders of the Muslim community

* **imam** spiritual-political leader in Shi'i Islam, one who is regarded as directly descended from Muhammad; also, one who leads prayers

Jafar al-Sadiq

died ca. 765
Founder of Jafari school of law

* **imam** spiritual-political leader of Shi'i Islam, one who is regarded as directly descended from Muhammad; also, one who leads prayers

Jafar al-Sadiq, a descendant of the Prophet Muhammad, was the sixth imam* of Shi'i Islam and the founder of the Jafari school of law, one of the five recognized schools of Islamic law and the major Shi'i school. During his lifetime, Jafar instructed hundreds of scholars in Islamic religion and other sciences.

Shi'i Muslims developed a concept of law that was different from that held by the Sunnis, the majority of the Muslim community. Sunni Muslims believe in four true sources for Islamic law: the Qur'an*, the hadith*, consensus or general agreement among Islamic jurists, and analogy*. Shi'i Muslims accept the authority of only the Qur'an and the hadith. They reject the opinions of the Sunni jurists in favor of the teachings of the caliph* Ali ibn Abi Talib and his descendants, known as the imams. Shi'is also believe that jurists may use independent reasoning (*ijtihad*) to determine the law in situations where the other sources do not provide clear guidance. Sunni Muslims, by contrast, feel that *ijtihad* has a much more limited role in Islamic law.

According to Jafari teachings, the descendants of Ali inherited the knowledge and authority to interpret the Qur'an and the hadith. This gave them a unique ability to determine appropriate Islamic law. Shi'i Muslims came to see the imams as without sin and infallible in matters of religion and considered them to be divine beings on earth. The Zaydi and Mustali Fatamid Ismaili schools of law arose from the same origins as the Jafari, but they are closer to Sunni religious practice.

For many years, Islamic jurists did not recognize the authority of Jafar's teachings or that of any other Shi'i jurists. In 1959, however, al-Azhar University in Cairo accepted the Jafari school as the fifth school of law along with the four traditional Sunni schools. (*See also* **Ali ibn Abi Talib; Ijtihad; Law; Shi'i Islam.**)

Jazeera, al-

Al-Jazeera is an Arabic-language satellite television network sponsored by the government of Qatar, a small nation bordering the Persian Gulf and Saudi Arabia. Operating 24 hours a day since 1996, al-Jazeera broadcasts to 22 Arab nations and has become one of the leading sources of news and information from and about the Islamic world.

Al-Jazeera grew out of a failed 1995 agreement between the British Broadcasting Corporation (BBC) and Orbit Communications, a company owned and operated by the government of Saudi Arabia. Orbit was to provide Arabic-language newscasts through the BBC's World Radio Network. The BBC insisted that it be free to report on any and all important issues in the Middle East. Saudi Arabia, however, refused to allow the station to cover news stories or offer opinions that reflected poorly on its government. Orbit ended the arrangement in April 1996 after the BBC aired a story on human rights that included footage of a Saudi-sponsored beheading.

Later that year, the amir of Qatar, Shaykh Hamad bin Khalifa al-Thani, hired most of the editors who had worked for the BBC's Arabic News Service and provided $150 million in funding to establish al-Jazeera. The money was intended to cover the costs of running the network for five years. After that time, al-Jazeera was expected to cover its expenses by selling advertising. Since then, however, the station has had a difficult time selling enough ads to pay for itself.

Although based in Qatar, al-Jazeera has a reputation for independence that has angered critics both inside and outside the Arab world. The United States was unhappy with what it considered al-Jazeera's anti-American coverage of the terrorist attacks on September 11, 2001, and subsequent messages from Osama bin Laden and other al-Qaeda leaders. Arab leaders also oppose al-Jazeera's uncensored news reports about political events in the Middle East. Saudi officials have called al-Jazeera's broadcasts "anti-Islamic." Kuwaiti officials believe the network is too sympathetic to Iraq, and Iran and Lebanon have also protested program content.

The fact that almost every Arab state has objected to al-Jazeera's programming at one time or another is one of the keys to its popularity. In most Middle Eastern countries, the government either owns or strictly controls the media. The press rarely carries stories critical of the government. Al-Jazeera, however, offers programs that go beyond the official government-sponsored point of view. Network programs, such as "The Opposite Direction" and "The Other Opinion," feature Arab politicians debating issues with Islamic militants as well as opponents examining both sides of the Palestinian-Israeli conflict. Al-Jazeera provides many Arabs with the only uncensored source of information about social and political issues in the region.

Because the government of Qatar sponsors al-Jazeera, some critics claim Qatar is using the station to promote its foreign policy. It is true that al-Jazeera has helped Qatar gain a great deal of political influence, especially given the country's limited economic and military strength. There is, however, less evidence that al-Jazeera promotes Qatar's political interests, and the Qatari government is careful to avoid interfering with al-Jazeera's day-to-day operations.

Recently, several Arab states, including Saudi Arabia, Tunisia, Jordan, Egypt, and Bahrain have tried to ban or limit al-Jazeera broadcasts in their countries. Others, however, such as Algeria, have avoided voicing concerns for fear that al-Jazeera will target them in broadcasts to the rest of the Arab world. (*See also* **Bin Laden, Osama; Newspapers and Magazines; Radio and Television.**)

Jerusalem

Along with Mecca and Medina, Jerusalem is one of Islam's three holiest cities. Known in Arabic as al-Quds (the Holy), this ancient city is also considered sacred by the world's two other major monotheistic* religions, Judaism and Christianity. Over the centuries, Jerusalem has been an important pilgrimage* site for all three faiths. The modern nation of Israel now occupies Jerusalem and claims the city as its capital, which has created ongoing controversy and conflict between that nation and the Islamic world.

A Sacred City. Muslims consider Jerusalem sacred because several events of significance to the Islamic faith occurred there. Jerusalem is also the home of the Temple Mount. According to tradition, this is where the patriarch* Abraham built an altar and prepared to sacrifice his son to show his obedience to God. This is an important site for Muslims because they, like the Jews, consider Abraham the father of their religion. The Temple Mount is also the site where the Hebrew king Solomon constructed his famous temple, which was later destroyed by the Babylonians.

* **monotheistic** refers to the belief that there is only one God

* **pilgrimage** journey to a shrine or sacred place

* **patriarch** male head of a group

Jerusalem

The sacred city of Jerusalem is home to monuments deemed holy by Jews, Christians, and Muslims. The Dome of the Rock, the oldest existing Islamic monument, and the Western Wall, a place of prayer sacred to the Jewish people, are shown here. Because of these holy sites, Jews and Arabs have long fought over control of the city.

The Qur'an* describes the night Muhammad was taken, by the angel Gabriel, to "the farthest mosque," which tradition interprets to be Jerusalem. This connection to the Prophet's Night Journey gives Muslims another reason to revere the city. After Islamic forces first defeated the Romans and took control of Jerusalem in 635 C.E.*, they restored the Temple Mount and built the Al-Aqsa Mosque* at the southern end of the site. Muslims later built the Dome of the Rock, a shrine* at the center of the Temple Mount, to mark the location from which Muhammad ascended to heaven, as well as the site of Abraham's sacrifice and Solomon's temple.

Jerusalem's status as the capital of the ancient Jewish kingdom and the site of Solomon's temple also makes it a holy site to Jews. For Christians, Jerusalem was the location of several significant events in the life of Jesus, including the Last Supper, his trial, Crucifixion, and Resurrection. The Church of the Holy Sepulchre marks the site of the Resurrection and is considered the most sacred place in Christendom. The fact that the city plays such an important symbolic role in all three religions has made it a prize worth fighting over for many generations of believers.

The Coming of Islam. Jerusalem was the capital of the ancient kingdom of Israel, founded by the Jewish people during biblical times. King David, the father of Solomon, established his capital here, and the Jews called Jerusalem the City of David. The Romans later conquered Israel, and in 135 C.E., they

expelled all Jews from the city following a number of local uprisings. In the 200s, the Roman Empire split into eastern and western sections, and Jerusalem came under the control of the eastern empire. After the western empire fell in 476, the eastern part became known as the Byzantine* Empire.

In 635 Muslim armies captured Jerusalem from the Byzantine Romans. The Muslims began to restore the city's many holy places, which had been badly neglected under Byzantine rule. The Umayyad rulers had political plans for Jerusalem but eventually chose the city of Damascus as the capital of their empire. The Umayyads later allowed Jews to return to Jerusalem to pray. For many years, Jews, Muslims, and Christians lived together peacefully in the city. This situation changed dramatically, however, during and after the Crusades of the Middle Ages.

In 1095 Pope Urban II called for Christian leaders of Europe to mount a military expedition to recapture the Holy Land from the Muslims. Armies from several countries answered his call and left Europe for the long journey to Palestine. By 1099 the Christian crusaders occupied Jerusalem. Christian forces remained in control of the city until Muslim leader Saladin recaptured it in 1187. Saladin's successors, the Mamluks, then took over Jerusalem and made it a center of Sunni* Islam. Although European Christians led a series of additional crusades over the next two centuries, they failed to recapture Jerusalem.

Bitter Disputes in Modern Times. The Ottoman Turks, who had conquered the Byzantine Empire in 1453, took control of Jerusalem from the Mamluks in 1517. They held the city until 1917, when British forces captured it during World War I. The Ottoman Empire fell after the war, and Great Britain governed the city from 1922 until the state of Israel was created in 1948.

When British forces withdrew from Palestine, Jerusalem was to come under the control of the United Nations. The intention was for the city to be separate from Israel and surrounding Arab states and have its own assembly elected by the citizens. These plans ended in 1948, however, when Jordan seized East Jerusalem and Israel occupied West Jerusalem, marking the beginning of the first Arab-Israeli war.

Israel and Jordan both refused to consider making Jerusalem an international city. During the fighting, the Israeli government expelled tens of thousands of Palestinians from West Jerusalem. Jewish settlers arrived to occupy many of the neighborhoods once inhabited by Palestinians. From 1948 to 1967, the city was split between Arab-controlled East Jerusalem and Israeli-controlled West Jerusalem. In 1967 another war erupted between Israel and the Arab states. Israeli forces seized East Jerusalem and declared the newly united Jerusalem to be the capital of Israel. Very few countries recognized Israel's right to control the entire city. The United Nations passed a resolution calling for Israel to end its occupation of Jerusalem and the other territories it captured during the 1967 war. Israel refused, however, to obey the U.N. resolution and today still controls all of Jerusalem. Palestinians who hope to establish their own independent nation in the region claim East Jerusalem as the capital of that state. The dispute over control of Jerusalem continues to be one of the most bitter aspects of the current Arab-Israeli conflict. (*See also* **Abraham; Arab-Israeli Conflict; Crusades; Mecca; Medina.**)

* **Byzantine** refers to the Eastern Christian empire that was based in Constantinople

See map in Israel (vol. 2).

* **Sunni** refers to the largest branch of the Muslim community; the name derives from sunnah, the exemplary behavior of the Prophet Muhammad

Jerusalem's Old City

The Old City, in East Jerusalem, is the city's historic heart and soul. Surrounded by ancient stone walls, the Old City has Jerusalem's greatest concentration of religious and historical sites, with over 300 synagogues, churches, mosques, and other religious monuments. Within the Old City's walls, a diverse population lives and works. Arabs, Jews, and Christians in traditional, modern, and religious dress mix with tourists from all over the world. Narrow cobblestone streets remain as they have for centuries. Markets line many areas of the Old City, giving it a crowded and busy atmosphere.

In recognition of its important place in history and in the traditions of numerous ethnic and religious groups, the United Nations in 1981 designated Jerusalem's Old City as a World Heritage site.

Jesus

Regardless of religious beliefs or the faiths to which they belong, most scholars who have studied the evidence acknowledge Jesus of Nazareth as a great leader and teacher. In Christianity, Jesus is the central figure revered as both the son of God and as one aspect of God himself in the Holy Trinity (the father, the son, and the Holy Spirit). Christians also revere Mary, the mother of Jesus. Muslims see both Jesus and Mary as important figures in God's plan for humanity, but their beliefs about them differ significantly from those of Christians.

The Qur'an mentions Jesus 25 times and credits him with many of the same miracles described in the New Testament, such as healing the sick. Muslims do not, however, worship Jesus as God. They see him, instead, as a special type of prophet—a messenger sent by God to bring his word to humans. God guarantees success on earth to messengers, and the words of these messengers, including Moses and Muhammad, are recorded in the scriptures. Moses' message from God is preserved in the Old Testament, or the Torah*. Jesus' message is recorded in the New Testament, or the Gospels. Muhammad's message comes to believers in the Qur'an.

Muslims also differ from Christians in their views about the nature of Jesus. For example, Muslims do not consider Jesus to be the son of God, nor do they believe in the concept of the Holy Trinity. For Muslims, the trinity is a form of polytheism—a belief in many gods. As a monotheistic* religion, Islam preaches that God exists in only one form. Muslims do not recognize Jesus as the son of God, but they also do not believe that he was conceived by a human father. In Islam, Jesus' conception is seen as a miracle from God.

Muslims do not believe in the Crucifixion and Resurrection of Jesus. Christians view the Crucifixion as a necessary sacrifice that Jesus made to save all humans from original sin, the state all people are born into because Adam and Eve sinned. Muslims do not believe in the idea of original sin, so they see no need for such a sacrifice. They believe that all people are responsible for their own salvation through their actions. The Qur'an states that God himself actually took Jesus up to heaven.

Mary is also a significant and popular figure in Islamic belief. The Qur'an calls her one of the four perfect examples of womanhood. In fact, the Qur'an mentions Mary more times than does the New Testament and provides more information about her life. The Qur'an includes an entire chapter devoted to and named after Mary.

According to the Qur'an, God "breathed a life" into Mary and "made her and her son a token for mankind." It was God's will that Mary give birth to Jesus. She did so knowing that, when she became pregnant, she would be accused of having sexual relations outside of marriage. Muslims revere her for sacrificing her repuation to bring Jesus into the world. The Qur'an states that the infant Jesus defended Mary's reputation by telling others that she was innocent of any sin.

Muslims often see a connection between Mary and Fatimah, the daughter of Muhammad. Fatimah was the founder of the line of imams* who were believed to possess divine truth. She is thus associated with the divine wis-

* **Torah** first five books of the Old Testament, constituting the holy scripture of Judaism

* **monotheistic** refers to the belief that there is only one God

* **imam** spiritual-political leader in Shi'i Islam, one who is regarded as directly descended from Muhammad; also, one who leads prayers

dom, or Sophia, from which humans gain knowledge of God. Like Mary, Fatimah is seen as an example of perfect womanhood. (*See also* **Christianity and Islam; Fatimah; Prophets.**)

Jihad

Generally referring to an endeavor toward a praiseworthy aim, the term *jihad* has many meanings. Muslims use the term to refer to battles within themselves or to efforts to improve the Islamic community. In the West, jihad is often translated as "holy war." In books on Islamic law and in the Qur'an*, the word often refers to armed conflict in defense of Islam. This "jihad of the sword," however, is only one of four types of struggle. Muslims can also wage jihad of the heart, the tongue, and the hand, which involve purifying the inner self, supporting good deeds, and halting harmful actions. Many Muslims use the term to refer to a struggle against some type of undesirable situation, much as an American might use the phrase "war on drugs" or "war on poverty." This article focuses on the military aspects of jihad.

* **Qur'an** book of the holy scriptures of Islam

Historical Concepts of Jihad

Various religious beliefs and historical circumstances have led to the development of the different meanings of jihad. Early interpretations are rooted in the statements of the Qur'an and hadith*, while later ones are derived from the reasoning of Islamic thinkers.

Martial Origins. The concept of jihad arose from the climate of war that pervaded pre-Islamic Arabia. Local tribes fought constantly; their battles were halted only by the occasional truce. Many Qur'anic verses refer to war and to the obligation of Muslims to fight unbelievers in combat. These verses discuss such matters as who can claim exemption from military service, whether one should fight during the holy months, how prisoners should be treated, and when and how one should make peace. The Qur'an states that harsh punishments in the hereafter await Muslims who refuse to fight. Those killed in battle, however, enjoy special privileges in paradise.

* **hadith** reports of the words and deeds of Muhammad (not in the Qur'an, but accepted as guides for Muslim behavior)

The Qur'an has puzzled many with its conflicting messages on jihad. Scholars have expressed confusion about whether one should fight only if attacked, or if one should initiate battle with unbelievers. Some early verses suggest the first interpretation, but later ones express the opposite view. In the second surah*, for example, Muhammad states that Muslims should "aggress not: God loves not the aggressors." In surah 9, he exhorts Muslims to "slay the idolaters wherever you find them," and to "lie in wait for them at every place of ambush." Partly in response to the Christian Crusades*, medieval* Islamic thinkers decided that the verses commanding Muslims to fight the unbelievers in all circumstances overruled those that justify only defensive warfare.

* **surah** chapter of the Qur'an

* **Crusades** during the Middle Ages, holy wars declared by the pope against non-Christians, mostly Muslims

* **medieval** refers to the Middle Ages, a period roughly between 500 and 1500

Medieval Interpretations. Islamic jurists developed a doctrine of jihad in the few hundred years following the death of Muhammad. They based

Jihad

A member of the Islamic Jihad displays a Qur'an during a demonstration in the West Bank town of Ramallah. Behind him, a banner displays a portrait of Osama bin Laden, the terrorist leader who has encouraged attacks against the United States.

* **caliph** religious and political leader of an Islamic state

these ideas on the Qur'an, the hadith, and the actions of the early caliphs*. The doctrine states that there should be a single Islamic nation that rules the entire Muslim community, or *ummah*. This nation is referred to as *dar al-Islam*, or Land of Islam, where Islamic law is supreme. A second category of nations is *dar al-sulh*, or the realm of treaty, where rulers have agreed to protect Muslims and their allies and pay a tribute acknowledging peace with *dar al-Islam*. Everything that lies outside the *dar al-Islam* and *dar al-sulh* is considered *dar al-harb*, or Land of War.

In this view, the *ummah* has a collective duty to wage jihad to expand the *dar al-Islam*. A caliph organizes and leads the struggle. If too few people take part in the struggle, the entire *ummah* is considered sinful. For his part, the caliph must ensure that the *ummah* attacks the enemy at least once a year after the conquests have ended to keep the concept of jihad alive. A group of Shi'i* Muslims, known as Twelvers, believes that only a rightful imam* may lawfully lead an expansionist jihad, although no such imam has existed on earth since 873. All Muslims, however, consider a defensive jihad just. As with the Arabian tribes that fought around the time of Muhammad, warriors are expected to follow the Islamic code that prohibits them from killing children, women, clergy or religious authorities, and old people.

Believers who wage jihad must meet certain conditions before they may lawfully attack unbelievers. They must first request that the enemy convert to Islam. If the enemy agrees, the Muslims may not attack, but must ask the enemy to move to the holy city of Medina. If the enemy refuses to convert, the leader of jihad must ask the people to agree to pay a tax to show their submission to Islam while remaining free to practice their own faith. The Qur'an limits this option to People of the Book, specifically Christians and Jews, who practice monotheism* according to their own holy scriptures. If the enemy refuses to convert or pay the tax, Muslims must engage them in battle.

Some Muslims feel that the concept of jihad excludes the possibility of peace. Medieval doctrine, however, follows the example set by Muhammad, who made a truce with the Meccan Arab armies. Some Islamic schools of law argue that a truce must end after a certain period of time, lasting for no longer than ten years. Others suggest that the caliph has the right to break or extend the truce whenever he wishes. All medieval writings, however, emphasize the importance of keeping the idea of jihad alive.

Modern Variations. Since the 1800s, several new and competing interpretations of jihad have arisen. The so-called apologetic interpretation of jihad developed in response to Western colonialism in the Muslim world. This view of jihad states that one may fight only to resist persecution or aggression. The first Muslim to propose this theory was the Indian thinker Sayyid Ahmad Khan.

Ahmad Khan developed his concept of jihad in response to the distrust the British felt for Muslims, who had taken part in rebellions against their rule. Because Islamic Mughals had ruled the region before the British, the officials feared that Muslims would use the concept of jihad to try to overthrow them. They began favoring Hindus over Muslims in the government, granting them key positions. In order to ensure employment for educated Muslims, Ahmad Khan argued that the Qur'an obliged only believers to participate in jihad to protect themselves against active oppression. Because the British allowed Muslims to practice their faith, jihad against them remained prohibited.

Some Muslims developed other views on jihad to adapt it to European standards of war. The modernist approach argues that the Qur'an and hadith do not divide the world into *dar al-Islam* and *dar al-harb*. A true jihad aims only to protect lives, property, or honor, and should not be fought to conquer peaceful nonbelievers. Those who support the modernist view feel that jihad should serve as a form of defensive struggle not unlike the "just war" of Western societies.

A third approach arose as a reaction to apologetic and modernist interpretations. The revivalist view argues that modern theorists have drained the

* **Shi'i** refers to Muslims who believe that Muhammad chose Ali ibn Abi Talib and his descendants as the spiritual-political leaders of the Muslim community

* **imam** spiritual-political leader in Shi'i Islam, one who is regarded as directly descended from Muhammad; also, one who leads prayers

* **monotheism** belief that there is only one God

life and vitality from the concept of jihad. Revivalist thinkers argue that Muslims should wage jihad against rulers who turn their societies away from the word of God. They do not advocate the enforcement of Islam, stating that the Qur'an calls for freedom of worship, but urge Muslims to topple regimes that lack religious principles.

The most radical revivalists call for the overthrow of corrupt governments within the Islamic world itself. Muslim law, however, prohibits revolt against Islamic rulers except in certain circumstances, such as when a leader abandons his beliefs. Many Muslims throughout history have accused their rulers of becoming heretics, or unbelievers, in order to justify waging jihad against established regimes.

Jihad in Practice

Throughout Islamic history, Muslims have waged jihad for a number of reasons. In the mid-1900s, many groups formed to promote the overthrow of their own governments, which were considered tyrannical and, therefore, un-Islamic. Jihad against Israel and its supporters has become popular, as well as the overthrow of regimes that some Muslims consider to be secular*.

* **secular** separate from religion in human life and society; connected to everyday life

Functions of Jihad. The concept of jihad serves several purposes for Muslims. Most importantly, it motivates them to fight against nonbelievers and to spread their faith. This is based on the belief that only Islam will allow people to live in peace and harmony. To provide an incentive for Muslims to fight, the Qur'an states that those killed in jihad will enjoy certain privileges in the afterlife. Becoming a martyr erases one's sins, enabling an individual to enter heaven and have a place near the throne of God.

Islamic leaders also use jihad to justify their reign. This function became important after 750, when the Islamic empire split into several factions, each under a different caliph. Each of these rulers waged war against unbelievers to show himself as a true leader of the Islamic community. Islamic leaders often cited the rules of jihad to show that their policy towards foreigners met the standards outlined in the Qur'an.

Jihad Organizations and Mujahidin. Since the mid-1900s, groups in several Middle Eastern countries have included the word *jihad* in their names to indicate their willingness to battle their own governments or those they deem heretical. Lebanon's Organization of the Islamic Jihad is probably the best known. It has claimed responsibility for kidnappings and attacks against Westerners and Israelis. This title, however, is just one of the names used by a Lebanese group, Hizbullah, so that it can deny taking part in such activities and thus shield itself from retaliation by Western military forces.

Other groups include the Islamic Jihad Movement based in Palestine and Egypt's Islamic Jihad Community. The former emerged in 1987 and takes part in violent attacks against Israel. The latter, formed in 1979, attempts to overthrow Middle Eastern leaders whom the group sees as betraying Islamic principles in favor of Western ideas and lifestyles. In the mid-1980s, the organization splintered into different groups.

Groups whose names contain the term *mujahidin*, "those who wage jihad," have also arisen in some countries. Iran's mujahidin emerged in the 1960s to overthrow the regime of Reza Shah Pahlavi. Consisting mainly of

When Believers are Unbelievers

The revivalist jihad movement has its roots in arguments made by the Islamic scholar Ibn Taymiyah. By the early 1300s, the Mongols had conquered the Middle East. Many Arabs resisted Mongol rule, although some Mongol leaders had converted to Islam. Since the Qur'an forbids revolt against a rightful ruler, Muslims sought a way to justify an attack on the Mongols. They approached Ibn Taymiyah with their problem. Ibn Taymiyah pointed out that the Mongols applied their own civil law rather than the *shari'ah,* or Islamic law. In his opinion, this invalidated their political legitimacy since the primary task of a Muslim ruler is to implement Islamic law. In 1981 Egypt's Islamic Jihad Community used the same reasoning to justify their assassination of President Anwar Sadat.

students and intellectuals, the organization called for freedom of the press, elected councils in towns and workplaces, and complete equality for all citizens. Thousands died in Ayatollah* Khomeini's Islamic Revolution in Iran in the early 1980s, but those who survived continued to fight against the Iranian government.

In Afghanistan, regional groups united under the title of Mujahidin arose to expel the Soviet occupiers in 1979. After the Soviets were defeated in 1989, the various Mujahidin leaders engaged in civil war as they competed for control of the country. This continued until an extremist group called the Taliban (meaning "students") arose in 1994. Some of the Mujahidin chiefs formed the Northern Alliance and attempted to overthrow the Taliban. On September 11, 2001, the United States accused the Taliban of harboring terrorists involved in the attacks on the World Trade Center and the Pentagon. With the help of the Northern Alliance, the United States drove the Taliban out of the capital and helped establish a new government in Afghanistan. (*See also* **Afghanistan; Arab-Israeli Conflict; Hamas; Hizbullah; Iran; Khomeini, Ruhollah al-Musavi; Mujahidin; Muslim Brotherhood.**)

* **ayatollah** highest-ranking legal scholar among some Shi'i Muslims

Jordan

Jordan is a Middle Eastern country bordered by Syria to the north, Israel to the west, and Saudi Arabia to the south and southeast. It also shares a small border with Iraq to the east. Due in part to its shared border with Israel, Jordan has played a central role in Arab-Israeli relations since the mid-1900s.

History and Government

A series of different cultures, including the Roman Empire, the Ummayad caliphate, the Mamluk kingdom, and the Ottoman Empire, controlled the area now known as Jordan until just after World War I (1914–1918). Jordan, historically part of Syria, was created by the British in the aftermath of the World War I. It achieved partial independence in 1928 and full independence in 1946.

A Historical Overview. Jordan was part of the Ottoman Empire from 1517 until the end of World War I. The Ottomans sided with Germany during the war, and when they were defeated by the Allied Powers (Great Britain, France, Russia, and the United States), the Ottoman Empire collapsed. After the war, the Allies divided the former Ottoman-controlled territories in the Middle East among themselves. The lands that today make up Israel and Jordan came under British control. The British divided the region into two parts. Lands to the west of the Jordan River were called Palestine. Those to the east of the river became Transjordan.

The modern state of Jordan first emerged in 1921 as the amirate of Transjordan. Although the country was still formally under British rule, it gained partial independence in 1928. During World War II (1939–1945), Transjordan sided with the Allied Powers (Great Britain, France, the Soviet Union,

See map in Gulf States (vol. 2).

and the United States) against the Axis Powers (Italy, Japan, and Germany). Jordan achieved full independence from Britain in 1946 after the war had ended and named King Abdullah ibn al-Hussein as its first ruler.

In 1948 the United Nations divided Palestine into what was supposed to be two states—one for Jews and one for Arabs. Israel immediately declared statehood, sparking the first Arab-Israeli War. The portion of Palestine still under Arab control united with Jordan and seized the eastern part of Jerusalem during the war. Three years later, King Abdullah was assassinated and his son, King Talal ibn Abdullah, assumed the throne. After less than a year in power he abdicated* and his son King Hussein ibn Talal took over.

When an Arab-Israeli war broke out in 1967, Israeli forces captured eastern Jerusalem and seized territory held by Jordan on the west bank of the Jordan River. Since that time, Israel has occupied the territory known as the West Bank. In the wake of Israel's occupation of the West Bank, thousands of Palestinian refugees fled across the border to Jordan. In 1988 Jordan formally ended its legal and political ties to the West Bank, and six years later, King Hussein signed a peace treaty with Israel. When King Hussein died in 1999, he was succeeded by his son King Abdullah II, who continues to rule.

The Government Takes Shape. In 1928 Transjordan adopted a constitution and a system of government headed by a king and an elected parliament*, or National Assembly. The parliament consists of two houses. In the lower house, members are elected by the voters. In the upper house, members are chosen by the king and approved by members of the lower house.

The country's first elections took place in 1929. In 1952 Jordan adopted a new constitution under which the king shares executive power with a prime minister and several cabinet* members. The king has the power to declare war and make treaties. He may also call the lower house of parliament into session, close its sessions, or suspend its activities.

Jordan's legal system consists of separate courts for civil and religious matters. Civil courts rule on cases of civil and criminal law, while religious courts deal with such issues as marriage, divorce, and inheritance. A supreme court handles appeals of lower court rulings and interprets the law. Tribal courts hear cases brought by Jordan's nomadic* population.

Politics and Islam

Political parties first emerged in Jordan during the 1920s and 1930s but were not truly effective. Since 1946, when Jordan gained full independence, Islamic parties have played a key role.

The Emergence of Political Parties. A number of early secular* parties in Jordan sought independence from Britain. They were limited, however, by British influence over the government and a general lack of political experience. Increased Western influence in the Middle East, combined with the creation of Israel, strengthened political activity in Jordan. These factors also contributed to the emergence of more radical* political parties in the country.

The most prominent political party in Jordan, the Muslim Brotherhood, is officially registered as a social and religious organization, but it has also

* **abdicate** to give up a throne or other high office

* **parliament** representative national body having supreme legislative power within the state

* **cabinet** individuals appointed by a head of state to supervise departments of government and to act as official advisers

* **nomadic** wandering from place to place in search of food and pasture

* **secular** separate from religion in human life and society; connected to everyday life

* **radical** favoring extreme change or reform, especially in existing political and social institutions

been very successful in politics. After declaring its support for King Abdullah I early on, the Muslim Brotherhood has been able to operate freely and continues to support the government. Under the slogan "Islam is the solution," the group calls for reforms based on Islamic law and values, and it aims to end corruption and Western influence in Jordan. Its main goals are to develop a national education program based on Islamic principles, to promote economic development, to work for a just distribution of wealth, and to advance Muslim unity.

Political unrest, including some riots, forced King Hussein to declare martial law in 1957. He also outlawed political activity by secular parties, which led to increased influence for the Muslim Brotherhood. After limited elections were held in 1962, the government lifted martial law and allowed political parties to operate again. Political turmoil, however, led to another ban on political parties in 1963. Wars with Israel in 1967 and 1973 kept tensions high and general elections were cancelled in Jordan for more than 20 years.

In 1989 King Hussein ended military rule and political parties were once again allowed to operate freely. General elections were held later that year, and the Muslim Brotherhood won 40 percent of the seats in the National Assembly. Two years later, the king invited a leader of the Muslim Brotherhood to form a cabinet. Members of the party were chosen to head five important ministries, including education and justice. The Muslim Brotherhood retained much of its political power in the elections of 1993 and 1997 as well.

Other Influential Islamic Groups. Although they have no legal status, other groups that claim significant membership include the Islamic Liberation Party, the Islamic Holy War Party, Hamas, Muhammad's Army, and the Muslim Youth Movement. They are considered threats to public order because they have called for the overthrow of Arab governments in the region in hopes of replacing the current regimes* with Islamic governments.

The Islamic Liberation Party believes that Islam should guide all aspects of life. Its goal is to replace secular governments with Islamic caliphates*. The party refuses to participate in social, religious, or charitable activities, which it feels distract from its political aims. The Liberation Party attempted an unsuccessful coup* in 1969. The Islamic Holy War Party, Muhammad's Army, and the Muslim Youth Movement are less popular than the Islamic Liberation Party. Nonetheless, members of these groups have been accused of trying to overthrow the government. Hamas, a Palestinian group that seeks the destruction of the state of Israel, is prohibited from political activity in Jordan.

A number of nonpolitical, purely religious Islamic groups also operate in Jordan. Sufi* orders, which came to Jordan from surrounding countries, stress proper religious conduct and reject materialist values. Their members come from all levels of Jordanian society and have increased the awareness of Islam among average citizens. Another prominent religious group, the Jama'at al-Tabligh, is a religious organization that calls for a return to the Qur'an* and early Islamic practices. The group traces its roots to India and followers are required to spend an hour each day, or one day a month, preaching the word of God. (*See also* **Arab-Israeli Conflict; Hamas; Muslim Brotherhood.**)

An American Queen in Jordan

In 1977 American-born Lisa Najeeb Halaby, just a few years out of college, was casually introduced to King Hussein at an airport ceremony in Jordan. Halaby was in the country visiting her father, who was working there. The king, whose third wife had recently died, soon struck up a friendship with 26-year-old Halaby. Being a well-known international figure, it was difficult for King Hussein to find time to be alone with Halaby. According to her, "We courted on a motorcycle. It was the only way we could get off by ourselves." After a six-week relationship, the king proposed to Halaby and they were married in June 1978. After the marriage, Halaby took the name Noor al-Hussein, meaning "Light of Hussein." Queen Noor, as she is called, became the first American-born queen of an Arab nation.

* **regime** government in power

* **caliphate** office and government of the caliph, the religious and political leader of an Islamic state

* **coup** sudden, and often violent, overthrow of a ruler or government

* **Sufi** refers to Sufism, which seeks to develop spirituality through discipline of the mind and body

* **Qur'an** book of the holy scriptures of Islam

Judaism and Islam

Founded in Arabia during the early 600s, the teachings of Islam reflected the influence of ancient religions practiced in the Middle East, including Judaism, Christianity, and Zoroastrianism. From the early days of Islam, Muslims have had a complex relationship with Jews. The two religious traditions interacted in many areas, such as scripture* and belief, society and politics, and culture and intellectual life. Jews generally enjoyed fair treatment in Islamic societies. The founding of the Jewish state of Israel in 1948 and subsequent displacement of Palestinians, however, severely strained the relationship between the Jewish and Muslim communities.

Common Ground. Islam considers itself the culmination of the monotheistic* traditions. Muhammad's revelations supported the religious concepts, commanded practices, and established institutions of Judaism. Both religions are monotheistic, and their followers believe that God is the creator, sustainer, and ruler of the universe. They also share a belief in divine revelation, prophecy, scripture, angels, and Satan. Islam and Judaism emphasize moral responsibility and accountability. The Muslim community accepted the Jewish practices of ritual worship and fasting, which existed in pre-Islamic* Mecca. The Qur'an* mentions popular figures from sacred Jewish literature, such as Joseph, Noah, Moses, and Solomon, and identifies them as prophets*.

Judaism and Islam stress practice in addition to belief, and therefore, law rather than theology* is the principal source of instruction for Jews and Muslims. Peace is central to both faiths, as demonstrated by similar greetings meaning "peace be upon you": *shalom aleichem* in Judaism and *salaam alaikum* in Islam.

Jews and Muslims believe they are children of Abraham, although they belong to different branches of the same family. Jews are the spiritual descendants of Abraham and his wife Sarah through their son Isaac. Muslims trace their lineage to Ismail, Abraham's firstborn son by his Egyptian servant, Hagar.

Both religions believe that they have a special covenant with God. Although Muslims recognize the Jewish prophets and the Torah*, they maintain that Islam supersedes Judaism. Muslims believe that God sent a revelation to Moses, but the messages of the Torah were corrupted versions of the original revelation. For Muslims, the Qur'an is the literal, complete word of God, revealed one final time to the Prophet Muhammad as guidance for all humankind. Despite the differences, the Qur'an grants Jews a special status within Islam as *ahl al-kitab* (People of the Book), because they possess sacred scripture. Regardless of the degree to which the Torah may have been altered, it was once God's word.

Opposing the Prophet. After Muhammad received the first divine revelation in 610, he began to preach a message of monotheism and social equality in Mecca. He experienced limited success in converting people to his beliefs and encountered fierce persecution. In 622 Muhammad led a small group of followers to the city of Medina, where he established the first Islamic community.

Muhammad dictated a document commonly referred to as the Constitution of Medina (ca. 622–624). The constitution contained laws that regulated both social and political life, and it established standards for the treatment of Jews and other religious groups living in the *ummah* (community of faithful Muslims). Eventually Jews (and later, Christians) were granted the status of a protected non-Muslim minority, or *dhimmi*. This was an inferior legal status relative to Muslims, but it permitted Jews to follow their own religious practices, including the observance of Jewish religious law, and granted them control over the internal affairs of their community. Moreover, Muslims offered *dhimmi* the security of life and property and defense against their enemies. In exchange, Jews had to pay special taxes, follow certain regulations regarding dress, occupation, and residence, and pledge their political support to the Muslim ruler.

Given their shared roots, it was natural to expect that the Jews would accept Muhammad's message and become his allies. The Jews of Medina, however, had strong ties to the polytheistic* Quraysh tribe of Mecca, who fiercely opposed the Prophet. Their support of Muhammad's enemy caused him to take action against the Jewish tribes of Medina. In modern times, Muslim activists have cited this as evidence of the Jews' rejection and betrayal of Islam, and Jewish activists have used it as evidence of Islamic opposition to Judaism.

Mutual Benefits. Following the Prophet's death in 632, Islam spread beyond Arabia to the rest of the Middle East and to other parts of the world. During the 600s, the great Jewish communities of Babylonia, Palestine, and Egypt came under Islamic rule. Wherever Muslims took control, Jews usually became a protected religious minority. Occasionally, Jews were treated harshly in Muslim societies, but this was the exception, not the rule.

The cultural and intellectual interchange between Jews and Muslims was profound. They contributed to and learned from one another in the fields of theology, philosophy, law, mysticism*, and poetry. Jewish scholars helped Muslim rulers collect and translate great works of science, medicine, and philosophy from both East and West.

Assured of a protected status, Jews sometimes relocated to Islamic lands during periods of Christian persecution. For example, during the Middle Ages, many Jews moved from Europe to Muslim-ruled Andalusia, the southernmost region of Spain, to escape a class system that prohibited them from improving their position in society. Due to the greater tolerance of Muslim governments, Jews were able to prosper as small landholders in Spain. During the 900s, Jews worked in Andalusia as translators, engineers, physicians, and architects in the court of the caliph*. Jews also fled from Europe to Muslim countries during the Inquisition—a period when Catholic courts persecuted Muslims and Jews, who were considered heretics*.

Equal Rights. Beginning around 1800, France, Great Britain, and other Western nations established themselves as colonial powers in the Middle East. In some regions, they introduced a policy of equal rights for minorities. This was a direct challenge to the long-standing institution of *dhimmah*, protection of the rights of non-Muslim minorities. The leaders of the Ottoman Empire responded by passing laws that gave *dhimmi*, including Jews, equal status with Muslims. Although these rules were not universally accepted and

Changing Direction

The Qur'an is considered the final installment in monotheistic revelation. As such, it incorporates many beliefs and customs of Judaism. For example, it initially adopted the Jewish practice of facing the holy city of Jerusalem during prayer. Soon after Muhammad's emigration to Medina, however, he had a revelation that Muslims should no longer face Jerusalem during prayer, but the site of Abraham's and Ismail's sanctuary, the Kaaba in Mecca, instead. This simple change affected all Muslims and marked Islam as a distinct alternative to Judaism, despite the many similarities that remained between the two faiths.

* **polytheistic** refers to believing in more than one god

* **mysticism** belief that spiritual enlightenment and truth can be attained through various physical and spiritual disciplines

* **caliph** religious and political leader of an Islamic state

* **heretic** person whose belief or practice is contrary to established religious doctrine

applied throughout the empire, they reflected the real changes being implemented by the Western powers. By the end of World War I in 1918, Jews had become full citizens in most Middle Eastern Islamic countries.

During the 1920s and 1930s, the Western presence in the region continued. Feelings of nationalism* grew among Muslims living in Western-controlled countries. As a growing number of Muslims joined the movement for independence, some Jews became supporters of Zionism (the movement to create a Jewish state in Palestine). This, in turn, led to increasing tension between Muslims and Jews.

Radical Change. The establishment of the state of Israel was a critical turning point in relations between Muslims and Jews. After World War II ended in 1945, those Jews who had survived Nazi persecution in Europe urgently pressed for the creation of a homeland in Palestine, a territory that Arabs had inhabited for centuries. After massive immigration into Palestine from Nazi-occupied Europe, Israel proclaimed its independence on May 14, 1948. Neighboring Arab countries, rejecting its claim to statehood, invaded the new Jewish nation. War lasted until the United Nations was able to broker a peace agreement in 1949. As a result of the war, about 600,000 Arabs, living in the part of Palestine that had come under Israeli control, fled their homes. Major conflicts between Israeli and Arab forces occurred again in 1956, 1967, 1973, and 1982.

Within 20 years of the first war, the majority of Jews in Muslim countries migrated to Israel, and to a lesser extent, North America and Europe. In subsequent years, relations between Jews and Muslims were influenced by the politics of the Arab-Israeli dispute and growing feelings of anti-Semitism*. For some Jews and Muslims, the struggle over Israel is based on religious, not political, claims to the land.

The role of the remaining Jews in Islamic countries has been controversial. Many Muslims believe that citizenship should be tied to religious affiliation, as it was in the past. They argue that Muslims must lead a state governed by Islamic law, because only Muslims are capable of interpreting Islamic law. In Pakistan, Sudan, Afghanistan, and Iran, non-Muslims do not have the right to hold high-level government positions.

Strict interpretations of Islam have led to persecution and discrimination against religious minorities under some Muslim governments, such as under the Taliban in Afghanistan. The legacy of Muhammad's attacks against the Jews of Medina for betraying him has been used by Hamas and Osama bin Laden to further their anti-Semitic aims. They argue that the Jews of Israel want to undermine Islam as their ancestors did in Medina during Muhammad's time.

In sharp contrast to these views, some Muslims support greater religious tolerance. In their opinion, religious pluralism* is the basis of Islam, and Islamic societies benefit from opening the political system to followers of other faiths. To support their position, they cite passages in the Qur'an and the practices of Muhammad and the early caliphs that demonstrate a tolerant attitude toward Jews and other religious minorities in the community. (*See also* **Abraham; Andalusia; Arab-Israeli Conflict; Christianity and Islam; Islam: Overview; Jihad; Minorities; Taliban.**)

* **nationalism** feelings of loyalty and devotion to one's country and a commitment to its independence

* **anti-Semitism** hostility toward and discrimination against Jews

* **pluralism** condition of society in which diverse groups maintain and develop their traditional culture or special interests

Justice

The Qur'an* describes the ideal Muslim society as one that is based on the unity and equality of all believers. In such a community, moral and social justice triumph over the oppression of its powerless and needy members. The concept of justice is central to the Islamic worldview, and as such, it has generated heated debate among Muslim legal and religious scholars since the early 600s. After colonial powers occupied most parts of the Islamic world during the 1800s, Western ideas about justice influenced the discussion.

Leveling the Playing Field. The people of pre-Islamic* Arabia were organized into tribes, each of which generally was concerned with the well-being of its members. Self-interest also motivated individual behavior. Muhammad's message of social justice, as revealed to him by God and described in the Qur'an, signaled the creation of a new order.

Muhammad preached that all Muslims belong to a single universal community called the *ummah*. Members of the *ummah* should care for and protect one another, regardless of social and economic status or tribal affiliation. Although Islam regards wealth as a product of hard work and God's blessing, prosperous Muslims have a responsibility for the poor and needy. Ideas about the redistribution of wealth are tied to the belief that everything belongs to God, and human beings are merely caretakers for God's property.

The Qur'an emphasizes the need to care for those who are considered outcasts. Under the tribal system of Muhammad's time, this group included widows, orphans, and poor people. Muslims can meet this requirement by setting aside a portion of their wealth for the poor. This practice, called *zakat*, is one of the five Pillars of Islam. All Muslims who are able must give 2.5 percent of their net worth annually. The Qur'an and sunnah* also permit Muslims to use arms in defense of poor people and those who have been wronged, especially those who have been driven out of their homes unjustly. In addition, the Qur'an forbids usury (the lending of money in return for high rates of interest) because such a practice takes advantage of the poor.

Pondering Weighty Issues. During his lifetime, Muhammad served as the leading legal authority, administering justice according to the will of God. After his death, Muhammad's followers argued about the proper way to ensure political justice. For Sunnis*, it involved choosing a ruler through *ijma* (community consensus). For Shi'is*, political justice could only be guaranteed by acknowledging the Prophet's son-in-law Ali ibn Abi Talib and Ali's descendants as the imams* of the Muslim community.

During the Middle Ages*, Islamic scholars continued to debate the concept of justice, in particular the issue of God's control over human activity. At the center of the discussion was the question: If God is responsible for human actions, how can He justly punish people for their evil deeds? Some scholars argued that people control their own actions and are, therefore, responsible for them. Others claimed that God predetermines all actions. In either case, Islam teaches that people can justly be held accountable for their actions. Another debate focused on the question of whether ideas about justice can be determined objectively by reason or only by revelation*.

* **Qur'an** book of the holy scriptures of Islam

* **pre-Islamic** refers to the Arabian Peninsula or to the Arabic language before the founding of Islam in the early 600s

* **sunnah** literally "the trodden path"; Islamic customs based on the exemplary behavior of Muhammad

* **Sunni** refers to the largest branch of the Muslim community; the name derives from sunnah, the exemplary behavior of the Prophet Muhammad

* **Shi'i** refers to Muslims who believe that Muhammad chose Ali ibn Abi Talib and his descendants as the spiritual-political leaders of the Muslim community

* **imam** spiritual-political leader in Shi'i Islam, one who is regarded as directly descended from Muhammad; also, one who leads prayers

* **Middle Ages** period roughly between 500 and 1500

* **revelation** message from God to humans transmitted through a prophet

Separating Religion From Justice

During the mid-1900s, an Egyptian liberal named Khalid Muhammad Khalid wrote a highly controversial book called *From Here We Start*. In his book, Khalid argues that social justice can be achieved only if religion and the state remain separate. He accused the *ulama* of exploiting people's devotion to religion in order to maintain their own wealth and social standing. In his opinion, they promoted superstition instead of reason, and poverty instead of wealth. Khalid concluded that the meddling of religion in society would "drag the whole people down" because it would "breed an instinct of following." In the late 1900s, Khalid adopted a less secular position, advocating a greater role for religion in issues of social justice.

* **polygyny** practice of having more than one wife at the same time

* *ulama* religious scholars

Prominent scholars identified the central principles of Islamic justice. They claimed that justice prevails when both parties involved in a transaction give and take equally. They maintained that determining whether an act is just depends on the context in which it occurs. Consequently, they believed that Islamic law must remain flexible and take into consideration differing circumstances when settling matters of justice.

Breaking With the Past. By the 1800s, governments throughout the Islamic world had become weak. Ultimately, Western colonial powers took control of many Muslim regions. This led to the development of two major schools of thought on the question of justice: the modernist and the traditionalist.

Modernists sought to reform Islamic law, taking into account the social changes brought about by modern life. Traditionalists believed that the ideas of modernists reflected the influence of Western societies and would compromise Islamic principles. They favored instead a return to traditional ideas and practices. The modernists wanted to adopt Western-style laws on divorce and economic equality. Traditionalists argued that Western codes did not give sufficient recognition to biological differences between men and women.

Many countries under European control adopted Western-style legal codes. Egypt's new civil codes combined Islamic, Arab, Turkish, and European law. Iraq and several other Arab nations adopted these codes. The major exception to this trend was in the area of family law. Most Islamic countries allowed traditionalists to decide issues related to marriage, divorce, and other personal matters. Although Tunisia abolished polygyny* in 1956, family law in Pakistan and the Gulf states remained virtually unaffected by modernists.

Social Justice. During the colonial period, the ruling governments generally ignored the condition of the Muslim populations they controlled. To some extent, the *ulama** also neglected the problems of poor Muslims. Issues of social justice came to the forefront of Muslim debate during the early 1900s. Industrialization and other economic changes in the Islamic world brought peasants from the countryside to the urban areas looking for work. This migration led to overcrowding in the cities and high rates of unemployment. It also increased the tensions that already existed as a result of colonialism. Such issues were addressed by a new generation of social and religious reformers in many parts of the Muslim world.

Among the earliest was Egyptian schoolteacher Hasan al-Banna (1906–1949), who founded the Muslim Brotherhood in 1928 as an organizational and religious solution to the plight of poor Muslims. In his view, Islam was a social movement that could improve all aspects of life. His message of social and economic justice soon spread to the rest of the Arab world.

Sayyid Qutb (1906–1966), a member of the Muslim Brotherhood, was also an advocate of Islamic social justice. During the mid-1900s, he wrote a book called *Social Justice in Islam*. In this work, Qutb argues that the Islamic idea of social justice applies to a person's material and spiritual well being. People cannot focus on spiritual matters if their basic needs—food and shelter—are not met. One way of ensuring the material well-being of the members of the community is through mutual responsibility. This means that individuals should participate in their community, and the community, in turn, should feed and protect its poor and defenseless members.

Inspired by Qutb, some reformist groups have become militant. They stress Islam's message of social justice as well as the need to rise up against oppression as a way to attract followers from the lower classes. Hamas and Hizbullah, for example, link the issue of social justice with the empowerment of the poor and weak and argue that the poor must rebel against unjust rulers. (*See also* **Law; Muslim Brotherhood; Qutb, Sayyid.**)

Kaaba

The Kaaba, a shrine* located near the center of the Grand Mosque in Mecca, is the most sacred place in the Muslim world. It is also called the "House of God." Millions of Muslims throughout the world turn toward the Kaaba five times each day when they pray. In addition, Muslims bury their dead with their heads pointing toward the Kaaba.

The shrine is also the primary destination of Muslims during the hajj*. Pilgrims visiting Mecca walk counterclockwise around the Kaaba seven times. This ritual imitates angels walking around God's heavenly throne and symbolizes for the pilgrims their entry into the presence of God.

The Arabic word *kaaba* means "cube" and reflects the cube shape of the gray stone structure. The Kaaba measures about 33 feet wide, 50 feet long, and 45 feet high. Its corners coincide with the four points of the compass. The interior of the Kaaba is bare, except for three pillars supporting the roof and silver and gold lamps hanging from the ceiling. During most of the year, the Kaaba is covered with a woven black cloth that has verses from the Qur'an* embroidered on it.

According to popular Muslim tradition, Adam built the Kaaba as a copy of the heavenly house of God. Its destruction during Noah's Flood left only the foundation. The Qur'an says that Ibrahim (Abraham) and his son Ismail

* **shrine** place that is considered sacred because of its history or the relics contained there

* **hajj** pilgrimage to Mecca that Muslims are required to make once in their lifetime

* **Qur'an** book of the holy scriptures of Islam

Considered by Muslims to be the most sacred site on earth, the Kaaba in Mecca is the primary destination during the hajj. In this recent photo, thousands of Muslims participate in the ritual circling of the shrine, walking counterclockwise around the Kaaba seven times.

See color plate 1, vol. 3.

* **idol** object of worship

* **monotheistic** refers to the belief that there is only one God

* **covenant** solemn and binding agreement

built the shrine. By the time of Muhammad, however, the Kaaba had come under the control of the Quraysh, the major tribe of Mecca, and was used as a shrine for idols* of their gods. In 630, when Muhammad triumphantly returned from exile to his native Mecca, he rid the Kaaba of its idols and restored the monotheistic* religion of Abraham.

The Black Stone of Mecca, a sacred stone that is possibly a piece of meteorite, is fixed into the wall in the eastern corner of the Kaaba. It measures about 12 inches in diameter. When pilgrims walk around the Kaaba, they often try to touch or kiss the stone. Worn down by centuries of contact, the stone's cracked and broken pieces are now held together by a wide silver band. Tradition says that Adam received the stone when he and Eve were expelled from paradise so he could obtain forgiveness of his sins. Muslims believe that Abraham and Ismail later placed the stone in the Kaaba when they rebuilt it. The stone is a symbol of God's covenant* with Abraham and Ismail and with the Muslim community itself. According to tradition, the stone was originally white but turned black after absorbing the sins of the many pilgrims who have touched it. (*See also* **Abraham; Hajj; Ismail; Mecca.**)

Karbala and Najaf

* **Shi'i** refers to Muslims who believe that Muhammad chose Ali ibn Abi Talib and his descendants as the spiritual-political leaders of the Muslim community

* **shrine** place that is considered sacred because of its history or the relics contained there

* **Sunni** refers to the largest branch of the Muslim community; the name derives from sunnah, the exemplary behavior of the Prophet Muhammad

* **mosque** Muslim place of worship

The two holiest cities in Iraq, Karbala and Najaf, are located in the central part of the country. Both cities contain important Shi'i* shrines* and have served as centers for political opposition to repressive rulers.

Karbala's religious significance stems from the Battle of Karbala, which occurred in 680 between the rival Sunni* and Shi'i Muslims. Husayn ibn Ali, the Shi'i leader, was the grandson of Islam's founder, the Prophet Muhammad. Greatly outnumbered by enemy forces, Husayn and his followers were massacred at Karbala. His tomb is one of the most important Shi'i shrines and the city is second only to Mecca as a pilgrimage destination for Shi'i Muslims. Husayn's half brother, al-Abbas ibn Ali, is also buried there, and many people visit his shrine believing in its miraculous healing powers. Many elderly Muslims travel to Karbala to die, believing that the city is one of the gates to paradise. Karbala serves as a symbol of defiance against unjust authority. Since its founding, the city has been a place of refuge for people fleeing from tyrannical rulers in the region.

Located south of Baghdad (Iraq's capital), Najaf has been an important religious center for Shi'i Muslims since the 700s. The mosque* in the city's center contains the tomb of Ali ibn Abi Talib, the spiritual founder of Shi'i Islam and son-in-law of Muhammad. As such, his tomb is also an important pilgrimage site.

Many Shi'i religious scholars have lived in Najaf and have used the city as a base from which to teach and spread the traditions of Shi'i Islam. Najaf eventually became a center of learning for Shi'i Islam. In the late 1800s, the city of Qom, in Iran, temporarily replaced Najaf as the center of Shi'i learning. With the rise of the Ayatollah Khomeini in the 1970s, however, Najaf regained its status as a focal point for Islamic studies and political activism. Throughout the last decades of the twentieth century, religious scholars and activists in Najaf led movements against secular* governments in Iraq and Iran. (*See also* **Husayn ibn Ali; Khomeini, Ruhollah al-Musavi; Shi'i Islam; Sunni Islam.**)

*secular separate from religion in human life and society; connected to everyday life

Kashmir

Situated in the extreme northern frontier of the Indian subcontinent, Kashmir is a mountainous region that has been the subject of dispute between India and Pakistan since 1947. Bounded by China, India, Pakistan, and Afghanistan, Kashmir covers an area of more than 85,000 square miles. India controls almost two-thirds of the territory, which constitutes the state of Jammu and Kashmir. Pakistan administers about one-third of the region, known as Azad (Free) Kashmir and the Northern Areas. After the Sino-Indian War of 1962, China occupied a portion of eastern Kashmir. The territory has approximately 12 million inhabitants. They are predominantly Muslim, but Hindus* make up a significant minority.

The Province of a Prince. The early history of Kashmir was dominated by clashes between Buddhism* and Brahmanism*, as rulers who followed one religion persecuted members of the other. From the 800s to the 1300s, Hindu dynasties* controlled the region, and for several centuries, Kashmir thrived as a center of Hindu culture. During the early 1300s, the leaders of Kashmir began to embrace Islam. Well-known *ulama** from Central Asia visited the area and preached to the masses, converting thousands of Kashmiris to Islam. By the end of the 1400s, most of the inhabitants of region were Muslim. Kashmir remained under Muslim rule for almost five centuries.

In 1819 Ranjit Singh, the Sikh* ruler of Punjab, conquered Kashmir. After winning the first Anglo-Sikh war, Great Britain gained rights to the territory. In 1846 the British named Raja Gulab Singh the maharaja, or "ruling prince," of Kashmir. Singh founded the Dogra dynasty, which controlled the territory until 1947. For the British, Kashmir provided a buffer zone between colonial India and the empires of Russia and China to the north. Muslims, however, suffered under Hindu rule. Despite being the majority of the population, they encountered severe oppression, including heavy taxation, forced labor without wages, and discriminatory laws.

Choosing Sides. In 1947 Great Britain divided the subcontinent into two independent states, the predominantly Hindu India and Muslim Pakistan. According to the terms of the partition plan, the maharaja Hari Singh could choose whether Kashmir would become part of Pakistan or India. Muslims, accounting for almost 80 percent of the population, favored Pakistan. Singh postponed the decision, however, hoping to retain the region's independence. His Muslim subjects revolted, and hundreds of tribesmen from Pakistan invaded Kashmir to support the rebels. The maharaja agreed to join India in 1947 on condition that the government provide military aid and permit the people of Kashmir to vote on their political status in the future.

A full-scale war between Pakistan and India resulted. The Pakistani government claimed that Muslim-majority Kashmir was a natural extension of

*Hindu refers to the beliefs and practices of Hinduism, an ancient religion that originated in India

*Buddhism religion of eastern and central Asia based on the teaching of Gautama Buddha

*Brahmanism ancient and orthodox form of Hinduism

*dynasty succession of rulers from the same family or group

*ulama religious scholars

*Sikh refers to Sikhism, a branch of Hinduism that rejects caste and idolatry

Constitution Without Clout

Unlike the rest of the states of the Indian Union, the state of Jammu and Kashmir has its own constitution. The constitution does not give Jammu and Kashmir much independence, however. In fact, the state remains under the tight control of the government of India. Under the constitution, the governor of Kashmir and all 12 judges of its high court are appointed by the Indian president. The only officials elected by the Kashmiri people are a council of ministers and members of the state's legislature. The Indian government also controls all legislation relating to Jammu and Kashmir's defense, foreign policy, and internal communications.

its own territory. The leaders of India argued that they had gained the legal right to rule Kashmir, based on their agreement with Hari Singh.

In January 1949, the United Nations negotiated a ceasefire and mediated the dispute. Later that year, India and Pakistan established a line of control to divide Kashmir. The boundaries that they established remain virtually unchanged today. In 1965 war erupted again between the two countries, followed by another ceasefire agreement. India and Pakistan agreed to seek a peaceful solution to the dispute, but fighting flared up repeatedly throughout the following decades.

Domestic Conflict. In addition to the rival claims of India and Pakistan to the territory of Kashmir, violent unrest has plagued the Indian-ruled portion of the region. From 1947 to 1953, the state of Jammu and Kashmir enjoyed considerable autonomy* under Shaikh Abdullah. In 1953, however, the Indian government arrested and imprisoned him. Despite promises to the Kashmiri people and to the United Nations, India never allowed the Kashmiris to exercise their right to determine their political status. Instead, the government declared Jammu and Kashmir to be an integral part of India. The Indian government did little to develop the infrastructure* and economy of the only Muslim-dominated state within India. Moreover, a growing emphasis on secularism* produced a religious backlash and contributed to the popularity of Islamic political parties.

In 1987 the Indian government prevented an alliance of several Islamic political parties from coming to power in Jammu and Kashmir, thus triggering a powerful mass resistance against Indian rule. Leading the armed struggle is the Hizbul Mujahidin, a group that is committed to jihad* and seeks to join the Indian portion of Kashmir with Pakistan. The Indian government alleges that Pakistan finances the armed struggle. Pakistan denies the charges, claiming that it provides only moral and diplomatic support. In response to the uprising, India has significantly increased its military presence in the area. According to the reports of various human rights groups, Indian security forces have committed terrible acts of violence against the people of Jammu and Kashmir. Authorities estimate that more than 30,000 people have died in the conflict. By 1998 India and Pakistan had developed nuclear weapons, making resolution of the decades-old dispute over Kashmir more urgent than ever. (*See also* **India; Pakistan; South Asia.**)

* **autonomy** self-government

* **infrastructure** basic facilities and institutions that a country needs in order to function

* **secularism** belief that religion should be separate from other aspects of human life and society, especially politics

* **jihad** literally "striving"; war in defense of Islam

Khadija

565–ca. 623
Wife of the Prophet Muhammad

Khadija bint Khuwaylid was the first wife of Muhammad, the prophet to whom the Islamic faith was revealed. Khadija and Muhammad were married for 24 years and had several children together, including Fatimah. Muslims revere Khadija and Fatimah, considering them to be among a few perfect women in history.

Khadija's father had been an honored leader of the Quraysh tribe of Mecca (in present-day Saudi Arabia). He was one of the most successful Quraysh merchants of his time, with a considerable talent for business and the accumulation of vast wealth. His daughter Khadija inherited both his business sense and his great wealth, and successfully carried on the family business after her father's death in 585.

By 595 Khadija had been married and widowed twice. At age 40, she hired Muhammad to lead a trade caravan to Syria. He was a distant cousin, and although he was only 25 years old, he was known as an honorable and trustworthy man. He did such an excellent job, earning Khadija twice the profit she had expected, that she hired him to lead her next caravan as well. Soon thereafter, Khadija proposed marriage to Muhammad, and he gladly accepted.

Khadija is honored by Muslims not only because she was the Prophet's first wife, but also because she was well-respected in her own right. During her lifetime, Khadija was known as "the pure one." She fed and clothed the poor and provided financial assistance to family members. She was the first person with whom Muhammad shared his revelations*, which form the cornerstone of the Islamic faith, and the first to publicly accept him as the Messenger of Allah. Khadija provided Muhammad with moral support when few others believed in him. Coming from an important family, Khadija used her great wealth to help Muhammad pursue his calling and establish Islam throughout Arabia.

* **revelation** message from God to humans transmitted through a prophet

Despite many hardships, Khadija and Muhammad had a happy marriage. When Muhammad began to teach about the new faith of Islam, he and his family were persecuted for their beliefs. Nonetheless, Khadija remained devoted to her husband. By the time she died, Khadija had spent all of her fortune helping Muhammad establish Islam. (*See also* **Fatimah**; **Muhammad**.)

Khariji

The Khariji movement began in 656 when Ali ibn Abi Talib, Muhammad's son-in-law and the fourth caliph* of Sunni* Islam, agreed to negotiate rather than continue a long, drawn-out battle with Mu'awiyah, a rebellious general. Believing that negotiation constituted a rejection of the Qur'an*, several of Ali's followers broke away and became known as Kharijis (seceders). Ali engaged in battle against the newly formed group and was later assassinated by a Khariji seeking revenge.

The early Khariji movement attracted many Bedouins* and southern Arabian tribesmen, but non-Arabs also joined the movement. Initially, Khariji centers included Basra (Iraq), South Arabia, and upper Mesopotamia. Arab armies also carried the Khariji doctrine to North Africa where many Berbers* adopted its teachings. At one time, more than 20 different Khariji sects* existed in the Islamic world.

Kharijis typically rejected compromise and were steadfast in their faith. Their world consisted of two groups—believers and nonbelievers. Nonbelievers were all considered sinners and could include Muslims who did not accept the Khariji philosophy, as well as non-Muslims. Sinners, including imams* and caliphs, were subject to exile or death unless they repented. Khariji beliefs have influenced modern extremist movements, such as al-Qaeda, that promote the violent overthrow of Islamic leaders who accept Western ideals.

* **caliph** religious and political leader of an Islamic state

* **Sunni** refers to the largest branch of the Muslim community; the name derives from sunnah, the exemplary behavior of the Prophet Muhammad

* **Qur'an** book of the holy scriptures of Islam

* **Bedouin** nomad of the desert, especially in North Africa, Syria, and Arabia

* **Berber** refers to a North African ethnic group that consists primarily of Muslims

* **sect** religious group adhering to distinctive beliefs

* **imam** spiritual-political leader in Shi'i Islam, one who is regarded as directly descended from Muhammad; also, one who leads prayers

A small but significant minority of Muslims still belong to the sect. There are about one million Kharijis, now known as Ibadis, primarily in Oman and North Africa. (*See also* **Ali ibn Abi Talib; Qaeda, al-.**)

Khayyam, Umar

ca. 1048–1129
Mathematician, astronomer, and poet

During his lifetime, Umar Khayyam was known as a scholar of mathematics, philosophy, astronomy, law, medicine, and history. After his death, Khayyam was also recognized for his poetry. Born in Neyshabur, Persia (now Iran), his last name means "tentmaker," which may have been his father's trade. Khayyam's early education included instruction in philosophy and the sciences, and he devoted the rest of his life to the pursuit of knowledge.

Umar Khayyam established his reputation in mathematics with several important works including *Treatise on Demonstration of Problems in Algebra* and commentaries on the work of the famous Greek mathematician Euclid. Khayyam's work influenced European mathematicians for several centuries after his death.

* **sultan** political and military ruler of a Muslim dynasty or state

Khayyam also made notable contributions as an astronomer when Seljuk sultan* Malik Shah Jalal al-Din asked him to develop a solar calendar. Working in an observatory in Isfahan, a province in Persia, Khayyam developed an astoundingly accurate calendar that measured the length of the year as just over 365 days.

Umar Khayyam is best known in the West for his poetry. In 1859 British poet Edward FitzGerald translated a collection of Khayyam's *Rubaiyat* into English. A *ruba'i* is a quatrain, a verse of four lines with a rhyme scheme of *aaba.* Immediately popular, Khayyam's verse influenced European views on Persian poetry. His work is characterized by its simplicity of language and references to the subjects he knew well, such as astronomy, metaphysics, and science.

By the 1800s, more than 1,200 quatrains had been attributed to Umar Khayyam. Modern scholars believe that only about 100 of these were actually written by him. (*See also* **Astronomy; Literature; Mathematics; Philosophy.**)

Khomeini, Ruhollah al-Musavi

1902–1989
Leader of the Islamic Revolution in Iran

* **Shi'i** refers to Muslims who believe that Muhammad chose Ali ibn Abi Talib and his descendants as the spiritual-political leaders of the Muslim community

* **shah** king (Persian); ruler of Iran

* **calligraphy** artistic, stylized handwriting or lettering

Ruhollah al-Musavi Khomeini was an Iranian Shi'i* cleric and leader of the Islamic Revolution that overthrew the shah* of Iran in 1979. Khomeini led the country for the next ten years as Iran's religious and political authority, advocating the formation of an Islamic republic.

Religious Leader and Outspoken Critic. Khomeini was born in the village of Khomein in central Iran. Both his father and grandfather were Shi'i religious leaders. As a child, Khomeini studied Arabic, Persian poetry, and calligraphy* at an elementary religious school and later attended other Islamic schools where he continued his religious education. As a Shi'i scholar and teacher, Khomeini produced writings on philosophy, law, and

The Ayatollah Khomeini led the Islamic revolution that ousted the shah of Iran in 1979. As the country's religious and political leader during most of the 1980s, Khomeini enforced Islamic law strictly.

ethics*. He later gained recognition as an ayatollah, signifying his status as a religious guide.

By the 1930s, Khomeini's teachings had attracted a large following of students. He became an outspoken critic of Iranian leader Reza Shah Pahlavi, giving public lectures opposing the shah's secular* reforms and urging Muslim clerics to unite against Western influence.

In the late 1940s, Khomeini's interest in politics increased. Influenced by his early religious training, he retained a conservative* worldview and embraced the concept of revolution against injustice in the name of God. Teaching that holiness came through action, Khomeini believed that Muslim clerics should be politically active, and by the 1960s, he was Iran's leading spokesman for an Islamic government.

* **ethics** set of moral principles or values

* **secular** separate from religion in human life and society; connected to everyday life

* **conservative** generally opposed to change, especially in existing political and social institutions

The ayatollah continued to criticize Iran's government, then led by Reza Shah Pahlavi's son Muhammad. Khomeini believed that Israeli and American influence had corrupted the shah. Muhammad Reza Shah Pahlavi, in turn, feared Khomeini's growing influence and had him arrested, sparking antigovernment riots. Exiled by the shah in 1964, Khomeini settled in the Shi'i holy city of Najaf in Iraq. When Iraqi leader Saddam Hussein forced him to leave the country in 1978, Khomeini moved to a suburb of Paris for a brief period.

The Road to Revolution. While in exile, Khomeini continued to oppose the shah's regime*. He built up his following in Iran through writings and taped speeches, and he developed ties with left-wing Iranian student groups. Khomeini's encouragement greatly strengthened long-standing opposition to Iran's American-backed government. Many people resented the shah's use of terror against opponents of his harsh policies. They also believed his economic policies benefited only his wealthy supporters. The peasants suffered as unemployment soared. Tensions finally boiled over in 1978 when millions of Iranians rose up against the government. Having lost the loyalty of the army, the shah fled the country in January 1979. Khomeini returned to Iran two weeks after the shah's departure, where he was hailed him as the leader of the revolution. A new constitution proclaimed Iran an Islamic republic. Khomeini sought to harness the forces of revolution to strengthen his position. His followers established the Islamic Republican Party (IRP). Khomeini and the IRP clashed with rival political leaders in Iran, but the ayatollah eventually gained the upper hand over his opponents. Using imprisonment, torture, and murder, Khomeini eliminated many who had worked for the shah's government and others perceived to be enemies of the revolution.

Religious and Political Authority. Khomeini solidified his position as Iran's leader in the fall of 1981. He had no interest in compromises or the sharing of power and made sure that his followers controlled Iran's three branches of government—a government dominated by Muslim clergy. As an expert on Islamic law, Khomeini had final authority. Some of his supporters even called him imam*.

Khomeini headed an oppressive regime, continuing with imprisonment and executions of political opponents. Much of the westernized middle-class fled the country as the government strictly enforced Islamic law. Women had to wear *hijab** in public and many were forced give up their jobs. The government banned alcohol and Western music and closed theaters and other places of entertainment. Non-Muslim Iranians faced arrest and persecution.

In foreign policy, Khomeini sought to export his Islamic revolution. He urged Muslims to overthrow pro-Western secular governments. The regime in neighboring Iraq was one of his first targets, and in 1980, the two nations went to war. The conflict dragged on for eight years and took a heavy toll on both sides. Thousands of Iranians died in combat and from Iraqi missile attacks. Ignoring the cost, Khomeini remained steadfast in his determination to overthrow Saddam Hussein. In 1988, faced with heavy internal unrest, Khomeini finally agreed to end the war.

In 1989 Khomeini issued a fatwa* against Salman Rushdie, author of *The Satanic Verses,* calling the book's portrayal of the Prophet Muhammad blasphemy*. He called for Muslims to assassinate Rushdie and the book's

---

* **regime** government in power

A Practical Necessity

Millions of Americans remember the Ayatollah Khomeini for his role in the Iranian hostage crisis. In November 1979, with Khomeini's approval, Iranian students seized the U.S. Embassy in Tehran. They held embassy personnel hostage for more than a year. Many Muslims criticized this action as distorting the message of Islam. The Qur'an calls for prisoners to be treated with respect and be released as soon as possible. The holy book also forbids taking prisoners except during a state of war. Khomeini, however, justified the taking of hostages as a practical necessity for the Islamic revolution.

* **imam** spiritual-political leader in Shi'i Islam, one who is regarded as directly descended from Muhammad; also, one who leads prayers

* **hijab** refers to the traditional head, face, or body covering worn by Muslim women

* **fatwa** opinion issued by Islamic legal scholar in response to a question posed by an individual or a court of law

* **blasphemy** lack of respect toward God, a religion, or something considered sacred

publishers. Although many Muslims throughout the world agreed with his evaluation of the book, most did not accept the fatwa as the correct response.

The charismatic Khomeini, nonetheless, retained his popularity with Iran's Shi'i population. A massive and tumultuous outpouring of grief followed his death in 1989. Shortly before he died, Khomeini had accepted a greater level of democracy in Iran's government, which helped facilitate a smooth transfer of power to his successor. Khomeini's revolution was one of the most significant political movements of the 1900s. (*See also* **Hostages; Iran; Iraq; Islamic State; Revolution; Rushdie, Salman.**)

Khums

See *Taxation.*

Khutba

See *Sermon.*

Koran

See *Qur'an.*

Kosovo

Kosovo is a region of southwestern Serbia in the former Yugoslavia. The majority of its population is Albanian and most of Kosovo's Albanians are Muslims. Christian Serbs comprise the second largest group in Kosovo. Tensions between these two groups have brought violence and unrest to the province for decades and continue to divide the region.

The Region's History Unfolds. During the 1300s, Kosovo was the center of the Serbian empire and home to many churches and monasteries. All of that changed in 1389, when Ottoman forces advanced into the region. Serbs and Ottoman Turks engaged in a fierce battle for control of the region. Although the Serbs lost the battle and ceded control of Kosovo to the Turks, they vowed to reclaim their land and reestablish their former glory.

During the 1400s, the Ottoman Turks ruled most of the Balkan region of southeastern Europe while increasing Islam's influence there. Many Christian Serbs left Kosovo and others converted to Islam.

By the late 1600s, immigrants from Albania, Serbia's neighboring province, began moving to Kosovo in great numbers. In fact, ethnic Albanians eventually outnumbered Serbs in Kosovo. While Serbian cultural influence in the area weakened, Albanians often resisted Ottoman rule.

Ethnic Tensions Rise. By the 1800s, Ottoman power in the region had begun to decline and Serbia broke away from the empire. Looking to avenge the loss of Kosovo, Serbian forces regained control of the province during the Balkan Wars of 1912 and 1913. Ethnic Albanians, however, who made up a significant portion of the population, did not welcome the change in government. Instead, they sought to merge Kosovo with Albania.

Kosovo

In 2001, the Yugoslav government turned former president Slobodan Milosevic over to the International Court of Justice for encouraging his troops to commit atrocities against Muslims during the conflict with Bosnia. Milosevic appears on a large screen in the pressroom of the Congress building in the Dutch city of The Hague answering those charges.

* **regime** government in power

* **Sufi** refers to Sufism, which seeks to develop spirituality through discipline of the mind and body

* **autonomy** self-government

When ethnic tensions erupted into violence, both Serbs and Albanians in Kosovo suffered heavy casualties. After World War I (1914–1918), Western nations redrew the map of the Balkan region, allowing Serbia to retain Kosovo while merging Serbia, Croatia, and Slovenia to form Yugoslavia.

During the 1920s, in hopes of regaining an ethnic majority in the region, Serb leaders encouraged more Serbs to move to Kosovo. Ethnic Albanians resisted and the fighting continued. After World War II (1939–1945), Josip Broz Tito's communist government took over Yugoslavia, crushing any attempts by ethnic Albanians to separate Kosovo from Serbia. Tito's regime* also suppressed the practice of Islam, outlawing public worship and Sufi* brotherhoods.

Many Serbs fled the province, and by 1950 the ethnic Albanian population in Kosovo had become the majority. In the 1960s, the communist regime relaxed its attitude toward Islam and Albanian nationalism in Kosovo, becoming more tolerant. Albanians maintained control over education, the court system, and the media. Meanwhile, calls for Albanian independence increased. President Tito granted Kosovo autonomy* in 1974 and a revised constitution established a high degree of self-government for the six republics of Yugoslavia—Bosnia, Croatia, Macedonia, Montenegro, Slovenia, and Serbia (including Kosovo).

One Land, Two Kosovos. When Tito died in 1980, his communist government lost power, and ethnic conflict in Kosovo increased. In 1989 Serbian president Slobodan Milosevic revoked Kosovo's autonomy and suppressed Albanian influence in the region. After his army occupied Kosovo, he dissolved the assembly and closed Albanian language schools. Although Milosevic's Serbian government was officially in control, the Albanian ethnic majority had its own government with its own elections. In fact, by 1990, more than 85 percent of Kosovo's population was Albanian.

By 1992 Croatia and Slovenia had broken away from Yugoslavia's Serb-dominated government and gained international recognition of their independence. President Milosevic vigorously opposed these moves toward independence and war engulfed the region. Serb forces massacred Muslims in Bosnia. Albanians in Kosovo initially used nonviolent tactics to resist Serb occupation until, frustrated by a lack of success, they formed the Kosovo Liberation Army (KLA). The KLA fought back against the Serbs and gained control of about 40 percent of Kosovo by 1999. When the Serbs launched a campaign of retaliation, thousands of ethnic Albanians fled the province.

After President Milosevic refused to accept a peace deal negotiated by the North Atlantic Treaty Organization, NATO warplanes bombed Yugoslavia. Milosevic responded by launching a vicious campaign designed to rid Kosovo of ethnic Albanians. NATO bombings continued until Milosevic agreed to withdraw his forces. NATO then sent an international peacekeeping force into the region to maintain order.

The violence in Kosovo, though rooted in ethnic tensions, also has religious undertones. Serb Christians have been fighting Albanian Muslims for centuries. Events in Kosovo have attracted the attention of Muslims throughout the world. Islamic agencies have tried to aid Kosovo's refugees but have faced resistance from Serb authorities. NATO intervention also divided the Islamic world when, resenting any extension of Western power in the Muslim world, Iraq, Libya, and Algeria condemned the organization's air strikes. Most Islamic nations, however, supported NATO's efforts to stop the fighting.

The extent of Islam's current influence in Kosovo is difficult to assess. Ethnic violence has overshadowed discussions of religion. Though most ethnic Albanians are Muslim, some reject Islam as an outdated remnant of the Ottoman Empire. Others have begun to identify themselves as Islamic nationalists. (*See also* **Albania; Bosnia; Europe.**)

Human Rights or Power?

The United States and other Western nations played an important role in NATO's decision to bomb Serbia as a means of ending the conflict in Kosovo. NATO's actions caused many Muslims to further resent the United States and the West for what they saw as selective Western interference in Islamic affairs. Some critics believed that the NATO bombing of Serbia was more about the extension of Western power than about protecting human rights. Some Muslims wondered why NATO acted to help Kosovo but did nothing to stop violence against Muslims in Chechnya (Russia) and Kashmir (India). Ironically, some Muslims praised President Milosevic's resistance to American power, even as he killed many Kosovar Muslims.

See *Ahmadi*.

Lahori

Latin America

Many Latin Americans associate Arabs (Muslim and non-Muslim) with *turcos*. The term refers to immigrants from the former Ottoman Empire* who arrived in Latin America in the late 1800s and made their fortunes by engaging in unethical business practices. After al-Qaeda's devastating attacks on the United States on September 11, 2001, the word *turco* depicted Arabs, especially Muslims, as terrorists.

Despite these stereotypes, the highly diverse Islamic community in Latin America extends beyond Arabs to include Muslim immigrants and their children, diplomats from various Islamic countries, and a small group of converts. Latin American Muslims are both Sunni* and Shi'i*, and they form part of a growing pan-American Muslim consciousness in this predominantly Christian region. The Latin American Muslim Unity website claims that area

* **Ottoman Empire** large Turkish state existing from the early 1300s to the early 1900s

* **Sunni** refers to the largest branch of the Muslim community; the name derives from sunnah, the exemplary behavior of the Prophet Muhammad

* **Shi'i** refers to Muslims who believe that Muhammad chose Ali ibn Abi Talib and his descendants as the spiritual-political leaders of the Muslim community

Muslims number more than six million. Muslim communities are most prevalent in Brazil and Argentina, but Islam is also gaining ground in Mexico, Peru, Panama, Venezuela, and other countries.

A Volatile Beginning. People of Islamic background were among the explorers, traders, and settlers who traveled to the Americas beginning in the late 1400s. Many Muslims, displaced by the Christian reconquest of Spain in 1492, migrated to Portuguese- and Spanish-controlled parts of the Americas. The Christian governors in the colonies viewed the increasing numbers of Muslims as a threat to their authority, however, and had many of them killed. According to some Latin Americans who have recently converted from Catholicism to Islam, becoming a Muslim signifies a return to their Moorish* origins and the nearly 700 years of Muslim rule in Spain.

The first wave of Muslims in Latin America consisted of slaves from the West African countries of Ghana, Dahomey (now Benin), Mali, and Nigeria. They were transported to the region between the mid-1500s and mid-1800s to work on Brazilian and Caribbean plantations. Although most of the African slaves converted to Christianity, some secretly maintained their faith in Islam. The second wave of Muslims in the region occurred in Guyana and Suriname. After the abolition of slavery, the British transported thousands of Indians to Guyana to work as indentured servants*. A significant number were Muslims. Similarly, the Dutch settled thousands of Muslims from Indonesia in Suriname. The contracts for these workers stated that they could return to their homelands after completing five years of service. Many of them decided to remain in Latin America, however, because they did not earn as much money as they had expected.

At the end of the 1800s, Arab Muslims from Middle Eastern countries began to arrive in Latin America, seeking to improve their economic condition and to avoid being drafted into the Ottoman army. Most Arab Muslims had hoped to migrate to the United States, but strict immigration policies forced them to settle in Argentina, Brazil, or elsewhere.

Historically, Muslims in the overwhelmingly Catholic countries of Latin America were unable to preserve their religious beliefs, practices, and institutions. Since the 1970s and the beginning of an Islamic revival in the Muslim world, however, the governments of Iran and Saudi Arabia have supported Muslims in Latin America by helping them build mosques and encouraging them to spread Islam.

Mexico's Muslims. Current statistical information on the number of Muslims in Mexico is limited and in dispute. Some scholars have estimated that there are only about 1,000 Muslims in the entire country. In 1986 writer M. Ali Kettani reported that the Islamic community totaled about 15,000 people. Most Muslims are either Sunni or Shi'i, although Sufis, Qadianis, and some members of the Baha'i religion also live in Mexico. The Islamic community is largely concentrated in Mexico City, but small groups of Muslims are dispersed throughout the country. An active Shi'i community in the state of Chihuahua assists the Iranian Embassy by translating its literature into Spanish.

Most scholars agree that the first Muslims in Mexico were Arabs from the Ottoman Empire who arrived during the late 1800s. Early immigration records are incomplete, however, because the Ottoman government prohibited Muslim emigration, forcing many to leave in secret. Once they arrived

* **Moorish** refers to the Moors, Spanish Muslims descended from the Arab conquerors

* **indentured servant** one who agrees to work for another for a certain number of years, usually in return for travel expenses, room, and board

in Mexico, many feared that admitting their religion was risking deportation. Preliminary research shows that the majority of Muslim immigrants settled in northern Mexico, primarily in the states of Coahuila and Durango, because the region had a reputation for religious tolerance and Muslims had established social networks in the area. Records also indicate that Shi'i families tended to migrate from Syria and Lebanon to Torreón, Coahuila.

Today, members of the first generation of Muslims in Torreón continue to observe many aspects of the Islamic faith. They know Arabic and can read the Qur'an*, and they have generally maintained the custom of marrying first cousins. The children of the immigrants, by contrast, are familiar with the translated version of the Qur'an, and they are less likely to marry within the family. Many of those who marry outside the faith, however, have a Muslim wedding.

* **Qur'an** book of the holy scriptures of Islam

The Muslims of Torreón do not strictly adhere to the principles of Islam nor do they actively spread the faith in their community. Prior to the building of a mosque in the late 1980s, they gathered at a private home to pray and celebrate holidays. The Suraya mosque, completed in 1989 and granted official status as a religious association in 1993, is not fully used.

The Muslim Center de México (MCM), located in Mexico City, functions as an umbrella organization for Sunni Muslims throughout the country. Its members have developed a comprehensive program to teach the public about Islam. With support from the Embassy of Saudi Arabia, the MCM rents a large home in Mexico City that serves as a prayer hall. Between 80 and 100 men of all nationalities attend the prayer service. Employees of the embassies of various Islamic countries, including Algeria, Egypt, and Indonesia, occasionally participate in MCM activities. The Shi'i community of Mexico City receives support from the Embassy of Iran. The embassy sponsors an annual book exhibition and holds conferences on Islam.

In 2002 the *Houston Chronicle* reported that between 200 and 500 Tzotzil Indians had converted to Islam in the southernmost state of Chiapas. The Sheik Hamden Bin Rashid Al Makoum mosque near San Cristóbal de las Casas hosts approximately 40 Tzotzil families who converted to Islam from evangelical* Protestantism. Esteban López and Aurillano Pérez, immigrants from Spain and founders of the Muslim community, are members of the Murabitun, a largely European group of Muslims who adhere to Sufism*. Most Muslims dismiss them as a cult*, and the Muslim Center de México notes that approximately one-half of the recent converts have broken away from the Murabitun and are seeking support from legitimate Muslim groups in Mexico City.

* **evangelical** characterized by religious zeal and dedication to the spread of religion, usually Christianity

* **Sufism** Islamic mysticism, which seeks to develop spirituality through discipline of the mind and body

* **cult** religion generally considered to be unorthodox or fake

Slavery and Struggle. The history of Islam in Brazil dates to a period between the 1500s and 1700s, when a small group of Mandika slaves who had converted to Islam were brought from Africa. The first large influx of African Muslim slaves arrived in Brazil during the early to mid-1800s. Primarily Hausas and Yorubas, they were forced to work in mines, on cotton, coffee, and sugar plantations, and in cities. The slaves gained notoriety for their involvement in a series of more than 20 revolts in Bahia, a sugar-producing province in northeastern Brazil where the majority of Muslim slaves toiled.

João José Reis wrote about a Brazilian Muslim slave uprising in Salvador, the capital of Bahia. In 1835 hundreds of Muslim slaves poured into the streets of Salvador to confront soldiers and armed civilians in an attempt

Islam in the Inner City

On the streets of East Harlem in New York City, a group of Latino Muslims confronts gang activity, drug dealing, prostitution, and AIDS. They are members of the Alianza Islamica (Islamic Alliance), the first Latino Muslim Association founded in the United States. In addition to efforts to improve the community, the mosque sponsors religious and cultural affairs, many of which reveal the blend of Arab, Spanish, and American influences that comprise Latino Islam. Hispanic Muslims trace their cultural ancestry to North Africa, the land of the Moors, and celebrate the history of Islamic Spain.

to win their freedom and return to Africa. Muslim preachers, who had promised to protect their followers, led the movement. After almost four hours of fighting, the rebellion was crushed. Nearly 70 slaves died, and 500 received punishments that varied from the death penalty to whippings, imprisonment, and hard labor. According to Reis, the Muslim slaves were united by their shared faith. Nevertheless, the brutal repression disrupted and dispersed the Muslim community. Islam did not gain a following among African Brazilians, who developed a religion that mixed Catholicism with African tribal traditions.

Today the majority of Muslims in Brazil are the descendants of Lebanese immigrants who arrived in the country after World War II (1939–1945). According to an article in *The Economist* (November 3, 2001), approximately one million Muslims live in Brazil. The country has about 30 mosques. The International Institute for the Study of Islam in the Modern World newsletter reports that there are eight mosques in the city of São Paulo, seven of which are Sunni. Despite the large population of Muslims in Brazil, the Islamic community lacks books about Islam in the Portuguese language.

According to Brazilian historian Andre Gattaz, Muslims in this predominantly Catholic country are hesitant to admit their faith. Only 22,000 admitted to being Muslim in the 1991 census. Although 10,000 Muslims reportedly live in the Foz do Iguacu area, only about 200 attend Friday prayers at the mosque. Foz do Iguacu is located in the region where Brazil, Argentina, and Paraguay meet, an area that has been linked to Islamic terrorists.

Speculation and Suspicion. According to Mujamad Hayer, director of the Office of Culture and Islamic Diffusion, there are between 650,000 and 700,000 Muslims in Argentina. More than one-half of the Muslim population is of Syrian descent, and therefore, most follow the Sunni branch of Islam. Notably, former president Carlos Saúl Menem, whose family was from Yabrud, Syria, converted to Catholicism, but his son Carlos Jr. identified himself as an Argentine Muslim. Carlos Jr. died in 1995 and was buried in an Islamic cemetery, symbolizing the importance of religion among Muslim immigrant families in the country.

The Islamic Center of Buenos Aires has tried to promote a moderate version of Islam in this country of almost 38 million people, most of whom are Roman Catholic. Nevertheless, Argentines and others regard the Islamic community with some suspicion. In 1982 members of the Shi'i minority established their headquarters at the A'Tauhid Mosque with funds from the Embassy of Iran. After July 18, 1994, this group came under scrutiny for the bombing of the community center of the Argentine-Israeli Mutual Association (known by its Spanish initials, AMIA), which resulted in the death of almost 100 people. Although many speculated about local connections that would implicate members of the Islamic community in Argentina, no one was ever charged with the attack.

According to the Latin American Muslim Unity website, King Fahd of Saudi Arabia reportedly donated between $10 and $15 million to build an Islamic Center in Argentina. Some view this move as questionable after the 1994 AMIA bombing and the bombing of the Israeli Embassy in 1992, which killed 29 people. (*See also* **Ahmadi; Baha'i; Shi'i Islam; Sunni Islam.**)

Law

Law is central to the practice of Islam, and following the law is the ultimate expression of faith and submission to God. Islamic law is comprehensive, instructing Muslims in the performance of their religious obligations and providing guidelines for daily living. Legal manuals typically devote their first chapters to Islamic rituals, such as prayers and fasting, then address such topics as marriage, divorce, and financial transactions. Aside from establishing laws, Islamic tradition also classifies certain acts as praiseworthy or blameworthy, establishing a code of ethics not enforceable by law, but encouraged among believers.

All Muslim regulations are based on *shari'ah*, Islamic law as established in the Qur'an* and the sunnah*. *Shari'ah*, which means "the path leading to the watering place," determines how Muslims should behave, both publicly and privately. Muslims view shari'ah as unchanging, revealed to Muhammad by God, and not subject to alteration. Interpreting or understanding the divine will and expressing it in legal codes is referred to as *fiqh*, a term that includes all attempts to form concrete rules and to make correct legal decisions. Scholars practice *fiqh* in their attempts to adapt divine law to contemporary situations.

In cases where the Qur'an and sunnah, which is based on the hadith*, do not provide specific answers to a legal question, scholars rely on other methods. Sunni* Muslims sometimes use *qiyas* (reasoning through analogy*) and *ijma* (consensus among scholars) to form laws. To decide whether Muslims may consume alcoholic beverages, for example, scholars looked to the Qur'an. The text prohibits wine on the grounds that it alters an individual's mental state. Because other alcoholic drinks have the same effect, scholars extended this ban to them, as well. Scholars practicing *ijma* gather to discuss a certain issue and take a formal position on it. This tradition derives from Muhammad's remark that his community would never agree on an error. Like Sunni Muslims, members of the Shi'i* branch use the Qur'an and hadith as the basis of law. They also rely on the traditions of imams*, passed down in hadith collections. Shi'is place less emphasis on *qiyas* and *ijma*, sometimes rejecting them entirely.

Development of Legal Theories

Muhammad served as the first judge, using the Qur'an to resolve legal problems. After his death, the caliphs* of Medina continued the tradition. The expansion of the Muslim community led to the creation of various legal systems by the early 700s. In all parts of the Muslim world, local traditions influenced the ways in which scholars interpreted the Qur'an and hadith. Jurists differed primarily on how much emphasis they gave to reason over traditional sources. Some jurists viewed independent thought as an impure substitute for the guidance of Muhammad. Others believed that many of the hadith had come from figures other than Muhammad and that reason could serve as a valuable tool for applying *shari'ah* to a variety of circumstances.

Sunni Schools of Law. Sunni Muslims have four major schools of law: Hanafi, Maliki, Shafi'i, and Hanbali. These emerged in the 700s and 800s.

* **Qur'an** book of the holy scriptures of Islam
* **sunnah** literally "the trodden path;" Islamic customs based on the exemplary behavior of Muhammad
* **hadith** reports of the words and deeds of Muhammad (not in the Qur'an, but accepted as guides for Muslim behavior)
* **Sunni** refers to the largest branch of the Muslim community; the name derives from sunnah, the exemplary behavior of the Prophet Muhammad
* **analogy** comparison based on resemblance
* **Shi'i** Muslims those who believe that Muhammad chose Ali ibn Abi Talib and his descendants as the spiritual-political leaders of the Muslim community
* **imam** spiritual-political leader in Shi'i Islam, one who is regarded as directly descended from Muhammad; also, one who leads prayers
* **caliph** religious and political leader of an Islamic state

The Hanafi school originated in the city of Kufa in Iraq, where Muhammad's companion Abd Allah ibn Masud served as a jurist and teacher of Abu Hanifah (699–767), who established the basis for the Hanafi School. Abu Hanifah encouraged the use of reason as well as tradition in making legal decisions. His reliance on the judgment of scholars resulted in the labeling of his followers as the People of Opinion. Abu Hanifah became the first jurist to formulate rules concerning contracts, and allowed both parties significant leeway. He also ruled that a woman past the age of puberty could marry without the approval of her guardian. He advised against punishing spendthrifts, concluding that adults should be able to do as they pleased.

Abu Hanifah attracted many students, several of whom became prominent jurists. By the 900s, scholars had compiled an impressive body of literature on Hanafi traditions. The Hanafi was the dominant school of law during the Abbasid caliphate* (750–1258) and the Ottoman Empire (1300–1922). Modern jurists consult Hanafi law when ruling on personal status matters and when issuing fatwas*. Hanafi is the most widespread school of law in Islamic countries, practiced by Muslims in Jordan, Iraq, Lebanon, Egypt, India, and several other nations.

The Maliki school originated in Medina. Malik ibn Anas (713–795) is viewed as the founder of the school, based on the traditions transmitted in the community in Medina. He placed more emphasis on tradition than reason, often concluding a legal point with the words, "And this is the rule with us." He stated firmly that he would not deviate from the teachings of his masters or from the *ijma* of the scholars of Medina. Malik did, however, use reason to form opinions in cases that had no precedent*.

The Maliki school is more conservative than the Hanafi school, especially regarding women. Maliki law prohibits a woman of any age from marrying without the consent of her marriage guardian. A young girl's father or paternal grandfather has the right to give her away in marriage without her consent, and, in some cases, even against her wishes. Muslims from North Africa studied Malik's teachings in Mecca and spread them throughout their own regions. Maliki serves as the predominant school of law in Morocco, Algeria, Tunisia, and Libya. It also has followers in Egypt, Sudan, Kuwait, and West Africa.

Muhammad ibn Idris al-Shafi'i (767–820) founded the third Sunni school. After he had memorized the Qur'an and traveled with a desert tribe famed for its poetic traditions, al-Shafi'i studied under Malik and became an expert on the first two Sunni schools of law. He believed that Maliki and Hanafi jurists placed too little emphasis on traditional sources in their rulings. He stated that custom had obscured the original intent of Islamic law. Al-Shafi'i wrote a seven-volume work describing his doctrines, discussing such topics as personal status, financial transactions, religious observations, and punishment. He attacked those who failed to accept the authority of the Qur'an and hadith and denounced the use of personal preference as a tool of law. The Shafi'i school gained prominence in Egypt and became the official school of the Ayyubid dynasty (1169–1252). Its influence remains strong in Palestine and Jordan, and it continues to have followers in Egypt, Pakistan, Indonesia, and other Muslim countries.

Founder of the Hanbali school, Ahmad ibn Hanbal (780–855), also emphasized tradition, valuing the Qur'an and the sunnah over the work of later

* **caliphate** office and government of the caliph, the religious and spiritual leader of an Islamic state

* **fatwa** opinion issued by Islamic legal scholar in response to a question posed by an individual or a court of law

* **precedent** prior example that serves as a model

See map in Sunni Islam (vol. 3).

Muslim scholars. Ibn Hanbal acknowledged five sources of law, each to be used only in the absence of advice from the preceding one: the Qur'an and sunnah; fatwas issued by Muhammad's companions that agree with the Qur'an and sunnah; the sayings of companions that correspond with the Qur'an and sunnah; traditions with a weak chain of transmission or no name attached to them; and reasoning by analogy. The Hanbali tradition is the official school of law in Saudi Arabia and Qatar. It also has followers in Iraq, Syria, and Palestine.

Other legal schools also emerged among Sunni Muslims, but attracted smaller followings and have disappeared. Sunni Muslims believe in the authenticity of all four of their schools of law. A Sunni may follow any one of them or use different traditions for different cases. Some scholars combine principles from various schools to form new legal doctrines.

Shi'i Legal Schools. Shi'i scholars differ from Sunnis in their faith in the imams and their rejection of non-Shi'i rulings. They use the same sources as Sunni Muslims but also rely on traditions passed down from the imams. The dominant Twelver branch places special emphasis on the authority of the twelfth and Hidden Imam, Muhammad al-Mahdi. According to legend, the Mahdi went into hiding when he was seven years old and lost contact with his followers at the age of 75. Protected by God, he continues to live in seclusion, waiting to return to the world and bring order to Muslim society. Twelver Shi'is view the Mahdi as infallible and place as much value on his teachings as on the Qur'an and the sunnah.

The Twelvers and other Shi'i groups advocate the use of reason only when it is needed to interpret traditional sources. Jurists practicing *qiyas* must try to reach conclusions that best correspond with *shari'ah* until the Mahdi returns to provide divine guidance on the issue. Many Shi'i sects believe that a fully qualified *mujtahid* (legal scholar) can serve as a representative of the imam and has the right to exercise judgment on cases not covered in traditional sources. *Mujtahids* may not decide a case by consensus, however, unless they include opinions issued by the twelfth imam or his associates.

Named after the sixth imam, Jafar al-Sadiq, the Jafari *madhhab** is the major Shi'i school of law. It originated from hadith-like reports on the imams and emphasizes their teachings. Minor schools of law have also developed among Shi'is. The Akhbari school places a heavy emphasis on the hadith and allows jurists to enforce their own judgments only when they correspond with precedents set by the imams. The Usuli school, on the other hand, allows jurists to deliver reasoned rulings on most cases. The Shaykhi school also grants *mujtahids* a great deal of freedom, promoting a nonliteral interpretation of traditional sources.

The Islamic Revolution in Iran in 1979 had a strong influence on Shi'i legal thought. Revolutionary leader Ayatollah* Ruhollah al-Musavi Khomeini established a government in which a Shi'i jurist serves as the spiritual leader of the country *(faqih)*. This person represents the Mahdi and has the final say in all legislative, executive, and judicial decisions. Khomeini served in this position for 10 years until his death in 1989. He earned the support of many Iranians and inspired Shi'i Muslims in other countries. However, some Shi'i jurists rejected his ideas and relied on earlier sources in their legal decisions.

* *madhhab* school of thought developed by a particular imam

* ayatollah highest-ranking legal scholar among some Shi'i Muslims

Islamic Legal System

Muslims have developed a complex legal system, and their approach to law varies widely from region to region. Scholars in some states advocate harsh, traditional punishments, while others adopt a more moderate approach. Jurists in some countries rely heavily on the Qur'an and other traditional texts. Many, however, were influenced by Europeans in the 1800s and made alterations based on Western secular* legal systems.

Study of Law. Islamic jurists and scholars practice *fiqh*. *Fiqh* includes all attempts to understand *shari'ah* and to translate it into specific rules. *Fiqh* involves elaborating on details of the law, delineating specific standards, justifying them by reference to divine authority, debating them, and writing books and treatises on them. In contrast to *shari'ah*, which never changes, *fiqh* is imperfect and subject to revision.

Muslim scholars have developed two types of *fiqh* literature: *furu al-fiqh* and *usul al-fiqh*. *Usul* authors discuss the origins of law and assess the effectiveness of various reasoning techniques. They concern themselves with the roots of Islamic law. *Furu* literature covers the rules themselves, as well as various legal cases. *Furu* authors discuss regulations pertaining to religious matters such as prayer, charity, fasting, pilgrimage, and jihad*, as well as social and economic matters such as inheritance, marriage, divorce, land ownership, and injury compensation. Works of *furu* typically classify actions as mandatory, recommended, permitted, abhorred (detested), or prohibited, although many other categories exist. Certain *furu* authors are noted for their clarity and skill. One scholar possessed a style so dazzling that an admirer described his treatise as "woven on a magician's loom."

Fiqh literature emphasizes the importance of *ijtihad*, which refers to the struggle that a jurist undergoes to determine the correct ruling on a case. To perform *ijtihad*, a scholar must work to the best of his or her ability to interpret traditional texts. The scholar must consult the Qur'an and the sunnah, and, if no answer presents itself, must use analogy or another reasoning technique to find a solution. If leading scholars agree on the resulting decision, it becomes an accepted rule. *Ijtihad* allows for the possibility of disagreement among scholars. It grants jurists flexibility in reaching a decision and gains legitimacy from Muhammad's alleged statement that "difference of opinion among my community is a sign of the bounty of Allah." Modern reformers often use *ijtihad* to rid the legal code of outdated laws and practices.

Court Systems. The Qur'an uses the term *hukm* to describe the act of judgment. *Hukm* refers to both the power to pass laws and to render a legal decision. In early Islamic societies, a *qadi* (judge) typically fulfilled these tasks. In most communities, the governor appointed *qadis* and determined their realm of influence. The governor had the final say in any disputes arising in court. Judges appointed numerous deputy judges and subordinate officials to help them with their caseloads.

In *qadi* courts, most cases followed the same procedure. Muslims typically appeared before judges without lawyers or other representatives. The defendant and prosecutor both stated their case. If the defendant admitted no guilt, the judge assumed his or her innocence. The prosecutor would have to produce two witnesses to testify to the defendant's guilt. Adult males with good reputations typically filled these roles, but women could testify in certain cases, with two females serving in the place of one man. *Qadis* did not accept written or physical evidence, no matter how condemning. If the prosecutor failed to prove his case, the judge offered the defendant the oath of denial, which, if taken properly, resulted in a favorable verdict. If the defendant refused to take the oath, the prosecutor won the case.

Around the 800s, Islamic societies developed additional courts. Officials realized that one *qadi* could not hear the case of every Muslim who ignored, for example, the ban on wine. They set up *mazalim*, injustice courts that exercised more flexibility than the *qadis* in their application of the rules. Injustice courts handled complaints against government officials. They also dealt with issues of criminal law not directly related to *shari'ah*. Local police and market inspectors handled petty crimes, administering punishments according to local custom rather than the dictates of the Qur'an.

The justice system in the Islamic world relies on fatwas as well as courts of law. Issued by muftis (scholars), these written opinions can influence government and judicial policy. Abu Saud, the grand mufti of Istanbul, used fatwas to regularize tax-collecting activities and marriage practices and to limit the authority of the sultan. Other muftis have issued fatwas on such subjects as contracts and punishments. Jurists sometimes use fatwas to justify certain legal positions, and some *qadis* seek advice from muftis.

Issuing Punishment. Islamic law has three broad categories of punishment for those convicted of a crime: *tazir*, *qisas*, and *hudud*. *Tazir* punishments include a wide range of offenses not covered in the Qur'an. Because *qadis* decide on *tazir* punishments, they vary widely. They can range from small fines to long prison sentences. Those who assault others, either in an act of homicide or another physical violation, receive *qisas* (retaliation). The laws of *qisas* dictate that the criminal suffers the same treatment as the victim. The victim or his or her family decides how to carry out the *qisas*, and whether to demand *diyah* (compensation) in the place of physical punishment.

The Qur'an specifically prescribes punishments for six types of crimes. *Hudud* (fixed) punishments are harsh. Desertion of Islam and highway robbery warrant death; married adulterers receive death by stoning and unmarried adulterers receive 100 lashes; thieves suffer the amputation of a hand; and those who accuse others of adultery without proof or consume alcohol receive 80 lashes. Many Muslim nations, such as Jordan, Egypt, Syria, and Lebanon, refuse to implement *hudud*. Others, such as Pakistan, Sudan, and parts of Nigeria, continue to impose *hudud* punishments for certain offenses. Many human rights activists oppose these practices. Those who support the use of *hudud*, however, argue that their societies need strict punishments to maintain social order. Some maintain that the punishments are mostly symbolic; they are rarely carried out, and they serve more to promote respect for the law than to actually harm offenders.

Modern Reforms

The invasion of European forces into Muslim countries in the late 1700s caused Muslim jurists to alter their legal systems. Muslims sensed that their society was in a state of decline and felt the need for reform. Some sought to update

Women's Rights in Malaysia

Muslim feminists protest what they consider the unequal application of the law in many parts of the Islamic world. In countries that enforce *hudud* punishments, for example, women are much more frequently stoned for adultery than men, despite the Qur'anic requirement that both parties receive punishment. In 2002 the government of the Malaysian state of Terengganu proposed a bill that would require rape victims to produce four male witnesses to the crime or receive 80 lashes for making a false accusation. If an unmarried woman became pregnant, even by rape, she could face 100 lashes or death by stoning. The federal government condemned the bill, as did Malaysian women, who typically enjoy the same opportunities as men. The Terengganu chief of police refused to enforce the *hudud* punishments on the grounds that they violate the federal constitution.

legal codes in accordance with Western models. Other Muslims resisted change, viewing reform as a compromise of God's will. These scholars worked to reinstate legal systems based on a strict interpretation of the Qur'an.

Western Influence. The Ottoman Empire introduced European procedures into its court system in the 1830s and 1840s. Ottoman leaders later added European laws to the empire's commercial, penal*, and maritime* codes. In the 1860s, the Ottomans implemented the Ottoman Code of Obligations (also referred to as the *Mecelle*) This document covered rules covering property, contracts, and legal procedure. The *Mecelle* also contained nearly 100 principles derived from *shari'ah.* Other Muslim countries followed the Ottoman example, establishing Western-style codes and limiting the power of religious courts.

* **penal** refers to punishment
* **maritime** refers to sea trade

When the Ottoman Empire fell after World War I (1914–1918), the new Turkish government encouraged secular reform. President Mustafa Kemal Atatürk adopted a European legal system in 1926, believing that the nation needed to embrace Western ideas in order to survive. Turkey established the most secular legal code in the Islamic world.

Egypt was also at the forefront of Islamic legal reform. The French introduced their legal tradition to the country in the early 1800s, and Muhammad Abduh (1849–1905) emerged as Egypt's most important legal reformer in the late 1800s. He believed that the legal system should combine Islamic traditions and modern ideas. He stated that rules governing worship should remain unchanged, but that regulations for everyday life should be adjusted to reflect modern realities. Abduh opposed polygyny*, for example, on the grounds that it lead to unjust treatment of women.

* **polygyny** practice of having more than one wife at the same time

Egypt's Abd al-Razzaq al-Sanhuri (1895–1971) served as one of the most influential Muslim legal reformers of the 1900s. An expert in Islamic and Western law, al-Sanhuri wrote civil codes that combined Islamic, Arab, Turkish, and European law. Egypt, Iraq, and several other Arab nations adopted these codes.

Other Muslim countries adapted their legal practices to those imposed on them by colonial powers. The reforms adopted in India, for example, reflect both Islamic and British traditions. The law that applied to Muslims, Anglo-Muhamaddan law, had its roots in Islamic doctrine but relied on the English language and British judicial methods. British and British-trained judges determined the scope and application of Islamic law. They typically respected Islamic civil codes but enforced their own criminal code. British judges rarely overturned the decisions of the great Islamic jurists. After the British left the region in 1947, the Muslims maintained a separate civil code.

India produced many legal reformers. Indian writer and activist Sayyid Ahmad Khan (1817–1898) was influential in the Indian Islamic world. He questioned the reliability of hadith as a source of law and sought to update Islamic rules to conform to modern social norms. For example, he believed that Islamic banks should charge moderate interest, claiming that the Qur'an prohibited exorbitant interest rates. Poet and philosopher Muhammad Iqbal (1877–1938) also took up the call for legal reform in India. He believed that the legal system was bogged down with the outdated writings of medieval jurists. He called for *ijtihad*, urging Muslim jurists to use their own reasoning to interpret early authoritative sources. Iqbal encouraged scholars to exercise caution when applying the hadith and stated that Islamic law should meet the needs of modern society.

Recent Developments. In the 1900s, legal reform in the Islamic world mainly centered around family codes. To minimize objections from conservatives*, legislators often implemented reforms indirectly. To prevent child and forced marriages, for example, new laws required spouses to register their marriages and to be certain minimum ages. Tunisia adopted the most radical* family law reforms. In 1956 its government abolished polygyny and gave women and men equal rights in divorce. Both India and Pakistan passed similar legislation, although Pakistan's reforms were later reversed. The 1926 Turkish Civil Code gave marriage partners equal rights in divorce and child custody. Egypt and Syria also reformed their divorce laws and expanded women's rights in family matters.

Reforms provoked strong opposition in the Islamic world. Muslim legal experts had a lower status than Western-trained professionals. Conservative Muslims protested the replacement of Islamic doctrines with European-based codes. In the 1970s and 1980s, a religious revival movement spread through much of the Islamic world. Revivalist groups demanded the repeal of Western laws, stating that *shari'ah* as traditionally codified should serve as the foundation of the state's legal system. Pakistan, Iran, the Sudan, Afghanistan, and Saudi Arabia restored *hudud* punishments to their legal codes. Other countries resisted the influence of revivalists. Egypt, for example, passed a law in 1976 prohibiting alcohol, but provided exceptions that limited its impact. As a concession to conservatives, the government amended the second article in the constitution to describe *shari'ah* as "the principal source," rather than "a principal source," of legislation.

The law still inspires debate across the Islamic world. Moderates and conservatives continue to oppose one another on reform measures. Followers of Sunni and Shi'i schools of law, however, have shown an interest in overlooking their differences. Internationally, diplomatic leaders and legal scholars have opened discussions to bring more uniformity to the legal codes of modern Muslim nations. (*See also* **Abduh, Muhammad; Ahmad Khan, Sayyid; Capital Punishment; Fatwa; Ijtihad; Iqbal, Muhammad; Islamic State; Jafar al-Sadiq; Justice; Women and Reform.**)

* **conservative** person generally opposed to change, especially in existing political and social institutions

* **radical** favoring extreme change or reform, especially in existing political and social institutions

Lebanon

A small country on the Mediterranean Sea, Lebanon shares borders with Syria and Israel. Lebanon has a population of 3.5 million, of which 70 percent is Muslim, and 30 percent constitutes a powerful Christian minority. Before the 1970s, Lebanon was a prosperous nation in which Muslims and Christians lived in relative harmony. A 16-year civil war, however, devastated the nation and left the Lebanese struggling to recover.

History and Government

Phoenicians settled in Lebanon around 3000 B.C.E.*, where they became great explorers and traders. Throughout most of their history, Phoenician kings paid tribute* to more powerful foreign rulers. Many empires laid claim to

* **B.C.E.** before the Common Era, which refers to the same time period as B.C.

* **tribute** money or other goods paid to a dominant power or local government

Lebanon

Shoppers look over merchandise at a street market in Beirut, the capital of Lebanon.

 See map in Gulf States (vol. 1).

See map in Gulf States (vol. 1).

* **c.e.** Common Era, which refers to the same time period as A.D.

* **Sunni** refers to the largest branch of the Muslim community; the name derives from sunnah, the exemplary behavior of the prophet Muhammad

* **Shi'i** refers to Muslims who believe that Muhammad chose Ali ibn Abi Talib and his descendants as the spiritual-political leaders of the Muslim community

* **Crusades** during the Middle Ages, the holy wars declared by the pope against non-Christians, mostly Muslims

* **Ottoman Empire** large Turkish state existing from the early 1300s to the early 1900s

the region, including the Egyptian, Assyrian, Babylonian, Persian, Greek, Roman, Umayyad, Mamluk, Ottoman, and French.

Arab and Christian Influence. In the 600s C.E.*, a Christian community identified with Saint Maron developed in northern Lebanon. Around the same time, both Sunni* and Shi'i* communities took shape in the area. Later a Shi'i offshoot group called the Druze attracted followers. Sunnis tended to settle in the towns and cities along the coast, while the Druze and various Shi'i groups occupied the mountains and rural areas in the south and northeast. Maronite Christians lived in both the towns and countryside.

Although Lebanon underwent a brief period of Christian rule after the First Crusade*, it was mainly a province of the Muslim empires and was generally considered a part of its neighbor Syria. The Ottoman Turks conquered the region in the early 1500s. Under the rule of the Ottoman Empire*, Beirut became a thriving international port, with silk as the main export. The French and other Europeans established trading posts throughout Syria, concentrating in Beirut. They sent missionaries who built schools for Christians, training them for top positions in the government and in society. The French influence grew in Lebanon, and Christian communities flourished. By the 1800s, some Sunni princes had even converted to the Maronite faith.

After World War I (1914–1918), the Christian presence in Lebanon became even stronger. During the war, the Ottomans had fought with the Germans and lost to the Allied forces led by Britain and France. French forces occupied Lebanon, and in 1923, the League of Nations granted France a mandate* to rule Syria and Lebanon. The Maronites welcomed the French, and the French rewarded them with high government positions. Many Muslims, however, resented French authority and wanted to unite Lebanon with the rest of the Arab world. They also struggled to create a balance of power within Lebanon that would accurately reflect the diversity of the region. In 1926 the Lebanese legislators created a constitution that began the division of power between the three largest religious groups. The president was to be a Maronite Christian; the prime minister, a Sunni Muslim; and the speaker of the assembly, a Shi'i Muslim.

Lebanon gained independence from France in 1946. The country enjoyed a period of peace, although some Muslims resented the Christian leanings of the National Assembly. Civil war almost erupted in 1958, when Muslims rioted for the inclusion of Lebanon in the United Arab Republic. President Camille Chamoun ordered the army to attack the rioters, but the commander refused, fearing that the army—composed of Christians and Muslims—would fall apart. The United Nations helped to resolve the conflict with the use of U.S. forces, and General Fouad Chehab became president in the next election. A relatively tranquil period followed, in which Chehab gave Muslims more seats in the government and helped to modernize the Muslim areas of Lebanon.

Civil War and International Conflict. Despite President Chehab's efforts, tensions between religious groups continued. As increasing numbers of Lebanese moved from rural to urban areas, cities became filled with people of different sects who established their own communities. The gulf between rich and poor widened, and many Muslims resented the wealth and stature of their Christian neighbors. Muslims also fiercely opposed the government's decision not to take part in the Arab-Israeli wars of 1967 and 1973. These wars sent Palestinian refugees flooding into Lebanon, resulting in greater resistance of the Lebanese population against Israel and against their own government. By the early 1970s, Palestinian refugee camps crowded the Lebanese border. Impoverished and exploited for cheap labor, the Palestinians bonded with poor Lebanese Muslims and began to form militia* groups.

Members of the Palestinian Liberation Organization (PLO) staged raids into Israel, bringing Israeli reprisals. Frustrated with the inaction of the Lebanese government, Israel attacked PLO camps in Lebanon. Christian militias joined in the attacks. These compounded existing tensions with the Druze, who sought a greater share of power, and the Syrian government, which did not accept the separation of Lebanon from Syria. By 1975 Lebanon was engaged in a full-scale civil war with multiple factions and shifting alliances. Battles raged daily, and the central government, which had never had a strong grip on the region, all but dissolved.

Arab nations held a summit meeting in October 1976 to resolve the crisis. They established an Arab League peacekeeping force composed mainly of Syrians to try to halt the fighting. The peacekeepers failed to end the war, however, and PLO raids into Israel continued, causing the Israelis to invade Lebanon in 1978 and to occupy southern Lebanon in 1982. In 1989 the Lebanese government met in Saudi Arabia and formed the Ta'if Accord, which guaranteed equal power for Christians and Muslims in government.

* **mandate** order issued by the League of Nations authorizing a member nation to establish a responsible government in a conquered territory

* **militia** group of citizens organized for military service

* **infrastructure** basic facilities and institutions that a country needs in order to function

* **militant** aggressively active in a cause

* **cabinet** individuals appointed by a head of state to supervise departments of government and to act as official advisers

Druze Struggle for Power

Druze political power in Lebanon peaked in the 1600s under Fakhr ad-Din II (1572–1635), a ruler widely considered to be the father of modern Lebanon. Fakhr ad-Din united feuding religious groups and gained control over northern Lebanon. Unsure of Ottoman support, he signed a treaty with Ferdinand I, the Duke of Tuscany, in which the leaders agreed to protect each other in case of Ottoman attack. When the Ottoman sultan learned of the arrangement, he ordered the governor of Damascus to attack Fakhr ad-Din. Fakhr ad-Din fled to Tuscany and returned five years later to defeat the governor. He then hired Italian architects, engineers, and scientists to design and build Lebanon's defenses. By 1631 Fakhr ad-Din had taken over most of Syria, Lebanon, and Palestine. Alarmed by his growing power, Sultan Murad IV attacked and finally defeated Fakhr ad-Din in 1635.

The agreement ended the civil war, but much of Lebanon lay in ruins. Israeli troops remained in occupation in the southern part of the country. The war had crippled the economy, damaged the infrastructure*, and led to the deaths of around 150,000 Lebanese and 20,000 Palestinians. Anti-Israeli forces continue to thrive in Lebanon, including the militant* Hizbullah party, which led the resistance against Israeli occupation. Israel withdrew from southern Lebanon in the summer of 2000, although conflict continues between the two nations over the disputed territory of Shebaa Farms.

Lebanon's New Government. The 1926 constitution that reserves political positions for each major religious group remains in effect. The Ta'if Accord, however, reduced the power of the president, giving more control to the cabinet*. The prime minister serves as head of government, assisted by the cabinet, which he chooses after consulting with the president and members of the assembly. The National Assembly consists of one house with 128 members elected by popular vote. Voters choose parties rather than individual candidates, and each party wins a number of seats based on the percentage of votes it receives. Party leaders then choose members to represent the party in the assembly. The National Assembly elects the president for a six-year term.

Like many other countries in the Islamic world, Lebanon has separate courts for civil and criminal matters. Three national courts deal with civil affairs, and one handles criminal cases. Among the Muslim population, each sect has its own religious courts that deal with personal status issues such as marriage, divorce, and inheritance.

Islam in Lebanon

Lebanese society has a high level of religious diversity, and the Lebanese government officially recognizes 18 religious groups. Lebanon has five main Muslim sects: Sunni, Shi'i, Druze, Alawi, and Ismaili. Among those groups, only the Ismailis lack representation in the National Assembly. The others enjoy varying amounts of political and social influence.

Sunni Muslims. Sunni Muslims constitute only about 20 percent of the Lebanese population, but they served as the country's dominant Muslim group until the 1980s. Sunnis live mainly in coastal cities, such as Beirut and Tripoli. The Ottomans favored the Sunnis in their administration, and the Sunnis led the drive for independence from France in the 1940s. Their historical dominance is reflected in the constitution, which calls for a Sunni to hold the powerful position of prime minister. A Sunni cleric also serves as the official leading jurist (mufti) of Lebanon, issuing formal opinions on legal and religious matters. Sunnis enjoy a high social and economic status in the country and have greater access to educational opportunities, health care, and sanitation services than do the other Muslim groups. Few Sunni leaders organized militia groups during the civil war.

Shi'i Muslims. Until the 1900s, most Shi'i Muslims lived in rural areas of Lebanon. They mainly inhabited the mountains of southern Lebanon and the Bekáa Valley in the north. Those in the north lived as tribal nomads, while the southern Shi'i were farmers. During the 1900s, Shi'i numbers grew significantly, and large groups moved to the cities. By the 1980s, the Shi'is had become the largest religious group in Lebanon, calling into question the constitutional arrangement that gives more political power to Sunnis and Maronite Christians. Many Shi'is became part of the middle class and worked to create better schools for Shi'is in both rural and urban areas. In 1967 the Lebanese government voted to create a Supreme Shi'i Council, granting it authority independent of the Sunni mufti. Shi'i leaders also established the Movement of the Deprived, which serves as a dynamic force in Lebanese politics.

Druze. The Druze, an offshoot of the Ismaili sect of Shi'ism, make up about seven percent of Lebanon's population. Originally from Egypt, the Druze remained united during the Lebanese civil war, unlike other religious groups in Lebanon. In the Druze community, *ajawids* (religious leaders) handle moral and civic issues. Each Druze village meets weekly to pray and discuss local problems. *Ajawids* confer with one another to resolve major issues affecting the community. Although important in the local community, *ajawids* have not played a major role in national politics.

Alawi. The Alawi are small in number but exercise some influence in Lebanon because they serve as the ruling group in neighboring Syria. In 1992 they won their first seats in the National Assembly. The Alawi venerate the fourth caliph* Ali, observe Christian and Persian holidays, and use sacramental wine in their religious ceremonies. Because of these practices, some Muslims consider the Alawi apostates*. Within Alawi society, amirs serve as political leaders, and imams* guide religious services. (*See also* **Alawi; Arab-Israeli Conflict; Druze; Hizbullah; Palestine Liberation Organization; Refugees; Syria.**)

* **caliph** religious and political leader of an Islamic state

* **apostate** person who abandons his or her religious faith

* **imam** spiritual-political leader in Shi'i Islam, one who is regarded as directly descended from Muhammad; also, one who leads prayers

Libraries

Islam has a rich literary tradition. Beginning with the command to "Read!" in the Qur'an*, Muslims are encouraged to always strive for improvement, and Allah tells them that the best way to improve is through the acquisition of knowledge. During the Middle Ages, the Muslim world housed many of the world's largest collections and served as a storehouse of knowledge from ancient Greece and Rome. In modern times, however, Islamic libraries and library practices have fallen far behind those of the West.

Early Muslim Libraries. The practice of storing written materials in the Islamic world began with donations by individuals of Qur'anic manuscripts to mosques. The first mosque collections appeared during the Umayyad dynasty* (661–750).

The second Abbasid caliph*, Abu Jafar al-Mansur, established a translation bureau in Baghdad (in the late 700s) that became the leading library of the day. In addition to translating texts from other cultures, it became a clearinghouse for the learning of the Islamic world. Other rulers of the period established similar centers. It is estimated that the caliph's library

* **Qur'an** book of the holy scriptures of Islam

* **dynasty** succession of rulers from the same family or group

* **caliph** religious and political leader of an Islamic state

Libraries

* c.e. Common Era, which refers to the same time period as A.D.

* parchment writing material made from the skin of sheep or goats

in Córdoba, Spain, held some 400,000 books. The rise of the *madrasah* (institute of higher learning) brought with it the development of academic libraries.

The large-scale production and acquisition of books by libraries became possible when paper became more widely available. Invented in China around 105 C.E.*, paper eventually replaced parchment* and reached the Muslim world in the mid-700s. The production and distribution of books led to the increased importance of the professional *warraq*—a paper dealer, copyist, and bookseller—who was sometimes a scholar and author in his own right.

Ibn al-Nadim, a famous *warraq*, produced a landmark work in 987. Titled *al-Fihrist*, this monumental work contained a description of every book al-Nadim had ever handled, seen, or otherwise knew of. It remains a significant source for the history of the literary culture of that era.

Muslim Libraries Decline. Over time, the great library collections of the Islamic world were dispersed through lack of care or by becoming part of another collection. Books were lost in fires and floods and by natural decay. There was also the deliberate destruction of volumes by the Mongol invaders (in the 1200s) and the Spanish Inquisitors (after the Reconquest of Spain, completed in 1492). Furthermore, during the period of European colonialism, thousands of Islamic manuscripts were removed to libraries and private collections in the West.

The books and manuscripts that remained in the Islamic world were generally poorly organized, making it difficult to find information. Traditional methods for the care and cataloging of books had become outdated. Colonial powers had set up and maintained modern libraries in Muslim countries. Even after independence, European professionals continued to dominate librarianship in the former colonies.

Modern Library Issues. In recent years, library education has progressed in Islamic countries, enabling Muslim librarians to assume leadership. Pakistan and Egypt are notable for their library studies programs and for sending trained Muslim librarians to teach others in the Gulf region. There is, however, no single accepted classification or cataloging system to bring standardization to Muslim libraries. Some Muslim countries use a modified version of the Dewey Decimal Classification, while others use the Library of Congress Classification. Many Muslim librarians have proposed various Islamic classification schemes, but none has proved suitable for general use.

Despite the importance of literacy in the Islamic world, public libraries are not a high priority for many Muslim countries. While some countries have a national library in their capital, it often serves as the main public library, as well. Turkey, Jordan, Pakistan, and Malaysia have founded public libraries, and Lahore and Kuala Lumpur opened public libraries especially for children.

Automation, networking, and freedom of access to information are some of the most significant issues currently facing public libraries in the Islamic world. Several groups have formed to address these issues, but progress has been slow. Saudi Arabia and other Persian Gulf states have created an on-line database, called GULFNET, to make information more widely available to Muslim libraries. (*See also* **Arabic Language and Literature.**)

Libya

Libya is an oil-rich country that shares borders with Egypt, Tunisia, Algeria, Sudan, Chad, and Niger. Its population of more than 5 million is of mixed Arab-Berber* ancestry, and an overwhelming majority of Libyans are Sunni* Muslims.

Historically, the part of North Africa now known as Libya consisted of three distinct regions separated from one another by harsh deserts: Tripolitania in the northwest, Cyrenaica to the northeast, and Fezzan in the southwest. Before Libya became an independent nation in 1951, its history revolved around these regions and their major cities, the tribes in the area, and a series of foreign invasions. Since 1969 Colonel Mu'ammar al-Qaddafi has attempted to create a distinct Libyan state and identity based on his unique concept of Islam.

Hard-Fought Freedom. During ancient times, various groups conquered and settled the region, including the Greeks, Phoenicians, Carthaginians, and Romans. The ancient Egyptians applied the term *Libya* to a single Berber tribe, and the Greeks used the word to refer to most of the land west of the Nile River. Nevertheless, the name did not refer to the territorial boundaries of modern Libya until the mid-1900s.

After Arab armies conquered Egypt in 642 C.E.*, they extended their raids to the west. Although the townspeople and farmers of the coastal areas readily accepted Arab rule, the nomadic Berber tribes of the interior resisted Arab political domination. By 705, however, the region that now includes Morocco, Algeria, Tunisia, and Libya was incorporated into the Muslim empire.

A succession of Arab and native dynasties* ruled the land for the next 800 years. The people who lived in North African cities and towns embraced

* **Berber** refers to a North African ethnic group that consists primarily of Muslims

* **Sunni** refers to the largest branch of the Muslim community; the name derives from sunnah, the exemplary behavior of the Prophet Muhammad

* **c.e.** Common Era, which refers to the same time period as A.D.

* **dynasty** succession of rulers from the same family or group

Bedouin tribes from Arabia and Egypt invaded Libya in the 1000s, introducing a distinctive culture to the country. Here, nomadic Bedouins on horseback wear their traditional robes.

* **Bedouin** nomad of the desert, especially in North Africa, Syria, and Arabia

* **Sufi** refers to Sufism, which seeks to develop spirituality through discipline of the mind and body

* **shaykh** tribal elder; also, title of honor given to those who are considered especially learned and pious

Islam relatively rapidly. By contrast, the nomads of the desert did not convert to Islam until after the 1000s, when Bedouin* tribes from Arabia and Egypt invaded the region. Even then, the Berbers maintained elements of independent tribal identity.

During the 1500s, the Ottoman Turks defeated the Arabs and extended their authority over Tripolitania, Cyrenaica, and Fezzan. France invaded neighboring Algeria in 1830, threatening Turkish domination in North Africa, which led the Ottomans to strengthen their direct control over the regions of Libya. Such events generated both anti-Western and anti-Ottoman sentiment among the people. Leading the opposition movement were members of the Sanusi, a Sufi* brotherhood founded in 1837 by Algerian religious scholar Sayyid Muhammad ibn Ali al-Sanusi.

With its headquarters in Cyrenaica, a region largely isolated from European and Ottoman influence, the Sanusi spread rapidly across Libya. They formed alliances with local *shaykhs** and tribal leaders who controlled trade routes from the Sahara to the coast of Egypt. By the late 1800s, the Sanusi was the leading political and religious force in Libya.

In 1911 Italy launched a war against Turkey, claiming control of Tripolitania, Cyrenaica, and Fezzan. Although the Ottomans surrendered in 1912, the local population defied Italian occupation. Resistance to colonial rule, led by Umar al-Mukhtar, remained strong over the next years. During the 1920s, an estimated 25 percent of the Libyan population perished in the fighting.

After its defeat in World War II (1939–1945), Italy lost control of its African colonies, including the provinces of Tripolitania, Cyrenaica, and Fezzan. Several years later, the United Nations granted the provinces independence, and in 1951, they were united to form the kingdom of Libya. The head of the Sanusi at that time, Idris al-Sanusi, became the country's king. In 1953 Libya joined the Arab League.

A Revolutionary Leader. The young country faced many challenges, including extreme poverty and an underdeveloped economy. The discovery of oil in 1959 provided much-needed revenue, but the previous pattern of foreign domination continued as King Idris permitted Western oil companies to lease huge tracts of land. Idris proved incapable of effectively managing the growing demands of an oil economy and the strong feelings of nationalism* in Libya. In 1969 a group of army officers led by Mu'ammar al-Qaddafi seized power in a coup*.

As head of the Revolutionary Command Council and the leader of the newly proclaimed Libyan Arab Republic, Colonel Qaddafi broke diplomatic ties with Great Britain and the United States and nationalized* the oil industry, banking, and other segments of the economy. Qaddafi declared that Libya would observe *shari'ah**, and he instituted a socialist* system of government.

Focused on the idea of Arab unity and determined to spread his concept of government outside Libya, Qaddafi attempted to form alliances with Egypt, Syria, and other nations. Qaddafi's anti-imperialist* views led him to support acts of terrorism by such groups as the Irish Republican Army, the Basques in Spain, and Palestinian resistance organizations.

During the administration of President Ronald Reagan, the United States actively opposed Qaddafi. The U.S. government banned the import of Libyan oil in 1982. In 1986, in retaliation for a terrorist attack in Germany attributed to Libya, American planes bombed the Libyan capital of Tripoli in a failed attempt to remove Qaddafi from power. In 1988 the United States accused Libya of planning the destruction of a Pan Am passenger jet over Lockerbie, Scotland. When Libya refused to cooperate in the investigation of this event, the United Nations imposed sanctions* on the country.

During the 1980s, the Libyan economy declined as a result of various internal and external factors, including tribal opposition in Cyrenaica, declining oil prices, U.N. sanctions, and the U.S. embargo on oil-producing equipment and military sales to the country. In recent years, Qaddafi has adopted a more moderate attitude toward the West, and Libya has become a mainstream North African state. As of 2003, its per capita gross domestic product (GDP) was the highest in Africa.

Distinctive Political System. The official name of Libya is the Socialist People's Libyan Arab Jamahiriyah. A *jamahiriyah*, or state of the masses, refers to a system of government in which the people hold decision-making power. In theory, Libya is a direct democracy in which the people are represented by the General People's Congress (GPC). The GPC consists of 750 members from locally elected or appointed committees. These representatives elect both the head of state (the premier) and the premier's cabinet*. Under this system, Qaddafi has no official title. Nevertheless, the govern-

Not Without a Fight

When the Italians invaded Libya in 1911, they envisioned a swift, effortless military campaign. They did not anticipate a powerful popular insurrection in Cyrenaica. Umar al-Mukhtar, a tribal elder of the Sanusi and a veteran fighter, used a combination of religious authority, skill, and personal appeal to unite local tribes in a fierce struggle against the Italian troops. For almost ten years, his small guerrilla force confounded the Italians, who were better equipped and greater in number. In the end, however, the superiority of the occupiers became apparent, as they forced the Bedouin population into concentration camps and cut off their supply lines. In September 1931, the Italians captured al-Mukhtar and executed him. Although the resistance movement soon crumbled, Libyans still regard al-Mukhtar as a national hero.

* **nationalism** feelings of loyalty and devotion to one's country and a commitment to its independence

* **coup** sudden, and often violent, overthrow of a ruler or government

* **nationalize** to place an industry under government control

* *shari'ah* Islamic law as established in the Qur'an and sunnah, the exemplary behavior of the Prophet Muhammad

* **socialist** refers to socialism, the economic system in which the government owns and operates the means of production and the distribution of goods

* **imperialist** refers to an empire

* **sanction** economic or military measure taken against a nation that acts in violation of international law

* **cabinet** individuals appointed by a head of state to supervise departments of government and to act as official advisers

ment has little or no actual power. Libya is essentially a military dictatorship with Colonel Qaddafi as its unofficial head.

Against the Establishment. When Qaddafi seized power in 1969, he declared Islam to be the guiding force in Libya. But his version of Islam differed significantly from that of the country's Sunni religious leaders. Although Qaddafi called for the implementation of *shari'ah*, his regime follows a two-track approach to governing. Traditional Islamic law applies only to spiritual matters. *Ijtihad* (independent reasoning) is used to find solutions to issues not covered in traditional sources of law. It also applies to social conditions that have changed with modern times. In effect, Qaddafi declared that anyone—not just traditionally-trained jurists—could interpret the law.

Qaddafi also rejects *ijma* (community consensus), hadith*, and parts of the sunnah* and has declared them unnecessary to Islam. Furthermore, like other rulers of Muslim countries, Qaddafi passed laws that gave the government control of *waqf*, the donations that are the primary means of financial support for religious organizations. By imposing his alternative views of Islam and by criticizing the *ulama**, Qaddafi has effectively weakened the cultural and political influence of Libya's traditional religious leaders.

In 1973 Colonel Qaddafi declared the beginning of an Islamic-based cultural revolution. He outlined his ideas in the *Green Book*, which proclaimed a Third Universal Theory of political action that would replace both communism* and capitalism* in his country. The revolution reached its peak in 1977 with the creation of the Jamahiriyah. In addition, Qaddafi further elaborated his alternative interpretations of Islam. He declared that the Qur'an was the only source of Islamic law and that the pilgrimage to Mecca was no longer one of the five Pillars of Islam. Qaddafi's "reforms" served his political as well as his religious purposes, giving the regime greater legitimacy in secular* matters and freeing it from the restrictions of Islamic doctrine and tradition.

Islamic revivalists* have expressed their opposition to Qaddafi by attacking military posts and government officials. Qaddafi has responded with a brutal campaign of repression against such activities, including public executions of the opposition movement's followers and the closing of Muslim institutions believed to be fronts for extremist groups. His secret police imprisoned dozens of opposition figures at the university in Benghazi in 2000 on similar charges. (*See also* **Arab League; North Africa; Ottoman Empire; Qaddafi, Mu'ammar al-; Sanusiyah.**)

* **hadith** reports of the words and deeds of Muhammad (not in the Qur'an, but accepted as guides for Muslim behavior)

* **sunnah** literally "the trodden path"; Islamic customs based on the exemplary behavior of Muhammad

* *ulama* religious scholars

* **communism** political and economic system based on the concept of shared ownership of all property

* **capitalism** economic system in which businesses are privately owned and operated and where competition exists in a free-market environment

* **secular** separate from religion in human life and society; connected to everyday life

* **revivalist** calling for the return to traditional values or beliefs

Literature

Throughout the Islamic world, literature has always been held in high esteem. The Islamic world did not produce prose in the forms familiar in the West—novels, short stories, and dramas—until modern times. Instead, Muslim writers commonly used poetry, essays, and anecdotes to communicate their ideas.

As the Muslim empire spread across the Middle East into Asia and across North Africa into Spain, it incorporated diverse groups of people. The literary traditions of these groups, many of which were based on ancient cul-

One of the greatest Persian poets, Firdawsi, recounted the history of Persia's kings in his version of *Shahnameh,* or *The Book of Kings.* The poem, which this drawing illustrates, is one of the most renowned works of Persian literature.

See color plate 7, vol. 3.

tures and languages, became part of the rich body of Islamic literature. This entry covers Persian, Turkish, Urdu, and African literature as well as contemporary Muslim works.

Persian Literature

With the expansion of the Muslim empire, Arabic became the dominant literary language in many areas. Over time, however, local languages regained favor as the medium of artistic expression. This was especially true in Persia (present-day Iran), whose literary tradition has influenced many surrounding regions. Outside of Iran, Persian literature has come from Afghanistan, the Indian subcontinent, Central Asia, and Turkey.

Poetic Forms. Some of the most important verse forms associated with Arabic poetry originated in Persia. These include the *masnavi* or *mathnawi* (a rhyming couplet) and the *roba'i* or *ruba'i*, a type of quatrain (four-line verse). Poets used the *masnavi* to compose very long stories with thousands of verses, including romances, legends, and histories. The best-known example of the *ruba'i* is *The Rubaiyat* of Umar Khayyam (died ca. 1129).

Persian literature also adapted Arabic literary forms. The *qasidah,* which comes from pre-Islamic* Arabia, became the chief poetic form in Persian works. The *qasidah* consists of 20 to 100 verses and maintains a single end rhyme through the entire piece. This type of poem begins with a brief introduction, usually about love, which is followed by the description of a journey. Poets end a *qasidah* by praising their patron*, tribe, or themselves. The *ghazal*, a love poem of 5 to 12 verses, probably originated as an extended version of the opening portion of the *qasidah.*

Regional Muslim rulers, such as the Samanids (819–1005), the Ghaznavids (977–1186), and the Seljuks (1038–1194), often sponsored the work of Persian poets, whose panegyrics* helped to legitimize Islamic regimes. Persian court poets did not create works as a means of expressing personal experience or original insights. Rather, they used poetry as a way of demonstrating their skill at handling familiar subjects and forms.

Rudaki (died 940), a poet of the Samanid court, is considered the father of the new type of Persian poetry that emerged after the spread of Islam. Daqiqi (died ca. 980) is another major poet of this period, one who excelled in describing events from daily life. In fact, Daqiqi was the first poet to attempt a verse adaptation of the *Shahnameh* (Book of Kings), the epic history of Persia's kings from mythical times to the reign of Khosrow II (590–628) and the overthrow of the Sassanians by Arab forces. Daqiqi completed only 1,000 verses, though, before his violent death. Firdawsi (ca. 935–ca. 1020), considered the greatest of the Persian poets, incorporated Daqiqi's work into his own version of *Shahnameh*, which he completed in 1010. This poem, which contains almost 60,000 verses in short rhyming couplets, remains one of the most celebrated works of Persian literature. Anvari (1116–1189) earned particular renown for panegyrics in the *qasidah* form. His *Tears of Khorasan* laments the destruction of Khorasan (largely in northeastern Persia) by invaders and the fading glory of the Seljuk dynasty.

Poets in the Azerbaijan region favored the themes of courtly romance. In their works, heroes are consumed by thoughts of physical passion but channel their love into the worship of an ideal but unattainable woman. A common motif involves the unfulfilled lover whose only comfort is wine. Nizami (died 1209) is considered the most important poet of this genre*. His famous *Khamsah* (Quintet) includes the story of Majnun, whose intense desire for the unattainable Layla drives him mad. Nizami's work introduced everyday language into the elevated tradition of Persian poetry. One of the greatest Persian-language poet in India was Amir Khosrow (1253–1325). Sometimes called "the parrot of India," he wrote numerous works, including five long poems in the style of Nizami.

* **pre-Islamic** refers to the Arabian peninsula or to the Arabic language before the founding of Islam in the early 600s

* **patron** person of wealth and influence who supports a writer, artist, or scholar

* **panegyric** poem of elaborate praise

* **genre** style or type, especially in literature and art

Art and Architecture

PLATE 1

Akbar (1556–1605) consolidated and expanded the Mughal Empire, bringing all of India and Afghanistan under his control. He made his court a center of culture, encouraging scholars, poets, musicians, and artists. This Mughal illustration from 1560 shows a scene of luxurious court life during Akbar's reign.

PLATE 2

Geometric design plays a major role in Islamic art. Artists use circles, triangles, hexagons, and squares to create ornate patterns to express and reinforce the unity of the Islamic world vision. This illustration comes from a Moroccan Qur'an tablet.

PLATE 3

Calligraphy—artistic, stylized lettering—is the most highly regarded form of art in the Islamic world. The practice of calligraphy gained special importance in the 600s when scribes made copies of the Qur'an. The first copiers used Kufic, the script with squarish letters shown here.

PLATE 4
A mihrab is a semicircular niche in the wall of a mosque that indicates the direction of Mecca. It guides the faithful by placing them in the proper position for prayers. These geometric tiles adorn the mihrab of a mosque in Cairo.

PLATE 5
Not all mosques follow traditional Islamic designs. In Kuala Lumpur, Malaysia, the Asv-Svakirin Mosque blends in with the soaring Petronas Towers, the world's tallest buildings.

PLATE 6
Built between about 687 and 692 by the Umayyad caliph Abd al-Malik, the Dome of the Rock in Jerusalem is one of the oldest monuments of the Islamic world. The eight-sided building is faced with marble and vibrant blue tiles. The tiles date from a renovation by the Ottoman Turks in the 1500s.

PLATE 7
The great Turkish architect Sinan (1491–1588) designed the Mosque of Sultan Selim II at Edirne when he was in his 80s. He regarded the mosque complex with its enormous dome as his masterpiece. The four tall minarets that rise from the corners of the mosque emphasize the upward thrust of the building.

PLATE 8

The Safavid dynasty ruled Iran from 1501 to 1722. The country became a great power and center of culture under Abbas I, who assumed power in 1588 and made the town of Isfahan into an elegant capital city. Among the architectural monuments of Isfahan are ornate mosques and palaces, gardens, and the Khaju bridge and dam (1650) shown here.

PLATE 9
This palace in Saudi Arabia, with its curves and turrets, is made out of dried mud.

PLATE 10

Djenné in southern Mali flourished as an African trading center from the 1200s to the 1600s. Djenné's Great Mosque, at least the third on the site, was completed in 1907. The massive structure consists of sun-dried mud bricks, plastered over with mud, and palm wood supports. Repair and replastering of the mosque takes place at an annual spring festival.

PLATE 11

Construction of the Great Mosque of Córdoba began in 785. The area shown here, built two hundred years later, expands on the mosque's original design of two-tiered arches set on columns. The use of double arches made it possible to raise the height of the building.

PLATE 12

The Court of the Lions (1354) is part of the Alhambra palace of Granada, one of the glories of Islamic architecture in Spain. A fountain supported by marble lions sits in the center of the courtyard that is lined with airy arcades.

PLATE 13

A series of gardens, many with pools, enhance the palace of Alhambra. The geometric pattern of this formal garden is created by clipped hedges and pathways.

PLATE 14

The Mughal ruler Shah Jahan built the Taj Mahal about 1630 in Agra, India. Dedicated to the memory of his beloved queen, the beautifully proportioned structure is covered with white marble and inlaid colored stones. A long reflecting pool leads up to it.

PLATE 15

This enamelled glass mosque lamp, made in the early 1300s, was dedicated to the Mamluk ruler Baybars II. Quotations from the Qur'an decorate the lamp.

Devotional Poetry. Beginning in the 900s and 1000s, Sufi* poets wrote works expressing their longing for divine inspiration and connection. They used the imagery of secular* love poetry, including wine and drinking, to convey their love of God. During the early 1200s, Muslims developed the first major genre to focus on religious devotion. The *mawlud*, a poem recited on the birthday of the Prophet Muhammad, usually depicts the marvelous events that surrounded the birth of the last messenger of God. A *mawlud* may also describe the miracles or special qualities of the Prophet. In addition to the *mawlud*, devotional poetry can take the form of a narrative ballad that recounts the acts of Muhammad, the first four caliphs*, or Sufi saints.

The most renowned Persian mystic* poet is Jalal al-Din Rumi (1207–1273). Rumi wrote more than 70,000 verses of poetry, using ordinary language to convey God's presence in all of creation. His six-volume masterpiece, *Masnavi*, includes spiritual exclamations, stories, and parables*. This work gained enormous popularity in the Persian- and Turkish-speaking world, and it has been widely translated. Sufis sometimes refer to the *Masnavi* as the "Qur'an* in Persian."

Prose. Persian culture also introduced prose to the Islamic artistic tradition. *Adab* literature, usually short narrative works meant to both teach and entertain, originated in Persia. Writers used many types of stock characters, ranging from rulers and judges to misers and party-crashers. A work of *adab* might include verses from the Qur'an, poetry, or passages from the hadith*. The master of *adab* literature was al-Jahiz (died 869), whose *Book of Misers* blends Persian and Arabic elements.

In addition to romances, myths, and fables, Persian prose included histories, commentaries on the Qur'an, legal texts, and scientific works. Al-Biruni (973–1048), a distinguished scholar, knew Hebrew, Turkish, Sanskrit, Persian, and Syriac as well as Arabic. He wrote works of history, astrology, and astronomy. Umar Khayyam, best known for his poetry, was also a scientist and mathematician. He wrote works of philosophy, law, history, medicine, astronomy, and mathematics, but few of his prose works have survived.

Turkish Literature

Throughout history, speakers of Turkic languages have inhabited the lands from present-day Mongolia to the north coast of the Black Sea, the Balkans, eastern Europe, Anatolia, Iraq, and part of North Africa. Pre-Islamic Turkish literature developed as an oral tradition and dealt primarily with such themes as nature and natural disasters, historical legends, war, heroes, and love.

After the Turks began to convert to Islam during the early 900s, Turkish writers incorporated Arabic and Persian elements into their work. Even so, some early works from this period emphasize the distinctiveness of the Turkish language. The *Kutadgu Bilig*, written by Yusuf Has Hacib during the 1000s, presents views on religion, politics, and education. Written almost entirely in Turkish, the book contains very few Arabic or Persian terms. Similarly, Kasgarli Mahmud created *Divan-i Lugat-it Turk* (The Dictionary of Turkish Languages) to prove that the Turkish language was the literary equal of Arabic. The book includes 7,500 words from different Turkish dialects, gleaned from ancient legends and poems.

* **Sufi** follower of Sufism, which seeks to develop spirituality through discipline of the mind and body

* **secular** separate from religion in human life and society; connected to everyday life

* **caliph** religious and political leader of an Islamic state

* **mystic** one who seeks to experience spiritual enlightenment and truth through various physical and spiritual disciplines

* **parable** story that teaches a religious or moral lesson

* **Qur'an** book of the holy scriptures of Islam

* **hadith** reports of the words and deeds of Muhammad (not in the Qur'an, but accepted as guides for Muslim behavior)

See color plate 3, vol. 2.

Select Audience. From the 1000s to the mid-1800s, Turkish literature developed along two different paths. Divan literature, which relied heavily on Persian and Arabic influences and used complicated language, was popular among the members of the educated upper class. Folk literature, by contrast, addressed the concerns and interests of the common people.

Divan literature is considered the most important literary contribution of the Ottoman period (ca. 1300–1918). The writers of this genre produced mostly poems but also wrote histories, letters, and travel books. Fuzuli (ca. 1495–1556) is the best-known Divan poet. Dehhani, Kadi Burhaneddin, Nesimi, and Ahmedi were the earliest masters of this literary form.

Beginning in the 1400s, elements of Persian poetry became evident in Divan literature. *Mevlut*, a religious poem written by Suleyman Celebi, is a well-recognized example of this period. During the 1500s, the Ottoman capital of Istanbul became a celebrated cultural center that attracted large numbers of visitors and immigrants. The influx of foreigners not only enriched the Turkish literary tradition, but also eventually transformed Turkish into the Ottoman language, which was more complex and difficult to understand.

By the 1700s, Divan poetry began to adopt more elements of common language and experience, increasing its appeal among the Turkish masses. The poet Nedim, the most celebrated Divan writer of this period, produced works that expressed the poetic elements of daily experience. Prose works, too, sought a simpler language. In practice, however, this language differed considerably from regular speech. By the 1800s, the influence of Western culture had seriously weakened the Divan tradition, which was gradually replaced by modern Turkish literature.

Wide Appeal. The folk literary tradition reflected the influence of Islam, especially the mystic philosophy of the Anatolian Sufis. Folk literature relied on pre-Islamic literary elements, simple Turkish language, and sometimes, musical accompaniment. Important folk works include the *Dede Korkut Stories*, believed to have originated with the minstrel (singer of verses) Dede Korkut. The twelve stories in this collection refer to the early years of Islam in Turkey. They include elements of Muslim and shamanistic* beliefs, as well as references from ancient Turkish legends and Greek mythology.

The folk tradition also produced religious works, known as Tasavvufi (Sufi) folk literature. The mystic poet Yunus Emre, who lived during the 1200s, is considered the most important writer in this tradition.

* **shamanistic** refers to the tribal practices of an individual acting as a medium between the physical and spiritual worlds; also, use of sorcery or magic to heal sickness or influence events

Urdu Literature

By the 1000s, northwestern India and the region that is now Pakistan had experienced a flowering of Islamic literature in the Persian language. However, in the military camps, Urdu developed as a new language that combined elements of Persian with Hindi, a northern Indian language. Early works of poetry and prose in Urdu drew heavily from Persian sources and models. Mirza Ghalib (1797–1869), considered the greatest Indian poet of his period, wrote in Urdu as well as in Persian. Ghalib specialized in *ghazal*, *masnavi*, and *qasidah*. His work questions the hardships of the physical world, but acknowledges the absolute power of God in all creation. Ghalib became poet laureate of India's last Mughal emperor, Bahadur Shah II, in 1850.

During the 1800s and 1900s, Muslim writers from the Indian subcontinent produced a wide range of works dealing with Islamic themes. Many advocated socio-political reform in response to their loss of power to Great Britain and to a perceived sense of spiritual and religious decline within the Islamic community. In 1879 Altaf Husayn Hali published the *Musaddas*, an epic poem that contrasts the past achievements of Islamic civilization with its status under colonial rule. The poem introduced a new stage in the history of Urdu poetry in which the themes of revivalism and political romanticism dominated. Reformist writer Nazir Ahmad (died 1912) was a pioneer in the development of the Urdu novel. His most famous book, *Mir'at al-arus* (The Bride's Mirror), focuses on the plight of women in Muslim society.

The events leading up to the establishment of Pakistan as a separate Islamic state also influenced Urdu literature. The work of poet and political writer Muhammad Iqbal (died 1938), who was known as the spiritual founder of Pakistan, had a profound impact on the Muslim community. Iqbal wrote in a direct style that appealed to Indian Muslims. Among his major poems in Urdu are *Shikva* (The Complaint), *Javab-i shikva* (Answer to the Complaint), and the collection entitled *Bang-i dara* (The Call of the Caravan Bell).

African Literature

When Islam spread through North Africa during the mid- to late 600s, the region became Islamized and Arabized—that is, the local peoples of the area adopted the Arab language and customs. North Africa produced several important literary figures. Arab geographer al-Idrisi (1100–ca. 1165) wrote a travel book titled *The Delight of Him Who Wishes to Traverse the Regions of the World*. The Egyptian poet Sharaf ud-Din al-Busiri (died 1296) composed two long poems in praise of the Prophet Muhammad, the *Burdah* and the *Hamziyah*, which became famous throughout Africa and are still recited. Ibn Battutah (1304–ca. 1368) explored India and other parts of Asia as well as the Niger region of Africa. Scholars believe that he visited almost every Muslim country of his time, covering some 75,000 miles. In 1353 he arrived in Morocco, and at the request of the sultan*, he recounted his adventures to a scribe. The resulting work, *Rihla* (Travels), describes the people, places, and events of his journeys. *Rihla* provides important geographical and historical information about the medieval* Muslim world.

Arab and Persian traders and missionaries* brought Islam to East Africa beginning in the 700s. As the native Bantu people mixed with the Muslim population, they incorporated numerous Arabic and Persian words into their language. Eventually, a distinctive language and culture known as Swahili emerged. Swahili literature, which dates to the early 1700s, became one of the first traditions in equatorial Africa to develop the epic. It also developed devotional forms, especially for Muslim sung worship. In addition, Swahili literature produced scholarly works of history, law, theology, and ethics.

Modern Trends

In the modern era, literature from the Islamic world has adapted to deal with new genres and themes. Fiction became prominent during the 1800s and 1900s, and writers began to use the novel to explore broad social themes

Mystic Super Star

The best-selling poet in the United States is a Muslim mystic who died 700 years ago. Jalal al-Din Rumi wrote about divine love, human experience, and the natural world with such passion that his work continues to resonate in this modern, high-tech society. An English translation of his poems, *The Essential Rumi,* has sold more than 250,000 copies and was the most successful poetry book published in the Western world during the 1990s. A second collection, *The Soul of Rumi,* also topped the charts. Clothing designer Donna Karan has used Rumi's words as background in her fashion shows. Madonna, Demi Moore, and Martin Sheen have recorded songs based on Rumi's poems. His work has even inspired space age architecture. Working with Rumi's theme of the unity of the elements (earth, wind, water, and fire), Nader Khalili designs buildings for future colonies in space.

* **sultan** political and military ruler of a Muslim dynasty or state

* **medieval** refers to the Middle Ages, a period roughly between 500 and 1500

* **missionary** person who works to convert nonbelievers to a particular faith

Loya Jirga

* **nationalism** feelings of loyalty and devotion to one's country and a commitment to its independence

* **parody** piece of writing that imitates an original work to achieve comic effect or to ridicule it

* **blasphemy** lack of respect toward God, a religion, or something considered sacred

* **fatwa** opinion issued by an Islamic legal scholar in response to a question posed by an individual or a court of law

* **assassination** murder of a politically important person

* **conservative** generally opposed to change, especially in existing political and social institutions

such as urbanization, nationalism*, migration, and women's rights. Other genres, such as drama and screenplays, also appealed to Muslim writers.

Muslim writers in Western countries, such as the United States and Great Britain, have attracted considerable literary attention. Contemporary Arab American poets write in a wide array of voices and styles and deal with such themes as cultural identity and immigrant status. Samuel Hazo, a poet of Lebanese and Syrian ancestry, founded the International Poetry Forum in 1966, and in 1993, he became the State Poet of Pennsylvania. Younger Arab American poets compete in poetry "slams" and have even experimented with rap forms. In 1999 the first Arab American Writers Conference, held in Chicago, drew a wide range of literary figures.

Salman Rushdie, a native of India who moved to Great Britain and then to the United States, has earned both acclaim and harsh criticism for novels with political themes, such as *Midnight's Children.* In 1988 Rushdie published *The Satanic Verses*, a novel that recounts the adventures of characters representing the Prophet Muhammad and his family. Denounced as a parody* and blasphemy* by the Islamic community, the novel led the Ayatollah Khomeini to issue a fatwa* calling for Rushdie's assassination*. Hanif Kureishi, a native of Great Britain, has written short stories, screenplays, and novels that deal with the challenges of the British Asian community. His short story "My Son the Fanatic," which concerns the conflict between a secular immigrant and his ultra-conservative* Muslim son, was adapted as a critically acclaimed film. (*See also* **Arabic Language and Literature; Iqbal, Muhammad; Khayyam, Umar; Rumi; Rushdie, Salman; Sufism.**)

Loya Jirga

The traditional tribal council of Afghanistan is known as *loya jirga.* For centuries, Afghan leaders have convened tribal councils to select new leaders, adopt or amend their constitution, declare war, and settle other important matters of state. The term *loya jirga*, from the country's Pashtu dialect, means "grand assembly."

Representatives from every part of Afghanistan—chosen in a two-stage process—participate in the *loya jirga.* A leadership council in each district meets to pick electors, people who will later cast ballots for delegates to attend the *loya jirga.* The electors then vote among themselves to determine who will represent each district. The number of delegates allotted to a district depends on the size of its population. This selection process has generally resulted in an assembly that includes almost all of Afghanistan's major ethnic and religious groups.

Women, however, constitute the largest single group that historically has been largely absent from *loya jirga*, reflecting societal attitudes toward their participation in the political process. Only a few women were represented at the *loya jirga* held in 1964 and 1977. In 2002, however, 160 of the 1450 seats were reserved specifically for women. Seats were also reserved for minorities, scholars, and representatives of other groups who might otherwise have little or no presence at the council.

Traditionally called by the ruler and limited to his initiative, *loya jirga* have had a significant impact on Afghan history. In 1747 Ahmad Shah Durrani, founder of the Durrani dynasty in Afghanistan, summoned a *loya jirga* to establish independent rule in the country. Amir Amanullah called one in 1921 to ratify his treaty with Great Britain. *Loya jirga* were convened in 1949 and 1955 to promote nationalist claims to tribal lands in Pakistan, and one was called in 1964 to ratify a new constitution.

Today Afghans hope that future *loya jirga* will provide them with a stable government after years of war and civil turmoil. In 2002, following the overthrow of the ultra-orthodox Taliban regime*, an emergency *loya jirga* was summoned to appoint a transitional government to lead the country for up to two years, until a fully representative government could be elected through free and democratic elections. (*See also* **Afghanistan; Taliban.**)

* **regime** government in power

Madhi

See *Messianic Traditions.*

Madrasah

The term *madrasah* originally referred to an institution of higher learning that specialized in Islamic studies, particularly law. In modern times, the term also includes elementary-level schools teaching Qur'anic* knowledge. At one time, *madrasah*s were the most important centers of learning in the Muslim world. *Madrasah*s declined during the age of Western colonialism but experienced a revival in many parts of the Islamic world in the mid-1900s.

* **Qur'anic** refers to the book of the holy scriptures of Islam

Centers for Wandering Scholars. In the early days of Islam, mosques served as schools, with Muslims gathering in study circles. Mosques hosted the first *madrasah*s and some provided housing for students. Eventually, *madrasah*s emerged as independent institutions. They featured a building that served as both a school and a residence for students and teachers. Most had libraries and provided food and medical care. Wealthy patrons* made charitable donations (*waqf*) of land or urban rental property to support *madrasah*s. The revenues from these properties paid the teachers' salaries and funded the students' education.

*Madrasah*s were established by a variety of Muslim groups, including Sunnis*, Shi'is*, and followers of various schools of legal thought. Some Islamic rulers tried to suppress certain *madrasah*s or to control them by confiscating the *waqf* properties that supported them. Others, such as the Seljuk* vizier* Nizam al-Mulk (died 1092), encouraged the growth of different *madrasah*s. Nizam al-Mulk supported all major schools of Sunni law and created the first large network of schools in the Middle East.

The subjects taught in *madrasah*s varied from one school to the next. They mainly focused on Islamic law, with the Qur'an, hadith*, and Arabic grammar as alternative topics of study. Some eventually incorporated secular* subjects, such as literature and the sciences, into the curriculum. Students frequently traveled to different *madrasah*s, gaining certificates from

* **patron** person of wealth and influence who supports a writer, artist, or scholar

* **Sunni** refers to the largest branch of the Muslim community; the name derives from sunnah, the exemplary behavior of the Prophet Muhammad

* **Shi'i** refers to Muslims who believe that Muhammad chose Ali ibn Abi Talib and his descendants as the spiritual-political leaders of the Muslim community

* **Seljuk** refers to the Turkish dynasty that ruled much of the Middle East from the 1000s to the 1200s

* **vizier** Muslim minister of state

* **hadith** reports of the words and deeds of Muhammad (not in the Qur'an, but accepted as guides for Muslim behavior)

* **secular** separate from religion in human life and society; connected to everyday life

Madrasah

Despite their decline during Western colonization, *madrasahs* experienced a revival in many Muslim countries in the mid-1900s. Today, some *madrasahs* offer a broader curriculum that includes instruction in secular subjects. In this photo, a teacher reviews her students' work in a *madrasah* in Jakarta, Indonesia.

* **stipend** money paid for services or to defray costs

* **mullah** Muslim cleric or learned man

each before settling down to study with a particular teacher. *Madrasah*s were highly informal and did not offer a degree program or a graded curriculum. The relationship between student and teacher had primary importance. Along with knowledge of the subject matter, the teacher would convey to the student religious insights and a mode of behavior that signified a certain scholarly rank. Because they had their own funding and provided students with small stipends*, *madrasah*s became a popular destination for poor Muslims who would otherwise lead a life of manual labor. Many of these students became teachers, legal experts, and government administrators.

Decline and Revival of Islamic Education. Beginning in the late 1700s, European forces invaded Muslim countries, damaging the *madrasah* system. In order to advance in government or secure a high-ranking position in society, Muslims needed a Western education. Islamic governments founded secular elementary schools, high schools, and universities, all of which offered a modern curriculum and employed Western teachers and teaching methods. Some *madrasah*s added subjects taught in secular schools to their curriculum but continued to lose students. In many Muslim countries, a rift developed between the *ulama* (religious scholars) and the Western-trained intellectuals, who debated various interpretations of religious texts and the role of religion within the state.

The leaders of many Islamic countries revised their educational systems in ways that affected *madrasah*s. Under Mustafa Kemal Atatürk, Turkey closed its *madrasah*s in the mid-1920s. Iran's *madrasah*s survived modernizing efforts by Reza Shah Pahlavi but lost much of their influence. Even sons of Iranian mullahs* sought the economic advantages of a secular education. The famous mosque-university al-Azhar in Cairo lost students to modern schools, and the government responded by passing a law in 1961 introducing secular subjects. In addition to traditional Islamic sciences, al-Azhar added such subjects as engineering, business administration, and medicine.

In the mid-1900s, however, *madrasahs* regained some of their former importance. The growing movement for a pure Islamic state led to a revival of traditional forms of education throughout the Muslim world. Even Turkey, which retains a secular constitution, experienced an increase in *madrasah*s at the middle and high school level. Waves of Muslims immigrating to England, France, and Germany have established *madrasah*s in Europe. Many new religious universities and centers have also opened in the Muslim world, such as the Islamic Research Institute in Damascus, the International Islamic Universities in Islamabad and Kuala Lumpur, and the African Islamic Center in Khartoum.

***Madrasahs* in Southeast Asia.** *Madrasahs* play a major role in Southeast Asian countries such as Indonesia, Malaysia, Singapore, and Thailand. The *madrasahs* in these nations exist within an educational system called the *pondok pesantren*. Derived from the terms for "inn" and "religious students," *pesantren* are boarding schools that teach various aspects of theology*. In Indonesia, some 40,000 *pesantren* teach about 8 million students, mostly in rural areas.

Most *pesantren* admit male students, who live together in a *pondok* (dormitory), where they cook their own meals and wash their own clothes. A few admit women, and others have separate dormitories for men and women. Students travel among the *pesantren* to study different subjects, earning a certificate from each teacher. They return to their home school once a year. Each *pesantren* is headed by a teacher-leader *(kiyayi),* who serves as the driving force behind the school, and most *pesantren* decline following the death or departure of the *kiyayi.*

The *pondok pesantren* operate solely through personal donations. The Indonesian government, however, sponsors state-run *madrasahs* that prepare students for higher religious education after they have learned secular subjects. These *madrasahs* operate at the elementary, middle, and high school levels. Since the 1970s, the government has added secular subjects to the elementary school *madrasahs*. Around 70 percent of the instruction in these schools and 30 percent of the instruction in the high schools revolves around nonreligious subject matter.

Singapore boasts nearly 40 *madrasahs*, each offering either elementary or secondary education. In the 1970s, secular subjects were added to the curricula of these schools. *Madrasah* students can take the same examinations as students from secular schools. Those who wish to travel to the Middle East for higher education must complete a year at Madrasah al-Junied al-Islamiiah, the only one of Singapore's *madrasahs* from which al-Azhar accepts certificates.

Because Thailand has a tiny Muslim population (around 4 percent), Muslim schools encourage students to spread Islam by preaching in remote areas. In the 1960s, Thailand's government worked to standardize *madrasahs*. It converted all of the country's *pondoks* into private schools, helping to set their courses of study. It has also developed programs to send students to Middle Eastern universities. (*See also* **Atatürk, Mustafa Kemal; Azhar, al-; Education; Religious Scholars; Universities.**)

See color plate 3, vol. 1.

* **theology** study of the nature and qualities of God and the understanding of His will

Little Sultan's Big Legacy

One of the Muslim world's most architecturally distinct *madrasah*s is the Sultan Hasan school in Cairo. Built in the mid-1300s, it has a modernistic decor with bare walls and recessed windows. The building consists of a courtyard surrounded by four halls, each of which represents one of the four Sunni schools of law. Students and teachers live in these halls and study the school of law that their hall represents. The large tomb of the *madrasah's* founder, Sultan Hasan, occupies a central place in the building. In most *madrasah*s, the patron lies in a small grave in a corner. Interestingly, the founder of this mosque had a short career. He came to power as a child and lost his throne at age 16. He regained it at 23, but his enemies murdered him just three years later.

Magic and Sorcery

The Hidden World of the Jinn

According to Islamic belief, a parallel world exists on the earth that is inhabited by supernatural creatures called *jinn*. The term *jinn* derives from the Arabic word *janna*, which means "to hide." Indeed, these creatures are usually invisible to humans, although, according to folk belief, they can take human form. *Jinn* are similar to people in certain ways. They eat, drink, marry, produce children, and even die, but they live much longer than humans. God gave *jinn* the ability to control the minds of others, and they are often accused of causing insanity in humans. If a *jinn* uses its powers for evil, however, it must answer to God on the Day of Judgment. *Jinn* are capable of becoming Muslim and being saved. The non-Muslim *jinn* form part of the army of Iblis, the rebel who represents the power of evil and is an enemy of God and humanity.

Many people associate the practice of magic with evil, and historically, magicians, wizards, witches, and sorcerers have been accused of being followers of the devil. A similarly negative attitude toward magic exists in many Muslim societies. Educated Muslims generally dismiss magical practices as the superstitions of the uneducated and criticize them as *bidah* (innovation, or even heresy*). Nevertheless, a belief in spirits, charms, curses, and the evil eye is still widespread in popular Islamic culture.

Good Versus Evil. The Bedouin* tribes that inhabited Arabia during the time of Muhammad believed that spirits lived in all natural objects and that they could either help or harm humans. People were particularly concerned with the spirit beings known as *jinn*, which they believed were responsible for a wide range of illnesses. As a result, they sought to gain the favor of the *jinn* or to control them through the use of magic.

As Islamic communities developed, Muslims adopted some elements of pre-Islamic belief and practice. They distinguished between two types of magic: *al-ruhani* (spiritual magic) and *al-simiya* (natural magic). *Al-ruhani* was further divided into high and low magic. High, or divine, magic depended on the supernatural powers of God, angels, and other helpful spirits. It was used for positive purposes, such as to protect one from misfortune. Low, or satanic, magic worked through the devil or other evil spirits to carry out sinister purposes. A practitioner of low magic was called *sahir* (sorcerer). *Al-simiya* depended on natural materials, such as certain perfumes and drugs, rather than on supernatural agents for their effect.

Practitioners of magic are believed to have special knowledge and techniques for controlling supernatural forces. They typically use their powers in response to requests from clients. A person who is suffering from an illness, for example, might seek a cure from a magician. Although respected for their knowledge and creative powers, magicians are also feared for their ability to harm their enemies. Thus, the magician occupies a moral "gray area" in Islamic culture.

The Power of the Verse. The use of amulets, or charms, which are believed to guard the wearer against evil or misfortune, is widespread in the Muslim world. An amulet often consists of a verse from the Qur'an* written on a slip of paper and placed inside a piece of jewelry. This practice traces its origins to the Prophet Muhammad, who used to recite religious formulas from the Qur'an. Today amulets are a popular type of jewelry worn by Muslims.

Magicians have developed other methods for applying the spiritual power of the Qur'an. Some practitioners write passages from scripture on small pieces of paper, which their clients may burn and then rub their bodies with the ashes. They may also soak the bits of paper in water to dissolve the ink and then drink the liquid to receive the magic in the verse. Similarly, some magicians write verses on the inside of a clay bowl, dissolve the writing in water, and have their clients drink the liquid as a cure for illness. Several Qur'anic passages are especially favored for these purposes.

In addition to the sacred text, Muslims believe in the power of objects to cure disease or prevent misfortune. Such objects include water from the

Zamzam Well in Mecca and pieces of the cloth cover of the Kaaba*. Relics of Muslim saints are also thought to have special powers.

Warding off the Evil Eye. Many Middle Eastern societies (as well as others in the Mediterranean region) believe in the power of the evil eye. According to this belief, an envious person glancing or staring at someone else's prized possession may damage or destroy it. Children and animals are considered particularly vulnerable to the evil eye. Although most educated Muslims consider the evil eye to be superstition, others insist that it is a real phenomenon, citing a reference to it in the Qur'an. Muhammad reportedly permitted magicians to use spells to avert the effects of the evil eye.

According to tradition, Muslims can defend themselves against the evil eye in a variety of ways. Reading scriptures or other holy writings is one method. They can also wear hand-shaped amulets—the hand is supposedly effective in fighting off attacks by the evil eye. Because boys are considered more vulnerable to the evil eye than girls, parents may dress a boy in girls' clothes to protect him.

People may also use magic to attack their enemies openly. An individual may curse someone by calling on the name of a supernatural being. Curses that include the names of God or of saints are intended to punish sinners, not to harm innocent people. In Morocco, some people place curses called *ar* on others to force them to carry requests against their will. (*See also* **Hajj; Health Care; Relics.**)

* **Kaaba** literally "House of God"; Islamic shrine in Mecca

Mahdiyah

The Mahdiyah movement arose in the late 1800s in the region of present-day Sudan. Its name derives from its leader, Muhammad Ahmad al-Sayyid Abd Allah (1844–1885), who claimed that he was the "Expected Mahdi." According to Muslim tradition, a Mahdi is a figure who will deliver the Islamic community from injustice and restore its purity of faith. The Sudanese Mahdi attracted devoted followers, waged war against the rulers of the Nile region, and succeeded in establishing an Islamic state in the Sudan.

Son of a shipbuilder from northern Sudan, the Mahdi lived near Khartoum and studied religion from an early age. Deeply attracted to Islam's mystical* tradition, he shunned higher education and adopted Sufism*. The Mahdi also opposed several government policies. A province of the Ottoman Empire, Sudan was governed by Egypt, which in turn came under the control of Britain. The Sudanese people had little in common with the ruling party, which imposed harsh regulations on them. For example, many were flogged when they could not pay their taxes. The Mahdi believed that the Turkish-Egyptian rulers had alienated the Sudanese and had completely abandoned Islam. In 1881 he publicly proclaimed himself the Mahdi and declared a jihad* against all corrupt governments. Although the Mahdi had only unsophisticated weapons, he attracted huge numbers of dissatisfied Sudanese subjects. By late 1883, the Mahdi and his followers had destroyed three Egyptian armies and seized almost all of the territory that had been under Egyptian occupation. His army captured enormous stores of money, jewels, and military weapons.

* **mystical** refers to mysticism, the belief that spiritual enlightenment and truth can be attained through various physical and spiritual disciplines

* **Sufism** Islamic mysticism, which seeks to develop spirituality through discipline of the mind and body

* **jihad** literally "striving"; war in defense of Islam

119

Only the capital city of Khartoum held out against the Mahdi's forces. In early 1885, however, the city fell. The Mahdi's troops killed the city's British governor, General Charles Gordon, despite the Mahdi's order to spare his life. They also massacred many citizens of Khartoum. After taking the city, the Mahdi—anxious to avoid the spiritual contamination of "the city of the Turks"—established a new capital across the river at Omdurman. Having seized the government printing press, the Mahdi sent out letters and warnings to his followers concerning every aspect of life. He preached sermons and issued proclamations but had his chief officers perform the more routine functions of government. The Mahdi's reign lasted only six months. He died of a sudden illness and was buried in Omdurman, where his tomb (*al-Qubbah*) towered over the city.

The Mahdi's followers continued his efforts to create a pure Islamic society. His successor, Abd Allah ibn Muhammad (known as the Khalifah, or successor to Muhammad) dealt with challenges to his leadership, as well as serious famine in the country. Internal conflicts between communities near the Nile and the nomadic tribes of the interior caused trouble, and corruption among judges and tax collectors plagued the Khalifah's rule. In August 1889, Anglo-Egyptian forces defeated the Mahdist army at Tushki, bringing the jihad to an end. Nine years later, the Anglo-Egyptian armies broke up the remaining Mahdists at the battle of Karari. The Khalifah fled to Kordofan (in central Sudan), but British forces hunted him down and killed him a year later. For the next 56 years, Sudan remained under Anglo-Egyptian rule. Sporadic Mahdist uprisings occurred during the first few decades but eventually disappeared.

The Mahdiyah movement gave the Sudanese a sense of common identity and national goals. It led to the creation of an Islamic state that pushed back powerful forces and extended from the Red Sea to Central Africa. The Mahdi served as an inspiration to Muslim nationalists* and reformers in other countries. He influenced later Islamic political movements such as the Ansar religious movement, which was established by the Mahdi's son Abd al-Rahman and led to the creation of the Ummah Party in 1945. The party derives most of its support from the former Mahdist strongholds of Kordofan, Darfur, and White Nile provinces. (*See also* **Central Africa; Messianic Tradition; Sudan.**)

* **nationalist** one who advocates loyalty and devotion to his or her country and its independence

Majlis

See *Government.*

Malaysia

Formed in 1963, Malaysia includes 11 states on the Malay Peninsula, which lies south of Thailand, and Sarawak and Sabah on the island of Borneo. The vast majority of the country's population of 22 million lives in Malaya, the name for the part of Malaysia that occupies the peninsula.

Located at the crossroads of important trade routes, Malaysia exemplifies ethnic, linguistic, cultural, and religious diversity. Malays and native people constitute about 58 percent of the population. Chinese and Indians are substantial minorities. More than half of all Malaysians are Muslim. Minority groups practice Buddhism*, Hinduism*, Christianity, and other religions.

The role of Islam in Malaysia reflects the divisions in the country's population. After independence, the government tried to limit the influence of Islam in the public sphere, ensuring that minority communities were fairly represented within the political system. Over the years, however, Malaysia's identity has become increasingly tied to Islam.

Prime Location. During the 100s and 200s C.E.*, Indian traders and priests settled the Malay Peninsula. Over the next millennium, the Indians established small kingdoms in the region. In the process, they adapted the beliefs of the native people to traditional Hindu and Buddhist practices. During the 1200s, Arab and Indian merchants brought Islam to the region. Sunni* Islam, with its emphasis on social equality, appealed to the peasant and merchant classes.

Around 1400 Prince Paramesvara (ruled 1403–1424) founded the state of Melaka (also known as Malacca) on the southwest coast of the Malay Peninsula. After he converted to Islam and became a sultan*, the capital city (also called Melaka) became an Islamic center and a critical point in the trade network of Southeast Asia. At the height of Melaka's influence, its harbor accommodated more ships than any other port in the known world.

The people who lived in and around Melaka, who were mostly Muslims, began to call themselves Malays. As a result, the term *Malay* became associated with individuals who practiced Islam and spoke a version of the Malay language. By converting to Islam, followers of Hinduism or Buddhism could also identify themselves as Malay. Although Islam dominated the region, it did not completely replace the practices of pre-Islamic cultures. Instead, the Malays incorporated rituals and beliefs from Hinduism and native religions.

Islam did not expand to Sarawak and Sabah until the 1400s and 1500s. It spread among the people who lived along the coast, but the inland population retained their native folk religions until the 1900s.

By the early 1500s, Europeans began to exert power in Southeast Asia. In an effort to dominate the spice trade, the Portuguese conquered the city of Melaka in 1511. Under the Portuguese, the regional economy declined. In 1641 the Dutch captured Melaka and attempted to revive its trade network, but the city never completely recovered its former prestige.

Except for Melaka, Westerners remained uninterested in northern Borneo and the other areas of Malaya until the late 1700s. At that time, the British East India Company purchased an island off the northwest coast of Malaya. In 1824 the British obtained Melaka from the Dutch. The Pangkor Treaty of 1874 imposed British rule on the Muslim states of the Malay Peninsula. The British allowed the sultanates to retain a symbolic political role and to rule on matters related to Malay religion and customs.

Between 1800 and 1941, Malay society became significantly more pluralistic*. Several million Chinese immigrated to Malaya, Sarawak, and Sabah to work on plantations, in mines, and as merchants. The rubber estates of Malaya employed many Tamils, an ethnic group from southern India.

Achieving Independence. Malay religious leaders and scholars objected to Western culture and sought to fight it by strengthening the Islamic iden-

* **Buddhism** religion of eastern and Central Asia based on the teaching of Gautama Buddha

* **Hinduism** ancient religion that originated in India

* **C.E.** Common Era, which refers to the same time period as A.D.

* **Sunni** refers to the largest branch of the Muslim community; the name derives from sunnah, the exemplary behavior of the Prophet Muhammad

* **sultan** political and military ruler of a Muslim dynasty or state

Stepping Down

Malaysia's prime minister, Dr. Mahathir bin Muhammmad, has led the country for more than two decades. But in 2002, he surprisingly announced that he would leave office on October 25, 2003. Dr. Mahathir, who trained as a family physician, brought prosperity and stability to Malaysia but also earned his share of criticism. Under his administration, Malaysia's economy expanded and modernized. The tallest buildings in the world, the Petronas Towers, soar above Malaysia's capital city of Kuala Lumpur, and serve as symbols of his legacy. At the same time, however, Dr. Mahathir has provoked criticism for stifling political dissent and for controlling the media.

* **pluralistic** refers to a condition of society in which diverse groups maintain and develop their traditional culture or special interests

121

tity of the masses. By the early 1900s, a politicized Islamic movement arose. Its leader, Shaykh Tahir Jalal al-Din (1869–1957), called for Islamic reform throughout the entire region. Reformers established schools that introduced modern subjects and a new method of religious education. They also used magazines and newspapers to communicate their ideas. These tactics had far-reaching social and political consequences. Reformers called attention to questionable religious practices, the social and economic inferiority of the Malay community as compared to non-Muslim immigrant populations in urban centers, and the injustice of colonial rule.

During World War II, the Japanese occupied Malaya and Borneo from 1942 to 1945. The occupation aggravated tensions between the Muslim and non-Muslim populations and also generated feelings of nationalism*. In 1948 the British formed the Federation of Malaya. As nationalists pressed for independence, Muslim reformers urged the creation of an Islamic state. On August 31, 1957, the federation achieved independence. The arrangement gave Malays significant political power, but the Chinese maintained their strong economic base and they gained important rights as citizens. In 1963 Malaysia came into being, with the inclusion of Malaya, the island of Singapore (until mid-1965), Sarawak, and Sabah.

Although the Malaysian constitution established Islam as the nation's official religion, the new government was committed to maintaining a secular society. Over the next decade, however, Islamic organizations intensified their pressure on the government. As a result, the nation's leaders focused on the educational, social, and economic development of the Malay Muslims.

A Balancing Act. During the 1950s, an Islamic political organization called the Partai Islam Se-Malaysia (PAS) emerged. This group, which began as a cultural association, became the country's long-term opposition party. It advocated a relatively moderate style of Islamization of social and political life. During the 1970s, a more radical* *da'wah* (missionary) trend developed through the activities of youth organizations in secular educational institutions. The da'wah movement spurred a resurgence of Islamic consciousness. It attracted professionals, teachers, and students who were frustrated with corruption in government and society. They denounced Western materialism and called for a return to Qur'anic* teachings.

The *da'wah* movement led to the emergence of three major groups in addition to PAS. The Malay Muslim Youth League (ABIM), founded in 1971, worked for the Islamization of the individual, family, community, and state. The Darul Arqam supported workshops, clinics, and schools and stressed economic independence and Qur'anic social values. It also supported segregation of the sexes. The Tabligh emphasized preaching and appealed to the educated segments of society.

The Malaysian government considered these activist groups a threat to the nation's multiethnic balance and secular values. Since the early 1980s, the government has sought to control *da'wah* activity by creating its own more moderate Islamic institutions. Prime Minister Mahathir bin Muhammad declared Malaysia's economy to be based on Islamic principles, and he founded an Islamic bank and other businesses. The government established the International Islamic University, increased aid to Muslim schools, and gave Muslim judges equal status to civil judges. Although the authorities

* **nationalism** feelings of loyalty and devotion to one's country and a commitment to its independence

* **radical** favoring extreme change or reform, especially in existing political and social institutions

* **Qur'anic** relating to Qur'an, the book of the holy scriptures of Islam

See color plate 5, vol. 2.

---

have yielded to some of the demands of *da'wah* groups, they continue to protect the rights of the substantial non-Malay population in the country.

The role of women in Malaysian society is also controversial. Moderate leaders call for full employment for women and modest forms of dress. More radical groups, however, want to restrict women to certain professions, such as nursing, teaching, and social work. They also call for women to wear the veil and to be segregated from men. A feminist group in Malaysia, Sisters in Islam, insists that the Qur'an guarantees gender equality. (*See also* **Colonialism.**)

Malcolm X

1925–1965
African American Muslim leader

* **militant** aggressively active in a cause

* **Sunni** refers to the largest branch of the Muslim community; the name derives from sunnah, the exemplary behavior of the prophet Muhammad

* **Pan-Africanism** movement to connect African Americans with their cultural and religious history in Africa

During the 1960s, Malcolm X (formerly Malcolm Little) rose through the ranks of the Nation of Islam, a militant* religious group that promotes the formation of a separate African American nation, to become one of the most prominent and controversial figures in the United States. A formidable critic of American society, particularly the racist practices of whites, Malcolm X challenged the civil rights movement and its notions of integration and nonviolence. Toward the end of his life, however, he converted to Sunni* Islam and shifted his focus to Pan-Africanism*.

Born in Omaha, Nebraska, Malcolm Little had a turbulent childhood. When he was just six years old, the Ku Klux Klan, a white supremacist group, burned his family's home in Lansing, Michigan. Shortly thereafter, his father was murdered and his mother was confined to a mental institution. Malcolm and his seven siblings spent many years in foster homes. At the age of fifteen, he became involved in the world of drugs and crime, which eventually led to imprisonment in Massachusetts.

During his incarceration (1946–1952), Little experienced an intellectual and social transformation. He read a variety of books about history, philosophy, politics, and religion, and improved his speaking skills. In 1948 he embraced the teachings of Elijah Muhammad, the leader of the Nation of Islam, and discarded his last name for the symbolic X (ex-Christian, ex-Negro, ex-slave). Particularly attractive was Elijah Muhammad's claim that God is a black man who will liberate African Americans and destroy their white oppressors.

Malcolm's social experiences, intellectual accomplishments, and dedication to Elijah Muhammad enabled him to advance rapidly within the Nation of Islam. In 1952 he began organizing Muslim temples in New York, Philadelphia, and Boston, as well as in the southern and western United States. Elijah Muhammad soon recognized Malcolm's abilities and charisma* and appointed him the leader of Temple Number Seven in Harlem (New York City), the largest and most prestigious temple aside from the organization's headquarters in Chicago. Malcolm X became the national representative of the Nation of Islam, and under his direction, its membership greatly increased.

Preaching the message of black identity, pride, and independence across the United States and around the world, Malcolm X became a favorite media personality. He challenged Dr. Martin Luther King's emphasis on nonvi-

* **charisma** personal charm or appeal that arouses loyalty and enthusiasm

Malcolm X

Malcolm X, African American Muslim and spokesman for the Nation of Islam, spoke to reporters in 1964. Malcolm X was a highly controversial figure who challenged the civil rights movement and its ideals of integration and nonviolence.

See color plate 8, vol. 3.

* **hajj** pilgrimage to Mecca that Muslims are required to make once in their lifetime

olence, encouraging followers to defend themselves by any means possible. As Malcolm X became more involved in domestic and international politics, however, his worldview gradually changed, and he began to question the teachings of Elijah Muhammad and the Nation of Islam. He instituted Arabic instruction in Temple Number Seven. Testing his leader's policies of political inaction and avoidance of contact with Sunni Muslims, Malcolm spoke out on a variety of civil and human rights issues. He also maintained close contact with Muslim diplomats.

Elijah Muhammad and other officials within the Nation of Islam became uneasy about Malcolm's success and concerned about the potential threat to their power. After Malcolm made controversial public comments on the assassination of President John F. Kennedy (November 1963), he was suspended. In 1964 Malcolm X left the Nation of Islam to establish the Muslim Mosque, Inc., and the Organization of Afro-African Unity. After participating in the hajj*, Malcolm X converted to Sunni Islam and changed his name to El Hajj Malik El-Shabazz. The experience also led him to shift his focus from forming a separate black nation to Pan-Africanism.

Tension between Malcolm's followers and members of the Nation of Islam led to threats against his life. On February 21, 1965, while delivering a speech in New York City, he was shot and killed by members of the Nation of Islam. Some have accused the U.S. government of arranging his murder. (*See also* **Elijah Muhammad; Farrakhan, Louis; Nation of Islam.**)

Malik ibn Anas

ca. 713–795
Founder of school of Islamic law

Malik ibn Anas, a scholar in Medina, specialized in Muslim law. His teachings became the basis for one of the four main Sunni* schools of Islamic jurisprudence—the Maliki school.

Born in Medina around 713, Malik ibn Anas spent his entire life in that city, traveling only to Mecca to fulfill his hajj* obligation. In Medina, he studied with the city's leading teachers of jurisprudence and devoted his own life to learning and teaching. He became an expert on the hadith*, and was known for giving judgments that were conscientious and fair. Many scholars attended the lectures that he gave at the Prophet's mosque. Malik believed that the faithful in Medina adhered most closely to the original teachings of Muhammad. Among his writings was a compilation of the religious and legal customs of Medina, which he published in a book titled *al-Mutawatta* (The Beaten Path). The first book of its kind, *al-Mutawatta* became a foundation of Muslim legal practices.

Some legal scholars, however, disagreed with Malik ibn Anas, and in time, four distinct schools of legal thought emerged. The Hanafi school, which became the most widespread, followed relatively liberal* methods of legal interpretation. The Maliki school was distinguished by its reliance on the traditions of Medina. The Shafi'i school combined elements from Hanafi and Maliki teachings but placed more emphasis on the practice of the Prophet Muhammad than on establishing new applications of Islamic principles. The Hanbali school, which placed great importance on tradition, became the basis of Wahhabi Islam in Saudi Arabia. The Maliki *madhhab* (schools of legal thought) became prominent in Medina, Egypt, and North Africa.

Although the Maliki school was considered conservative, its followers actively debated controversial issues such as free will and predestination*. In addition to law, Maliki scholars also studied grammar, linguistics, mathematics, astronomy, and medicine. Maliki instruction and study flourished especially in the cities of al-Qayrawan and Tunis in North Africa. (*See also* **Creed**.)

* **Sunni** refers to the largest branch of the Muslim community; the name derives from sunnah, the exemplary behavior of the Prophet Muhammad

* **hajj** pilgrimage to Mecca that Muslims are required to make once in their lifetime

* **hadith** reports of the words and deeds of Muhammad (not in the Qur'an, but accepted as guides for Muslim behavior)

* **liberal** supporting greater participation in government for individuals; not bound by tradition

* **predestination** doctrine that God alone determines whether a Muslim goes to paradise or to hell

Mamluk State

In the 800s and 900s, Islamic rulers came to rely on slave soldiers as the basis for their military power. Called *mamluks* (an Arabic word meaning "owned"), these slave soldiers were usually of non-Muslim origin but converted to Islam as part of their education and training. In later centuries, the slave soldiers themselves took control of the state and ruled as powerful sultans* in the Muslim world. From 1250 to 1517, the Mamluk state centered in Egypt was the most successful of these slave sultanates. It controlled Egypt, Syria, southeastern Asia Minor, and western Arabia.

The Mamluk state emerged when a small group of army officers staged a revolt against al-Salih Ayyub, heir of the last Ayyubid sultan. They assassinated al-Salih Ayyub in 1249 and designated one of their own to be the new leader. The first two Mamluk sultans, Aybak and Qutuz, faced rebellion from their own soldiers, as well as challenges from Ayyubid princes in

* **sultan** political and military ruler of a Muslim dynasty or state

Syria. Qutuz's lieutenant, Baybars, became famous for his victory over invading Mongols in Palestine. Soon afterward, he murdered Qutuz and seized power for himself.

Ruling as sultan from 1260 to 1277, Baybars established the foundation for the long-lasting Mamluk state. He defeated the Mongols who had destroyed Baghdad in 1258, stopping their conquest of the Middle East. The Abbasid caliphate* had come to an end with the Mongol conquest of Baghdad, and Baybars installed an Abbasid prince as his caliph in Cairo. He fought a series of wars with states established by crusaders*, bringing an end to their power.

Until around 1340, when the Black Death* devastated the populations of Egypt and Syria, the Mamluk state enjoyed a period of prosperity. Agricultural output had been high, and trade between the countries of the Mediterranean region and South Asia had brought great wealth to the government. The Mamluk sultan was acknowledged as the highest ruler of Sunni* Islam because of his control of all four holy cities (Mecca, Medina, Jerusalem, and Hebron). Under Mamluk rule, the cities of Cairo, Damascus, and Aleppo flourished as major centers of art and culture. The Mamluk elite supported *waqfs**, facilitating the development of a sophisticated religious and academic class in these urban centers. Cairo, in particular, attracted scholars from all over the world to its acclaimed schools.

The Mamluk state flourished as the undisputed military power of the central Muslim world until the mid-1400s. But the Mamluk economy never fully recovered from the famines and plagues it had suffered earlier. The sultanate implemented short-term measures to recover the state's former glory, but the Mamluks were unable to deter the formidable military threat of the Ottoman Empire*. In 1516 the Ottoman ruler Selim I defeated the Mamluks at the battle of Marj Dabiq in Syria. Cairo fell to Selim the following year. This military campaign ended Mamluk rule, but the Ottoman monarch permitted some of the Mamluks to remain in power. He appointed Mamluks as governors over various provinces and allowed them to maintain their private armies. In fact, when Napoleon Bonaparte's troops invaded Egypt in 1798, they fought Mamluk soldiers. Mamluk power did not completely end until 1811, when Muhammad Ali Pasha took control of Egypt and killed the Mamluk leaders. (*See also* **Egypt; Ottoman Empire.**)

* **caliphate** office and government of the caliph, the religious and political leader of an Islamic state

* **crusader** person who participated in the holy wars against the Muslims during the Middle Ages

* **Black Death** refers to the disease that killed millions of people in Europe and the Middle East in the mid-1300s

* **Sunni** refers to the largest branch of the Muslim community; the name derives from sunnah, the exemplary behavior of the Prophet Muhammad

* *waqf* donation of property for charitable causes

* **Ottoman Empire** large Turkish state existing from the early 1300s to the early 1900s

Markets

See *Bazaar.*

Marriage

* **Qur'an** book of the holy scriptures of Islam

* **chastity** purity in conduct and intention; also, abstention from sexual intercourse

* **sunnah** literally "the trodden path"; Islamic customs based on the exemplary behavior of Muhammad

For Muslims, marriage is essentially a religious duty. The Qur'an* notes that Allah created men and women to be companions for each another and to produce children. In addition, marriage is believed to guard against sexual temptation and to be a means of ensuring chastity*. Although Islam permits divorce under certain circumstances, the Qur'an and sunnah* emphasize the seriousness of divorce and view it as a last resort.

In Islamic culture, marriage is an important religious duty. This wedding celebration in Kurdistan—unlike in some Muslim countries— includes both men and women.

* **polygyny** practice of having more than one wife at the same time

Living in Harmony. Before the rise of Islam in the early 600s, Arabs lived in a traditional, patriarchal (male-dominated) society. Women were considered to be property, and no limitations on polygyny* existed. Islam brought some reforms, particularly with regard to the status of women. The Qur'an recognized a woman's right to choose her own marriage partner, and it set limits on the practice of polygyny. A man could have as many as four wives, if he could provide for and treat them equally.

Islam characterizes the relationship between a husband and a wife as complementary. The husband's primary responsibility is to support and protect the family. The wife cares for and disciplines the children and maintains the home. Although Islamic law teaches that the husband and wife are equal before God, women are subordinate to men. According to the Qur'an, rights are proportional to responsibilities, and men are regarded as having greater responsibilities outside the home. Nevertheless, the Qur'an counsels spouses to honor a bond of mutual "love and mercy" in their marriage and encourages them to "dwell in tranquility."

Drawing Up the Contract. Issues affecting the family, including marriage, divorce, and inheritance, became central to Islamic law, which developed in the 700s and 800s. Based on Qur'anic principles, family law has generally remained in force through the centuries. Nevertheless, interpretation of the law and practices vary significantly from one Muslim country to another.

* **monotheism** belief that there is only one God

* **scripture** sacred writings that contain revelations from God

Marriage is a contract between a man and a woman or between a man and a woman's legal guardian (*wali*), who is always a male and usually her father. Islamic law requires four conditions for a valid marriage—an offer, an acceptance, a minimum of two competent Muslim witnesses, and a marriage gift. The law prohibits certain categories of marriage partners, such as the marriage of close relatives. Some regulations reflect concerns about the faith of the future children. Although the husband is the head of the household, the children spend most of their time with the mother, and therefore, they are likely to adopt her religion. A Muslim man may marry a woman who practices Judaism or Christianity, because these religions are based on monotheism* and divine revelation as recorded in scripture*. The law forbids marriage between a Muslim woman and a non-Muslim man, however, because the man assumes responsibility for the religious instruction of the older children.

Traditionally, Muslim families arrange marriages. The mother seeks suitable wives for her sons. Once a potential bride is chosen, her legal guardian assumes responsibility for the arranging of the marriage contract. Despite the Qur'an's prohibition of forced marriages, traditional Islamic law allows a father to force his daughter to marry a man of his choice without her knowledge or permission, and he can refuse to allow her to marry at all. In practice, parents usually ask their daughter whether she agrees with their choice of spouse. Moreover, most Muslim countries have passed laws to prevent the guardian from compelling his daughter to marry. In addition, modern lifestyles are replacing the traditional custom of arranged marriages, as men and women meet their future mates through mutual friends, contact at the workplace or university, or while traveling.

The marriage contract usually sets the *mahr*, an amount of money or property that the prospective husband must pledge to legally validate the marriage. Some men agree to pay the *mahr* in two parts, half at the time of the marriage and the other half in the event of divorce or their death. Ideally and by law the *mahr* is intended as a gift from the groom to the bride for her to use as she sees fit. In practice, however, some families take the *mahr*, and some husbands reserve it for their own use.

* **pre-Islamic** refers to the Arabian Peninsula or to the Arabic language before the founding of Islam in the early 600s

* **Sunni** refers to the largest branch of the Muslim community; the name derives from sunnah, the exemplary behavior of the Prophet Muhammad

* **Shi'i** refers to Muslims who believe that Muhammad chose Ali ibn Abi Talib and his descendants as the spiritual-political leaders of the Muslim community

Spouse for a Day. Muhammad reportedly recommended the pre-Islamic* practice of temporary marriage, or *mutah*, to his soldiers and companions. Soon after the Prophet's death, however, Sunni* Muslims rejected the custom. Shi'i* law, by contrast, still permits temporary marriages.

A *mutah* is usually associated with a private, verbal contract between a man and an unmarried woman, whether she has never been married, is divorced, or widowed. The parties must specify the length of time—whether one hour, one year, or 99 years—that the marriage will last. In addition, the contract must indicate an amount of money to which the woman is entitled. A man may enter as many temporary marriages as he desires without jeopardizing his right to have as many as four wives. A Shi'i Muslim woman, by contrast, is permitted only one temporary marriage at a time. A single woman may arrange a *mutah*, but only with her father's permission.

The Islamic government of Iran actively promotes temporary marriages, known as *sigheh*. During the Iran-Iraq war of the 1980s, the government encouraged *sigheh* for war widows as a way for them to obtain companionship and financial support. Today Iranian clerics and government leaders continue to endorse temporary marriage as an acceptable alternative to sexually promiscuous behavior, especially among young people who cannot yet afford marriage. Despite the official approval of *sigheh*, the practice remains very controversial. Many Iranians regard temporary marriage with ambivalence, and some consider it to be little more than legalized prostitution.

Although some Muslims hope that *sigheh* will liberalize sexual attitudes in Iran, women who engage in the practice face negative consequences. The fact that a woman has entered into a *sigheh* means that she is no longer a virgin, and this can hurt her future marriage prospects. Although some young couples enter temporary marriages, *sigheh* usually occurs between older men and divorced women.

Attempts at Reform. The formulation of marriage and divorce laws in the contemporary Middle East is part of an ongoing debate that has persisted since the late 1800s. During the period of colonial rule, some Westerners identified the inferior status of Muslim women under Islamic law as the central cause of poverty and backwardness of Muslim society. Muslim reformers held similar views. Egyptian Muhammad Abduh (1849–1905) argued that a Muslim man's unrestricted right to polygyny and divorce created an unstable environment in which to raise children. Another Egyptian reformer, Qasim Amin (1865–1908), believed that women's rights were central to progress and favored reforms in marriage laws. Feminist writer Malak Hifni Nasif (1886–1918) denounced polygyny, early marriage for girls, and the custom of marriage between older men and young girls. Even the Muslim Brotherhood, founded as a movement to reassert religious tradition and resist British occupation, sought reform in marriage and divorce laws.

During the 1900s, some Muslim governments passed legislation that introduced changes to family law. For example, the Tunisian Code of Personal Status, enacted in 1956, established a minimum age for marriage, abolished polygyny and the right of guardians to contract marriage without the woman's consent, and imposed conditions on a husband's right to divorce. In general, however, modern legislation regarding marriage and divorce has done little to correct the inequalities in Islamic family law in traditional societies. Moreover, Islamic political movements have worked to limit further reforms in family law by insisting on strict application of *shari'ah**. They associate the desire for changes to Islamic family law with Western values and cultural imperialism*. With the resurgence of revivalism, those who want to liberalize the law run the risk of being labeled infidels*. (*See also* **Divorce; Family; Law; Women and Reform.**)

Henna and Money Hats

Wedding ceremonies in the Muslim world incorporate a rich array of local traditions. Among the Bedouin, a nomadic desert people, a traditional wedding lasts for an entire week. First, the fathers of the bride and groom meet to make formal arrangements. Before the wedding, friends of the bride apply henna, a reddish brown dye, to her hands and feet in elaborate patterns that symbolize beauty, luck, and health. Music, songs, and dance follow. Men and women enjoy the celebration in separate areas. In fact, the bride and groom do not set eyes on each other until the ceremony is over. In most regions, the bride and groom wear special wedding garments. During the mid-1800s, brides from the villages of Palestine wore a headdress embellished with hundreds of coins and strings of colored beads. In some villages, the "money hat" was shared by brides who borrowed it for their weddings.

* *shari'ah* Islamic law as established in the Qur'an and sunnah, the exemplary behavior of the Prophet Muhammad

* *imperialism* extension of power and influence over another country or region

* *infidel* unbeliever; person who does not accept a particular faith

Martyrdom

Islam grants a special status to those who lose or sacrifice their lives in the service of their religion. Such a person is a martyr, or *shahid*, the Arabic term for "witness." To die in defense of Islam is considered the highest form of witness of faith in God.

Martyrdom

A mural on a street in Tehran, Iran, pays homage to those who died for their country. In Islam, to die as a martyr in the defense of religion or country is a great honor.

* **Qur'an** book of the holy scriptures of Islam

* **scripture** sacred writings that contain revelations from God

* **hadith** reports of the words and deeds of Muhammad (not in the Qur'an, but accepted as guides for Muslim behavior)

The Qur'an* contains many passages that honor martyrs. It states: "Whosoever obeys God, and the Messenger—they are with those whom God has blessed. Prophets, just men, martyrs, the righteous; good companions they!" Scripture* teaches the virtue of martyrdom: "Say not of those who die in the path of God that they are dead. Nay rather they live." Moreover, according to the hadith*, the Prophet Muhammad clearly indicated his support of martyrs. Like other major religious traditions of the world, Islam admires self-sacrifice for a higher moral, ethical, or spiritual idea or cause.

The Promise of Reward. In Islamic teaching, a martyr's motives must be religious. In the hadith, the Prophet noted: "Whosoever partakes of the battle from desire of glory, or in order to show his courage, is no martyr." Instead, "a martyr is only he who fights in order that Allah's Word may be prevalent." Islam also makes an important distinction between suicide and martyrdom. Muslims are forbidden to commit suicide. According to tradition, the punishment for such a deed is the unending repetition of the act by which the individual took his or her life.

The theme of martyrdom is closely associated with the theme of rewards in the afterlife, which are elaborated in popular traditions. Unlike ordinary Muslims, after they die martyrs do not have to undergo the intimidating review of their deeds by the angels Munkar and Nakir. A martyr proceeds directly to the highest station in paradise, near the throne of God. According to some Muslim traditions, martyrs are so devoted to their faith that they would leave the bliss of paradise and return to earth so that they may be martyred again—up to ten times.

Different Set of Qualifications. The religious leaders of Sunni* Islam traditionally discouraged the deliberate pursuit of martyrdom, which they considered equivalent to suicide. Sunni scholars taught that a life of good deeds was equal to or even preferable to martyrdom. Individuals who performed acts of worship, prayer, and charity could qualify for the status of martyr, depending on how perfect and pure their motives were when they performed such acts. Indeed, Sunni theologian Abu Hamid al-Ghazali (died 1111) wrote: "Every one who gives himself wholly to God in the war against his own desires, is a martyr when he meets death going forward without turning back. So the holy warrior is he who makes war against his own desires, as it has been explained by the apostle of God." In addition, collections of hadith identify several types of death that confer martyr status. These include death in an epidemic, by drowning, by fire, and in childbirth.

Despite Sunni opposition to the idea of dying to become a martyr, scholars respected the jihad* of the early community at Medina against their Arab opponents in Mecca. Moreover, Sunnis recognize the early martyrs of Islam. In general, Sunni tradition values martyrdom less as a means of individual salvation or happiness in the afterlife than as a way for individuals to defend the Muslim community.

The Burial Site. The ideal of martyrdom is a vital element of belief for Shi'i* Muslims. Twelvers, the largest subgroup of Shi'i Muslims, recognize a long list of martyrs, beginning with Abel (the son of Adam and Eve who was killed by his brother Cain) and including Muhammad and eleven of the twelve imams*. The first imam, Ali ibn Abi Talib, was murdered, and each of his successors suffered persecution or death at the hands of a caliph* or the caliph's supporters.

Shi'is make annual pilgrimages to *mashhads*, the gravesites of notable martyrs, especially the imams. They believe that their devotion to the imams will grant them forgiveness of their sins, and they also regard the shrines as places where they can share in the holiness of the imams. Weeping for the martyrs has special religious value, as does enduring the same type of suffering that the martyrs experienced, such as extreme thirst and hunger.

Of all the imams, Husayn ibn Ali is considered one of the most important. He not only suffered the torments of thirst and hunger in the desert, but he also was slaughtered in an ambush by his enemies at Karbala (in

* **Sunni** refers to the largest branch of the Muslim community; the name derives from sunnah, the exemplary behavior of the Prophet Muhammad

* **jihad** literally "striving"; war in defense of Islam

* **Shi'i** refers to Muslims who believe that Muhammad chose Ali ibn Abi Talib and his descendants as the spiritual-political leaders of the Muslim community

* **imam** spiritual leader in Shi'i Islam, one who is regarded as directly descended from Muhammad; also, one who leads prayers

* **caliph** religious and political leader of an Islamic state

present-day Iraq). His tomb was probably the first *mashhad*. The tombs of other imams are also regarded as important holy sites.

Various Muslim rulers donated great riches to expand and decorate the *mashhads* of the imams. Towns and cities grew up around the *mashhads*. In addition, the sites have become centers of Shi'i learning, and Muslims have established important *madrasahs* (colleges for higher studies) nearby. Many Shi'is seek their final resting place in the holy surroundings of the beloved imams, as demonstrated by the growth of large cemeteries at all the *mashhads*.

A New Understanding. Beginning in the 1700s and 1800s, much of the Muslim world came under colonial rule. Muslim soldiers who died in wars of independence were referred to as martyrs, leading to a new understanding of martyrdom.

Since the late 1900s, Muslims have identified all struggles in defense of Islamic land as jihad, and those who lose their lives in such a struggle as martyrs. In the war between Iran and Iraq during the 1980s, for example, both Sunni Iraqi leaders and Shi'i Iranians relied heavily on the ideal of martyrdom to motivate their troops. Iranians created martyr cemeteries for soldiers who died in the conflict and for the clergy and others who died during the 1979 revolution.

By the beginning of the twenty-first century, martyrdom had taken on controversial dimensions as Islamic extremists introduced the use of suicide bombing against civilian targets, particularly in Israel, but also in the United States and elsewhere. Instead of merely dying for their faith, these martyrs use their deaths to kill as many of their enemies as possible. Critics condemn this practice as terrorism* and argue that the perpetrators of such acts violate the teachings of Islam and are not martyrs. Those who support such actions, however, believe that the self-sacrifice of suicide bombers honors the faith and is a necessary form of resistance to the oppression of the Islamic community.

Although most suicide bombers are young single men, teenagers have begun to volunteer for these missions. The practice of recruiting adolescents and children as Islamic martyrs has aroused widespread criticism. Even so, between 70 and 80 percent of Palestinians continue to support suicide bombing as a tactic against Israeli occupation of the West Bank and Gaza Strip. (*See also* **Afterlife; Arab-Israeli Conflict; Karbala and Najaf; Shrine; Suicide; Terrorism.**)

* **terrorism** use of violence against people, property, or states as a means of intimidation for political purposes

Maryam Jameelah

1934–
Islamic revivalist

* **revivalist** calling for the return to traditional values or beliefs

Born Margaret Marcus to a Jewish family in New Rochelle, New York, Maryam Jameelah became a unique voice in the Islamic revivalist* movement. She grew up in a nonreligious household but developed a keen interest in spiritual matters. While attending New York University, she began to explore different faiths. Disappointed with what she considered the hypocrisy of most religions, she became attracted to Islam. Jameelah was especially inspired by two books—*The Road to Mecca* and *Islam at Crossroads*—by Muhammad Asad, a Jewish convert to Islam.

To the disapproval of her family and friends, Jameelah officially converted to Islam in 1961. Soon after, she began to write for the *Muslim Digest* of Durban, South Africa. Jameelah debated with critics of Islam, and sought to express Islam's pure nature. Her work brought her into contact with the writings of Mawlana Sayyid Abu al-Ala Mawdudi (died 1979), founder and leader of the Jamaat-i Islami (Islamic Party) of Pakistan. The two began a correspondence, discussing issues related to Islam and to Jameelah's conflicts with her family. (These letters were published in 1986.) Mawdudi urged Jameelah to move to Pakistan to live among Muslims. In 1962 Jameelah traveled to Pakistan, settling in Lahore and becoming a member of Mawdudi's household. She married Jamaat-i Islami member Muhammad Yusuf Khan, becoming his second wife.

While in Lahore, Jameelah continued to write and to promote the work of Jamaat-i Islami. Much of her writing focuses on perceived differences between Western and Islamic values. Critics claim that she uses isolated incidents of moral wrongdoing to condemn the West. Jameelah's work, however, has helped develop revivalist thought in some countries.

Jameelah elaborated on her views in an open letter to her parents, published in 1986. In it, she tells her parents that they live in a collapsing society and that the lack of a strict moral code has led to widespread divorce, pollution, substance abuse, and other problems. Islam provides joy, she wrote, because it is based on absolute truth. Americans and Europeans place too much emphasis on science, which makes mistakes and therefore does not serve as a proper foundation for human society.

Maryam Jameelah continues to live and work in Lahore. She has written several books, including *Is Western Civilization Universal?*, *A Manifesto of the Islamic Movement*, and *Islam and Orientalism*. (*See also* **Women and Reform.**)

See *Mosque*.

Masjid

Mathematics

Muslim scholars have made invaluable contributions to the study of mathematics, and the Islamic world served as the center of scientific learning throughout the Middle Ages*. Until around the 1100s, Europeans relied on basic Roman systems to calculate measurements and conduct business. Muslims, however, made efforts to acquire the knowledge of the ancients. In the 700s, wealthy Muslims hired scholars to translate Greek, Indian, and Persian works into Arabic. Mathematicians were especially influenced by the Greek writings that treated mathematics not only as a practical discipline, but also as a philosophy. They studied and developed several fields, including arithmetic*, algebra*, geometry*, optics, music, and astronomy*.

Arithmetic. Muslim mathematicians made their first advances in the field of arithmetic. The people of ancient Mesopotamia relied mainly on three

* **Middle Ages** period roughly between 500 and 1500

* **arithmetic** mathematical branch that involves the computation of real numbers

* **algebra** branch of mathematics in which letters representing unknown numbers are combined in accordance with the rules of arithmetic

* **geometry** branch of mathematics that includes the measurement of solids, surfaces, angles, lines, and points

* **astronomy** study of celestial bodies

Mathematics

* **abacus** device for making arithmetic calculations, consisting of a frame and rows of beads or counters that slide back and forth

tools for mathematical calculations—the abacus*, finger reckoning (counting), and a system involving letters created by the Babylonians. Scribes and secretaries used finger reckoning to work with simple sums. The abacus helped with addition, subtraction, multiplication, and division. Used for astronomy, the Babylonian letter system involved sexagesimals, or figures based on the number 60. The Babylonians used letters to symbolize certain amounts and created astronomical and time tables based on their calculations. The 24-hour day, 60-minute hour, and 60-second minute have their roots in this system, as does the study of angles and arcs.

In the 800s and 900s, Muslim scholars produced works that dramatically changed the practice of arithmetic. Muhammad ibn Musa al-Khwarizmi, for example, studied Indian mathematics and adapted its concepts in his work. He created the numerical system that we use today: Arabic numerals, number groups based on units of ten, and the numbers one through nine. He used the Indian zero to indicate the absence of a number. Al-Khwarizmi's work inspired Europeans to adopt Hindu-Arabic numerals instead of the more unwieldy Latin ones. In the 900s, Abu al-Hasan al-Uqlidisi developed a decimal system that included fractions and a decimal point. He also completed the first successful treatment of the cube root.

Other Muslim scholars also contributed to the study of arithmetic. In addition to preserving systems used by the ancient Greeks, Hindus, and Babylonians, they developed algorithms* (the name taken from a Latinized version of al-Khwarizmi's name), along with operations involving irrational numbers (numbers that cannot be expressed as fractions) and root extraction (determining the numbers that equal a certain number when multiplied by themselves a specified number of times). In the mid-800s, Thabit ibn Qurrah formulated a rule for finding amicable numbers, a pair of digits in which each represents the sum of the divisors of the other.

Algebra. Al-Khwarizmi made some of his most important contributions to the study of algebra, a word stemming from the Islamic *al-jabr* (operation). He developed elaborate systems for determining unknown quantities (variables) from known ones. He provided formulas for solving different types of equations, attempting to create a theory for the solution of all problems. His work had a large impact on Muslim and European mathematical theory. Other scholars made further advances, working with expressions involving powers of the unknown, coefficients (numbers multiplied with an unknown quantity), polynomials (certain equations consisting of one or more terms), congruence (in which two numbers equal each other), and decimal fractions.

The Persian mathematician and poet Umar Khayyam (1048–1131) made some notable discoveries, forming a broader system of numbers than that used by the Greeks. Later scholars wrongly attributed many of his ideas to the French mathematician and philosopher Rene Descartes. Sharaf al Din al Tusi, another scholar whose work Europeans mistakenly attributed to their own, developed rules to help determine the positive roots of arbitrary equations. Al-Tusi introduced a new discipline—algebraic geometry—that relies on equations to study curves. Other Muslims used geometry to explain algebraic procedures, and vice versa.

Algebra had many practical uses in the early Islamic world. It aided Muslims in the distribution of inheritance, a process governed by complex laws. Merchants and surveyors also used algebra to chart areas and make navigational decisions. Muslims in certain fields used the discipline for unorthodox purposes—one scholar determined all the possible Arabic words that could be created with a maximum of five letters and assembled a compilation of all valid selections.

Geometry. To Muslim scholars, the Greek mathematician Euclid served as the primary authority on the subject of geometry. Khayyam had thoroughly studied Euclid's writings, criticizing and expanding them. He pioneered the use of conic equations (equations dealing with cones or conic sections) to solve cubic equations (equations dealing with cube roots), as well as the use of curves and geometric figures in certain equations. Other Muslim scholars focused on conic sections, determining the area and volume of flat and three-dimensional figures and studying the properties of mirrors made from conical parts. Muslim mathematicians also developed non-Euclidean theorems, influencing Europeans in their creation of non-Euclidean geometry.

Geometry had many practical uses in the Muslim world. Ibn Qurrah and Ibrahim ibn Sinan used it to design curves for sundials. Geographers applied geometric laws in determining the latitude and longitude of specific places,

* **algorithm** set procedure for solving a mathematical problem

Powerful Patrons

Mathematicians in the Islamic world benefited from the patronage of the nobility and ruling classes. In the early 800s, the Abbasid caliph al-Mamun built a translation and research facility in Baghdad. Called the House of Wisdom, this center greatly advanced the pursuit of mathematical knowledge. Wealthy individuals, such as the Banu Musa—three brothers who wrote influential treatises on mechanics and geometry—also patronized scholars. Even the Mongols promoted academics in the Islamic lands that they conquered. They built observatories and supported the work of mathematicians. The Mongol leader Ulugh Beg made great advances in trigonometry in the 1400s.

the distance between cities, and the direction from one city to another. Medieval artisans* and astronomers also benefited from advances in geometry.

Optics. Muslim scholars made their most significant contributions to mathematics in the field of optics. The mathematician Ibn al-Haytham overturned the Greek belief that vision arises from contact between the eye and an object. He stated that the eye does not sense an object directly, but light reflected from the object forms an image that the eye perceives. Al-Haytham wrote seven highly influential books on his theories. Subjects covered by al-Haytham and other Islamic mathematicians include the study of vision, the reflection of rays on mirrors, the burning of mirrors and lenses, and the creation of atmospheric phenomena such as rainbows. In the late 900s, the Muslim scholar Abu ibn Sahl completed a study on lenses, exploring different types of curves and the geometrical methods that one could use to draw them. One of his discoveries is referred to in Western countries as the law of Snellius, after the European who drew the same conclusion in 1621. Another Muslim scholar, Kamal al-Din al-Farisi, explained the occurrence of rainbows by analyzing the properties of a glass filled with water.

Astronomy. Muslim astronomers gained knowledge from a wide variety of sources, including Babylonian, Indian, and Persian texts. They studied star movements, created instruments and tables to chart the motions of heavenly bodies, and sometimes practiced astrology*, although the two fields diverged during the Middle Ages. Many of the other mathematical fields developed to accommodate the needs of astronomers, especially trigonometry*. Scholars worked to understand the rotation of the seasons, the movements and position of the planets, the location and size of constellations, and how to navigate by charting celestial bodies. The desire to make astrological predictions also drove scholars to study the heavens. Many, however, denounced astrology and separated themselves from the field.

The Greek-Egyptian mathematician Ptolemy served as the most influential of the ancient astronomers. Muslim scholars immersed themselves in his works. Al-Khwarizmi used both Ptolemaic and Indian sources to create the first original Arabic text on astronomy. He drew up tables for the movements of the sun, moon, and planets. Other Muslim scholars noted flaws in ancient texts and developed non-Ptolemaic models, combining different astronomical traditions to form new approaches. Observatories sprung up in major Islamic cities, including Baghdad, Cairo, and Damascus.

For medieval Muslims, astronomy served many purposes. Al-Khwarizmi calculated the new moon's time of visibility, which helped Muslims to devise a calendar based on monthly cycles. Muslim astronomers also formulated methods for locating the direction of Mecca, enabling architects to build mosques facing the holy city and to indicate which direction Muslims should face while praying. Al-Tusi invented the linear astrolabe*, an improvement on an earlier instrument used by ancient sailors. This device, sometimes the size of a pocket watch, enabled astronomers to determine the position of the sun and other stars in relation to the horizon. Other Muslims produced plane projections of spheres, allowing for the creation of maps of the hemispheres. In the 1300s, the Syrian scholar Ibn al-Shatir created an astrolabe that that could solve all problems of spherical astronomy in five different ways.

Islamic Math in Europe. Before the 1100s, Europeans had a limited understanding of the mathematical sciences. They relied on cumbersome Latin methods until scholars translated Muslim works into Latin. These texts enabled Europeans to radically expand their mathematical capabilities. By the 1500s, the center of math research had shifted from the Islamic world to Europe. Muslims, however, had greatly enriched the fields of algebra, geometry, optics, and astronomy, and their translations of Greek, Persian, and Indian texts preserved the knowledge of ancient scholars. Recent discoveries of untranslated Muslim works hold the promise of further mathematical discoveries. (*See also* **Astronomy; Khayyam, Umar; Music; Numerology.**)

Mawdudi, Sayyid Abu al-Ala

1903–1979
Islamic thinker and activist

One of the most influential figures in the revivalist* movement, Sayyid Abu al-Ala Mawdudi interpreted Islam as a vehicle that would transform society and politics. As the founder and leader of Jamaat-i Islami (the Islamic Party) for more than 30 years and the author of an impressive number of articles and books, Mawdudi has inspired thinkers and activists throughout the Muslim world. His influence is evident in the ideas of Egyptian activist Sayyid Qutb (1906–1966).

* **revivalist** calling for the return of traditional values or beliefs

Sayyid Abu al-Ala Mawdudi was born in Aurangabad, India, and raised in a devout Muslim family. His ancestors played a prominent role in the conversion of many Indians to Islam. Mawdudi's father provided his children with a traditional education, which included Arabic, Urdu, and religious texts. Mawdudi later studied a more modern curriculum at a local *madrasah* (college for higher studies).

As a teenager, Mawdudi exhibited a keen interest in writing and politics, and he focused on the issue of India's independence from Great Britain. In 1919 he joined the Khilafat movement, which sought to influence the British government to preserve the authority of the Turkish ruler as caliph*. During the early 1920s, Mawdudi increased his knowledge of Muslim political thought. He also learned English, read Western books, and pursued a formal religious education, gaining recognition as a major Islamic intellectual.

* **caliph** religious and political leader of an Islamic state

In 1924 the Turkish government abolished the caliphate. Mawdudi became convinced that the decline of Muslim power stemmed from the corruption of Islam by other cultures and that Muslims could restore their community by re-establishing Islamic institutions and practices. To purify Islam, Indian Muslims would have to sever their cultural, social, and political ties with Hindus*.

Mawdudi advocated an Islamic state governed by true believers who base their rule on the Qur'an* and sunnah*. He believed that God alone should have total sovereignty in the state. Moreover, the government should enforce Islamic moral order in the state's legal, political, and economic affairs. With this agenda, Mawdudi recast the meaning of Islam so that social action became a requirement for faithful Muslims, and religion itself became the vehicle of social action. Despite his radical* ideas, Mawdudi advocated

* **Hindu** refers to the beliefs and practices of Hinduism, an ancient religion that originated in India

* **Qur'an** book of the holy scriptures of Islam

* **sunnah** literally "the trodden path"; Islamic customs based on the exemplary behavior of Muhammad

* **radical** favoring extreme change or reform, especially in existing political and social institutions

a moderate approach and he condemned the use of violence. He believed that social change would result from gradually taking over the centers of political power, not from mobilizing the masses to topple the existing political order.

During the late 1930s, Mawdudi became intensely involved in politics, particularly the struggle for Indian independence. Despite his call for cultural purity, Mawdudi did not support the Muslim League's efforts to create a separate Muslim state in India. He characterized the league's work as too secular*. To advance his own religious political agenda, Mawdudi founded the Jamaat-i Islami in 1941. After Britain partitioned India in 1947, Mawdudi campaigned to base Pakistan's laws on traditional Islamic interpretation. He rejected efforts to modernize Islamic laws as anti-religious. Pakistan's leaders identified him as an enemy of the state and imprisoned him several times from 1948 to 1967. During the last decade of his life, Mawdudi focused on writing. He died in 1979. (*See also* **India; Islamic State; Pakistan; Qutb, Sayyid.**)

* **secular** separate from religion in human life and society; connected to everyday life

Mawlawiyah

* **Sufi** refers to Sufism, which seeks to develop spirituality through discipline of the mind and body

The Turkish Sufi* order known as the Mawlawiyah was founded in the 1200s, in Anatolia. The order is also known by its Turkish name—Mevlevi—and as whirling dervishes, reflecting their distinctive style of vigorous dancing during meditation rituals.

Following Rumi. Jalal al-Din Rumi, the founder of the Mawlawi order, was known to his followers as Mawlana (Mevlana in Turkish), meaning "Our Master." Rumi was born in 1207 the city of Balkh in what is now Afghanistan. His father, Baha Walad, was a religious scholar and Sufi master. When Rumi was a boy, his family settled in the Seljuk capital of Konya (in present-day Turkey). Baha Walad was a respected legal scholar and preacher, and Rumi inherited his father's appointments after Baha Walad died.

Rumi studied Sufism under his father's former disciple, Burhan al-Din al-Tirmidhi. Rumi prospered in his career as a legal scholar and judge, but a wandering mystic* named Shams-i Tabrizi attracted his attention in 1244. Rumi believed the mystic would lead him to a deeper knowledge of God, but Rumi's family and students became jealous of his devotion to Shams. After several years, the wandering mystic disappeared. Some scholars believe that Rumi's students probably murdered him with the knowledge and consent of both Rumi's son and his principle disciple.

Following the disappearance of his spiritual mentor, Rumi withdrew from public life and dedicated himself to guiding his Sufi disciples and writing poetry. His poetry inspired generations of Sufis seeking mystical inspiration. The Mawlawi order adopted Rumi's 26,000-verse work, the *Masnavi*, as its primary mystical text.

Salah al-din Zarkub, a fellow disciple of Burhan al-Din al-Tirmidhi, led the order immediately after Rumi's death. Husam al-Din became the third Mawlawi leader, and Rumi's son Sultan Walad was next in succession. Since Walad's death, a descendant of Rumi has almost always headed the Mawlawiyah.

* **mystic** one who seeks to experience spiritual enlightenment and truth through various physical and spiritual disciplines

Distinctive Rituals. The Mawlawi order is known for two important ceremonies. The first is a lengthy orientation process to initiate new members. The *sama* (audition) ritual is another distinctive feature of the Mawlawi order. This meditation ritual traces its roots to Rumi, with new elements added by his descendants.

See color plate 11, vol. 3.

The *sama* takes place in a circular room with a wood floor. The room is generally surrounded by galleries for guests and a separate one for musicians. A Sufi leader summons participants to ritual prayers, after which they listen to hymns and readings from the *Masnavi*, accompanied by music. In the next phase, musicians beat a simple rhythm while the participants and the ritual leader walk in a circle, performing a complex series of bows and salutes. In the final phase, the participants perform a ritual dance consisting of several cycles. Using their left foot as a pivot, the participants whirl in a counterclockwise direction with their right palm facing up and their left palm facing down.

The dance is a devotional practice that has important mystical meaning for the Mawlawiyah. It is part of a quest for a direct spiritual experience of God. The upturned right hand symbolizes receipt of divine grace. The downturned left hand represents God's blessings being passed to humanity. The entire ritual simulates the order of the universe.

Lasting Influence. For more than 700 years, the Mawlawiyah emphasized the importance of the arts and greatly influenced the development of Ottoman culture. Mawlawi followers produced significant works of art, music, and poetry. Ottoman sultans* included members of the order in their courts.

* **sultan** political and military ruler of a Muslim dynasty or state

Mawlawi influence was especially strong in Turkey and in cities with large Turkish populations. The order's influence declined after 1925, when Turkey dissolved all Sufi brotherhoods. Although weakened, the Mawlawiyah survived in scattered communities throughout Turkey, the Middle East, and Europe. In the 1990s, Mawlawi leaders sought to revive the Sufi order in North America. In the Middle East and Turkey, Rumi remains a revered figure as both a spiritual leader and a poet whose works are enjoying a revival. Scores of admirers visit his tomb in Konya each year. (*See also* **Literature; Rumi; Sufism.**)

Mawlid

See *Muhammad, Birthday of*.

Mecca

Located in the Sirat Mountains of western Saudi Arabia, the city of Mecca is the holiest place in the Islamic world. The Prophet Muhammad was born in Mecca, and it is the site of the Kaaba* and the destination of the annual Muslim pilgrimage. Every Muslim who is able, both physically and financially, must make a pilgrimage to Mecca once in his or her lifetime. Furthermore, tradition dictates that Muslims must face Mecca during their daily prayers.

* **Kaaba** literally "House of God;" Islamic shrine in Mecca

See color plate 1, vol. 1.

* **polytheistic** believing in several gods

* **monotheism** belief that there is only one God

* **hajj** pilgrimage to Mecca that Muslims are required to make once in their lifetime

* **sultan** political and military ruler of a Muslim dynasty or state

* **medieval** refers to the Middle Ages, a period roughly between 500 and 1500

In the late 500s, Mecca was a major center of trade and commerce as well as the site of the Kaaba, a religious shrine that housed hundreds of gods and goddesses worshipped by the tribes in the region. A small group from within the Quraysh tribe controlled the political and economic affairs of the city. Born around 570, Muhammad prospered as a merchant in the caravan trade of Mecca. After Muhammad received a calling to become a prophet of God, he began to preach against the polytheistic* practices of the people and against the inequality between the wealthy elite and the poverty-stricken masses. Muhammad's claim to be a prophet challenged the authority of the ruling class, and his emphasis on monotheism* threatened to wipe out the city's profits from religious pilgrimages. As a result, the Meccans actively persecuted him and his followers. In 622 Muhammad and his followers emigrated to Medina.

While in Medina, Muhammad received revelations indicating that Mecca should be the direction (*qibla*) for prayer and the site of the hajj*. In response to attacks on his followers and their families, Muhammad initiated a series of battles against the Meccans. In 630 the Prophet Muhammad established Muslim authority in Mecca. He cleansed the Kaaba of its idols and reinstated the "religion of Abraham" to the city.

Because the trade routes of the new Islamic empire did not pass through western Arabia, Mecca lost much of its commercial importance. Closed to non-Muslims, the city's chief sources of income included donations, gifts to the shrine and its overseers, and the hajj. Control of the city returned to the local aristocracy, the *sharifs*, men who could claim to be descended from the Prophet through his daughter Fatimah and her husband Ali ibn Abi Talib.

In 1250 the Mamluk sultans* of Egypt seized control of the region. Mecca regained some commercial importance and wealth, as trade through the Red Sea developed between India and the East and the countries of the Mediterranean region. In 1517 the Ottoman Turks gained authority over Islam's holy land. During World War I (1914–1918), the Ottomans joined Germany in the fight against the Allied Powers (France, Great Britain, Russia, Italy, Japan, and later, the United States). Supported by the British, Sharif Husayn ibn Ali led an armed revolt against the Turks in 1916. Mecca soon fell to Husayn's forces, and he proclaimed himself king of western Arabia. Husayn ibn Ali retained the throne until 1926, when Mecca became part of the kingdom of Saudi Arabia.

In 1926 Mecca still looked like a medieval* town of narrow streets and crumbling buildings. During the 1950s, the Saudis enlarged the mosque and improved the pilgrimage facilities, and Mecca experienced rapid growth. Today Mecca is a modern city, although it is still transformed annually by the pilgrimage, which attracts millions of Muslims from all over the world. (*See also* **Hajj; Kaaba; Medina.**)

Medicine

* **Qur'an** book of the holy scriptures of Islam
* **hadith** reports of the words and deeds of Muhammad (not in the Qur'an, but accepted as guides for Muslim behavior)

Medicine in the Islamic world has undergone many changes since the time of Muhammad. In the early Islamic world, doctors relied mainly on three sources—the Qur'an* and the hadith*, folk remedies, and the writings of Greek physicians. Colonization altered Islamic medicine as Europeans brought

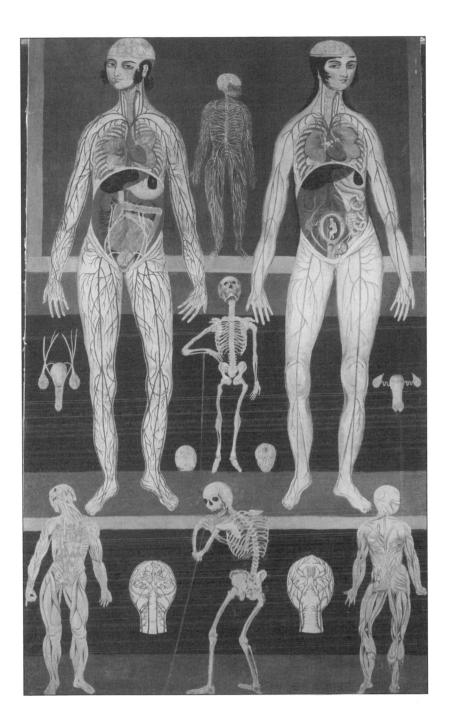

Early Islamic scholars praised the study of the body, which they saw as a way to reveal God's design. These illustrations of the human body appeared in a Persian anatomical study from the 1800s.

See color plate 13, vol. 3.

their own methods of healing to Muslim regions. Islamic doctors learned these new practices and adapted them according to religious doctrine. In the twenty-first century, Muslim health professionals struggle to balance Western techniques with Islamic traditions.

Healing in the Early Islamic World

In the early Islamic Middle East, cures for common disorders relied mainly on pre-Islamic* traditions. As in Europe, bloodletting and cupping (drawing blood to the surface of the skin with heated cups) served as popular heal-

* **pre-Islamic** refers to the Arabian Peninsula or to the Arabic language before the founding of Islam in the early 600s

* **elixir** substance believed to have special properties, such as the ability to prolong life; medicinal mixture

* **liniment** liquid or semiliquid preparation applied to the skin

* **salve** healing cream or ointment

* **medieval** refers to the Middle Ages, a period roughly between 500 and 1500

* **pharmacology** study of medicinal drugs

* **B.C.E.** before the Common Era, which refers to the same time period as B.C.

* **C.E.** Common Era, which refers to the same time period as A.D.

* **caliphate** office and government of the caliph, the religious and political leader of an Islamic state

ing methods. Muslims also used broths, elixirs*, liniments*, salves*, and powders prepared with natural ingredients, such as herbs and milk. To treat broken bones, they massaged the afflicted area, rubbed it with an ointment, and immobilized it. Medieval* Islamic physicians had little success with surgical procedures, however. Their knowledge extended to lancing boils, and they usually failed to save those suffering from major internal wounds.

Popular medicine relied on magical as well as natural cures. As in many parts of the Mediterranean region, Muslims believed that supernatural forces such as the evil eye and *jinn* (spirits) affected personal health and could cause epidemics. To protect themselves from illness, Muslims wore charms, amulets, and talismans made from stones or animal parts. They also carried written magical sayings or kept them in their homes.

Early folk remedies were also influenced by the work of alchemists, who made valuable contributions to pharmacology* while seeking a method of changing common metals into gold. While mixing various elements, alchemists discovered numerous substances with healing properties. Many modern drugs have their origins in these findings, and modern chemists use processing methods developed by the alchemists.

Greek Humoral Medicine. Greek traditions influenced Islamic healing methods. Promoted by Hippocrates and other Greek physicians from around 400 B.C.E.*, the humors theory became the basis for medical practice throughout Europe and the Middle East. This tradition assumed the existence of four humors (bodily fluids)—blood, phlegm, yellow bile, and black bile. Each humor possessed certain qualities, such as warmth, cold, heat, and dryness.

Healers believed that disease stemmed from an imbalance within the humors, which they could correct by prescribing a medicine that possessed the deficient qualities. Black bile, for example, was considered cold and foul-smelling. An excess of this humor led to such complaints as dry skin, colds, and depression. For someone with too much black bile, a physician might prescribe a bath, exposure to sweet-smelling oils or harmonious music, or wine, which was thought to warm the blood and promote cheer. The popularity of the humors theory reached its height with the writings of the Greek physician Galen (129–216 C.E.*) but began to decline shortly thereafter.

Abbasid Caliphate. Research on science and medicine flourished during the Abbasid caliphate* (750–1258), and Islamic scholars revived humoral theories. They translated Greek texts into Arabic, creating encyclopedias, teaching texts, and self-help manuals based on the works of Galen. Islamic researchers added to his ideas, making major advances in the fields of pharmacology, ophthalmology (the study of eye disease), optics, surgery, and contagion, an area neglected by the Greeks. In the *Canon of Medicine*, the physician Ibn Sina (known as Avicenna in the West) assembled Galen's ideas into a unified system that influenced European as well as Islamic medicine.

Ibn al-Nafis (died 1288) correctly described the ways in which blood circulates through the human heart. Galen and Ibn Sina had suggested that blood moves through a hole in the left and right ventricles of the heart. Ibn al-Nafis argued that no such hole exists and that blood reaches the left ventricle of the heart from the lungs. Later European theories regarding blood circulation drew on the work of Ibn al-Nafis.

Muslim societies became famous for their hospitals, which treated all patients regardless of gender, religion, or social class. These facilities offered surgery as well as treatment for contagious diseases and mental illness. Some hospitals were equipped with pharmacies and medical libraries. In the early years of the Abbasid caliphate, hospitals existed primarily in Baghdad and other regional Islamic centers. During the 1100s and 1200s, the number of hospitals in the Muslim world increased dramatically. The Nuri hospital of Damascus and the Mansuri hospital of Cairo were among the prominent institutions of this period.

Influence of Muhammad. Islamic physicians did not only rely on Greek medicine, but also looked to the sayings of Muhammad as recorded in the Qur'an and the hadith. The Qur'an gives little advice on medicine, but many Muslims believe in a "medicine of the Prophet." Early collections of advice attributed to Muhammad include sayings on the curative power of honey and the medical properties of wolf's gall, and guidelines on whether one should flee from the plague, use passages from the Qur'an as charms, or consume *haram* (unlawful) substances to help cure illnesses.

Research on Muhammad's healing advice peaked in the 1300s, when the Syrian scholar Ibn Qayyim al-Jawziyah published the highly influential *Medicine of the Prophet*, a collection of medical reports. The book included information on both natural and magical remedies, and advice on such topics as doctor's fees, ethics, sexual intercourse, and singing. Humoral physicians denounced such works as quackery, but the collection enjoyed great popularity among most Muslims. *Medicine of the Prophet* continues to be a bestseller in some Arab countries, and many Muslims use herbal cures for headaches, stomach problems, and coughs. Some also use faith-based remedies such as uttering a prayer or a charm over a cup of water or milk before drinking it. Modern scholars have devoted much attention to certain cures advocated by Muhammad, especially the use of honey for various ailments.

Medicine in the Modern Islamic World

The invasion of colonial powers in the Muslim world in the late 1700s and 1800s brought Muslim doctors into contact with Western medicine. Ironically, Western medicine had developed largely as a result of the work of early Muslim physicians and scientists. Eager to expand their facilities, Muslim rulers founded European-style hospitals and training centers and hired European physicians to organize their health services. Western medicine also had an effect on Muslim scholars, who debated the moral implications of certain European practices. In Islamic countries as elsewhere, manuals on combating supernatural forces remain popular, and humoral medicine serves as a widely-used alternative to more modern cures, especially in India and Pakistan.

Spread of Western Methods. In colonized countries, European authorities administered medical services. They established modern hospitals and health facilities but placed them only in the European sections of cities. In Algeria and Egypt, for example, the organization of medical centers came to reflect the class structure of society. The French or British had access to the best hospitals; Jewish or Italian citizens were treated at second-rate fa-

Healing With Honey

Islamic tradition places a high value on the use of honey as a medicine. In a hadith, Muhammad stated: "Honey is a remedy for every illness and the Qur'an is a remedy for all illness of the mind, therefore I recommend to you both remedies, the Qur'an and honey." The Qur'an describes bees as issuing "a drink of varying colors, wherein is healing for mankind." Studies in the United States and other countries have revealed honey to have many benefits. On wounds, it inhibits the growth of bacteria and reduces inflammation. It eases the severity of diarrhea, helps lower cholesterol, and soothes sore throats and coughs. Rich in vitamins and minerals, it contains high levels of antioxidants—substances believed to prevent certain diseases. Islamic and other scholars continue to research the curative properties of honey.

cilities; and Muslims received care at third-rate centers only. Most Muslims had no exposure to modern medicine and continued to consult herbalists, bonesetters, midwives, and spiritual healers.

After some Islamic countries gained independence in the mid-1900s, most governments required that physicians receive Western-style medical training. They gave traditional healers second-class status and expanded medical schools, hospitals, and public health systems throughout the Muslim world. Muslim countries have achieved widely varying levels of westernization in their medicine. Oil-rich nations, such as Saudi Arabia, have spent billions on modern medical facilities, while poor countries, such as Pakistan, lack basic supplies.

Western medicine has provided Islamic societies with many benefits, such as a drop in child and infant mortality. Some Muslims, however, remain skeptical of European methods. They claim that Western doctors treat individual symptoms rather than the person as a whole. They also believe that financial interests override patient care in many situations. Some scholars have called for a return to Islamic values and for increased use of herbal and spiritual remedies. In 1981 Muslim physicians held the First International Conference on Islamic Medicine to promote Muslim principles in health care. Some Muslim countries, such as Jordan, have created modern Islamic hospitals that resemble their Western counterparts except that the staff wears traditional dress and observes Muslim codes of behavior.

Ethical and Religious Debate. In many parts of the Muslim world, the *ulama** have commented on Western medical practices and debated their compatibility with Islamic values. In Saudi Arabia, for example, citizens asked the *ulama* to rule on the legality of organ transplants. The scholars stated that such donations are legal in cases where the donor or next of kin provides written consent. An Egyptian scholar, asked about cosmetic surgery, stated that beauty is a gift of God and that Muslims should alter their appearances only to relieve physical suffering or psychological distress.

Pakistani philosopher Fazlur Rahman delivered many influential opinions on Islamic ethics and medicine. He expressed approval of dissection and organ transplants, stating that the needs of the living are more important than those of the dead. Regarding genetic engineering, he denounced those who would tamper with the will of God, but noted that people had made genetic alterations to plants and animals since the beginning of history and that genetic improvement of humans could occur as long as it did not lead to loss of life or dignity. Speaking on pregnancy, he cautioned against the donation of a sperm or egg cell by a person outside of the marriage, as such an act would classify as adultery under Islamic law. Finally, he expressed disapproval of the practice of keeping a person alive by artificial means, stating that the Qur'an emphasizes quality over quantity of life.

Many Muslim scholars have also delivered opinions on family planning. Some sanction the use of abortion within the first four months of pregnancy. Many Muslims, however, oppose abortion, stating that killing brings punishment in the afterlife and that children are divinely created. Approaches to combating sexually transmitted diseases have also created controversy. Reluctant to admit the occurrence of sexual promiscuity and gay sex in Muslim countries, many Islamic governments have taken inadequate measures to try

* *ulama* religious scholars

to halt the spread of HIV and AIDS. They have failed to implement educational programs or even to collect statistics on the disease, preferring to view it as a foreign danger. Many Muslim doctors, however, have encouraged governments to spread more awareness of AIDS and HIV. The development of prevention programs continues to expand within Muslim countries. (*See also* **Abortion; Ethics; Health Care; Ibn Sina; Magic and Sorcery; Science.**)

Medina

Medina, known in pre-Islamic times as Yathrib, is located in the Hejaz region of western Saudi Arabia. The city is 275 miles north of Mecca, the birthplace of Islam, and about 100 miles from the Red Sea coast. Medina and Mecca are Islam's two holiest cities.

In the 600s, Medina was an oasis* consisting of palm groves and farmsteads. The tribes who lived there, some Jewish and some polytheistic*, were in the midst of a civil war. Seeking to end the violence, some of the city's residents invited Muhammad, known as a charismatic holy man and just arbiter*, to move there. Muhammad and many of his followers, facing persecution in Mecca, migrated to Medina in 622. Muslims celebrate this journey as the Hijrah*; it marks the beginning of the Islamic calendar. Muhammad built the first mosque* in the city, which came to be called "the city of the Prophet (*madinat al-nabi*)." He resolved political disputes and sought to unite the city's residents into a single community.

Muhammad still had powerful enemies in Mecca. The Quraysh (the most powerful tribe in Mecca) had fought several battles against the Muslims. In 627 a Quraysh force of 10,000 attacked Medina. Muhammad only had 3,000 troops to oppose them. To strengthen Medina's defenses, Muhammad had a trench dug around the city. This tactic proved successful and the Muslim force prevailed in what came to be called the Battle of the Trench. Following the defeat of the Quraysh, several Arab tribes allied themselves with Islam.

Muhammad next moved to consolidate his power within Medina. On separate occasions, he exiled two disloyal Jewish groups and executed the adult males of a third group. These harsh measures crushed any further opposition among Medina's remaining non-Muslim residents. When the Quraysh later resumed hostilities, Muhammad marched out with a force of 10,000. He captured Mecca without bloodshed. More Arab tribes came over to his side, either as converts or as allies. At the time of Muhammad's death in 632, Medina was the capital of an Islamic empire that ruled Arabia.

Muhammad's successors governed from Medina until 661. Mu'awiyah, the first Umayyad caliph*, moved the Islamic capital to Syria. Medina declined in political importance over the following centuries. Egyptian and Ottoman governors usually administered Arabia from Jeddah, a city on the coast. In the 1800s, Medina finally regained political stature. It became an important Ottoman communication and military center. Telegraph and railroad lines connected the city with distant provinces. After the fall of the

* **oasis** fertile area in a desert

* **polytheistic** refers to believing in more than one god

* **arbiter** person with the authority to settle disputes

* **Hijrah** celebrated emigration of Muhammad from Mecca in 622, which marks the first year of the Islamic calendar

* **mosque** Muslim place of worship

See map in Gulf States (vol. 1).

* **caliph** religious and political leader of an Islamic state

Ottoman Empire, Arab leaders fought over the city. Abd al-Aziz ibn Saud captured Medina in 1925 and incorporated it into his kingdom, renaming the country Saudi Arabia after himself.

Medina has remained an important religious city throughout Islamic history. Muhammad's tomb is in Medina's chief mosque. The city also contains the tombs of the Prophet's daughter and the first three caliphs. Because millions of Muslims visit the tombs and shrines in Medina each year, the city has constructed a campground to accommodate the large number of visitors. Muslims consider Medina second in importance only to Mecca. Non-Muslims may not enter the city.

Today Medina is one of Saudi Arabia's largest cities. Most of its residents are Sunni* Muslims. Although it is a modern city with much recent industrial development, Medina's economy remains largely agricultural or tied to the pilgrimage industry. The city's religious status is still its most notable feature. (*See also* **Hijrah; Mecca; Muhammad; Saudi Arabia.**)

* **Sunni** refers to the largest branch of the Muslim community; the name derives from sunnah, the exemplary behavior of the Prophet Muhammad

Mehmed II

1432–1481
Ottoman sultan

* **sultan** political and military ruler of a Muslim dynasty or state

* **Byzantine** refers to the Eastern Christian empire that was based in Constantinople

See color plate 2, vol. 3.

* **fiscal** refers to financial matters

* **theology** study of the nature and qualities of God and the understanding of His will

In 1444 Sultan* Murad II, in an attempt to prevent a struggle for succession after his death, turned over the throne to his 12-year-old son, Mehmed II. During the next two years, internal and external crises threatened the reign of the child ruler, and Murad returned to the throne and restored order. He died in 1451, and Mehmed (then 19) regained the throne. The young sultan punished his opponents and gained control of the Janissaries, an elite military force.

Mehmed engaged in a program of conquests, establishing the Ottoman Empire as a major force. After strengthening the military, Mehmed marched on Constantinople, the Byzantine* capital. Supported by gigantic cannons, Mehmed and his army captured the city in May 1453. He changed the name of the city to Istanbul, made it the capital of his empire, and established a great mosque there. He encouraged subjects from other parts of the empire to come and populate his great city.

After defeating the Byzantines, Mehmed's prestige and popularity soared. He led several other successful campaigns and became known as Mehmed the Conqueror. The Ottoman Empire absorbed most of Asia Minor and the Balkans. His troops threatened eastern Europe, Russia, and Italy and his rapid conquests created some tensions in the region. Mehmed's continual wars of conquest undermined his attempts to improve the empire's economy.

Mehmed used Ottoman power to create a vast empire. He reorganized the government and employed Christians and Jews to administer the conquered lands. Mehmed established criminal and fiscal* law codes and promoted the sciences and theology*. But Mehmed was a harsh ruler, and after his death, discontented subjects placed his eldest son, Bayezid, on the throne, ignoring his favorite son. They also began a reaction to many of Mehmed's policies. (*See also* **Istanbul; Ottoman Empire.**)

Messianic Traditions

Like Judaism and Christianity, Islam has a messianic* tradition. According to hadith*, prior to the end of time, God will send a leader to the world to deliver his people from oppression. Called the Mahdi (divinely guided one), he will arrive when the world has reached its worst state of affairs. He will spread justice, restore the faith, and defeat the enemies of Islam.

Muslims agree on certain characteristics of the Mahdi. He will be from the Prophet's family and will bear the Prophet's name. His father's name will be the same as the name of the Prophet's father (Abd Allah). Miraculous signs will accompany his appearance, and he will bring great wealth, which he will distribute generously among the faithful. His reign, however, will last a relatively short time.

Longing for a Golden Age. The Muslim community faced its first political crisis when the Prophet Muhammad died in 632. His followers disagreed about who should succeed him. One group believed that the Prophet Muhammad had appointed his son-in-law, Ali ibn Abi Talib, and Ali's descendants as the imams* of the Muslim community. The majority, however, elected Abu Bakr, an early convert from Mecca, to become the first caliph*. The dispute eventually resulted in the division of Islam into two main traditions—Shi'i* and Sunni*.

After a period of unrest, Ali became the fourth caliph in 656, raising hopes among his supporters that his rule would restore Islam to its original state. Ali was assassinated, however, and his followers lost control of the caliphate. Thereafter, religiously oriented Muslims—particularly Ali's supporters (known as the Shi'is)—developed the concept of a perfect leader. He would redress the wrongs committed against the oppressed and establish justice, by which the Shi'is meant the abolition of the caliphate of their rivals and the return to pure Islam. They also believed that this messianic savior would convert the world to Islam.

Rallying the People. By the end of the 700s, Sunni Muslims accepted the historical caliphate as a continuation of Muhammad's earthly position as leader of the *ummah* (community of believers). They viewed the Mahdi as a future "caliph of God" who would not emerge until the end of time. Shi'is, by contrast, rejected the historical caliphate as human interference in the fulfillment of the divine plan. Shi'is eventually came to believe in a hidden Mahdi who would restore the ideal Muslim order.

For centuries, Shi'i Muslims interpreted contemporary events according to their messianic views. Each generation believed the Mahdi would soon appear and recruit them to launch a revolution under his command. Shi'i political leaders took advantage of these expectations to justify rebellion against Sunni governments. Some of these Shi'i movements, such as the Abbasid revolution in 750 and the Fatimid revolution during the 900s, were successful. Nevertheless, many of these attempts failed, and Shi'is eventually came to regard the Mahdi as future messianic imam who would appear when God commanded him to take charge of the world.

Shi'i Islam split into several branches based on differing views of the messiah. The Twelvers, or Imamis, recognize the spiritual leaders of eleven

* **messianic** refers to the messiah, the anticipated savior to be sent by God

* **hadith** reports of the words and deeds of Muhammad (not in the Qur'an, but accepted as guides for Muslim behavior)

* **imam** spiritual-political leader in Shi'i Islam, one who is regarded as directly descended from Muhammad; also, one who leads prayers

* **caliph** religious and political leader of an Islamic state

* **Shi'i** refers to Muslims who believe that Muhammad chose Ali ibn Abi Talib and his descendants as the spiritual-political leaders of the Muslim community

* **Sunni** refers to the largest branch of the Muslim community; the name derives from sunnah, the exemplary behavior of the Prophet Muhammad

Iranian Claims to the Mahdi

During the 1840s, young Iranian merchant Sayyid Ali Muhammad Shirazi angered Shi'i religious leaders with his claim to be the Hidden Imam. He promised a new religious order and led his followers, the Babis, in revolt. The government crushed the movement and executed Shirazi in 1850. During the 1860s, Mirza Husayn Ali Nuri, who had taken the title Baha Allah (meaning "glory of God"), adopted the Babis' social mission. Declaring himself a divine messenger, he founded the Baha'i faith and sought to create a united global order. Baha Allah attracted many followers, and the Baha'i community continued to grow even after his death in 1892. Today, it has more than seven million members worldwide.

* **heretic** person whose belief or practice is contrary to established religious doctrine

imams. They believe the twelfth imam, who disappeared, is the Mahdi. God is concealing the whereabouts of this imam for an unspecified period of time. Someday, he will return to dispense justice. The Seveners, or Ismailis, only recognize seven imams. They believe that the sixth imam, Jafar al-Sadiq, named his son Ismail to be his successor, but Ismail died before his father. After Jafar's death in 765, some Shi'is still considered Ismail to be the seventh imam and the Mahdi.

Enduring Expectation. Throughout Islamic history, a number of Muslim reformers have professed to be the Mahdi, particularly in times of social or political crisis. In 1495 Sayyid Muhammad, a Sunni Muslim of Jaunpur, India, claimed he was the messiah. Sunni jurists considered him a heretic* and had him executed.

Messianic revolts against colonial powers sprang up across the Islamic world during the 1800s in such places as India, Algeria, Senegal, Ghana, and Nigeria. Muslims yearned for a leader to deliver them from the oppression of the Europeans. In Sudan, Muhammad Ahmad ibn Abd Allah proclaimed himself Mahdi. The Mahdiyah, as his movement became known, sought to overthrow the British and Ottoman-Egyptian forces in the region and establish God's ideal rule on earth.

Some Shi'i Muslims believed that the Iranian Revolution of 1979 was a prelude to the Mahdi's return. On November 20, 1979, the Sunni Jahaymin al-Utaybi led a major messianic uprising in Mecca. The Saudi government crushed the movement. Many Muslims later believed the Persian Gulf War (1990–1991) was a sign of the end of time. Believers across the Islamic world still await the Mahdi and the creation of an ideal order. (*See also* **Ali ibn Abi Talib; Babism; Baha'i; Ismaili; Ithna Ashari; Mahdiyah; Shi'i Islam; Sunni Islam.**)

Metalwork

See *Art.*

Mevlevi

See *Mawlawiyah.*

Middle East

The region that includes the lands of southwest Asia and North Africa is frequently called the Middle East. The term itself did not appear until the late 1800s, when European imperial planners used it to refer to the area between the "Far East" and the "Near East." In the mid-1900s, the Middle East emerged as the most common label for a region with boundaries that varied according to the person or group describing the region. The broadest definition of the Middle East covers the region extending from Pakistan to Morocco; more limited definitions focus on the eastern Arab world, Turkey, and Iran. Although the term *Middle East* is relatively recent, this region with distinctive

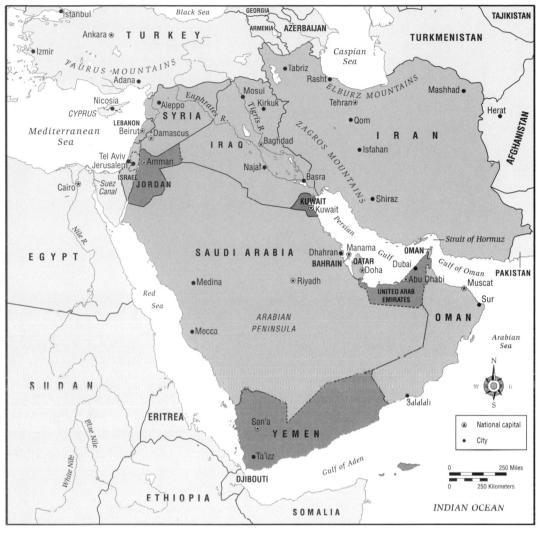

characteristics has been the center of the Islamic world since the Arab-Muslim expansion of the 600s.

Spread of Islam

Before the rise of Islam, Arabia consisted of various self-governing tribes and had no central leadership. In the early 600s, Muhammad unified much of the region under his rule. Muslim armies conquered other lands, and soon gained control over vast portions of the Middle East. Powerful caliphates* emerged, but the region proved difficult to govern. Warfare and upheaval repeatedly divided the Middle East.

The First Great Dynasties. By the time of Muhammad's death in 632, Muslim forces controlled the entire Arabian Peninsula. During the next three decades, Arab armies conquered Egypt, Syria, Iraq, and most of Iran. In 661 the Syrian governor Mu'awiyah wrested control of the Islamic caliphate away from Muhammad's family. Mu'awiyah established the Umayyad dynasty*, which was based in Damascus. Umayyad armies pushed through Iran to in-

The Middle East is a vague term that has been used to describe a region extending from Pakistan to Morocco. More commonly, the term refers to the countries shown here—Bahrain, Egypt, Iran, Iraq, Israel, Jordan, Kuwait, Lebanon, Oman, Qatar, Saudi Arabia, Syria, United Arab Emirates, and Yemen. It is the region in which Judaism, Christianity, and Islam arose.

* **caliphate** office and government of the caliph, the religious and political leader of an Islamic state

* **dynasty** succession of rulers from the same family or group

149

vade Central Asia and India. They also occupied North Africa and much of Spain. In less than a century, the Umayyad caliphate had united the Middle East and its neighboring regions under Muslim rule.

The Abbasids seized control of the caliphate in 750, choosing Baghdad as their new capital. Their supremacy did not last, however, and in the 900s, a powerful Shi'i* sect broke away and formed the Fatimid dynasty. Claiming descent from Muhammad through his daughter Fatimah, the rulers settled in Egypt and took over Syria, Palestine, parts of Africa, and Sicily. They failed, however, to topple the Abbasids, who also struggled with the Iranian Buyids and Seljuk Turks. In 1258 Mongols from the northeast invaded the Middle East and captured Baghdad, overthrowing the Abbasids. A powerful Mamluk state headed by former military slaves emerged to occupy Egypt, Syria, and western Arabia.

Clash of Empires. Mongol power waned in the 1400s, and two great empires reasserted Muslim control over the Middle East. The Ottoman Turks took Syria, Egypt, and Arabia away from the Mamluks. The Safavids arose in Iran and assumed control of the region. The two Muslim powers fought a long series of wars. One area of fighting involved control of Iraq, which became part of the Ottoman Empire after the collapse of the Safavid state in the 1700s.

Colonialism

The Islamic empires controlled the Middle East until around the early 1800s, when the industrial nations of Europe invaded the region. Ottoman strength had declined by this time, and the Qajar dynasty, which had succeeded the Safavids in Iran, was too weak to resist the colonial advance. Great Britain exerted its will in Egypt and competed with Russia for control of Iran. France established influence in Syria and Lebanon. Europe remained the dominant political force in the Middle East until the mid-1900s.

Islam and Reform. European colonization created new theological debates within the Middle East. Some Muslims believed that their regimes* had grown weak through corruption and that a return to Islamic roots would enable them to reclaim the power that they had held during the Middle Ages*. Most, however, asserted that only modernization based on Western models could bolster the Muslim states, giving them the force to challenge the Europeans. Islamic leaders adopted Western military technology and hired Europeans to train their armies and develop their scientific capabilities. They sought to balance tradition with the needs of the modern world.

The Iranian scholar Jamal al-Din al-Afghani emerged as an important teacher in the late 1800s. He believed that reason, which had once served as a major tenet of Islam, had become distorted by fanaticism and tyranny. This resulted in stagnation within the Islamic world. Al-Afghani promoted a return to the original principles of Islam, maintaining that such a move would enable Muslims to modernize their states and vanquish the Europeans. Al-Afghani's student and colleague, Muhammad Abduh, continued the campaign for reform and rationalization in the early 1900s, serving as the grand mufti* in Egypt.

Muslim political leaders, however, did not look to Islamic principles to modernize their countries. They worked instead to create stronger central gov-

* **Shi'i** refers to Muslims who believe that Muhammad chose Ali ibn Abi Talib and his descendents as the spiritual-political leaders of the Muslim community

* **regime** government in power

* **Middle Ages** period roughly between 500 and 1500

* **mufti** scholar who interprets Islamic law

ernments and to regulate religious practice. In Egypt, rulers placed the brotherhoods under strict state control. They banned such practices as ceremonial drumming, singing, and leaping, as well as several other practices. Egyptian and other Muslim leaders sent students to European universities, where they could study Western ideas and bring them back to Islamic countries.

Rise of Arab Nationalism. Prior to colonial rule, most Muslim lands had existed in a loose structure. Nomadic tribes and agricultural villages had little direct involvement with the rulers who were based in the cities. Europeans divided the Middle East into separate countries, giving many Muslims a newfound sense of national identity. Campaigns for religious reform also brought Muslims together, promoting Islamic activism and pride. Leading reformers, such as Hasan al-Banna, formed organizations that encouraged a practical, goal-oriented religion and promoted the creation of strong Islamic states. In the mid-1900s, young officers, administrators, and intellectuals joined nationalist* movements.

Independence and the Future

Most Middle Eastern countries gained their independence after World War II (1939–1945), when weakened European powers could no longer maintain control over them. Great Britain and France gave up their colonies in the 1940s and 1950s, creating boundaries that divided the region into self governing states.

In 1947 the United Nations announced a plan to partition Palestine, which had been under British control since the end of World War I. The plan called for the creation of two states—one for Jews and one for Arabs. Both sides rejected the plan. On May 14, 1948, Israel proclaimed its independence, and armed conflict between Arabs and Jews erupted. Thousands of Palestinians fled the region to seek refuge in Jordan, Syria, Lebanon, and other neighboring countries, as well as in the West Bank and Gaza. Many Palestinians continue to live in refugee camps.

In the early years of independence, rulers of Muslim countries worked to strengthen their nations. They established Islam as the official religion, made primary education mandatory, developed industry and infrastructure*, and worked to urbanize rural areas. Some leaders, such as Egyptian president Gamal Abdel Nasser, pushed for secularization* of the state.

Islamic Revival. Israel's victory over Arab forces in the Six-Day War of 1967 discredited the secular ideas promoted by Nasser. Some Muslims, known as "Islamists," urged a return to a strict Islamic government. Appealing to numerous discontented people, an Islamic revival swept across the region. The Islamists promoted economic fairness, the importance of family, and the veiling of women and criticized the corruption of secular governments. They pushed for the inclusion of Islamic principles in all aspects of society.

Despite the popularity of the revival movement, only two Middle Eastern nations formally adopted strictly Islamic governments—Iran and Saudi Arabia. In 1979 the Ayatollah* Ruhollah Khomeini led a revolution in Iran and gained control of the country. He sought to abolish secular and Western influences and created a constitution that mandates rule by divine law,

Islamists in Turkey

In 2002 people around the world were surprised to learn that the Islamist Justice and Development Party (AKP) won 34 percent of the vote in Turkey, granting it the majority in parliament. Some Turks viewed their new leaders with suspicion, fearing that they would violate the secular constitution. Western nations worried that Turkey would take a hostile attitude towards them. Party leader Recep Tayyip Erdogan assured Turkish citizens that the AKP would fight for human rights, democratic freedoms, and entrance into the European Union. He also guaranteed an end to the economic slump plaguing the country.

* **nationalist** referring to feelings of loyalty and devotion to one's country and a commitment to its independence

* **infrastructure** basic facilities and institutions that a country needs in order to function

* **secularize** to separate religion from other aspects of human life and society

* **ayatollah** highest-ranking legal scholar among some Shi'i Muslims

* **parliament** representative national body having supreme legislative power within the state

* **Sunni** refers to the largest branch of the Muslim community; the name derives from sunnah, the exemplary behavior of the Prophet Muhammad

as interpreted by Shi'i scholars. A Shi'i religious scholar heads the government, which includes a popularly elected parliament*. Saudi Arabia has a Sunni* monarchy with roots in a revivalist movement of the 1700s. The Saudi government differs from that of Iran, ruling by traditional Sunni law.

Islamist parties have thus far failed to seize power in other Middle Eastern states, where government and military leaders oppose them. The rulers of Iraq and Syria, for example, have violently suppressed oppositional religious movements. In Turkey, the 2002 election gave the Islamically oriented party the majority in parliament, but that party does not propose to alter the secular constitution.

The Twenty-First Century. The world's dependence on oil has secured a prominent role for the Middle East in the global economy. Vast petroleum resources have contributed to the wealth and political power of several Arab nations. Saudi Arabia owns around one-fourth of the world's oil reserves and is the largest oil exporter in the world. Iraq has the second largest oil reserve, and Iran, Kuwait, and several smaller Arab nations also export large quantities of oil and gas.

Despite its petroleum revenues, the Middle East faces serious challenges. Saudi Arabia, Syria, and Yemen struggle with rapid population growth, and many Middle Eastern nations suffer from water shortages, pollution, and overcrowded cities. Poverty grips large areas of the region as governments struggle to diversify their economies. Lebanon continues to recover from a 16-year civil war, and Israeli troops and Palestinians continue to clash in the Israeli-occupied territories. The United States toppled the regime of Iraqi leader Saddam Hussein in April 2003, leading to further unrest in the region. (*See also* **Arab-Israeli Conflict; Egypt; Gulf States; Ibn al-Arabi; Iran; Iraq; Israel; Jordan; Law; Lebanon; Saudi Arabia; Sufism; Syria; Turkey; Yemen.**)

Minorities

* **Qur'an** book of the holy scriptures of Islam

* **revelation** message from God to humans transmitted through a Prophet

Relations between Muslims and non-Muslims have historically taken shape according to the status and size of each group. The Qur'an* accepts the legitimacy of multiple religions, dealing most specifically with Judaism and Christianity. Members of these faiths are accepted as People of the Book, those who have received true revelation*. The Qur'an discusses the treatment of these and other non-Muslim peoples under Islamic rule.

Minorities in Muslim Societies

Treatment of non-Muslim minorities in Muslim societies and the nature of their relations with the Muslim majority have changed considerably since the early days of Islam. Minority groups have generally gained more rights over time, and the constitutions of many Islamic countries recognize the legal equality of people of all religions. Muslim scholars, however, continue to debate the degree of authority that non-Muslims should have in Islamic societies.

Muhammad and the Qur'an. Muhammad preached a message of monotheism* and social equality in Mecca. But he had limited success in converting people to his beliefs and faced fierce persecution. Muhammad and a small group of followers eventually settled in Medina, where he established the first Islamic community. He dictated a document commonly referred to as the Constitution of Medina (about 622–624), which established standards for the treatment of Jews and other religious groups living in the *ummah* (community of faithful Muslims). Under the constitution, these groups had autonomy* and full religious freedom, but Muhammad was the supreme arbiter* and leader. The situation changed when many of the Jews did not recognize Muhammad as a prophet of God and when some of the Jewish clans allied themselves with his Meccan enemies. Muhammad reacted by killing these Jews or expelling them from Medina.

The Qur'an commands Muslims to treat unbelievers fairly and decently, as long as the unbelievers do not attack them. It does, however, draw distinctions between different classes of unbelievers. Members of religions that received knowledge of God through scripture* are classified as *ahl al-kitab* (People of the Book). This category originally included only Christians, Jews, and Sabaeans, but later covered people of other faiths as well, such as Zoroastrians and Buddhists*. The Qur'an directs Muslims to have polite relations with *ahl al-kitab*. It does not, however, extend this courtesy to polytheists. According to tradition, Muslims may not even share food with people in this group. Furthermore, under certain circumstances, Muslims are instructed to fight hostile unbelievers until they either convert or submit to Islamic rule.

A contract of protection established the legal status of *ahl al-kitab*. These protected minorities, called *dhimmi*, enjoyed security from harassment by the state, freedom of movement, the right to own property, and the right to worship freely, as long as they practiced their religion discreetly. Muslims levied a *jizyah* (tax) on the *dhimmi* for the privilege of their protection. In the 700s, a document called the Pact of Umar set out additional restrictions on dress and hairstyle, worship, the construction and repairing of churches and synagogues, the height of houses, the use of animals, and other aspects of life to further distinguish between *dhimmis* and Muslims.

Variations in Practice. The actual degree of protection and legal rights enjoyed by *dhimmis* varied from one Islamic land to the next. Economic and political conditions often played a greater role than the letter of the law in determining how Muslims treated minorities. For example, Muslims enjoyed close relations with Christians and Jews in Islamic Spain and in Egypt under the Fatimid dynasty* (909–1171). Instances in which *dhimmis* enjoyed greater rights, however, were still seen by some Muslims as a violation of accepted standards.

Non-Muslims enjoyed a good deal of autonomy under Muslim rule, often forming separate societies within the larger culture. The Ottoman *millet* system, for example, ensured that each group existed in its own self-governing community with a leader who served as a representative to Muslim authorities. Non-Muslims frequently had their own religious, legal, social, and educational institutions that functioned alongside those of the state. Although most Muslim states did not have an official policy of segregation,

* **monotheism** belief that there is only one God

* **autonomy** self-government

* **arbiter** person with the authority to settle disputes

* **scripture** sacred writings that contain revelations from God

* **Buddhist** refers to the beliefs and practices of Buddhism, a religion of eastern and central Asia based on the teaching of Gautama Buddha

* **dynasty** succession of rulers from the same family or group

153

* **conscription** military draft

* **conservative** generally opposed to change, especially in existing political and social institutions

* **liberal** supporting greater participation in government for individuals; not bound by tradition

non-Muslims tended to fill jobs that were considered undesirable or unclean for Muslims.

As European influence in the Islamic world increased, the status of minorities in Muslim lands began to change. European powers acted as protectors of certain religious communities and put pressure on Islamic governments to grant greater rights to non-Muslims. In the mid-1800s, for example, the Ottoman Empire passed the Tanzimat laws that granted non-Muslims full legal equality. It also replaced the *jizyah* with the duty to perform military service or to pay a tax to avoid conscription*. Following World War I (1914–1918), Britain and France assumed direct control over much of the Islamic world, often resulting in greater privileges for non-Muslims than for Muslims.

An increased number of rights and privileges provided non-Muslims with greater economic opportunity. At the same time, non-Muslims came into closer contact with Muslims in social, business, and political situations. Social class became almost as important as religious and ethnic background as a way to identify oneself. Outside pressure made these new opportunities possible and also meant that minorities were particularly vulnerable without that pressure. As Muslim states demanded and won their independence, minorities in those countries lost the protection of the former colonial rulers.

Both Sides of the Issue. The current constitutions of most Muslim states grant legal equality to Muslims and non-Muslims. Most of these countries, however, base their legal systems on the principles of Islamic law, which applies to all citizens regardless of their faith. In many countries, the head of state must by law be Muslim, but some states guarantee minority groups a fixed share of the seats in their parliaments and assemblies.

Not all Muslims are satisfied with the current status of non-Muslim minorities. Some conservative* groups wish to bring back the rules relating to *dhimmi* and other restrictions. They believe that the rights non-Muslims have in any country should reflect their usefulness to the larger Muslim community. There are also more liberal* Muslim thinkers who seek full political and legal equality for non-Muslims. They would like to see Islamic law modified to eliminate distinctions between Muslims and non-Muslims.

Between these two positions is the view that those who perform the same duties in society should have the same rights, regardless of faith. Legal equality in this case is limited to the "non-religious domain." The problem is defining what is included in the religious domain, and what is not. For example, holding high government office in Muslim lands is seen by some as a religious function, which complicates the process of separating political equality from religious belief. In general, those holding this middle view argue that non-Muslims should be allowed to vote and to participate in politics if they also help to defend the state. However, the eligibility of non-Muslims to high political, military, or judicial positions should still be restricted.

Muslim Minorities in Non-Muslim Lands

About one-third of the world's Muslims live as minorities in non-Muslim lands. In some places, such as Palestine, Muslims were once in the majority, but eventually lost that position. In other places, such as Bosnia, Muslims once ruled as minorities and many remained there after that rule ended. Communities exist in non-Muslim lands, such as India, in which many people converted to Islam. Still others resulted from Islamic migration to non-Muslim regions, such as Europe and North America. Two key questions face these minority Muslim communities. The first concerns their duty to Islam and to each other in a non-Muslim land. The second deals with the relationship that exists between minority Muslim communities and the world-wide Muslim community, or *ummah.*

Relations With Non-Muslim Majorities. In some countries where Muslims live as minorities, the majority population is generally hostile to Islamic culture and there is little encouragement for tolerance. As a result, some Muslims give up some of their religious practices in order to assimilate into the mainstream culture. For those who do not wish to give up aspects of their faith, the history of Islam offers two choices of action. The first is migration to an Islamic land. The second is striving to preserve one's Islamic identity within the larger non-Muslim culture. The second option does not mean a complete separation from non-Muslims. The Qur'an commands Muslims to bring the word of God to all people. Thus, Islam encourages its followers to interact with non-Muslims, even as minorities in non-Muslim societies.

Members of Muslim minority communities have obligations to one another as well as to their faith. They are expected to support other Muslims in their beliefs and practices and to help one another cope with the pressures of living in a non-Muslim culture. These obligations have resulted in the creation of formal and informal organizations to serve the Muslim community and to promote traditional Islamic lifestyles and practices. Such groups have sometimes created suspicion among the non-Muslim majority, especially when they express radical or militant views.

Relations With the *Ummah*. Most Muslims in Islamic lands feel political and social obligations toward Muslim minorities abroad. They do not agree, however, on the nature of these obligations or on the best way to meet them. One model assumes that the *ummah* should treat such communities as Muslim colonies in the non-Muslim world. This view suggests that the *ummah* should take active steps to protect these communities. Yet modern political reality limits what the *ummah* can actually do for Islamic communities abroad. Governments in non-Muslim countries would probably view any significant efforts on behalf of Muslim minorities as interference with their internal political affairs.

A second model suggests that Muslim minorities in non-Muslim lands should be autonomous and treated as sovereign bodies equivalent to independent Muslim states. Many international Islamic organizations, such as the Organization of the Islamic Conference, exist to promote unity among Muslims regardless of where they live. But some of these organizations lack the power to act within their Muslim states, much less in the non-Muslim world. Still, the Qur'an requires that all Muslims have a duty to encourage one another to withstand pressure to abandon their faith, as well as to adopt the means to defend and spread the faith.

It is generally accepted that the *ummah* provide support that is relevant to the spiritual and cultural life of minority Muslim communities. But it is important that it does do so in a way that will not threaten the security or livelihood of Muslims in minority situations. The *ummah* should advise those minorities about how to advocate for their rights in a way that reflects the spirit and principles of their faith. This includes seeking methods that increase understanding and cooperation between Muslims and the majority cultures in which they exist. (*See also* **Christianity and Islam; Colonialism; International Meetings and Organizations; Judaism and Islam; Refugees; Ummah.**)

Missionaries

* **Qur'an** book of the holy scriptures of Islam

* **surah** chapter of the Qur'an

Many Muslims believe that they must call others to the faith. The Qur'an* advocates different forms of *da'wah*, which is broadly defined as an act of invitation or summoning. Surah* 16.125 of the Qur'an tells Muslims to "Invite to the Way of your Lord with wisdom and beautiful preaching, and argue with them in ways that are best and most gracious." The Qur'an prohibits forced conversion: "There is to be no compulsion in religion." It also stresses the legitimacy of other religions: "Whoever believes in God and the Last Day, and whoever does right, shall have his reward with his Lord." This verse refers to Christians, Jews, and members of other monotheistic* faiths. Muslims, therefore, vary in their dedication to converting others to their religion. Islamic missionary work in the modern era primarily focuses on other Muslims, in an effort to create an international community of believers (*ummah*).

* **monotheism** belief that there is only one God

Conversion of Non-Muslims. The Islamic empire spread across the Middle East, North Africa, and Spain in the 700s, and Muslims brought their religion to the areas they conquered. Most Islamic rulers did not force people to convert. They granted them the right to practice their faith as long as they paid a *jizyah* (poll tax). In many cases, non-Muslims were also required to wear clothes that distinguished them from Muslims and to restrict their public expressions of piety. Non-Muslims could not ride horses, bear arms, or build structures higher than those of Muslims. Many non-Muslims found it politically and economically advantageous to profess a belief in Islam. By the 900s, most countries in the Islamic empire had become predominantly Islamic. In other areas, such as East Africa, India, and Southeast Asia, people learned of Islam from traders, popular preachers, and Sufi* wanderers and converted because they found the doctrine appealing.

* **Sufi** follower of Sufism, which seeks to develop spirituality through discipline of the mind and body

* **crusader** person who participated in the holy wars against Muslims during the Middle Ages

Unlike Christians, Muslim religious leaders did not organize missionary expeditions. In fact, the Arabs lacked a term for conversion until they came into contact with Christian crusaders*, who traveled to the Islamic world to recapture Jerusalem from the Muslims and to spread their faith. They remained largely unsuccessful but tried again in the 1800s, after European powers had colonized much of the Islamic world. Western missionaries not only brought religious teachings to Islamic regions, but also established schools, hospitals, and other facilities. Some made their services free to Christians but charged high fees to Muslims in order to encourage conversion. As a backlash against this practice, Muslims established their own missionary movements and social welfare organizations.

In the early twenty-first century, most *da'wah* groups seek to unify Muslims, though some groups work to convert those of other faiths. In sub-Saharan Africa, for example, Christian and Muslim missionaries compete fiercely for converts. In the United States, African Americans have initiated campaigns to urge members of their communities to embrace the Muslim faith, sometimes promoting it as the religion of their ancestors. Muslim immigrant groups in Western countries have attracted followers by emphasizing Islam's link to Christianity and Judaism. Finally, sects such as the Ahmadi work to spread their version of Islam to both Muslims and nonbelievers.

Within the Muslim Community. Most *da'wah* groups focus on the Muslim community. After the Europeans took over much of the Islamic world, *da'wah* took on a political significance that it had not had since the early days of the empire, when the Abbasids used it to gain support from the Umayyads and the Ismailis used it to rebel against the Abbasids. In the late 1800s, the Ottoman sultan Abdulhamid II used the term *da'wah* to refer to the caliph's* duty to bring Muslims of all countries under his authority, much as the Pope had done with the Catholics. The sultan had turned *da'wah* into a tool to promote the political unity of Muslims. In a time of Western colonialism and increased Christian missionary activity, this politicized approach to *da'wah* gained popularity.

The rise of independent Muslim nations after World War II (1939–1945) inspired leaders to create state and international *da'wah* groups. Rulers such as Egypt's Gamal Abdel Nasser established international organizations to promote Islam, the Arabic language, and Arab nationalism*. Saudi Arabia established the Islamic University in Medina in 1961 to train *da'wah* workers and gave rise to the Muslim World League, which sought to unify the Muslim world and replace secular* society with a community based on Islamic principles. Some leaders, however, accused Egyptian and Saudi Arabian leaders of using missionary work to reinforce their own power rather than that of the Islamic community.

Some Muslims created nongovernmental *da'wah* movements based on their dissatisfaction with modern rulers. These Muslims often saw little difference between state leaders and Western colonial rulers. They viewed their governments as more concerned with modernization than with the revival of pure Islamic states. Some *da'wah* organizations continue to call for the overthrow of regimes that they deem too secular or unsupportive of pure Islam, urging members to withdraw from mainstream society to follow traditional Islamic practices and to call upon others to do so. Other nongovernmental groups work to spread Islam to areas in which Muslims constitute a minority. The Tablighi Jamaat brings Islamic teachings and practices to believers and nonbelievers living at the borders of Islamic nations. Other groups seek converts in Western communities to which Muslims have migrated.

Current *Da'wah* Trends. Once the work of individuals, *da'wah* is now dominated by organizations and institutions that pursue a variety of goals, such as attracting young people, building mosques, and promoting traditional practices. Academies in Saudi Arabia, Pakistan, and other countries train Muslims for missionary work. They create programs for the teaching of imams*, community leaders, and other professionals; they arrange seminars, lectures, and conferences; they establish libraries in prisons and hospitals;

Guidelines for *Da'wah*

Da'ee (Muslims practicing *da'wah*) work to determine the best methods for attracting converts. An article published in 1999 in *Nidaul Islam* magazine, offers guidelines based on the Qur'an and hadith. The authors cite the Qur'an as encouraging sincerity, eloquence, moral excellence, and a thorough knowledge of Islam. They also urge *da'ee* to preach during favorable times of the day, citing a disciple of Muhammad who said: "The Prophet used to take care of us in preaching by selecting a suitable time, so that we might not get bored." Brevity also serves as a virtue, as advocated by the Prophet in his statement that *da'ee* should "lengthen the prayer and shorten the sermon, for there is charm [in precise] expression." Effective *da'ee* also speak clearly, use parables to illustrate their points, and rely on visual aids when necessary.

---

* **caliph** religious and political leader of an Islamic state

* **nationalism** feelings of loyalty and devotion to one's country and a commitment to its independence

* **secular** separate from religion in human life and society; connected to everyday life

* **imam** spiritual-political leader in Shi'i Islam, one who is regarded as directly descended from Muhammad; also, one who leads prayers

they organize leadership and training courses for new Muslims; they publish literature and audio-visual material on the act of *da'wah*; and they communicate with other *da'wah* organizations. Some *da'wah* groups also promote social welfare, especially for refugees, and hope to expand their facilities to include medical care and education.

Despite the proliferation of *da'wah* organizations, the movement has met with only limited success. Its effort to unify Muslims has alienated some local groups. Muslim activists also find it difficult to penetrate communities in Africa and other areas in which Islam is relatively new. Muslims who immigrate to Europe and lose touch with their regional roots are more likely to accept organized Islamic movements, as are small mosques or societies eager to join a larger community. (*See also* **Ahmadi; Christianity and Islam; Conversion.**)

Modernism

* **regime** government in power

By the 1800s and early 1900s, Europe had gained control over much of the Muslim world from North Africa to Southeast Asia. Tendencies toward modernism appeared in the late 1800s in response to westernizing European regimes*. Islamic modernists advocated a flexible and continuous reinterpretation of their religion so that Muslims could reform education, law, and politics, making them more suited to modern life. Modernists also believed that Muslims could restore their political power by selectively adapting Western ideas and technology.

* **conservative** person generally opposed to change, especially in existing political and social institutions

* **jihad** literally "striving"; war in defense of Islam

* **secular** separate from religion in human life and society; connected to everyday life

Middle Ground. Colonial rule had severely undermined the political and cultural authority of the Islamic state and society. Muslims offered a variety of explanations for this condition as well as different ways to address it. Conservatives* linked the weakness of Muslim society with a movement away from traditional Islam. They called for a total rejection of Western values and culture, and some religious leaders urged Muslims to wage jihad* against colonial governments. At the other extreme were groups that blamed the situation on a refusal to abandon outdated ideas. In their view, Western secular* culture could be a model for modern Muslim nation-states. They promoted the separation of religion and politics and the restriction of Islam to personal matters.

Modernists offered an alternative response based on the concept of *ihya* (revival) and *tajdid* (renewal). They identified Europe's advanced scientific and technological knowledge and its political organizations as the major factors that enabled the West to colonize Muslim countries. They acknowledged the problems that prevailed in the Islamic world but rejected the argument that the underdevelopment of Muslim societies was attributable to Islam. In their view, Islamic countries had declined because of their unquestioning reliance on traditional practices. They noted that the early followers of Islam were flexible and willing to accommodate new ideas. Historically, Muslim centers of learning produced important works in the fields of law, education, and the sciences. In fact, Europe obtained much of its early scientific knowledge from Muslim Spain. These modernists concluded that a revival of the earlier Islamic commitment to science and learning would restore dignity and greatness to the Muslim world without damaging the integrity of Islam.

Renewal was another key concept of modernism. Reformers advocated a continuous reinterpretation of Islamic texts so that Muslims could develop institutions of education, law, and government suited to ever-changing conditions. They rejected the idea that *ijtihad* (independent reasoning) was no longer acceptable or necessary, arguing that the deteriorating state of the Muslim world served as proof that modern problems required modern answers. Modernists also asserted that reason is compatible with belief.

Modernism in the Middle East. One of the earliest modernists was a leading Egyptian educator named Rifaah Rafi al-Tahtawi (1801–1873). Drawing on the philosophy of the compatibility between reason and revelation, he called for the study of modern science and technology. He also urged jurists to use independent reasoning to adapt Islamic law to changing social conditions, and he promoted primary education for all boys and girls. Jamal al-Din al-Afghani (1838–1897) shared al-Tahtawi's views, but he also brought a new sense of activism and political resistance to the modernist movement. He encouraged Muslims to vigorously oppose European forces, rather than passively accept foreign domination. Al-Afghani believed that acquiring a modern education was a practical method of self-improvement and political reform. Although he succeeded in effectively spreading his message, he failed to persuade Muslim rulers to take action.

Egyptian scholar Muhammad Abduh (1849–1905), a disciple of al-Afghani, developed modernist ideas more fully, promoting a positive attitude toward modern learning and its application in society. A few years after Great Britain occupied Egypt in 1882, British officials appointed Abduh to reform Egypt's educational and legal systems. His opponents thwarted his attempt to blend customary religious education and modern learning at al-Azhar, the famous mosque-university in Cairo. Nevertheless, as mufti (chief jurist) of Egypt, he interpreted Islamic law broadly to demonstrate that Muslims could adapt to modern circumstances and still remain true to their faith.

India and Indonesia. As in the Middle East, European colonialism led to the rise of modernism in India. Following an uprising in 1857, Great Britain abolished the Mughal dynasty* and established formal political rule over India. Muslims were barred from governmental posts because of their support for the revolt. Writer and political activist Sayyid Ahmad Khan (1817–1898) emerged as a strong voice calling for reform. Motivated partly by his desire to convince the British that Muslims were loyal subjects, Ahmad Khan led a movement in support of Western scientific and political ideas. In 1875 he established a college to provide Muslims with a British education. Professors at the school promoted a flexible interpretation of Islamic law and sought to improve the status of women in Islamic society.

During the early 1900s, Indian modernists faced a new question: Assuming that India gained its independence from Great Britain, what would be the future role of Muslims as a minority among India's majority Hindu* population? Led by poet and political writer Muhammad Iqbal (1875–1938), one group called for a separate Muslim state in northwestern India. Another group, led by Islamic thinker Abu al-Kalam Azad (1888–1958), argued that Muslims and

A Variety of Voices

In some countries, such as Egypt and Tunisia, high-ranking officials in education and the government advanced modernist ideas. In the Ottoman Empire, by contrast, a group of lower-level bureaucrats known as the Young Ottomans called for a Western-style political system that limited the authority of the ruler by an elected parliament, or legislative body. They rejected, however, the Western habits and customs that had become popular among higher-ranking officials. Given their opposition to the wholesale adoption of European ways, the Young Ottomans justified the introduction of liberal political principles by claiming that such principles were inherently Islamic.

* **dynasty** succession of rulers from the same family or group

* **Hindu** refers to the beliefs and practices of Hinduism, an ancient religion that originated in India

Hindus should unite to oppose British rule and seek to form a single nation. Both groups agreed that Indian Muslims should live in a democracy.

Dutch colonialism fueled Islamic modernism in Indonesia. In 1912 Hadji Ahmad Dahlan (1868–1923) founded the Muhammadiyah, the country's most important modernist movement. The Muhammadiyah established a network of schools that combined modern scientific and religious instruction. In addition, it pushed for legal reforms through a return to the Qur'an*, sunnah*, and the use of *ijtihad* (independent reasoning). Confronted by local animist* and Hindu sects*, the Muhammadiyah gradually shifted its focus from spreading modernism to purifying religious practices among Indonesian Muslims.

Contemporary Challengers. Modernism has declined as a force for change in Islamic society. During the first half of the 1900s, the movement suffered from the perception that its members represented only the educated elite. Nationalists* and conservatives condemned modernists for compromising with Western colonial powers, maintaining that such actions prolonged foreign rule. The nationalists used this argument effectively to win popular opinion.

After Muslim countries achieved their independence, Islamic fundamentalism* emerged, posing yet another challenge to modernism. Although fundamentalist ideas have great popular appeal, the principles of modernism survive among many contemporary Islamic thinkers. (*See also* **Afghani, Jamal al-Din al-; Ahmad Khan, Sayyid; Colonialism; Education; Fundamentalism; Ijtihad; India; Iqbal, Muhammad; Science; Secularism; Technology.**)

Modesty

* **Qur'an** book of the holy scriptures of Islam

* **sunnah** literally "the trodden path"; Islamic customs based on the exemplary behavior of Muhammad

* **animist** refers to the belief that natural phenomena and objects have souls

* **sect** religious group adhering to distinctive beliefs

* **nationalist** one who advocates loyalty and devotion to his or her country and its independence

* **fundamentalism** in the general sense, a movement that promotes a literal interpretation of scripture; in Islam, politicization of religion under modern conditions to create an alternative public order

* **Qur'an** book of the holy scriptures of Islam

See color plate 13, vol. 1.

The Qur'an* strongly promotes the quality of modesty and discourages vain and arrogant behavior. The scripture states that Satan (Iblis) was once a high-ranking angel. But when God commanded the angels to honor Adam, Satan refused to comply, explaining that "I am better than [Adam]; you created me from fire and created him from clay." Satan's disobedience angered God, who cast him out of heaven. According to the Qur'an, Satan's fall from grace was a direct result of his vanity.

A Muslim who engages in vain or arrogant behavior, such as adopting an attitude of racial, gender, or class superiority, is regarded as embracing satanic logic. Although the Qur'an acknowledges that God has given some human beings more gifts or talents than others, it states that He created all humans from the same *nafs* (soul). Moreover, God introduced diversity into the world so that people could learn from one another and "compete with each other in goodness."

Islam teaches that those who believe that they are more powerful than others elevate themselves to the status of demigod. By submitting to such people instead of to Allah, Muslims commit *shirk*, the sin of believing in more than one god or in a god other than Allah. Any Muslim who engages in arrogant or vain behavior risks serious punishment both on earth and in the afterlife. The Prophet Muhammad reportedly said that a person with vanity in his or her heart, even if it weighs no more than a mustard seed, will not enter paradise. The Qur'an describes arrogant people as unjust, criminal, and unbelieving and warns that Allah will punish them in the afterlife. Scripture offers examples of arrogant nonbelievers whom God disgraced, defeated, or destroyed, including a Pharaoh and his chiefs.

Muslim jurists traditionally discouraged all types of behavior that might be considered immodest. For example, they advised Muslims not to strut vainly down the street, to raise their voices as a way of demonstrating superiority, or to live luxuriously. They used the example of the Prophet to support their counsel. Muhammad dressed and ate modestly. He also mended his own clothing, helped his wives with housework and child care, and assisted others, especially widows and unmarried women.

The Islamic emphasis on modesty and the increasing tendency to follow the patriarchal (male-dominated) tradition in the Islamic world led some Muslim legal scholars to demand that Muslim women cover their faces and avoid public life. In fact, during the time of the Prophet, women were not required to do either. Today, some jurists have determined that they cannot justify these practices. They have called for a return to moderation, which the Qur'an describes as the defining characteristic of the *ummah* (community of believers). (*See also* **Clothing; Hijab; Women.**)

Mongols

The Mongols were a nomadic tribal people from the steppes of Central Asia who established one of the largest empires in history during the early 1200s. Under their leader Genghis Khan and his successors, they conquered much of Asia, Russia, eastern Europe, and the Middle East. The Mongols dominated a large part of the Islamic world for about 200 years.

Mongol society was organized by alliances among different tribes. Periods of cooperation alternated with times of tribal warfare. Temujin, the son of a chief, became leader of the Börjigin (one of the Mongol peoples). In 1206 he was given the title of Genghis Khan (meaning "Lord of the Steppe"), by members of the grand assembly. Genghis Khan quickly established control over other Mongol tribes and began a series of military campaigns to conquer neighboring territories. By 1227 his empire covered all of Russia and China and much of eastern Europe.

The first conflict between Mongols and the Islamic world occurred in 1218. At first, Genghis Khan tried to make peace with the most powerful Muslim ruler in the region, the Khwarizmshah, who ruled a kingdom near what is now Afghanistan. When the Khwarizmshah refused a peace offering of 1,500 camels, Genghis Khan overran his kingdom and swept into Persia (present-day Iran). Although Genghis Khan died in 1227, his sons continued the military campaigns in the Middle East. In 1258 Genghis Khan's grandson Hulagu Khan captured Baghdad. He burned the city, killing the caliph* and his family and toppling the Abbasid caliphate that had ruled the Islamic world for 500 years. Only a defeat at the hands of Egyptian forces in Syria stopped the Mongols from overrunning the entire Muslim empire.

* **caliph** religious and political leader of an Islamic state

This illustrated manuscript from the late 1200s shows the attack of Baghdad by Mongol troops in 1258. The invaders burned the city and overthrew the Abbasid caliphate, which had ruled the Islamic world for 500 years.

* **patron** one who provides support or financial sponsorship to an artist or scholar

* **dynasty** succession of rulers from the same family or group

* **shari'ah** Islamic law as established in the Qur'an and sunnah, the exemplary behavior of the Prophet Muhammad

The Mongols owed much of their success to their nomadic lifestyle and their skill as horsemen. The military was an important part of Mongol society, and all Mongol men between the ages of 14 and 60 served in the army. Even the annual hunt for food was organized around the military and was aimed at providing training, as well as food, for the community. Life on the move prepared the Mongols for cavalry warfare and for changing direction on short notice. Mongol archers mounted on horses constituted a rapid and powerful attack force that amazed and demoralized their foes. The tactics of the Mongol warriors were often brutal but effective. If the people in a city accepted the conquerors, no harm came to them. If they resisted, however, the Mongols burned the town and slaughtered its inhabitants. For all their brutality in war, the Mongols were civilized rulers. They rebuilt the cities they had destroyed and became patrons* of the arts and sciences. They also kept subject peoples in place to administer the new government.

The Mongols tolerated all religions, but by the late 1200s the ruling dynasties* in Central Asia and the Middle East had converted to Islam. Mongol rulers attempted to use Islam as a political tool. For example, they rejected the use of *shari'ah* * for civil matters and restricted the ability of Muslim clerics to interpret *shari'ah* so that it would not conflict with Mongol civil law. This led the Islamic legal scholar Ibn Taymiyah to label the Mongols unbelievers, thus giving Muslims the right (and even the duty) to engage in jihad* against Mongol rule.

* **jihad** literally "striving"; war in defense of Islam

Following the death of Genghis Khan, the Mongol Empire split into four large states, each ruled by one of his sons. By the 1240s, the different branches of the family began to fight for control with one another. In addition, the leaders of the various states had become accustomed to the luxury of a more settled lifestyle. Over time, the states weakened, both militarily and economically. In the late 1300s, Tamerlane (Timur Lang), a Central Asian conqueror, seized power in one of the Mongol states. He hoped to gain control of the neighboring territories, and in the span of 20 years, he had conquered much of the old empire. In 1404 Tamerlane invaded China, but he died there the following year. His empire soon fell apart, marking the end of Mongol dominance in the region. (*See also* **Abbasid Caliphate; Ibn Taymiyah; Tamerlane.**)

Morocco

A North African country about the size of California, Morocco has existed as an Islamic region since the 700s. Its local name, al-Maghrib, means "sunset," after the ancient Arabic name for North Africa, Bilad al-Maghrib (Lands of Sunset). Morocco's population consists mainly of Arabs and Berbers, a native, nomadic people. Nearly 99 percent of the population is Muslim; 1 percent is Christian; and less than half of 1 percent is Jewish. Morocco has around 30 million inhabitants.

Morocco occupies a strategic position on the northwest coast of Africa, directly south of Spain and Portugal. It borders the North Atlantic Ocean and the Mediterranean Sea, with Algeria to the west and the Western Sahara to the south. Morocco controls the Western Sahara region but faces opposition from a local movement seeking independence. The Moroccan economy relies on agriculture, rock mining, food processing, textiles, and tourism. Droughts plague the region, sometimes causing economic instability. With a rapidly growing population, Morocco strives to increase its educational and economic opportunities.

Islamic Conquerors and Western Invaders

Around 1100 B.C.E.*, Phoenician traders established settlements around North Africa as they made their way to Spain seeking silver and tin. The Romans conquered the area in 146 B.C.E., followed by the Byzantines in 533 C.E.*. In 705 the Islamic Umayyad empire expanded to include North Africa. With two large armies from Egypt, the Umayyads suppressed the fiercely independent Berber tribes. Once conquered, the Berbers readily converted to Islam. They adopted the religion and then worked within it to justify rebellion against rulers they considered corrupt. The concept of jihad* inspired them in their struggles against caliphs*.

* **B.C.E.** before the Common Era, which refers to the same time period as B.C.

* **C.E.** Common Era, which refers to the same time period as A.D.

* **jihad** literally "striving"; war in defense of Islam

* **caliph** religious and political leader of an Islamic state

Berber Rights

Moroccan Berbers are taking part in a growing movement to protect their culture. Called Imazighen, or "free and noble men," Moroccan Berbers fight to establish their language, Amazigh, as the official language of Morocco. Even though 60 percent of Moroccans are Berber, Arabic is the national language. Moroccan schools teach only in Arabic, causing many Imazigh children to drop out in frustration. Berber activists blame the high dropout rate for the continued poverty of the Berbers and for the 56 percent Moroccan illiteracy rate. The government also prohibits parents from registering their children under non-Arabic names, such as Jurgurtha or Messina, the names of ancient Berber kings. In 2001 King Muhammad announced that he would establish a Royal Institute for Amazigh Culture and take steps to integrate Amazigh into the educational system.

* **dynasty** succession of rulers from the same family or group

* **Sufi** refers to Sufism, which seeks to develop spirituality through discipline of the mind and body

* **protectorate** country under the protection and control of a stronger nation

Morocco Under Muslim Influence. Berbers and Arab Muslims clashed on many issues. Umayyad rulers promoted the Islamic doctrine of equality among believers, but often betrayed this ideal in daily life. When recruiting Berbers to aid them in their conquest of Spain, for example, they gave them less pay and lower status than Arab warriors. Caliphs also took Berbers as slaves, especially women. In 740 a rebellion broke out in Tangier, and a Berber dynasty* began in southern Morocco. The Umayyads fought frequently with tribal groups but could not maintain a strong grip on the region.

In 1056 a group of Berber tribes united as the Almoravids (*al-murabitun*, meaning "those who stand together," particularly in defense of Islam). The Almoravids linked themselves to the Qur'anic idea of a holy war. They conquered Morocco, taking over most of North Africa and Muslim Spain. They turned the region into a trading zone with thriving urban centers. In the mid-1100s, the Berber Almohads (*al-muwahhidun*, meaning "those who affirm the unity of God") defeated the Almoravids, promoting a return to traditional Islamic values. Their leader viewed himself as Muhammad's heir and wanted to recreate the Islamic community as it had existed in the time of the Prophet.

The Almohad empire began to disintegrate in the mid-1200s, however. It no longer abided by the principles on which it had been founded, and the ruling class could not maintain power over the various tribes and religious groups. Other Berber tribes took over in North Africa. Cultural centers in Morocco flourished, and rulers financed the construction of elaborate mosques and schools. To the disapproval of the Almohads and other Islamic traditionalists, Sufi* mystic practices and organizations gained popularity, especially in rural areas. Moroccan Sufis emphasized discipline, silence, charity, sorrow, and humility. They were devoted to saints—holy people who they believed could intercede between God and humans, interpret dreams, and perform miracles.

Morocco remained politically fragmented with small tribes spread across the region and a lack of a strong central government until the 1600s, when the Alawi (*al-alawi*, or descendants of Ali, Muhammad's cousin and son-in-law) came to power. The Alawi dynasty unified Morocco and continue to reign in the region in the present day. They suffered internal chaos and economic instability but defended Morocco against the Ottomans, who took over neighboring Algeria and other North African states. The threat of invasion, however, did not end with the Ottomans. In the early 1900s, France and Spain took advantage of the Alawi's weakness and divided Morocco into protectorates*.

Resistance to the French and Spanish. In European-controlled Morocco, the sultan appeared to be in control. A French general, however, ruled middle and southern Morocco, and the Spanish established a puppet government (local government controlled by an outside authority) in the north. After suppressing a five-year rebellion in the 1920s, the Spanish had a relatively peaceful reign. Spain maintained friendly relations with the Moroccans, allowing them to receive their education in Arabic and encouraging them to attend Islamic universities in Egypt. Many Moroccans, however, joined General Francisco Franco in his attack on the Spanish Republic during the Spanish Civil War (1936–1939).

The French implemented harsher policies than the Spanish. They disarmed the Berber tribes, forced them to pay taxes, and seized their land. They also suppressed the ruling class, established a new court system, and allowed only a small number of Muslims to study at institutions of higher education. The French attempted to divide Moroccans by pitting the Berbers against the Arabs. Their plan backfired, however, meeting with resistance from both sides and leading to the creation of a unified nationalist* movement.

Moroccan nationalists began a serious rebellion against France after it fell to the Germans during World War II (1939–1945). The Alawi sultan Muhammad V refused to approve anti-Jewish legislation imposed by the Nazis and pushed for Moroccan independence. When the French exiled him in 1953, he became an instant hero to his people. Faced with increasing opposition from resistance groups in Algeria and other North African countries, the French restored the Moroccan sultan to the throne in 1955. The country became a constitutional monarchy, and Morocco declared its independence in 1956.

Foreign and Domestic Concerns

After the withdrawal of France and Spain, Morocco had to rebuild itself. The French had improved agriculture and communications, expanded industry, and built a modern infrastructure*. They had managed most of these activities, however, by taking land from native Moroccans and excluding them from the more rewarding endeavors. Once the Europeans left the region, the economy declined. Morocco went into debt and people rioted against the government. Moroccans worked hard to gain control of their economy. The French had secularized* the school system in many areas and had introduced Western dress and customs. Many Muslims took measures to return to traditional Islamic values.

When the sultan died in 1961, his son Hasan II succeeded him. Hasan triumphed over dissenting parties and claimed victory in a 1977 election that many viewed as manipulated. He established a strong central government, exerting more control over rural and tribal areas than previous rulers. Hasan won the approval of most Moroccans when he sought to recover the former Spanish colony of Western Sahara, a region dominated by Muslim Berbers in medieval* times.

Struggle Over Western Sahara. Morocco continues to engage in a struggle for control over Western Sahara. In 1957, the year after it gained independence, Morocco made a claim on the region and battled with Spanish colonizers. The struggle grew more complicated after Mauritania declared that it, too, had rights to Saharan land. Meanwhile, native Saharans began to rebel. Spain withdrew from the region in 1976, leaving the issue for Morocco and Mauritania to resolve.

By an agreement between the two countries, Morocco received the northern region, an area rich in minerals. Both Morocco and Mauritania faced opposition from the native Polisario Front, however, which pushed for Saharan independence. Mauritania made a peace agreement with the organization in 1979, and Morocco promptly seized its share of the Sahara. In 1988 Morocco and the Polisario Front accepted a United Nations peace proposal allowing Saharans to vote on whether to become part of Morocco officially or to accept the leadership of the Polisario Front. As of 2003, however, the vote has

* **nationalism** feelings of loyalty and devotion to one's country and a commitment to its independence

* **infrastructure** basic facilities and institutions that a country needs in order to function

* **secularize** to separate religion from other aspects of human life and society

* **medieval** refers to the Middle Ages, a period roughly between 500 and 1500

165

still not occurred. Large numbers of Moroccan settlers have moved into Western Sahara, pushing tens of thousands of native Saharans into refugee camps in Algeria and increasing tensions between Morocco and Algeria.

Political and Religious Issues. Moroccan Muslims continue to debate the merits of their government and the best way to practice Islam. Conservative* Muslims criticize Sufis for their festivals honoring the saints, which they believe take the focus away from God. They also frown on the use of music, dancing, and the mixing of men and women at religious gatherings. In the early 1900s, a Salafi* movement arose in Morocco. Members of this movement denounce Sufism and urge for a return to traditional Islamic values. They believe that God enabled the first Muslims to conquer much of the world because they obeyed his laws. When Muslims deviated from God's laws, he allowed the unbelievers of Europe to conquer them. If Muslims returned to the roots of their religion, they would once again prevail over their enemies. Members of the Salafi sect worked to gain Moroccan independence and attracted many followers.

Sultan Hasan died in 1999 and was succeeded by his son Muhammad VI. Educated in the West, Muhammad seeks to modernize Morocco. He has expressed interest in such reforms as a literacy program for rural women and changes in divorce laws that would aid women and provide equal division of property between spouses. Many conservative Muslims oppose Muhammad's ideas, but Islamist groups remain too divided on the issues to pose a serious threat to the government. (*See also* **North Africa; Salafi; Sufism.**)

* **conservative** generally opposed to change, especially in existing political and social institutions

* **Salafi** reform movements of the early 1900s that sought to restore Islamic doctrines to pure form

Mosque

* **Qur'an** book of the holy scriptures of Islam

* **prostration** act of lying facedown in respect, submission, or worship

According to the Qur'an*, a mosque is God's "sacred house," a setting for Muslims to perform rituals, and a "meeting place for the people." The term *mosque* derives from the Arab word *masjid*, meaning a "place for (ritual) prostration*." A *jami* is a congregational mosque used specifically for Friday prayers. In modern times, the words *masjid* and *jami* are used interchangeably. The term *musalla* designates informal areas and open-air spaces set apart for prayers. Although a mosque primarily serves as a place for formal prayer, throughout the history of Islam, its functions have been practical as well as spiritual.

History

Muhammad reportedly said: "The earth is a mosque for you, so pray wherever you happen to be when prayer time comes." Although Islam places few restrictions on the place of prayer, wherever Muslims have settled in large numbers, one of their first tasks has been to erect a mosque. As Islam spread, mosques appeared across the Middle East, North Africa, Central Asia, and the Indian subcontinent.

See color plate 8, vol. 1.

Spread Across the Empire. Muhammad built the first mosque in the courtyard of his house in Medina in 622. It was one of the events that marked the establishment of the Islamic community. Muslims assembled at this house-

mosque for prayer and to discuss business matters. The mosque became Muhammad's burial site.

The mosques of Medina, Mecca, and Jerusalem have special status in Islam. According to the hadith*, a visit to the Medina mosque will win Muhammad's intercession* on the Day of Judgment. The Kaaba, a shrine* located near the center of the Grand Mosque in Mecca, is said to be the earthly representation of God's throne in heaven. Muslims believe that the al-Aqsa Mosque in Jerusalem is the site of the Prophet's famous Night Journey.

Muslims built mosques nearly everywhere they settled. During the conquests of Iraq and North Africa in the 600s, advancing Arab armies created prayer spaces in the center of their camps. As military posts developed into cities, such as Basra and Kufa (in Iraq) and Fustat (on the future site of Cairo in Egypt), prayer spaces evolved into buildings. In some captured foreign cities, Muslims converted temples, churches, and palaces into mosques.

In the early period of Islam, the mosques in cities were usually one of two types. Large state buildings were used for Friday prayer and community assemblies. Muslim caliphs* and their appointed governors often established their residences close to these mosques. Small mosques were built and operated by various groups within the community. Both state and private mosques depended on donations and *waqf** endowments for support.

* **hadith** reports of the words and deeds of Muhammad (not in the Qur'an, but accepted as guides for Muslim behavior)

* **intercession** act of pleading for another

* **shrine** place that is considered sacred because of its history or the relics contained there

* **caliph** religious and political leader of an Islamic state

* *waqf* donation of property for charitable causes

As the Islamic empire grew, the number of mosques increased. For example, Fustat-Cairo had one congregational mosque during the 600s. By the 1400s, it had 130, along with several hundred additional small mosques. Other cities, such as Damascus and Aleppo in Syria and Fez in Morocco, followed a similar pattern. Beginning in the mid-1400s, the Ottomans took over much of the central Islamic world. During the reign of Mehmed II (ruled 1451–1481), they built almost 200 new mosques.

Both Shi'is* and Sufis* have played major roles in the construction of mosques over the tombs of the Prophet, his family, and other holy men and women. These tomb-mosques became pilgrimage sites, and some functioned as congregational mosques as well. During the late 1900s, Muslims built mosques at an unprecedented rate. Several factors contributed to this surge: the Muslim population greatly expanded during this period, Arab oil revenues boosted state and private support for mosques, and Muslims increasingly sought to maintain their identity in an ever-changing global society.

The Blueprint. The Islamic world is noted for its distinctive architecture, and the mosque is its most impressive example. Early mosque designers modeled their buildings on Muhammad's mosque-house in Medina. Unfired brick walls surrounded the spacious open courtyard, which contained rooms for the Prophet and his wives. The prayer area had a roof supported by columns made of the trunks of palm trees.

Mosque design has undergone many changes since the 600s, and the characteristics of mosques vary. Generally, the building includes a large open area—sometimes covered by a roof—for prayer. Mats or carpets cover the floor. The imam* delivers the Friday sermon from the *minbar*, a platform modeled on the stone structure that the Prophet ascended to give his sermons. The *minbar* stands next to the *mihrab*, a semicircular niche set into a wall of the mosque to indicate the direction of Mecca.

Islamic law requires Muslims to perform ritual washing (ablution) before prayer. Mosques contain *ziyadahs,* walls that hold the facilities for ablution. Outside the mosque stands the minaret, a tower from which the muezzin calls the faithful to prayer five times a day. In addition, mosques include a separate chamber for women, because female worshippers are not permitted to pray in the main area with men.

Mosque walls are decorated with mosaics*, verses from the Qur'an, and sometimes, the names of Muhammad and his companions. The buildings do not, however, include pictures, statues, or ritual objects.

Hub of Activity

All Muslims are required to practice the five Pillars of Islam; one pillar is prayer five times each day and community prayer in the mosque on Fridays. The mosque basically exists as a place for Muslims to perform these rituals. Even so, this institution serves a variety of other functions. Today, as in the past, mosques hold great social, political, and educational importance.

Community Connection. The Qur'an and sunnah provide two models for the connection between the mosque and society. One portrays the mosque as a place reserved for spiritual matters, and the other depicts it as the hub

Shi'i refers to Muslims who believe that Muhammad chose Ali ibn Abi Talib and his descendants as the spiritual-political leaders of the Muslim community

Sufi follower of Sufism, which seeks to develop spirituality through discipline of the mind and body

imam spiritual-political leader in Shi'i Islam, one who is regarded as directly descended from Muhammad; also, one who leads prayers

mosaic art form in which small pieces of stone or glass are set into cement to form a picture or pattern

of public affairs. Most mosques combine aspects of both models, to a greater or lesser degree. Some mosques may be situated in relatively isolated areas, while others are located in a capital city or in a busy neighborhood. Builders may design mosques as a composite complex. For example, the *Süleymaniye külliye* of Istanbul, built in the 1500s, consists of a congregational mosque, two schools, a hospital, a public bath, a public kitchen, fountains, housing, shops, cafes, and a cemetery, among other sections.

Historically, mosques had an established hierarchy*. At the top was the imam, an individual who had a thorough knowledge of the sacred Islamic texts. Religious scholars and jurists were also members of the core leadership. They often served as intermediaries between the ruler and the people. Village and tribal mosques sometimes incorporated devotion to holy men or women, usually deceased, who acted as intercessors with God. A chosen disciple or descendant of the saint was usually the unofficial leader in such settings.

Today mosques fall under either government or private sponsorship. In the case of a government mosque, the buildings and staff receive financial support from the state. The Ministry of Religious Affairs or its equivalent hires a professional preacher and monitors his performance. By contrast, a private mosque receives funds from charitable associations. The congregation usually sets the agenda and selects the preacher. Some private mosques attract a sizable following, and their preachers attain social and political prominence.

Although practices vary across the Islamic world, important rituals and ceremonies often take place in the mosque. Muslims commonly place the body of a deceased relative before the *mihrab* for funerary prayers. Believers frequently visit their mosques before and after the hajj* or a minor pilgrimage*. Mosques also serve as the centers for the collection and distribution of *zakat* (charity). Business agreements may be reached in a mosque. During times of crisis, Muslims gather at a mosque for mutual support and guidance.

Expression of Ideas. Since the days of Muhammad, the mosque has been a center of political activity. Early mosques were gathering places for political discussion and debate. Pious Muslim rulers placed great importance on building a central mosque, usually located near the palace.

In recent years, the mosque has become even more politically relevant for several reasons. Mosques provide a forum for the exchange of ideas and an opportunity to challenge the questionable practices of the authorities. Under oppressive regimes, a preacher may use his sermon to criticize the country's leadership. Since the 1970s, some Muslim rulers have elevated the importance of the mosque. Saudi Arabia's King Faysal and Iran's Ayatollah Khomeini, for example, attended Friday prayers and publicized these events. In the process, such leaders created a sense of cultural pride and encouraged other Muslims to follow their example. Globalization has enabled imams to relate local issues to international events. In this way, the mosque can shape a unified Muslim response to contemporary political issues.

In many Muslim societies, private mosques are the main focus of opposition to the government, and therefore, subject to increasing control. During the 1990s, for example, the Egyptian government attempted to incorporate many of these institutions into its administrative system. The authorities often pressure the imams of government-controlled mosques to avoid preach-

* **hierarchy** system of rank within an organization

* **hajj** pilgrimage to Mecca that Muslims are required to make once in their lifetime

* **pilgrimage** journey to a shrine or sacred place

A Link to the Past

The Great Mosque of Damascus is the oldest surviving stone mosque. Caliph al-Walid I (ruled 705–715) built the structure on a site that formerly housed a temple of the Roman god Jupiter, and later, a church of St. John the Baptist. Also called the Umayyad Mosque, the building was a monument to the greatness of Islamic civilization. Occupying an immense quadrangle, which measures 515 feet by 330 feet, its walls were once covered by dazzling mosaics depicting scenes from paradise. Rows of columns divide the worship hall into three long aisles, and marble grilles cover the windows. A foreign army destroyed the mosque in 1401. Arabs later rebuilt it, but in 1893, a fire damaged the structure once again. Although the mosque never regained its original splendor, it remains an example of early Muslim architectural achievement.

Mosque

See color plate 3, vol. 3.

*theology study of the nature and qualities of God and the understanding of His will

*sunnah literally "the trodden path"; Islamic customs based on the exemplary behavior of Muhammad

*shari'ah Islamic law as established in the Qur'an and sunnah, the exemplary behavior of the Prophet Muhammad

*scripture sacred writings that contain revelations from God

*secular separate from religion in human life and society; connected to everyday life

*nationalist refers to nationalism, feelings of loyalty and devotion to one's country and a commitment to its independence

ing about political topics. In some instances, government officials write the sermons to be delivered at the mosques.

Pursuit of Knowledge. From the beginning of Islam, the mosque has functioned as a center of religious education. At an early age, children learned to memorize passages from the Qur'an and hadith. At a higher level, mosques enabled Muslims to advance their religious knowledge through inquiry, debate, and discussion. In 978 the Fatimid dynasty established al-Azhar, a mosque-university, and it remains one of the world's oldest institutions of higher learning.

Early mosque education varied across the Islamic world. Communities and regions differed in their approach to the teaching of tradition, laws, and theology*. Moreover, certain branches of Islam incorporated their own ideas and practices. Nevertheless, most mosques emphasized a set body of religious knowledge consisting of the Qur'an, sunnah*, and *shari'ah**.

For centuries, mosques provided higher education in scripture* and law. Certain features were characteristic of the great Sunni mosques during the early 1800s. Revenues from *waqf* endowments and donations from wealthy Muslims financed the educational system. Although some students traveled great distances to study with respected religious scholars, most were from nearby towns and villages. Mosques attracted students from a wide range of economic backgrounds. For students from poor, rural families, a mosque education provided an opportunity for upward mobility. Young, affluent Muslims pursued a mosque education as an avenue to important government or religious positions.

Knowledge of classical Arabic was a requirement for mosque studies. Religious scholars lectured from a favorite pillar in the mosque with students gathered at their feet. After a student completed several years of study under a particular teacher, the teacher issued an *ijazah* (written statement) certifying that the student had successfully mastered certain texts and was qualified to teach them. Mosques did not have required courses, and students did not receive an official degree or diploma other than the *ijazah*.

Between 1850 and 1950, mosque education underwent major changes. Reformers of that period encouraged Muslims to pursue modern learning, arguing that a modern education was the key to overcoming European dominance. As Muslim countries achieved independence from colonial rule, their new governments reduced the power of the traditional religious authorities, which extended to education practices. Beyond these forces, however, economic and social changes were the primary causes of the decline of traditional mosque education. As younger Muslims embraced secular*, nationalist* ideas, this type of education declined in status and value. In recent decades, the modern Islamic university has become the preferred place for higher education in the religious sciences. Mosque education persists at the elementary level and in informal ways, such as adult instruction in the Qur'an and sunnah.

Building Boom. Muslims who settled in western Europe and North America during the early 1900s expressed little interest in establishing Islamic institutions. Many of them expected to earn enough money to be able to return to their native countries. Even when they decided to remain in the West, they lacked the resources to build mosques. Consequently, many held prayer services in their homes.

By the 1930s, Muslim immigrants sought more formal ways to observe their religious traditions and to affirm their social identity. Mosque construction began slowly, but after 1970, building activity increased significantly. Several factors caused the dramatic growth in the number of mosques and Islamic centers in Europe and North America. Muslim populations in the West increased. Muslim governments, rich from oil revenues and eager to cultivate Islamic communities abroad, provided the funding for mosque construction. Several European governments even supported the mosque movement, largely out of concern that minority Muslim populations would become angry and frustrated if they did not have a voice in the community.

By the beginning of the twenty-first century, the United States had an estimated 1,450 mosques, Islamic centers, and prayer halls. More than 5,000 were located in Europe, and almost one-half of them were in Germany. Mosques in the West vary in style. Muslims in the United States often convert former churches or other buildings into mosques.

For Muslims living in the West, mosques serve many of the same social, political, and educational functions that they did at home. In addition, they forge a sense of solidarity among the members of the minority Muslim population. Many turn to the mosque as a haven from discrimination and a place to receive moral support. At the mosque, Muslims affirm their shared values and reinforce their Islamic identity. (*See also* **Ablution; Architecture; Azhar, al-; Education; Imam; Minorities; Muhammad; Prayer; Rites and Rituals; Sermon.**)

Mughal Empire

From the mid-1500s to the mid-1700s, the Mughal Empire dominated most of the Indian subcontinent. At its peak, this Muslim dynasty* was one of the wealthiest in the Islamic world. Historians attribute much of the empire's success to a policy of religious tolerance toward non-Muslims, especially India's majority Hindu* population. During the late 1600s, a period of oppression and government mismanagement led to civil unrest and the eventual decline of the empire. Great Britain exiled the last Mughal ruler in 1857 and took control of the subcontinent.

Appreciating Diversity. The Mughal Empire was founded by a prince named Babur (ca. 1483–1530), who claimed descent from two great conquerors—Genghis Khan and Tamerlane (Timur Lang). Forced to leave his Central Asian kingdom, Babur seized control of the region of northwestern India known as the Punjab. By 1530 he ruled much of northern India. After Babur's death, his son Humayun lost control of the newly acquired Mughal territory in a war with Afghan rebels. Humayun regained the throne in 1555 but died shortly thereafter. His son Akbar succeeded him as emperor.

Akbar displayed outstanding military and political skills and established a lasting reputation as the greatest Mughal ruler. When he died in 1605, his empire consisted of Afghanistan and most of India. Even more impressive than his military conquests was his ability to unite the people under his rule. India consisted of many diverse cultures and religious traditions, and Muslims were only a small minority. Akbar recognized that he needed broad support to gov-

* **dynasty** succession of rulers from the same family or group

* **Hindu** refers to the beliefs and practices of Hinduism, an ancient religion that originated in India

See map in India (vol. 2).

ern effectively. He eliminated the *jizyah*, a tax traditionally imposed on non-Muslims. Convinced of the importance of maintaining good relations with the Hindus under his rule, Akbar appointed many Hindus to government posts and enlisted them in the army. Unlike earlier rulers, he allowed them to keep their own laws and customs. Showing respect for Hindu dietary laws, Akbar became a vegetarian and gave up hunting, his favorite pastime.

Akbar's policies reflected not only political reality but also his own religious commitment to spirituality, tolerance of other faiths, and recognition of universal religious principles. Although Akbar's pluralistic* policies won the acceptance of his Hindu subjects, they offended some Muslims. Conservative* Muslim leaders felt that granting Hinduism and other religions equal status with Islam was dangerous.

The Disintegration of an Empire. Akbar's son Jahangir maintained the political structure and tolerant policies of his father's reign. Jahangir's son Shah Jahan (ruled 1627–1657) also followed the general principles of Akbar's administration but was more conservative than his ancestors, stressing Islamic law rather than spirituality. Shah Jahan was a great patron* of the arts, and under his rule, architecture experienced a golden age. He built India's famous Taj Mahal in memory of his adored queen. A capable military leader, Shah Jahan expanded the boundaries of the Mughal Empire, but his military campaigns created significant economic problems.

The demise of the Mughal Empire began during the reign of Shah Jahan's successor, Aurangzeb. Worsening economic conditions led Aurangzeb to impose restrictions on non-Muslims within the empire. He removed them from government positions, and under pressure from the *ulama**, he reinstated the *jizyah*. Throughout the empire, Hindu temples and schools were destroyed. Aurangzeb also persecuted followers of a new Indian religious tradition, who were known as Sikhs*.

Aurangzeb's military conquests expanded the empire to its greatest size, but such growth came at a huge cost. To make up for the cost of his campaigns, he imposed heavy taxes on his subjects. Farmers, especially, were soon unable to bear the load, which led to a decline in agriculture, an important sector of the economy. As the state became poorer and rivalry between Muslims and Hindus increased, groups throughout the empire began to challenge Mughal authority.

The empire fell into decline after Aurangzeb's death in 1707. Persian and Afghan invaders attempted to conquer parts of northern India, and Sikhs and the Hindus from the mountainous regions continued to oppose Mughal rule. Moreover, the power of the Mughal emperors weakened as they allowed Great Britain to establish trading centers in the area.

By the 1750s, the Hindu Marathas had taken control of much of northern India, reducing Mughal authority to a small region around Delhi. In 1785 the Marathas captured Delhi, the seat of the empire, but by the early 1800s the British had established control over the city. The Mughal Empire continued as a British protectorate*. Following an uprising in 1857, Great Britain abolished the Mughal dynasty and established formal political rule over India. The authorities exiled the last Mughal emperor, Bahadur Shah II, to Myanmar (formerly Burma) for his part in the revolt. (*See also* **Akbar, Jalaludin Muhammad; India.**)

* **pluralistic** refers to a condition of society in which diverse groups maintain and develop their traditional culture or special interests

* **conservative** generally opposed to change, especially in existing political and social institutions

* **patron** person of wealth and influence who supports a writer, artist, or scholar

* *ulama* religious scholars

* **Sikh** refers to Sikhism, a branch of Hinduism that rejects caste and idolatry

See color plate 14, vol. 2.

* **protectorate** country under the protection and control of a stronger nation

Muhammad

ca. 570–632
Prophet of Islam

Although little is known about Muhammad's early life, his later experiences were carefully documented by contemporaries and by people in the generations immediately after. His actions form the content of the sunnah*, an essential source of Islamic law. Reports of Muhammad's character have inspired not only Muslims but also people of all religions. Many authors, from medieval* scribes to modern European biographers, have written about the Prophet.

* **sunnah** literally "the trodden path"; Islamic customs based on the exemplary behavior of Muhammad

* **medieval** refers to the Middle Ages, a period roughly between 500 and 1500

Life of the Prophet

Muhammad gave rise to one of the great world civilizations. His teachings united Arab tribes and eventually spread to every continent. Muslims view the Prophet as *rasul Allah* (God's Messenger) to Arabs and to all humankind. The Qur'an* serves as the main source of information about Muhammad. Other works include the *sirah* (biographical texts compiled in the century after the Prophet's death), the hadith*, and general histories composed around the same time as the *sirah.*

* **Qur'an** book of the holy scriptures of Islam

* **hadith** reports of the words and deeds of Muhammad (not in the Qur'an, but accepted as guides for Muslim behavior)

Childhood and Youth. Many legends have arisen around Muhammad's childhood. According to the *sirah* and hadith, Muhammad's mother Aminah emitted a light when she was pregnant, and a glow lit up the city of Busra in Syria when she gave birth. As a boy, Muhammad tended sheep and had protection from the sun by a large cloud that formed over his head. Various spiritual leaders declared that Muhammad would become a prophet. Favorable marks appeared on his back, and he sat under auspicious* trees while resting from his work.

* **auspicious** conveying a favorable omen

Although few details about the Prophet's childhood were recorded, scholars know that Muhammad was born in Mecca. His father died before he was born, and his mother died after he reached the age of six. Muhammad went to live with his paternal grandfather, who put him in the care of a nomadic tribe, as was the custom for young boys at the time. Muhammad was a quiet, reflective youth who occasionally spent nights in meditation in a cave in a hill. He often accompanied his uncle Abu Talib on trading journeys to Syria. On one such expedition, a wealthy widow named Khadija hired him to look after her goods. She was so impressed with the trustworthiness of the young man that she hired him to manage the business she had inherited. Eventually, she proposed marriage. The couple had four daughters who reached adulthood and at least three sons who died in infancy. Until Khadija died about 24 years later, Muhammad took no other wife.

Divine Inspiration. Muhammad had his first revelation* at about the age of 40, receiving a vision that he later identified as the angel Gabriel. The angel asked him to recite, but Muhammad did not understand the significance of the command. Gabriel repeated his request two more times, then declared Muhammad a messenger of God. Muhammad accepted his role and continued to receive revelations and transmit them to his followers until his death.

* **revelation** message from God to humans transmitted through a prophet

After Muhammad's appointment as God's messenger, he went on the celebrated Night Journey (*isra*). According to tradition, the Prophet embarked

Muhammad

* **Kaaba** literally "House of God"; Islamic shrine in Mecca

on a miraculous overnight voyage from the sanctuary near the Kaaba* to the Temple Mount in Jerusalem, where he experienced the Ascension (*miraj*) to heaven. During this event, Muhammad encountered the Prophets Abraham, Moses, and Jesus, prayed with them, and received instruction on the proper form of prayer. Muslims celebrate this event, which is mentioned in the Qur'an, on the 27th day of the month of Rajab.

Muhammad experienced divine inspiration in many ways. He received no visions after the first one but sometimes perspired on a cold day or heard the sound of a bell. Most often, he felt the presence of a message in his heart. Muhammad's friends and family accepted his new role, and joined him in prayers. In 613 Muhammad began to preach publicly. His early messages focused on the oneness of God, the terrors that await the proud or the greedy on the Day of Judgment, and the idea that people should exercise goodwill toward one another. He placed special emphasis on the practice of caring for the poor, especially orphans and widows.

Muhammad believed that his revelations stemmed from the same divine source as Jewish and Christian doctrine. The Prophet's revelations did not constitute a separate religion but conveyed the same ideas in a form suitable for the Arabs. Many of Muhammad's followers were neither Christian nor Jewish but believed in monotheism*. Some were poor members of weak clans, and others belonged to wealthy clans. All were dissatisfied with the materialistic* nature of Meccan society. Muhammad and his followers denounced the emphasis on competition and worldly goods in Mecca, which served as a center for trade and the destination of an annual Arab pilgrim-

* **monotheism** belief that there is only one God

* **materialism** belief in the high value of worldly goods and money

age. Merchants tried to quiet the Prophet by offering him a bride from a wealthy family, but he refused.

Polytheistic* Arabs mistrusted Muhammad for his assertion of the existence of only one God. Some accused the Prophet of practicing sorcery or being possessed by jinn (spirits). They challenged him to perform miracles and persecuted him and his followers when he refused. Several Qur'anic verses depict God as comforting Muhammad, telling him to have faith. The Meccans taunted Muhammad, boycotting his community and preventing his followers from buying food. Muhammad's clan withdrew its protection from him in 619, making him even more vulnerable to attack. In 622 Muhammad accepted an invitation from feuding clans in Medina, a city north of Mecca whose citizens had heard of his reputation as a just arbiter*. Muhammad and his followers embarked on the Hijrah* to Medina.

Journey to Medina and Battles With Unbelievers. News of the Prophet's journey spread to Medina by way of traders, and when Muhammad arrived, 75 people met him to profess their allegiance. They vowed to defend Muhammad, taking what became known as the pledge of al-Aqaba, which indicated their continuing support for him. The Prophet enjoyed life in the fertile climate of Medina and gained many more followers.

Upon arrival in Medina, Muhammad drafted an agreement with tribal leaders. It guaranteed religious freedom and mutual respect to all and required clans to fight together against enemies. Muhammad suffered a deep disappointment, however, when some of the Jewish tribes refused to accept him as a prophet. After powerful authorities rejected his claims, Muhammad broke away from Jewish and Christian tradition, establishing Islam as a separate religion. He and his followers turned away from Jerusalem when praying, facing Mecca instead. Muhammad exiled two Jewish clans, taking over their businesses and lands. He ordered the killing of the male members of another clan that had joined forces with his Meccan enemies, and forced the women and children into slavery.

The wealthy Quraysh tribe of Mecca continued to harass the Muslims, seizing and selling their property. The Prophet responded, sending out raiding parties to attack their caravans. The Meccans and the Muslims fought a major battle in 624 at Badr, where Muhammad's troops had intercepted a caravan led by the powerful leader Abu Sufyan. The Meccans sent a force three times as large as Muhammad's. Against all expectations, the Prophet's army prevailed, causing many to believe it had been divinely protected. Large numbers of Arabs converted to Islam, and Bedouin* tribes began to show greater interest in the religion. Muhammad's troops, however, suffered heavy losses at Abu Sufyan's hands the following year. Despite this setback, the Prophet ultimately gained control over Mecca.

Victory Over Mecca. In 628 Muhammad was inspired to make a pilgrimage to Mecca. Muhammad and his followers traveled almost 300 miles. They camped outside of town, where Meccan leaders rode to greet them. Muhammad and the Meccans agreed to a ten-year truce if he would wait until the following year to enter Mecca. Muhammad traveled back to Medina with his followers.

In the spring, Muhammad again led his followers to Mecca, where they finally completed their pilgrimage. Later that year, however, a Meccan army

* **polytheistic** refers to believing in more than one god

* **arbiter** person with the authority to settle disputes

* **Hijrah** celebrated emigration of Muhammad from Mecca in 622, which marks the first year of the Islamic calendar

See map in Middle East (vol. 2).

* **Bedouin** nomad of the desert, especially in North Africa, Syria, and Arabia

broke the truce by attacking a group of Muslims. Abu Sufyan and other clan leaders rushed to Medina to persuade Muhammad to refrain from launching an assault on their city. They agreed to peacefully surrender Mecca. In 630 Muhammad and his forces took control of Mecca without a fight. The Prophet quelled uprisings from neighboring clans, destroyed idols in the Kaaba and other shrines, and demanded that rich Meccans grant loans to his poorest followers. Muhammad established himself as ruler of the region and settled in Medina with his wives and children.

The following year, the "Year of Deputations," many tribes sent messengers to Muhammad's headquarters to pledge their loyalty to him. Meccans also converted to Islam in large numbers. Muhammad had gained control of Arabia, quickly suppressing any opposition. In 632 he embarked on his last pilgrimage to Mecca, called the Farewell Pilgrimage by his followers. On the return trip, he contracted a fatal illness. Knowing that he would not survive, he retired to the apartment of his youngest and favorite wife, A'ishah, who tended him throughout his illness. Muhammad died in June at the age of 60. His followers appointed A'ishah's father, Abu Bakr, as caliph*, or "successor" to the Prophet.

* **caliph** religious and political leader of an Islamic state

Muhammad's Character. The Prophet conquered a large part of the Arabian Peninsula, organized a community of believers in a major world religion, and set in motion the creation of a vast empire. Muslims consider him the last and the greatest prophet. They acknowledge, however, that he was human and are careful to avoid elevating him to supernatural status, as they believe the Christians did with Jesus. The Qur'an and hadith reveal Muhammad as a mortal with desires and limitations. Even after gaining many converts and defeating the Meccans, the Prophet agonized over the fact that he had not convinced every Arab of the truth of his teachings. In the Qur'an, God offers him words of comfort. God also reminds him that he has sinned, although He does not specify how. He tells the Prophet that he is mortal, and that, like everyone else, he will have to face the angels on the Day of Judgment.

The Qur'an reveals Muhammad to be charming, vigorous, and quick of thought and action, although gentle with children. The Prophet enjoyed the company of women and had at least nine wives. He also liked perfume and good food. His preference for nuts and honey influenced Muslims to use these ingredients for holiday meals and healthy snacks. Muhammad also had a humble and retiring side, as shown in God's instructions: "O believers, do not enter the apartments of the Prophet, unless you are given permission for a meal. . . . Do not linger for idle talk, for that would be an annoyance to the Prophet, and he would be shy to ask you [to leave]."

Modern scholars debate aspects of the Prophet's character. Some, for example, criticize him for having so many wives. Others find fault with his apparent eagerness for battle. The Prophet, however, lived in a society in which tribal warfare was commonplace, and where tribes were expected to conduct raids on their aggressors. Most battles fought by Muhammad were initiated by his enemies, and many of his armed expeditions resulted in a show of strength rather than in actual combat. A few scholars condemn the Prophet for his tactics, but most view him as using the methods of the time to found and shape a new community.

Muhammad's Impact on the Arab World

Islam had a huge impact on the Arabian Peninsula. It united warring clans, creating a civilization out of a fragmented society. The Islamic empire spread over the Middle East, Africa, and Europe, attracting many converts. Islamic law led to changes in everyday life. Muhammad promoted the development of inner spirituality. He preached an ethical code that would establish a just and peaceful society on earth and enable believers to gain divine favor on the Day of Judgment.

Influence on Society. Before Islam, Arabian society consisted of scattered clans and families. Muhammad worked to create the *ummah* (community of believers) that would transcend tribal loyalties. To accomplish this goal, he established the five Pillars of Islam: *shahadah* (profession of faith), *salat* (prayer), *zakat* (charity), *sawm* (fasting during the month of Ramadan) and *hajj* (pilgrimage to Mecca). Each pillar serves a certain purpose. Ritual prayer binds Muslims together. Charity promotes a sense of common welfare and responsibility for others. By declaring their belief in Islam and participating in the Ramadan fast, Muslims affirm their loyalty to the group and to Islamic values. The pilgrimage to Mecca—the location of the Kaaba—serves to remind Muslims of the roots of their heritage.

Muhammad also altered Arabian society by preaching the existence of one God. While Christians and Jews believed in monotheism, Arabian tribes placed their faith in many deities. They built shrines to different gods, believing them responsible for such domains as fertility and victory in battle. Muhammad destroyed these temples and idols, cautioning Arabs against creating images of the divine being. Instead of seeking favors from the deities, Muslims prayed to God for spiritual reasons.

In addition, Muhammad introduced a code of ethics to his followers. The Qur'an calls for justice, compassion, and mercy for the poor and vulnerable. It also establishes rules to deal with conflict. Before Islam, clans typically created their own laws, with responsibilities and rights determined by patriarchs*. Under Muslim rule, everyone had to follow certain modes of behavior. When settling feuds, for example, Muhammad encouraged members of families not to kill one another but to accept monetary compensation instead. If the family decided that they could only retaliate through bloodshed, the offended family could kill only the wrongdoer, not any other member of the family. This ruling provided a sense of security among families, as they knew that they did not have to fear mass vengeance for the misdeed of one person.

As well as taking steps to regulate criminal law, Muhammad imposed restrictions on financial transactions. The Qur'an prohibits the practice of collecting interest on loans and promotes fairness in business dealings and contractual agreements. Many schools of law emerged from Islamic doctrine, and the justice system of many Muslim countries relies heavily on the Qur'an and hadith.

Influence on the Family. Muhammad's teaching altered family life as well as Muslim society. Before Islam, families were highly patriarchal. Male heads of families arranged marriages to suit their interests rather than the wishes of the married couple. Women had inferior status and typically could not own property. Family life, however, varied considerably from group to group. In some tribes, women practiced polyandry (the practice of taking more than one

The Prophet's Advice

Many Muslims went to Muhammad seeking help for problems. The hadith contain the Prophet's advice on a wide range of matters, including dreams, conduct in battle, gift-giving, and medicine. According to one hadith, a nomad asked Muhammad what he should do if he came across a lost object. The Prophet told him to make a public announcement about it for a year, then to keep it for himself if no one claimed it. The man inquired about a lost sheep, to which Muhammad replied, "It is for you, for your brother [the owner], or for the wolf." When the nomad expanded the question to include camels, the Prophet lost patience and said, "You have nothing to do with it, as it has its feet [and] its water reserve and can reach places of water and drink, and eat trees."

*****patriarch** male head of a group

See color plate 1, vol. 1.

husband). In others, men had multiple wives who either lived together or in different tribes, receiving visits from the husband on a rotating basis. These various structures created a fragmented society, which Muhammad tried to unite.

The Qur'an outlaws marriage between close relations and discourages divorce. It views the husband as the head of the household but insists on the dignity and full humanity of women. It limits polygyny* to special cases and commands men to treat their wives fairly. It encourages harmonious, respectful relations between husband and wife. The Qur'an also gives women property and inheritance rights and enables them to receive support from their husband for a limited time after a divorce.

Issues for Biographers

Biographies of Muhammad have appeared in all languages, in both poetry and prose. Because of the prohibition against religious idolatry, there are few images of the Prophet. A biographical movie, *The Messenger,* was released in Lebanon in 1976 and approved by religious authorities. Made without shots of Muhammad or the sound of his voice, the film presents his story through the action and dialogue of his followers.

Most Muslims, however, learn about the Prophet through celebrations, such as Mawlid (Muhammad's birthday), and the commemoration of the Night Journey and the Ascension. On such occasions, Muslims express the virtues of the Prophet through prose, poetry, recitation of the Qur'an, and ritual movement.

Accuracy of Sources. Scholars writing the life of Muhammad confront a host of difficult issues. They must decide how to portray the Prophet and how to evaluate his actions. They face the task of sifting through a wide selection of materials to find accurate sources. They also have the chore of determining which stories constitute legend and which convey facts.

Many scholars suspect certain hadiths to have developed long after Muhammad's death. In order to promote certain political or religious agendas, some people may have written fictitious accounts of the Prophet. Biographers try to select only those stories that have a solid chain of transmission and that originate from reputable sources. The hadith collector al-Bukhari, for example, chose a mere 7,275 accounts from over 600,000. Muslims group biographies about Muhammad into two types: historical and narrative accounts (*sirah*), and anecdotal accounts illustrating correct thought or behavior (sunnah). The *sirah* serve as a major source for modern biographers, and the sunnah developed as the basis for Islamic law.

The Muslim writer Muhammad ibn Ishaq (died 767) created a *sirah* that became a base for all later biographies of the Prophet. It starts with the creation of the world and chronicles its history up to the time of Muhammad, demonstrating how Muhammad's life served as the fulfillment of the divine mission. It compares the Prophet to holy men in Christian and Jewish traditions. A shorter summary of this work, edited by Ibn Hisham (died ca. 827), became the standard biography that is widely used in the Islamic world.

Varying Interpretations. The Prophet represents different things to different people. Some Muslims view him as an arbiter of divine law. Others see him as a mystic*, philosopher, conqueror, or ruler. Until recently, Western authors have held critical views of Muhammad.

During the 1800s, a new trend emerged in Islamic scholarship. Certain Muslims, attracted to Western values, wrote biographies depicting Muhammad as embodying the ideals of modern civilization. Muslims view Muhammad as a model of Islamic behavior, showing how life can be lived in accord with God's revelation. (*See also* **A'ishah; Islam: Overview; Judaism and Islam; Khadija; Qur'an; Women and the Qur'an.**)

Muhammad, Birthday of

Mawlid an-Nabi, the birthday of the Prophet Muhammad, is a major religious and cultural festival throughout the Islamic world. Although no one knows the exact date of Muhammad's birth, celebrations occur on the twelfth day of Rabi al-Awnal, the first spring month in the Muslim calendar. Mawlid an-Nabi festivities include readings from the Qur'an, poetry, recitations of Muhammad's life and deeds, songs praising Muhammad's virtues, feasting, and distribution of food to the poor. However, not all Muslims celebrate this occasion.

The first recorded public celebration of the Prophet's birthday occurred in Egypt around the year 1100. Most Sunni* Muslims, however, trace the practice to the Iraqi city of Irbil in the year 1207. Al-Malik Muzaffar Ad-Din Kukburi, brother-in-law of the Egyptian sultan Saladin, arranged a month-long celebration in honor of Muhammad. Religious and political figures, scholars, musicians, and other travelers began to arrive in Irbil up to two months before the birthday. Jugglers and poets entertained the crowds. A large sacrifice of animals occurred two days before the feast, followed by a torchlight procession on the next night. The Prophet's birthday featured a public sermon, singing, gifts bestowed on high-ranking guests, poems, and a sumptuous meal.

Although religious leaders did not recognize it as an official holiday, the celebration of Muhammad's birthday soon spread across the Islamic world. Sufis* were particularly supportive of the practice. Many Muslims condemned it as idolatrous and heretical*. They denounced what they viewed as the Christian roots of the holiday, believing it was inspired by Christmas. Other Muslims, however, accepted the holiday with enthusiasm, and some groups began to celebrate the *mawlids* of various imams* and other religious figures. The Mawlid an-Nabi is currently a state holiday in every Muslim country, except Saudi Arabia. (*See also* **Muhammad.**)

* **Sunni** refers to the largest branch of the Muslim community; the name derives from sunnah, the exemplary behavior of the Prophet Muhammad

* **Sufi** refers to Sufism, which seeks to develop spirituality through discipline of the mind and body
* **heretical** characterized by a belief that is contrary to established religious doctrine
* **imam** spiritual-political leader in Shi'i Islam, one who is regarded as directly descended from Muhammad; also, one who leads prayers

Muhammad Khatami

1943–
President of Iran

In 1997 Shi'i* cleric Muhammad Khatami was elected as the fifth president of the Islamic Republic of Iran. He easily won his bid for reelection in 2001. His supporters praise him as a reformer and a moderating influence in Iranian society. Critics claim that he has taken few real steps toward promoting democracy in Iran.

Born in central Iran, Khatami is the son of a well-known religious leader. His varied and extensive education includes traditional religious study as

* **Shi'i** refers to Muslims who believe that Muhammad chose Ali ibn Abi Talib and his descendants as the spiritual-political leaders of the Muslim community

* **secular** separate from religion in human life and society; connected to everyday life

* **parliament** representative national body having supreme legislative power within the state

well as advanced degrees from Isfahan University and the University of Tehran, which were both secular* institutions in Iran. During the 1960s and 1970s, Khatami participated in political activities to oppose the pro-Western policies of Iran's leader, Muhammad Reza Shah Pahlavi. Following the Iranian revolution in 1979 and the establishment of the Islamic republic, Khatami won a seat in parliament*. In 1982 he became the head of the Ministry of Islamic Guidance and Culture. While serving in that post, Khatami removed some government restrictions on films, music, art, and literature. Fearing that his policies were un-Islamic, members of the Iranian parliament forced him to resign in 1992.

Five years later, Muhammad Khatami ran for president, promoting greater political tolerance and the creation of a civil society. He won around 70 percent of the vote. Khatami supports democracy and greater freedom in Iran in his public statements. However, he has been unable to enact serious reform because of the limitations on his authority under the Iranian constitution. Ayatollah Ali Khamenei, known as the Supreme Leader, controls the armed forces, judiciary, security, and other important government functions. (*See also* **Iran.**)

Muharram

See *Calendar, Islamic.*

Mujahidin

* **jihad** literally "striving"; war in defense of Islam

* **Shi'ism** branch of Islam that believes Muhammad chose Ali ibn Abi Talib and his descendants as the spiritual-political leaders of the Muslim community

* **Marxism** political philosophy that rejects capitalism and advocates a classless society

* **Qur'an** book of the holy scriptures of Islam

* **hadith** reports of the words and deeds of Muhammad (not in the Qur'an, but accepted as guides for Muslim behavior)

* **atheistic** denying the existence of God

* **imperialism** extension of power and influence over another country or region

* **capitalism** economic system in which businesses are privately owned and operated and where competition exists in a free-market environment

* **guerrilla** unconventional warfare

Many people associate the term *mujahidin* with Muslims who take up arms to defend their land against injustice caused by foreign powers or oppressive governments. The Arabic word is often translated as "warriors of God" or those who "engage in jihad*." Although the term *mujahidin* does not have an inherent connection with war, groups have fought under this designation in places as diverse as Albania, Bosnia, Chechnya, Kashmir, and Kosovo. This entry focuses on Iran and Afghanistan, two countries where mujahidin were particularly active during the late 1900s.

Redefining Islam. The Holy Warrior Organization of the Iranian People, better known as the Iranian Mujahidin, has functioned as the main opposition to the Iranian government for more than 30 years. Combining aspects of Shi'ism* and Marxism*, the movement interprets Islam—particularly the Qur'an* and hadith*—as a divine message for political, social, and economic revolution. Although the mujahidin reject the atheistic* position of Marxism, they support its stance against imperialism* and capitalism*.

A group of graduates from Tehran University founded the Iranian Mujahidin during the mid-1960s. Many of them had also studied the Qur'an under Ayatollah Mahmud Taleqani, a leading Iranian cleric and political activist. The young militants opposed the government of Muhammad Reza Shah Pahlavi, calling him an oppressive tool of the West. Inspired by guerrilla* movements in Cuba, Vietnam, and Algeria, the mujahidin especially admired Latin American revolutionary Che Guevara. Interpreting Islam as a

Mujahidin leader Ahmed Shah Massoud assembles his men to pray in the Panjshir Valley during the civil war in Afghanistan. Massoud was affiliated with the Islamic Society, one of the most influential mujahidin groups.

socialist* creed, the Iranian Mujahidin promoted armed struggle to free the people from political and economic injustice. Although the movement consisted mainly of college students, it also attracted teachers, engineers, and other professionals.

The Iranian Mujahidin interpreted Islamic teachings in accordance with their ideology*. They argued that the early Shi'i martyrs* had died for social equality and described military *jihad* as "liberation struggle." They referred to an imam as a "charismatic revolutionary leader," rather than a religious leader. Although devout Muslims, the mujahidin opposed traditional Shi'i religious leaders. They believed the traditional clergy had sapped Islam's revolutionary power.

In 1971 the Iranian Mujahidin launched a guerrilla campaign. They assaulted the government with a series of bombings and armed attacks. But the government fought back, and in 1972, the shah (king) imprisoned one of the movement's most important leaders, Mas'ud Rajavi. Arrests, executions, and gun battles claimed the lives of other key figures and members of the mujahidin. The movement suffered a major setback in 1975, when some members renounced Islam in favor of Marxism and formed a separate organization.

In 1978 the government released Rajavi from prison. Regrouping his followers, he then helped to remove the shah from power during the Iranian Revolution. The mujahidin wielded substantial political influence in the young Islamic republic. Iranian voters backed mujahidin candidates. The organization's supporters included trade unions, professional organizations, and regional parties. The movement's newspaper had a wide circulation, and the mujahidin used its popularity to push for sweeping social changes.

Although the mujahidin followed the practices of Shi'ism, they opposed the Ayatollah Khomeini's regime. They criticized the idea that the clergy had the divine right to rule and condemned Khomeini's attitude toward women and his interpretation of *shari'ah**. The ayatollah responded by restricting

* **socialist** refers to socialism, the economic system in which the government owns and operates the means of production and the distribution of goods

* **ideology** system of ideas or beliefs

* **martyr** one who dies for his or her religious beliefs

* ***shari'ah*** Islamic law as established in the Qur'an and sunnah, the exemplary behavior of the Prophet Muhammad

Mujahidin

* **coup** sudden, and often violent, overthrow of a ruler or government

* **communist** refers to communism, a political and economic system based on the concept of shared ownership of all property

* **sectarian** refers to a religious group that adheres to distinctive beliefs

* **conservative** person generally opposed to change, especially in existing political and social institutions

* **radical** favoring extreme change or reform, especially in existing political and social institutions

mujahidin activities. In 1981 Khomeini declared the mujahidin to be "enemies of God" and ordered his forces to eliminate them. Iranian police arrested, tortured, and executed members of the movement. Despite a counterattack by the movement's followers, more than 9,000 mujahidin died in Iran between 1981 and 1985. Rajavi and other leaders fled the country, and with the support of Iraqi leader Saddam Hussein, they established military camps in Iraq. Following the U.S. overthrow of Saddam's regime in 2003, the mujahidin organization entered a new phase as an opposition movement labeled a terrorist organization.

The Power of Perseverance. The rebel fighters who resisted Soviet control of Afghanistan from 1979 to 1989 are perhaps the best known of the mujahidin. In 1978 a coup* led by the People's Democratic Party of Afghanistan brought a communist* government to power. This regime met with strong resistance from most Afghans, and the following year it fell apart. Shortly afterward, the Soviet Union invaded Afghanistan to maintain communist rule. To defend their country and Islam, religious leaders launched a popular uprising against the Soviets. Afghans who had fled into exile in Pakistan, as well as thousands of young Muslims from other parts of the Islamic world, rushed to Afghanistan to support the uprising. Among the volunteers was Osama bin Laden, a recent college graduate from Saudi Arabia. Throughout the struggle in Afghanistan, bin Laden helped recruit soldiers and played a role in financing their training.

The resistance fighters received military and financial support from the United States, China, Pakistan, Saudi Arabia, and other countries. Although the Soviet forces had superior weapons and controlled the air space, the rebels remained an elusive foe. Eventually, the two sides reached a stalemate, as the Soviets dominated the cities and the guerrillas occupied the mountainous rural areas.

The Afghan movement was affiliated with numerous political parties, ethnic groups, and sectarian* organizations. Two rival alliances consisting of Islamic conservatives* and radicals* emerged. By the mid-1980s, they formed a single coalition and created a council with decision-making power, which enabled them to better coordinate their operations.

The mujahidin also obtained more advanced weapons, including U.S. antiaircraft missiles. As the rebels gained ground, Soviet casualties mounted. Public support for the war waned in the Soviet Union. In 1988 Soviet general secretary Mikhail Gorbachev decided to withdraw his forces from Afghanistan. The following year, after a decade of struggle, the mujahidin took control of most of the country.

The rebel victory did not, however, inaugurate a period of stability. The communists still clung to power in the capital city of Kabul, and the mujahidin continued to fight them. Finally, in April 1992, the mujahidin captured Kabul and declared Afghanistan an Islamic state.

War had devastated the country, crippling economic production and killing more than one million Afghans. In the face of such troubles, the mujahidin failed to create a new Islamic political system. Instead, rival groups seized control of sections of the country, enabling the Taliban to seize power in 1994. (*See also* **Afghanistan; Bin Laden, Osama; Jihad; Iran; Qaeda, al-; Taliban.**)

Mujtahid

See *Ijtihad.*

Mullah

See *Religious Scholars.*

Mulla Sadra

1571–ca. 1640
Persian philosopher

Sadr al-Din Shirazi, called Mulla Sadra, was born to a prominent family in the southern Iranian city of Shiraz. He began his education in his hometown, later traveling to Isfahan, a cultural and intellectual center in central Iran. There, he studied religion, science, philosophy, and jurisprudence* under several eminent scholars. After leaving Isfahan, he devoted himself to a life of asceticism* and inner purity.

Mulla Sadra wrote several important works on philosophy and spirituality. According to his theory, the universe—except for God—has both eternal and temporal origins. He believed that all things consist of varying gradations of being. Spiritual development can bring people closer to the source of all being, God. Mulla Sadra further taught that spirituality was a key component of political reform. In his most important work, *The Fourfold Journey*, he wrote that a leader needs a mystical knowledge of God in order to transform the world.

Along with his mentor Mir Damad, Mulla Sadra founded a mystical school of philosophy at Isfahan. Mulla Sadra opposed the intolerance of the *ulama**, which he believed undermined spirituality. Traditional Shi'i* scholars branded him a heretic*.

Despite opposition, Mulla Sadra attracted a large following. His students included several people who later became famous philosophers and scholars in their own right. Mulla Sadra's teachings inspired a cultural revival in Iran and extended his influence to India and Iraq. Many Iranians today still regard Mulla Sadra as their greatest philosopher and consider him one of the best theological* scholars. Mulla Sadra died around 1640 and is buried in Najaf, an Iraqi city with many important Islamic shrines*. (*See also* **Cosmology; Karbala and Najaf; Philosophy; Theology.**)

* **jurisprudence** science of law

* **asceticism** way of life in which a person rejects worldly pleasures to follow a spiritual path

* **ulama** religious scholars

* **Shi'i** refers to Muslims who believe that Muhammad chose Ali ibn Abi Talib and his descendants as the spiritual-political leaders of the Muslim community

* **heretic** person whose belief or practice is contrary to established religious doctrine

* **theological** refers to the study of the nature, qualities, and will of God

* **shrine** place that is considered sacred because of its history or the relics contained there

Music

Islamic music goes back to the Middle Ages* and can be examined as a performing art, a branch of science, and a medium of spiritual devotion. Middle Eastern and North African musicians sing and play a wide variety of instruments to intricate rhythms and melodies. They use music to celebrate both spiritual and secular* occasions. Muslim scholars have written extensively on music theory, and Sufis* have popularized the use of chanting and certain musical instruments. Contact with the West has influenced Islamic performers, and Muslim musicians have contributed to music in Europe and the United States.

* **Middle Ages** period roughly between 500 and 1500

* **secular** separate from religion in human life and society; connected to everyday life

* **Sufi** follower of Sufism, which seeks to develop spirituality through discipline of the mind and body

The Mawlawiyah (or Mevlevi), a Sufi order, uses music and dance as part of its religious ritual. The order is known as the Whirling Dervishes in the West.

See color plate 9, vol. 3.

* **Qur'an** book of the holy scriptures of Islam

* **hadith** reports of the words and deeds of Muhammad (not in the Qur'an, but accepted as guides for Muslim behavior)

* **Bedouin** nomad of the desert, especially in North Africa, Syria, and Arabia

Islamic Musical Traditions

The Qur'an* says little on the subject of music. The hadith* contain many statements condemning the art, although Muhammad displayed some tolerance for war marches, pilgrimage chants, and festival songs. Muslims generally interpret the hadith as cautioning against music for pleasure. Some consider music acceptable only for rituals and religious occasions, while others value it as a form of entertainment. Many Muslims view music as a means of connecting with God or of promoting religious values.

History and Origins. In pre-Islamic societies, music served as an inspirational force. For example, the Bedouins* had *shairs* (poet-singers), who they believed had supernatural powers. *Shairs* chanted verses to inspire the tribes in war and to praise them in times of victory. Female *shairs* accompanied warriors in battle, singing elegies (songs of sorrow) when they fell. Many Middle Eastern villages held dances and music and poetry competitions, attracting artists from neighboring regions. *Qaynat* (singing girls) performed in courts and taverns. Music also served practical functions. For example, camel drivers sang special songs as a charm against desert spirits.

After the rise of the Islamic empire, music served as a means of entertainment and became elevated to a high art form, despite Muhammad's warnings. Wealthy Muslims acquired slave musicians and held lavish concerts and competitions. Complex musical styles developed, and some musicians gained widespread fame. Islamic music reached its height during the Abbasid dynasty (750–1258), when every educated person played an instrument, and music became a subject of study for philosophers and scholars. The Persian singer, composer, and lute player Ish Aq, for example, wrote nearly 40 books on music and developed the first theories on Islamic musical styles.

Folk and Religious Uses. Music enhances both secular and religious occasions in the Islamic world. It often serves to commemorate weddings and other major life events. Music can also enliven tasks of labor, as in the case of the *fjiri* (pearl-diving songs) performed by groups of musicians in the Arabian Gulf. In some Islamic regions, musicians have maintained their traditional roles as poet-singers. In Arabian deserts, for example, Bedouin *shairs* continue to recite poetry accompanied by an upright fiddle. Poet-singers in central Turkey perform moral and devotional songs while plucking a long-necked lute called a *saz*.

Many religious practices in the Islamic world also involve music. The chanting of passages from the Qur'an has become a standard feature of worship. Muezzins* deliver the call to prayer five times a day in an improvised, melodic style. In some Muslim countries, music appears in plays that celebrate the lives of imams*.

Sufis have developed the most advanced musical traditions. Mystics* use both music and dance as vehicles for spiritual enlightenment. Early scholars, such as Abu Hamid al-Ghazali, (1058–1111) taught Muslims how to attain spiritual purification through careful attention to music. Sufi choruses engage in a musical tradition called *dhikr*, in which they repeat religious phrases while performing rhythmic body movements, singing hymns, and improvising melodies. The Mevlevi order in Turkey gained fame in the 1200s for its elaborate musical performances, its use of the *ney* (reed flute), and its creation of a religious dance involving whirling.

Influence of the West. Beginning in the late 1700s, Europeans colonized much of the Islamic world. Their musical traditions influenced Muslim artists and inspired leaders. The Egyptian ruler Muhammad Ali hired European musicians to teach band music at military schools, and Cairo opened its first opera house in 1869. Similar developments occurred in Turkey and Iran. The Turkish president Mustafa Kemal Atatürk even banned Ottoman classical music, hoping to promote Western styles. By the 1900s, many Middle Eastern composers and music teachers had undergone training in European music theory, notation, and teaching methods.

Traditionally highlighting solo performance, Islamic music began to take on Western elements, such as large ensembles and electronic amplification. Songs became shorter and some featured Western melodies and rhythms. Musicians began to use Western instruments, such as the cello, accordion, and saxophone. Western music has also been influenced by Islamic styles. Europeans have adopted such instruments as the lute and the kettledrum. Modern European and American pop artists use Middle Eastern instruments and rhythms, and Islamic music has gained in popularity in the West.

Features of Islamic Music

Islamic music has many distinctive characteristics. It typically features a solo singer or instrumentalist with a high level of skill and a mastery of many different techniques. The performer exhibits his or her talent through improvisation, the spontaneous invention of new melodies and themes. The

See color plate 11, vol. 3.

* **muezzin** person who calls the faithful to prayer

* **imam** spiritual-political leader in Shi'i Islam, one who is regarded as directly descended directly from Muhammad; also, one who leads prayers

* **mystic** one who seeks to experience spiritual enlightenment and truth through various physical and spiritual disciplines

See color plate 10, vol. 3.

Rapping for Ramadan

Just as Western music has gained popularity in the Muslim world, music with Islamic themes has attracted a following in the United States. Muslim rap groups, such as Native Deen in Washington, D.C., have won acclaim for their distinctive style and lyrics. Rapping to traditional drumbeats, Native Deen sings about such subjects as reciting morning prayers, wearing headscarves, and avoiding drugs. Muslim musician and actor Mos Def also works to promote Islamic values, portraying women respectfully in his videos and using Arabic terms in his songs. Muslim groups also encourage celebration of Islamic festivals. Native Deen's song "Ramadan" includes the lyrics, "Ramadan is here/The blessed month of the year/Fasting and not eating food/Acting nice and not rude/Instead of watching movies today/Let's go to the *masjid* (mosque) and pray."

structure of a song matters far less than detail and embellishment. Islamic music typically takes on an improvised, unformed quality, emphasizing the abilities of the performer over the composition as a whole. Soloists perform in several styles, such as *layali*, which involves long vocalizations of meaningless sounds, and *taqsim*, which is the instrumental equivalent.

Melody and Rhythm. Most Middle Eastern melodies, whether sung or played, are highly intricate. Textures include solo, unison (playing or singing the same melody with others), singing or playing in octaves, singing accompanied by a droning sound, and heterophony, in which two or more musicians play the same part with subtle differences. Islamic musicians rarely use harmony. While Western music relies on whole- and half-steps between notes, Islamic music makes use of a much wider range of intervals. Islamic music also features microtones—pitches created when notes are partially flattened or sharpened.

Islamic musical tradition relies on melodic modes, or *maqamat*. These dictate the scale patterns, units of measurement, and notes of emphasis used in each song. Over 100 *maqamat* exist in Islamic music. Each bears a title referring to a place, object, individual, or event. *Maqamat* also correspond with certain philosophical or emotional concepts, such as love. Musicians improvise within the confines of the *maqam*, but sometimes switch from one to another during a performance.

Rhythms in Islamic music also come in different modes, or *iqaat*. These are organized into cycles of strong beats, weak beats, and pauses. As with the *maqamat*, over 100 rhythmic patterns exist, and all are subject to improvisation. Musical styles, such as the North African *nawbah* and the Turkish *fasil*, have sections that share the same melodic mode but differ in rhythm and structure.

Middle Eastern Instruments. Musicians in the Muslim world have developed many different instruments. Islamic music typically makes heavy use of stringed instruments. The *oud* (short-necked lute, from which many wooden instruments evolved) predominates in classical music. Other stringed instruments include the *qanum* (zither), the Turkish *tanbur* (long-necked lute) and *kemence* (upright fiddle), and the Afghan *rubab* and the North Indian *sarod* (lutes with unplucked, resonating strings). Islamic musicians also use the Western violin. Muslim music also relies on certain wind instruments, such as the *ney* (flute), the *buq* (horn), the *nafir* (long trumpet), and instruments similar to the clarinet and oboe. Percussion instruments in the Arabic world include the Iranian *santur* (hammered dulcimer) and *dumbak* (hand drum), *sunuj* (cymbals), tambourines, snare drums, and kettledrums. (*See also* **Art**; **Sufism.**)

Muslim Brotherhood

* **nationalism** feelings of loyalty and devotion to one's country and a commitment to its independence

Founded in Ismailiyah, Egypt, in 1928, the Muslim Brotherhood is a popular Islamic reformist organization. From the beginning, the brotherhood's goals were both social and political—the organization promoted charitable causes as well as nationalism*, independence, and the reform of society according to Islamic principles.

The Muslim Brotherhood (in Arabic, Ikhwan al-Muslimun) grew into a significant movement in Egypt and beyond. Branches were established in such places as Syria, Jordan, and Sudan, and similar groups took shape in many parts of the Islamic world. To achieve their goals, various factions within the Muslim Brotherhood have used tactics ranging from social activism and support of existing regimes* to militancy and antigovernment violence. Although some governments have outlawed or restricted its activities, the brotherhood has mass appeal, and it remains a very important Islamic movement in the Arab world.

* **regime** government in power

Building the Organization. During the 1920s, Great Britain dominated political and economic affairs in Egypt. Anti-western sentiment grew as foreign business owners and managers prospered while Egyptian workers remained poor and secular* ideas appeared to threaten Islamic culture.

* **secular** separate from religion in human life and society; connected to everyday life

Egyptian schoolteacher Hasan al-Banna advocated a return to Islamic principles as the remedy for the economic and social concerns of Egyptian Muslims. In 1928 he founded the Muslim Brotherhood. Over the next several years, al-Banna and fellow members gathered support for the organization by vigorously preaching Islam in the mosques*, as well as in coffeehouses, workplaces, and homes across Egypt. The result was that the movement grew rapidly.

* **mosque** Muslim place of worship

During the 1930s, the organization began to pursue a political agenda. The brotherhood started a weekly newspaper, *Al-Nadhir* (The Warning), to spread its message throughout and beyond its membership. Al Banna communicated directly with the leaders of Arab governments. The Muslim Brotherhood raised money for Palestinian Arabs resisting Zionism (the movement to create a Jewish state in Palestine).

The brotherhood built its own schools, factories, and hospitals, and its members became active in various organizations, including the trade unions and armed forces. The brotherhood gained popularity, especially among the lower and middle classes in urban areas. Although teachers, skilled craftspeople, and merchants formed the base of its membership, the movement also drew support from lawyers, doctors, accountants, and industrial workers. By the 1940s, the organization had more than 500,000 active members and many supporters. Some even considered the Muslim Brotherhood "a state within the state."

Determined to support the Arab struggle in Palestine and to resist British imperialism*, the organization also established an armed unit. Acts of violence against British and Jewish targets in Egypt escalated, and inevitably, some Egyptians were killed or injured. In response, the Egyptian government outlawed the brotherhood in December 1948. Shortly afterward, a member of the organization assassinated Prime Minister Mahmud Fahmi al-Nuqrashi. The following year, Egyptian secret police killed al-Banna.

* **imperialism** extension of power and influence over another country or region

After the death of its founder, the Muslim Brotherhood placed an even greater emphasis on political issues. In 1952 a group of army officers led by Colonel Gamal Abdel Nasser seized control of Egypt in a coup*. As allies of these officers, the brotherhood hoped for direct participation in the new government. When they failed to achieve their objective, one of their members attempted to assassinate Nasser. In response, the government executed several leaders of the Muslim Brotherhood and imprisoned thousands of others, forcing the movement to operate in secret.

* **coup** sudden, and often violent, overthrow of a ruler or government

Activist Sayyid Qutb emerged as the brotherhood's leading spokesman during the late 1950s. In the writings he produced between two periods of imprisonment, he promoted a radical* version of Islam, calling for jihad* against pro-Western and secular governments. In 1966 Nasser had Qutb executed. Considered a martyr* by many, Qutb's writings helped inspire Islamic activist movements in the following decades.

After Nasser died in 1970, Anwar el-Sadat became the president of Egypt. He released members of the brotherhood from prison, hoping to gain the movement's support for his policies. Even so, Umar al-Tilimsani, the leader of the Muslim Brotherhood at that time, and Sadat were unable to agree on numerous issues, especially the question of peace with Israel. In September 1981, Sadat arrested al-Tilimsani, other leaders of the brotherhood, and members of other Islamic groups. A month later, a member of al-Jihad, an Egyptian militant group, assassinated Sadat.

During the 1980s and 1990s, the Muslim Brotherhood pursued a platform of political moderation and nonviolence. The organization's more radical elements broke away and formed militant Islamic groups. Brotherhood members made political alliances and gained seats in Egypt's parliament*. In recent years, the movement has experienced renewed appeal as part of widespread religious revival* in the Muslim world.

The Syrian Branch. Soon after the founding of the Muslim Brotherhood in Egypt, the movement spread to nearby countries. In Syria, the ideas of Hasan al-Banna found an eager audience. During the 1930s, the Syrian people were struggling to achieve national independence from French colonial rule. They also sought relief from their economic woes, the result of expanding European trade, high inflation, drought, and debt. Disappointed with the local leaders of the independence movement, they turned to newer reformist groups.

Working through schools and publications associated with the brotherhood, the Syrian organization promoted Islamic morals and education and encouraged anti-imperialist activities. It formed a strong constituency in urban areas, especially among artisans* and tradespeople. Syria gained its independence in 1946, and in 1954, the Brotherhood called for a government based on Islamic law. The Syrian branch of the Muslim Brotherhood, however, lacked a clear program of action.

In 1963 the Ba'th Party seized power, establishing a secular, socialist* regime. The new government brought a large number of people from the rural parts of Syria into the state bureaucracy*. The Muslim Brotherhood opposed the regime's policies, viewing them as a threat to Islamic principles and to the economic welfare of its members.

Tensions between the Syrian government and the brotherhood escalated during the 1970s. After Hafiz al-Assad became president and adopted a secular constitution, the brotherhood waged a jihad against the government. The organization particularly opposed the increased power that Assad had granted to his own rural-based community of Alawis, a religious minority, at the expense of the country's Sunni* majority, especially those who lived in the towns. The Muslim Brotherhood carried out large-scale demonstrations and armed attacks, which led to the government's banning of the organization in 1980. Two years later, the brotherhood sparked an armed uprising in Hama, its stronghold. Assad's troops crushed the revolt, and the influence of the brotherhood declined. It has not been a major opposition force in Syria since the defeat at Hama.

Ties to the Monarchy. During the 1940s, members of the Egyptian Muslim Brotherhood sought to establish branches of their movement in Palestine and Jordan. In 1946 the first Jordanian branch was formed. King Abdullah extended his approval to the brotherhood, which registered with the government as a charity, on the condition that its members abstain from political activity.

Initially, the members of the Jordanian Muslim Brotherhood focused on religious issues, including a return to Islamic values and the education of Jordanian society. Through acts of charity, such as the construction of health and welfare facilities, they were able to spread their message.

After the Arab-Israeli War (1948) and the Jordanian occupation of the West Bank (the section of Palestine west of the Jordan River), the organization's membership increased and its activities became more politicized. In 1957 King Hussein banned political parties. Although the brotherhood had often functioned as a political party, he permitted its members to continue their activities, believing that they would be strong allies for his regime. His assessment proved correct for nearly three decades. During the mid-1980s, however, the brotherhood began to criticize Hussein's government, charging it with corruption and immorality. Unwilling to tolerate an attack on the legitimacy of his rule, the king used arrests and other forms of harassment against members of the organization.

The rift between Hussein and the movement was short lived. In 1989 the king decided to hold free elections for the first time in more than 22 years. The brotherhood gained more than 25 percent of the seats in parliament. In 1991 the organization supported Iraq in the Persian Gulf War. Although unpopular with its Kuwaiti and Saudi financial supporters, this position increased the movement's appeal at home. The brotherhood's message remains popular in Jordan.

Key Player. The Muslim Brotherhood of Egypt spread its influence to neighboring Sudan during the 1940s, and the Sudanese branch of the movement was officially founded in 1954. Most of the new members came from the educated classes but had strong ties to more traditional Islamic values. They were devout Sufis* and strongly opposed communism*.

The movement was not a significant political force in Sudan until the mid-1960s. Led by Hasan al-Turabi, the brotherhood entered politics with the founding of the Islamic Charter Front (ICF) in 1964. The ICF joined other groups in urging the Sudanese government to outlaw the communist party and to adopt an Islamic constitution. In 1969, however, Jafar al-Nimeiri overthrew the government with the aid of Sudanese communists. The new regime arrested several brotherhood leaders, including al-Turabi.

During the mid-1970s, al-Nimeiri moved away from secular, nationalist policies and embraced Islam. The brotherhood reconciled with al-Nimeiri, enabling its members to gain important positions in the regime and to strengthen the organization and improve its finances. The brotherhood also helped persuade al-Nimeiri to adopt a program of implementing Islamic law in 1983.

Censoring the Message

Over the years, the publications of the Muslim Brotherhood have significantly influenced the course of public debate. Hasan al-Banna recognized the power of communication, both to spread his message and to refute negative reports about him and his organization. The Muslim Brotherhood has struggled against government censorship to produce a host of newsletters, magazines, and journals. In 1976 Egyptian president Anwar el-Sadat gave the brotherhood permission to distribute *Al-Dawah* (The Call), a publication that had been banned for 20 years. *Al-Dawah*'s opposition to Sadat's policies, including a peace treaty with Israel and his push to reform family law, however, led to another ban in 1981. Its successor, *Liwa' al-Islam* (The Banner of Islam), criticized Egypt's alliance with the United States in the Persian Gulf War (1990–1991), which led to its temporary ban.

* **Sufi** follower of Sufism, which seeks to develop spirituality through discipline of the mind and body

* **communism** political and economic system based on the concept of shared ownership of all property

Democratic forces overthrew al-Nimeiri in 1985, and the National Islamic Front (NIF), the brotherhood's political organization, took an active role in parliament as the major opposition party. Four years later, the leaders of a military coup established an Islamist* regime. The brotherhood supported the new government. The NIF gained control of the construction industry, the media, banking, transportation, and education. From their dominant position, the brotherhood helped shape debates on the proper role of Islamic law in Sudanese society and politics. (*See also* **Charity; Egypt; Jordan; Qutb, Sayyid; Sudan; Syria.**)

* **Islamist** referring to movement advocating reintegration of religion and politics; also one who advocates reintegration of religion and politics

Mut'ah

See *Marriage.*

Mu'tazili

The Mu'tazilis were members of an early school of Islamic thought that emphasized reason and God's justice and unity. They referred to themselves as "the people of [divine] justice and unity" and developed a formal school of theology* in the 700s. More than any other Muslim group, they drew from Greek philosophy and science.

Overall, the Mu'tazilis viewed reason and revelation* as complementary. They believed that God created a world, governed by logical rules, that functions independently. The Mu'tazilis argued against the belief that all human actions are predetermined. Instead, they taught that humans have free will. Stressing Qur'anic* claims that God will reward virtue and punish vice, the Mu'tazilis maintained that it would be unjust to reward or punish people for actions over which they have no control. However, humans choose their own path, and God rewards or punishes them accordingly.

The Mu'tazilis taught that God, human nature, and the universe all conform to laws that can be understood by human reason. Muslims should therefore use their intellectual powers to determine their actions. This idea alarmed traditional religious thinkers, who called for complete submission to Muhammad and the Qur'an. Equating an emphasis on rational thought with heresy*, the traditionalists branded the Mu'tazilis as "free thinkers."

The Mu'tazilis also stressed the unity of God. They maintained that the attributes of God described in the Qur'an—such as sight, hearing, knowledge, and will—are part of God's nature and do not exist apart from God. Furthermore, the Mu'tazilis rejected the dominant view of the Qur'an as uncreated, eternally existing with God. They argued that whereas God is eternal, the Qur'an—God's revelation—is created in time and place. Therefore, those who believe the Qur'an to be the uncreated word of God are sinning by ascribing eternity to something God has created. Qur'anic passages discussing this matter should not be taken literally.

The Abbasid caliph* al-Mamun tried to impose Mu'tazili doctrine on state officials in the early 800s. The Mu'tazili movement gained followers in Baghdad and Basra, where courts placed high value on the new interpretation of

* **theology** study of the nature and qualities of God and the understanding of His will

* **revelation** message from God to humans transmitted through a prophet

* **Qur'an** book of the holy scriptures of Islam

* **heresy** belief that is contrary to established religious doctrine or practice

* **caliph** religious and political leader of an Islamic state

the Qur'an based on logical argument and the study of natural laws. The movement, however, declined in the 900s. Traditional Sunni* thinkers preferred the Ashari school of theology, which emphasizes that God is all-powerful and wills human action. Nevertheless, the rational approach of the Mu'tazilis to religious doctrines continues to have appeal among Muslim intellectuals. (*See also* **Ali ibn Abi Talib; Ashari, Abu al-Hasan al-; Tawhid; Theology.**)

* **Sunni** refers to the largest branch of the Muslim community; the name derives from sunnah, the exemplary behavior of the Prophet Muhammad

Mysticism

See *Sufism.*

Najaf

See *Karbala and Najaf.*

Names and Naming

Customs for naming children were established early in the history of Islam. The Qur'an* instructed Muslims to "call them after their true father's names." As a result, the only name given to a child is the first name. The second name is always the father's name. For example, the Arabic name *Husayn ibn Ali* means "Husayn son of Ali." Other names, such as the name of the grandfather, may be added to the first two. These rules apply equally to boys and girls, and women keep their father's name after marriage. Muslim inheritance laws depended on these naming conventions, and until recently, such basic practices remained virtually unchanged.

* **Qur'an** book of the holy scriptures of Islam

Muslims carefully select a child's first name. Muhammad reportedly commanded his followers to "choose for your children pleasant and beautiful names." The Prophet even changed the name of an individual whose original name he considered to be unsuitable.

Parents do not necessarily give a child a name and register his or her birth immediately. This is especially true if the date of birth holds no special meaning or if the family has to wait for important relatives to gather for the celebration that follows the naming. The waiting period gives the family time to assess the child's personality and other characteristics in order to choose a suitable name. In the meantime, a male child usually is called Muhammad and a female child Fatimah, a practice based on religious tradition.

First names often are the names of important Islamic religious figures. For example, Ali, the name of Muhammad's son-in-law, is a favorite for Shi'i* boys. Many Sunni* Muslim girls are called A'ishah, the name of Muhammad's favorite wife. Also relatively common are names made up of combined words that express religious devotion. Muslims memorize and recite the 99 "most beautiful names of God," such as the All-Knowing and the All-Loving. Preceded by the words *Abd* or *Amat* (male or female servant), the names for God's attributes are often part of proper names, such as Abd al-Rahman, meaning "servant of the Merciful." At times, ethnic* or heroic names have surpassed in popularity those with religious significance. In ad-

* **Shi'i** refers to Muslims who believe that Muhammad chose Ali ibn Abi Talib and his descendants as the spiritual-political leaders of the Muslim community

* **Sunni** refers to the largest branch of the Muslim community; the name derives from sunnah, the exemplary behavior of the Prophet Muhammad

* **ethnic** relating to groups of people who share a common racial, national, tribal, religious, linguistic, or cultural background

* **honorific** giving honor or showing respect

* **hajj** pilgrimage to Mecca that Muslims are required to make once in their lifetime

dition, parents may select a name such as Sa'id, meaning "happy," in the hope that the child will develop that characteristic.

Another common Muslim practice is to give a person an honorific* name. For example, the title *sayyid*, meaning "lord, master, or prince," was used for the descendants of the Prophet Muhammad. A name may also distinguish a person from others who have a similar name. For example, someone with very common given and ancestral names might be given an additional name referring to his or her profession, such as al-Naqqash ("the painter").

In modern times, these naming practices have undergone changes. Under pressure to adapt to Western ways, many Muslims have started using simpler or shorter names. By contrast, African Americans who convert to Islam have generally adopted Muslim names. For example, Malcolm X, a prominent figure during the 1960s in the Nation of Islam, a militant Muslim religious group, was born Malcolm Little. After participating in the hajj*, Malcolm X converted to Sunni Islam and changed his name to El Hajj Malik El-Shabazz. (*See also* **Family; Rites and Rituals; Titles, Honorific.**)

Naqshbandiyah

* **Sufi** refers to Sufism, which seeks to develop spirituality through discipline of the mind and body

* **dhikr** Sufi chant for the remembrance of God

Naqshbandiyah refers to one of the most widespread and active orders within Sufi* Islam. Naqshbandi groups exist in most Islamic regions of Asia, but until recently they have not been common among Arabs. Naqshbandis are found in Turkey, Bosnia and some states of the former Soviet Union, and much of Southeast Asia, including the Philippines. The order is characterized by strict observance of traditional Islamic law, avoidance of music and dance, and a preference for silent *dhikr*. The order has tended to be politically active. For example, Naqshbandis were prominent in Afghanistan's resistance to the Russian invasion in the 1980s. In addition, several Naqshbandi leaders were important spiritual and intellectual leaders.

The Naqshbandiyah originated in the late 1300s in Bukhara, a city in present-day Uzbekistan, a republic in the former Soviet Union. Within 100 years, the order spread to adjacent areas of the Muslim world. A branch of the order, called the Mujaddidi, became especially popular. It was founded by Shaykh Ahmad Sirhindi, who was known as the first *mujaddid*, or "renewer," of Islam.

In the early 1800s, India emerged as an important center of the Naqshbandi order, largely because of a teacher named Ghulam Ali. Attracting followers from India, Central Asia, and the Middle East, his students continued to spread his teachings throughout the Muslim world. One of Ghulam Ali's students, Mawlana Khalid, began another branch of Naqshbandiyah, called Khalidiyah. Mawlana Khalid is sometimes considered to be the second "renewer" of Islam. He tried to centralize the Khalidiyah, making it a disciplined order focused on himself. In other ways, the Khalidiyah resembled the Mujaddidi branch. Khalidiyah spread quickly, reaching Southeast Asia within a few decades. In recent years, Naqshbandi teachers have become more prominent in the eastern Arab world and in North America. (*See also* **Sufism.**)

Nationalism

From the time of the American and French Revolutions in 1776 and 1789 respectively, nationalism has played a central role in modern politics. Although nationalism's role in the Middle East started much later, around the mid-1800s, it has played a similar role to that of nationalism in the West. Nationalism in the Arab world has given rise to an Islamic renaissance that has had an undeniable impact on politics.

Arab nationalism is not a static phenomenon that can be easily isolated and studied. It is, instead, a developing reality that is connected to a fluid, ever-changing, political life. As such, its meaning is complicated by its long history in different nations with various forms of government at different stages of development. Political and ideological interests can also produce different interpretations of nationalism. Scholars differ on what constitutes a nation—and, consequently, what defines nationalism.

The Many Faces of Nationalism. There are several definitions that can be used to understand the concept of nationalism. One definition favored by many Muslims says that nationalism is a mental state in which loyalty centers on the country or region. While attachment to a country, its traditions, and a regional authority is not restricted to modern thinking, nationalism turns such attachment into a feature for character building—privately and publicly—and for history making. Another definition of nationalism suggests that it is a mental and emotional state of a group of people who live within specific borders, speak the same language, have a common culture that expresses the ambitions of the group, and share the same common traditions—including, at times, religion. Another definition sees nationalism as expressing the desire to preserve national and cultural identity or the desire to protect and develop such an identity.

No matter which definition is favored, it is possible to say that nationalism is loyalty at some level to a state identified by its culture and a commitment to political movement toward achieving independence and progress. Nationalism derives from a nation's history a sense of power, which is supplemented by the need to defend itself in the present and achieve its goals in the future. Thus, nationalism singles out certain characteristics that distinguish it from other nations, such as language, territories, and a common history. While all nations have languages, territories, and histories, historical development specifies the main characteristics of each nation.

What Defines a Nation? Every nationalist movement aims at independence when a nation is under occupation or is subservient to another country in a multination state. The movement also aims for unity when a nation has been partitioned into many states. Nationalism strives to achieve political and social progress, but its goal in those areas differs from one society to another.

The many variables that factor into an understanding of nationalism are, perhaps, the product of different definitions of a nation. Some scholars define a nation as the people, or the vast majority of people, who reside in one state and are unified by a political and emotional power—nationalism. Others define a nation as a great number of groups that have coexisted on a

Nationalism

Growing nationalism in Islamic countries gradually led to their independence from colonial rule, as shown in this chart.

Egypt	1922	Somalia	1960
Iraq	1932	Kuwait	1961
Ethiopia	1941	Sierra Leone	1961
Lebanon	1941	Tanzania	1961
Jordan	1946	Algeria	1962
Syria	1946	Malaysia	1963
Bangladesh	1947	Gambia	1965
India	1947	Maldives	1965
Pakistan	1947	South Yemen	1967
Indonesia	1949	Bahrain	1971
Libya	1951	Qatar	1971
Morocco	1956	United Arab Emirates	1971
Sudan	1956	Guinea-Bisseau	1974
Tunisia	1956	Comoros	1975
Guinea	1958	Western Sahara	1975
Burkina Faso	1960	Djibouti	1977
Central African Republic	1960	Brunei	1984
Chad	1960	Albania	1990
Cyprus	1960	Azerbaijan	1991
Ivory Coast	1960	Kazakhstan	1991
Mali	1960	Kyrgyzstan	1991
Mauritania	1960	Tajikistan	1991
Niger	1960	Turkmenistan	1991
Nigeria	1960	Uzbekistan	1991
Senegal	1960	Eritrea	1993

specific land, creating an independent existence, and having an organization—a central government. A more elaborate definition claims that a nation consists of a complete material and emotional unity with a central and stable political authority within specific and settled borders, and whose population is largely united around certain ethics, feelings, and values. Another, more specific definition may describe a nation as a settled group of people that has gradually developed and is based on a language, designated land, an economic life, and a psychological makeup that is expressed in a unique national culture.

The Relationship Between State and Nation. Differences over the understanding of nationalism sometimes stem from the relationship between a state and a nation—that is, which one comes first and creates the other? It is easy to confuse the concept of a nation with that of nationality. A state can be composed of many nations, such as the Ottoman Empire*, but its citizens all have the same nationality. A nation takes time to develop. There are many Arab states but only one Arab nation. The rise and fall of a nation is a long historical process, while a state can be created and demolished by a single decision.

The relationship between a nation and a specific religion also forms a part of nationalism. While religion spreads beyond specific states and creates new bonds, opinions differ about whether religion should be considered among a nation's many characteristics. For example, some Arab nationalists

* **Ottoman Empire** large Turkish state existing from the early 1300s to the early 1900s

refuse to consider Islam as a factor in Arab nationalism, while others believe that Islam is a key component of Arab nationalism. Finally, the relationship between a nation and a race may also form a part of nationalism. A nation is a cultural entity and race is a biological one. Some people, however, use the two terms interchangeably, speaking of the Arab nation or the Arab race.

A Historical Overview. In the Middle East, prior to World War II (1939–1945), a few groups and organizations tried to spread Arab nationalist feelings by focusing on Islamic culture, Arab identity, and Arabic language and literature. Arab nationalists set up public and private political organizations that called for either autonomy or independence from the Ottoman Empire. Military activities followed and reached their peak during the Great Arab Revolution in 1916. Sharif Husayn ibn Ali of Mecca and other notable leaders headed the Arab nationalist movement at that time. The movement failed because it did not have the wide popular support needed to achieve unity and independence from British control in the Middle East. The Turkish nationalist movement, however, led by Mustafa Kemal Atatürk, was more successful. After World War I (1914–1918), Atatürk established a dictatorship in the name of the Turkish republic. After the collapse of the Ottoman Empire, he abolished the Islamic caliphate* and promoted nationalism based on secularism*.

During the colonial era after World War I, Arab nationalist forces moved toward complete independence and the establishment of an Arab national state. Among the nationalist trends that emerged was the religious nationalism that linked the concept of a nation with Islam. Arabism and Islam were seen as two components of a single nationalism that would unite all Arabs. Abd al-Rahman al-Kawakibi and Muhammad Rashid Rida were two ideologists behind this trend. They believed that the Arab nation was the custodian of Islam and that the caliphate should be filled by an Arab. In their view, Islam embodied the truth of Arabism, and Arabism guaranteed the preservation of Islam.

The Arab struggle took place within the borders of the existing states that were set up by the colonialist powers until the rise of the Arab Ba'th Party and the Egyptian revolution of 1952 that spread Pan-Arab nationalism and advocated social justice, unity, and independence. From independence until the 1970s, the state elites in many countries favored secular nationalism. With the notable exceptions of Saudi Arabia and Morocco, states generally separated themselves from Muslim religious concepts. In general, law and education passed from religious control to state control. Ibrahim al-Yazji and Ahmad Faris al-Shidyaq are two of the forces behind secular nationalism. At its beginning, secular nationalism was promoted by Christian Arabs who focused more on the language component than on religion. The Arabic language became the embodiment of Arab culture and common characteristics of Arabs. Attacks were focused on the Ottoman Empire and its persecution of the Arabs.

Although nationalist feelings dominated the Arab world until the 1970s, Arab unity has not been achieved, despite the tremendous popularity of Egyptian President Gamal Abdel Nasser, noted nationalist leader. Central to the Arab nationalist struggle have been the creation of the state of Israel in 1948 and the subsequent Arab-Israeli conflict. The only real practical outcome of Arab nationalism has been the creation of the Arab League, established 1945. The Arab League has been made ineffective, however, by sharp

* **caliphate** office and government of the caliph, the religious and political leader of an Islam state

* **secularism** belief that religion should be separate from other aspects of human life and society, especially politics

ideological and political differences among members, many of whom pay more attention to the survival of their own regimes than to the goals of the organization. After the Arab world freed itself from colonialism, the United States and the Soviet Union emerged as the main competitors for influence in the Middle East. Since then, Arab nationalism has been gradually replaced by Islamic fundamentalism. (*See also* **Arab League.**)

Nation of Islam

* **militant** aggressively active in a cause

The Nation of Islam is a militant* African American religious movement that originated in Detroit in the 1930s. The organization uses some of the symbols and features of mainstream Islam, but its central message is one of racial pride and separatism. The movement has played a significant role in bringing Islam to African Americans.

Founding Father. Wallace D. Fard, who is believed to have been an orthodox* Muslim born in Mecca in the 1870s, founded the Nation of Islam. Fard emigrated to the United States in 1930 and began selling goods in a poor Black neighborhood of Detroit. Along with the goods he sold, Fard delivered a religious message to his customers. He told them that their true religion was not Christianity, but the "religion of the Black men" of Africa and Asia. Basing his message on both the Christian Bible and the Muslim Qur'an*, Fard began to teach in the homes of his followers. He referred to himself as Farrad Mohammed, but he was also known as Wali Farrad, Professor Ford, and Master Fard. In 1931 his followers recognized him as the Great Mahdi, meaning "savior." They believed that he was a special messenger sent by God to help poor Black people living in the ghettos* of American cities.

* **orthodox** conforming to accepted beliefs and practices

* **Qur'an** book of the holy scriptures of Islam

* **ghetto** part of a city in which members of a minority group live, especially because of social, legal, or economic pressures

Fard eventually rented a hall that became known as the Temple of Islam, with its own rituals and style of worship. He established one school to

Members of the Nation of Islam, the militant African American religious organization, stand proudly in New York City in 1993. The movement has worked to make positive changes in African American communities since the 1930s.

See color plate 8, vol. 3.

train Muslims to spread his teachings and another school to train girls in home economics and proper Muslim behavior. He also organized a men's group whose members served as bodyguards and enforcers of Muslim rules.

Most Trusted Follower. Fard's most trusted lieutenant was Robert Poole (1897–1975), who became known by the Muslim name Elijah Muhammad. Poole joined the Nation of Islam in 1931, when he was about 35 years old. He rose rapidly through the ranks and soon became the chief minister. Fard's mysterious disappearance in 1934 led to a struggle for leadership within the organization. Elijah Muhammad took a group of his followers to Chicago, where he established Temple of Islam Number Two. It became the national headquarters of the Nation of Islam, and its members became known as black Muslims.

Throughout the 1940s, Elijah Muhammad reshaped the Nation of Islam. He promoted the notion that Fard was Allah and that he was Muhammad, the Messenger of God. Although he continued the basic teachings of Fard, Muhammad added a strong component of black nationalism to the message. He preached that the white man is a "devil by nature" and the cause of all the problems of black people. He argued that African Americans needed to form a separate black nation to be free of the white man's evil.

Under Elijah Muhammad's leadership, the Nation of Islam helped many African Americans to become economically independent and to develop a more positive cultural identity. The motto of the movement was "Do for Self." Black Muslims were expected to work hard, save money, avoid debt, improve themselves, abstain from alcohol and other drugs, eat a healthful diet, and follow a pure lifestyle.

The reputation of black Muslims for being disciplined and dependable helped many of them obtain jobs or start small businesses. Under Elijah Muhammad's leadership, black Muslims nationwide established more than 100 temples and thousands of small businesses.

Elijah Muhammad's message was very appealing, especially to poor African Americans and in the prisons where black Muslims preached. The hope and self-respect of some of these people had been virtually destroyed by centuries of racial prejudice and discrimination. Thousands of African Americans, especially young men, joined the organization.

From Prison to Leadership. Malcolm Little, a young man from New York City, first heard about the Nation of Islam while serving time in prison for petty offenses. He became a black Muslim and took the name Malcolm X. When he was released from prison in 1952, he began organizing Muslim temples around the country. He also founded the Nation of Islam's newspaper, *Muhammad Speaks.* Malcolm X advanced rapidly in the organization and soon rose to second in command, after Elijah Muhammad himself. Malcolm's charismatic* leadership inspired a surge in the Nation of Islam's membership, which soon claimed 500,000 people.

Malcolm X's views appeared radical* at first. For example, he challenged the ideas of Martin Luther King, Jr., concerning integration and nonviolence, urging Black Muslims to defend themselves "by any means possible." After participating in the hajj* and seeing Muslims of all colors and cultures worshipping together, Malcolm's worldview began to change away from those of Elijah Muhammad. In 1964 Malcolm X left the Nation of Islam to establish the Muslim Mosque, Inc. and the Organization of Afro-American Unity.

The Story of Yacub

The central story underlying the belief system of the Nation of Islam is about a black man, a scientist named Yacub. According to the story, Yacub rebelled against Allah by creating white people—a race of weak people who were allowed to temporarily dominate the world. The story goes on to say that there will one day be a battle between the forces of good and the forces of evil. In this battle, black people will be victorious and once again control the world under Allah's guidance.

The story of Yacub helped many black Muslims explain and rationalize the pain and suffering they endured as a racial minority in America and establish a more positive self-identity. African American Muslims who have adopted orthodox Islam no longer accept the story as part of their religious belief system.

* **charismatic** capable of arousing enthusiasm and loyalty

* **radical** favoring extreme change or reform, especially in existing political and social institutions

* **hajj** pilgrimage to Mecca that Muslims are required to make once in their lifetime

Tensions developed between Malcolm's followers and the Nation of Islam. In 1965 he was killed by members of the Nation of Islam. His influence, however, lives on, providing the basis for the Black Power and black-consciousness movements of the late 1960s and 1970s.

The Nation of Islam continued to prosper after Malcolm's departure but never experienced anything like the earlier surge in membership. Louis Farrakhan, a Boston minister and controversial figure, replaced Malcolm X as second in command in the organization.

Following His Father. Elijah Muhammad died in 1975, and one of his sons, Warith Deen Muhammad, succeeded him as the head of the Nation of Islam. Warith Deen made some drastic changes in the organization. He declared that whites should no longer be viewed as devils and that they could even join the movement. He also moved the organization in the direction of orthodox Islam, following the Qur'an and orthodox Muslim traditions. He changed the name of the organization and moved it into the mainstream of Islamic beliefs and practices. He decentralized the organization, making individual mosques* the prime focus for local Muslim groups. His followers in the United States still number in the hundred thousands.

Militant Followers. The direction taken by Warith Deen Muhammad led some of the more militant members of the Nation of Islam to form their own religious groups. Louis Farrakhan led the largest and most successful group. By 1978 Farrakhan had restructured the Nation of Islam based on Elijah Muhammad's original black nationalist and separatist views. But he changed the organization in other ways to reflect his own views. For example, under Elijah Muhammad, black Muslims did not vote or participate in politics, because he taught them they were a nation apart. Farrakhan believed that African Americans could be more effective working within the political system and he encouraged black Muslims to vote and even to run for office.

Under Farrakhan's leadership, the Nation of Islam has helped poor blacks by providing security patrols in drug-infested neighborhoods and establishing an AIDS awareness program. Farrakhan and his organization have also come under criticism for their outspoken views of whites, and especially Jews, as oppressors of black people. Farrakhan has successfully spread his message of black unity and independence through his newspaper, the *Final Call,* and recordings by rap groups, such as Public Enemy. In recent years, he has moved the Nation of Islam closer to orthodox Islamic practices. (*See also* **Elijah Muhammad; Farrakhan, Louis; Malcolm X; United States.**)

* **mosque** Muslim place of worship

Newspapers and Magazines

Printing presses were introduced in Islamic countries such as Egypt, India, Iran, and Turkey as early as the 1600s. Over the next several centuries, newspapers and magazines appeared throughout the Islamic world. In general, Muslim publications can be classified into two categories. Some cover general topics and include special sections or editorials about religious issues. Others are devoted almost exclusively to Islamic content and may operate with a license or in secret.

A New Medium. At the beginning of the 1900s, Islamic print media reflected a struggle of competing forces. Newspapers played an important role in spreading European ideas, such as nationalism* and secularism*. They were also a medium for the messages of the Islamic reform movement and the campaign against European imperialism*. The fight for independence in various parts of the Muslim world contributed to the growth of the press.

As the Islamic world achieved its independence from colonial rule, modern mass communication gained greater prominence in the new nation-states. Although government-supervised institutions typically operate radio and television stations, the press has enjoyed a fairly independent private status. The large number of press agencies in Muslim countries reflects the diversity of ethnic, linguistic, and geographical groups.

Arabic-Language Journalism. In terms of reputation and readership, Arabic-language publications are the most important segment of Islamic journalism. They carry news and information of general interest as well as interpretations and comments on current events. In addition, these publications raise cultural awareness and reinforce the norms of Muslim society. They also promote businesses and services and entertain readers.

Napoleon Bonaparte of France, who led his armies into Egypt in 1798, established that country's first newspaper. *Courier de l'Egypte* was designed to inform, instruct, and support the French troops. Around 30 years later, the first Turkish-Arabic newspaper was published in Cairo. *Al-waqa'i al-Misriyah* (Egyptian Events) was the official paper of the Egyptian government. The development of Arabic magazines began during the 1880s. While living in exile in Paris, political activist Jamal al-Din al-Afghani and his disciple Muhammad Abduh published the monthly *Al-urwah al-wuthqa* (The Firm).

Among the most important Islamic publications in the Arab world today are three Egyptian pro-government newspapers and two Egyptian anti-government magazines. Jordan, Kuwait, Lebanon, Morocco, Saudi Arabia, and Tunisia also have important publications. In the Arab world, newspapers generally focus on local issues. Political commentaries and editorials typically appear in these publications, and journalists generally report current events from a political perspective. Rivalries exist between national and opposition newspapers and between privately owned and government-controlled newspapers.

Turkish and Iranian Publications. The Turkish press has historically exerted influence throughout the Islamic world. In 1831 the first official Turkish newspaper, *Le Moniteur Ottoman*, was published in Constantinople (now Istanbul). Today, the most prominent Turkish newspapers are *Milliyet* and *Cumhuriyet*. Newspapers and magazines for Muslims who speak the Turkish language are available in the Central Asian states of the former Soviet Union.

Many newspapers were published in Iran during the early 1800s, but they appeared irregularly and were devoted largely to praising the country's rulers. Since the Islamic revolution of 1979, the Iranian government has provided licenses for the private ownership of newspapers and magazines. Many Iranian papers publish articles reflecting disapproval of government policies. Several of the Islamic newspapers published in Iran, such as *Al-majalis* (The Councils), have relatively large circulations.

* **nationalism** feelings of loyalty and devotion to one's country and a commitment to its independence

* **secularism** belief that religion should be separate from other aspects of human life and society, especially politics

* **imperialism** extension of power and influence over another country or region

No Kidding

Under the militant extremist Taliban regime, Afghan newspapers and magazines had no real freedom of the press—even cartoons were censored. Such restrictions did not deter Usman Akram from producing a monthly magazine that poked fun at the Taliban. Called *Zanbel-e-Gham* (Basket of Sorrows), the magazine was handwritten, photocopied in secret, and passed among friends. The Taliban regime fell in 2001, and Hamid Karzai became the country's new head of state. Under the new government, Afghan editors must still accept a certain degree of risk for political satire. But Akram continues to publish cartoons that comment on current political and social issues, such as corruption and inefficiency.

Asian Editions. The history of Islamic journalism in the Indian subcontinent dates to 1866, when writer and political activist Sayyid Ahmad Khan founded the *Aligarh Institute Gazette*. The journal contained articles about politics and social issues. Among the notable contemporary magazines are several English-language journals that focus on Islamic affairs, including the *Panjab Observer* and *The Moslem Chronicle*. A very popular women's magazine, *Tahzibunnisvan* (Manners of Women), is published weekly in Lahore.

More than 100 daily newspapers, most of which are in Urdu, circulate in Pakistan. Among the most important of these Urdu newspapers are the state-owned *Imroz* and the liberal* *Hurriyat*. The government-sponsored *Pakistan Times* is an influential English-language daily. Popular newsmagazines in Pakistan include *Takbir*.

Although Muslims account for only 20 million of China's 1.2 billion people, they publish more than 100 newspapers and magazines. Most of them are in Chinese, although several are in Arabic, Japanese, or English. These publications cover Islamic affairs and current issues. *Uhowa* is considered to be the most important Islamic magazine in China.

The Western Front. Lebanese and Syrians who immigrated to the United States at the beginning of the 1900s developed the first Islamic newspapers and magazines in North America. The most important of these today is a weekly bilingual newspaper called *Sada al-watan* (Arab American News), which is published in Dearborn, Michigan. It covers Islamic affairs from a Shi'i* perspective. Another popular bilingual newspaper is *Al-rayah* (The Banner), which is published in Philadelphia.

Islamic newspapers and magazines are also available in many parts of Europe. In 1972 Muslim students in London, England, established a monthly magazine called *Al-ghuraba* (The Strangers). Since 1983 the Islamic Center of London has published a monthly magazine. German Muslims may read *Alam al-Islam* (The Islamic World) or *Liwa' al-Islam* (Flag of Islam).

Younger Audiences. Illustrated magazines, consisting of cartoons and text, are the dominant form of children's literature in Muslim countries. Designed both to educate and to entertain, many of these publications have a religious orientation. Even secular magazines contain some religious material, such as verses from the Qur'an* and parts of the hadith*. Children's magazines may function as a political tool of a Muslim government, or they may be the product of an independent publisher. The most successful children's magazine in the Islamic world is *Majid*. It is produced in the United Arab Emirates but can be purchased in New York, Paris, London, and other cities with large Arab and Muslim populations. (*See also* **Literature; Radio and Television.**)

* **liberal** supporting greater participation in government for individuals; not bound by tradition

* **Shi'i** refers to Muslims who believe that Muhammad chose Ali ibn Abi Talib and his descendants as the spiritual-political leaders of the Muslim community

* **Qur'an** book of the holy scriptures of Islam

* **hadith** reports of the words and deeds of Muhammad (not in the Qur'an, but accepted as guides for Muslim behavior)

Nigeria

Located on the west coast of Africa, Nigeria is home to about 130 million people, making it the most populous country on the continent. Like many other modern African states, Nigeria has been greatly affected by European colonialism. Prior to colonial rule, the region consisted of several large states and kingdoms. Between 250 and 400 different ethnic* groups representing various cultures and religions reside within Nigeria's borders. This high level of diversity has influenced economic, social, and political conditions in the country, and conflicts between Muslims and Christians erupt frequently.

A Divided People. Issues related to religious and ethnic identity have significantly influenced the history of Nigeria, and they continue to affect its political climate. Of the hundreds of ethnic groups in the country, a few have achieved considerable social and political importance: the Hausa and Fulani in the north, the Yoruba in the southwest, and the Ibo in the southeast. As a dominant element in Nigerian society, religion shapes community values, but it also acts as a divisive force. About 50 percent of Nigerians identify themselves as Muslims. They are concentrated in the northern states. Christians, who make up about 40 percent of the population, dominate the southern part of the country. The remaining 10 percent of the population follow traditional religions. Christian and Muslim Nigerians have incorporated elements of traditional African spiritual practices into their religions.

Nigerian Muslims generally follow Sunni* traditions. Even so, the Muslim community reflects a variety of beliefs and practices. Two Sufi* brotherhoods, the Qadiriyah and the Tijaniyah, have substantial followings. In recent years, Sufis have encountered opposition from Islamic activists who advocate a return to the original sources of Islam—the Qur'an* and hadith*.

From Kingdom to Colony. By the 800s, Muslim merchants were spreading Islam to the cities and towns along the trans-Saharan trade routes. Eventually, Islam extended its reach to parts of West Africa. At that time, much of what is now Nigeria consisted of several large states and some smaller kingdoms. These included Borno, the Hausa states, the Yoruba states, the Edo state of Benin, and the kingdom of Nupe. During the 1000s, the ruler of Kanem— a kingdom located in the Lake Chad region—and his court adopted Islam. Several centuries later, internal political conflicts forced the ruling family to relocate to Borno (in northeastern Nigeria). Borno became a thriving center of Islamic culture. The kingdom endured until the mid-1800s.

To the west of Borno, the Hausa people established seven city-states. Strategically located at the crossroads of various trade routes, each city-state featured a market center. During the 1300s, clerics from Mali converted the ruling family of Kano to Islam, which gradually spread in Hausaland (northern Nigeria). Muslims in Kano and Katsina established mosques* and schools that became prominent in the Islamic world. Hausa rulers administered a form of Muslim law, but these practices were mainly limited to the urban areas. Pre-Islamic* cultural traditions dominated life in the countryside.

Around the same time, Fulani herders from the Senegal River valley migrated to the Hausa region in search of grazing land and water for their livestock. A group of Muslim Fulani settled in the cities, where they mixed with the local people and eventually assimilated* into the Hausa ethnic group. Devoutly religious and well educated, the Fulani served the Hausa kings as Islamic judges, teachers, and government advisers.

Shortly after 1800, a Fulani scholar named Usuman Dan Fodio declared a jihad* against the rulers of the Hausa city-states. He condemned them for allowing the people to mix Islamic and polytheistic* religious practices and

* **ethnic** relating to groups of people who share a common racial, national, tribal, religious, linguistic, or cultural background

* **Sunni** refers to the largest branch of the Muslim community; the name derives from sunnah, the exemplary behavior of the Prophet Muhammad

* **Sufi** refers to Sufism, which seeks to develop spirituality through discipline of the mind and body

* **Qur'an** book of the holy scriptures of Islam

* **hadith** reports of the words and deeds of Muhammad (not in the Qur'an, but accepted as guides for Muslim behavior)

* **mosque** Muslim place of worship

* **pre-Islamic** refers to the Arabian Peninsula or to the Arabic language before the founding of Islam in the early 600s

* **assimilate** to adapt socially and culturally to the larger population

* **jihad** literally "striving"; war in defense of Islam

* **polytheistic** refers to a belief in more than one god

* **shari'ah** Islamic law as established in the Qur'an and sunnah, the exemplary behavior of the Prophet Muhammad

* **caliphate** office and government of the caliph, the religious and political leader of an Islamic state

* **amirate** office or realm of authority of an amir

* **parliament** representative national body having supreme legislative power within the state

* **missionary** person who works to convert nonbelievers to a particular faith

* **nationalism** feelings of loyalty and devotion to one's country and a commitment to its independence

* **coup** sudden, often violent, overthrow of a ruler or government

Resisting Innovation

During the late 1960s and 1970s, the popular Sufi brotherhoods came under the attack of a reformist movement calling for a return to the basics of Islam. One of the movement's leading figures was Abubakar Gumi, a former judge of northern Nigeria. He condemned common Sufi practices, such as the worship of saints and the consumption of alcohol at celebrations, and worked to transform Nigeria into an Islamic state.

His followers formed a network called Izala to spread Gumi's message, which they did through effective use of radio and television. Gumi believed that every Muslim should have access to the Qur'an, and he translated the scripture into the Hausa language. By the time of his death in 1992, Gumi's translation had sold millions of copies.

for neglecting the observance of *shari'ah*. Between 1804 and 1808, Usuman Dan Fodio and his followers defeated most of the Hausa rulers and claimed their land. Usuman Dan Fodio became head of a caliphate*, with its capital in the town of Sokoto, in the northwest corner of Nigeria. By the mid-1800s, the caliphate consisted of about 30 amirates* and encompassed most of the northern region of Nigeria as well as parts of present-day Niger and Cameroon. A strong military and commercial power, the caliphate dominated the region throughout the 1800s.

The Yoruba had established the kingdoms of Ife and Oyo in the southern and western portions of Nigeria, and the kingdom of Benin emerged to the east. By the time the Portuguese arrived in West Africa in the late 1400s, these areas were important centers of trade. For a time, the ruler of Benin enjoyed the financial benefits of commerce with the Portuguese. He exchanged peppers, ivory, and slaves for European goods, especially guns and gunpowder. The slave trade on the Nigerian coast flourished for about 300 years. During that period, the Dutch, French, and English established numerous trading posts in West Africa.

In 1807 the British parliament* declared the slave trade illegal. The government of Great Britain sent naval forces to the West African coast to enforce the ban, which severely weakened Nigeria's former slave states. As trade in palm oil, cocoa, and other products increased, British companies moved into the region. In 1861 Great Britain established a colony in the coastal city of Lagos. Meanwhile, Christian missionaries* arrived in large numbers to convert the peoples of southwestern Nigeria.

During the mid-1880s, European powers divided Africa into various spheres of influence. Great Britain took control of Nigeria but encountered much resistance throughout the country. After a long, bloody war, the British secured their hold on southern Nigeria in 1897. Three years later, Great Britain declared the establishment of a colonial government in Nigeria, and shortly thereafter, conquered the Sokoto caliphate.

Independence and Instability. Great Britain administered Nigeria through a policy of indirect rule. Tribal chiefs, working under the supervision of European officials, controlled local government. The British retained many traditional Nigerian political institutions and generally respected local customs. As a result of missionary activity, Christianity and Western education spread rapidly in southern Nigeria. By contrast, Muslim leaders in the north resisted missionary efforts, and consequently, northern Nigeria developed much more slowly. The growing gap between the two regions led to political strife.

Throughout the early 1900s, opposition to British rule and feelings of Nigerian nationalism* increased. Great Britain granted Nigeria its independence in 1960, and the country became a republic three years later. National elections were held in 1964. Centuries-old regional divisions (related to economic and educational inequalities and ethnicity) quickly revived in the new nation. In 1966 the army seized power in a coup* and installed an Ibo officer to head the government. Northern officers staged a counter-takeover later that year. In 1967 civil war erupted when several Ibo states in the east declared their independence to form the Republic of Biafra. Peace was finally restored in 1970, after the loss of an estimated one million lives.

Oil was discovered in Nigeria during the late 1960s, and within a short period, the country became the fifth largest petroleum producer in the world.

Rapid growth, however, led to serious problems, including shortages of food and other necessities, crowding in the ports, and demands for an equitable distribution of oil profits. A severe drought and rising unemployment among Nigeria's unemployed agricultural workers added to the economic problems. Unrest caused further military takeovers. Military rule finally ended in 1979, when a new constitution and elected officials replaced the former military government. Civilian rule did not last long, however, as more coups by the military occurred in 1983, 1985, and 1993.

The oil boom of the 1970s also stimulated an Islamic revivalist* movement. Muslim students called for a return to the Qur'an and hadith as a way to strengthen Muslim identity in the face of secular* challenges. They urged the government to follow *shari'ah* and to recognize Muslim foreign policy interests. During the 1980s and 1990s, some Muslims became more militant* in their demands, which led to riots and street fighting between Christians and Muslims in the northern provinces.

* **revivalist** calling for the return to traditional values or beliefs

* **secular** separate from religion in human life and society; connected to everyday life

* **militant** aggressively active in a cause

Tensions Remain High. In 1999 Nigeria made another transition from military to civilian rule with the election of Olusegun Obasanjo, former general and head of state, as president. Nigerians adopted a new constitution, giving the president and state governments greater authority.

Civil violence continued to plague Nigeria. Bloody conflicts over land and resources occurred in both the north and south. Ethnic conflicts erupted between the Yoruba and Hausa peoples. By the end of 2001, about 12 northern states had adopted *shari'ah* as their legal code, which led to terrible rioting between Muslims and Christians. Many Christians fled the areas under Islamic law, while Muslims moved into these same areas. (*See also* **Qadiriyah; Sokoto Caliphate; Tijani; West Africa.**)

North Africa

Islam spread rapidly across North Africa in the years following Muhammad's death. After conquering Egypt in 642, Arab armies swept westward into lands inhabited by Berber tribes. Arabs called this region, which encompasses present-day Libya, Tunisia, Algeria, and Morocco, the Bilad al-Maghrib, or "Land of Sunset." By 705 Muslim armies had incorporated the Maghrib into the Muslim empire. Within several centuries, the region's native population converted to Islam and adopted many elements of Arab culture.

A Winning Strategy. Home to one of the world's oldest civilizations, Egypt was part of the Byzantine* Empire during the 600s. Its diverse population included thriving Jewish and Coptic Christian communities. The fertile lands along the Nile River provided abundant agricultural products, and the city of Alexandria, on the Mediterranean coast, served as an important seaport.

* **Byzantine** refers to the Eastern Christian empire that was based in Constantinople

With the growth of Islam, Muslims turned their attention to economic and political ventures in lands beyond the Arabian Peninsula. During the 630s, they attacked Byzantine and Persian cities in the north. Although Muslim armies captured key cities in Syria and Palestine, they worried that the Byzantines could launch a counterattack on Syria from their base in Egypt. To pre-

North Africa

vent this from occurring, Arab forces invaded Egypt in 639. Amr ibn al-As, an Arab general who had visited Alexandria as a child and knew of Egypt's great wealth, led an army of about 4,000 men into Egyptian territory. By 642, with the help of military reinforcements, these troops defeated the Byzantines and forced them to withdraw from Egypt. The Byzantine navy launched an attack on Alexandria in 645, but Muslim forces quickly suppressed it.

The Arab conquerors built a new fortified town called Fustat (later Cairo) on the banks of the Nile. Its Amr ibn al-As mosque* served as a religious and administrative center. But for many years, Fustat was the only town in Egypt with an Arab majority, and Islam took root in the country slowly. In accordance with Islamic law, Muslim leaders extended legal protections to Jews and Christians living under their rule. The Arabs actually discouraged conversion to Islam, because they collected taxes (*jizyah*) from non-Muslims. When local people eventually converted, the governors required them to continue paying the tax.

Egypt's tax revenues and grain harvests enriched the Arab rulers. The strategic location of the province also facilitated the expansion of the Muslim empire. During the mid-600s, Egyptian and Syrian fleets launched a series of attacks on the islands of Rhodes, Cyprus, and Sicily. These combined forces defeated the Byzantine fleet in a decisive battle at the Mediterranean port of Phoenix in 655. From their base in Egypt, Arab troops also expanded westward into Berber territory and southward along the Nile into East Africa.

Early Victories. Around 1100 B.C.E.*, Phoenician traders established settlements around North Africa as they made their way to Spain in search of silver and tin. They founded the city of Carthage (in what is now Tunisia) in 814 B.C.E. The Romans conquered the area in 146 B.C.E., and by the early 500s C.E.*, North Africa was under Byzantine control.

Beginning in the 640s, Muslim armies raided the lands west of Egypt. They did not attempt to formally establish Arab rule, however, until the rise of the Umayyad caliphate* in the 660s. Umayyad rulers realized that their

* **mosque** Muslim place of worship

* **B.C.E.** before the Common Era, which refers to the same time period as B.C.

* **C.E.** Common Era, which refers to the same time period as A.D.

* **caliphate** office and government of the caliph, the religious and political leader of an Islamic state

empire would never be secure from Byzantine invasion unless they brought the Maghrib under their control. In 670 Arab army commander Uqbah ibn Nafi led his troops into Tunisia. He established the fortified city of al-Qayrawan, which became the first center of Arab rule in the region and replaced Fustat as the base for further expansion in North Africa.

Venturing west of Tunisia, Arab armies encountered resistance from the Berber population. Abu al-Muhajir Dinar al-Ansari, who had assumed command of the Arab forces, was able to persuade the Berber king Kusaylah to accept Islam. Kusaylah presided over a group of tribes living in the area between northeastern Algeria and central Morocco. Because the king accepted the authority of the caliphate, he remained in power, and a period of peaceful relations followed. But in 681, Uqbah resumed command, and within a year, Muslim armies swept westward across Algeria and into Morocco, imposing direct Arab rule throughout the region. Under Kusaylah's orders, a group of Berbers ambushed Uqbah on his way back to al-Qayrawan. He died near Biskra (in present-day Algeria), becoming a folk hero of the Muslim conquest of the Maghrib.

The Arabs had no intention of yielding control of the Maghrib to the Berbers. In an effort to crush the rebellion, they sent two armies from Egypt to the region. Fierce resistance lasted for several years, but Arab armies eventually reoccupied al-Qayrawan. Moreover, they captured Carthage from the Byzantines. As a result of these victories and successful naval expeditions in the Mediterranean Sea, the Byzantines were forced to cede their remaining positions on the coast of North Africa. In 705 the Maghrib became an official part of the Umayyad caliphate.

Restoring Order. Once conquered, the Berbers readily converted to Islam. They soon discovered, however, that Arab rulers had betrayed the ideals of the faith. Although Islam emphasizes the equality of believers and rejects the concept of privilege based on social class or race, the Arabs ruled as elites. They treated the Berbers as *mawali* (clients) instead of equals, paying Berber soldiers less than Arab warriors and requiring Berbers to supply slaves to the Arab ruling class.

Frustrated by this mistreatment from fellow Muslims, the Berbers used Islamic teachings to justify rebellion. War broke out in 740, when Berber fighters defeated the Arab army near Tangier, Morocco. By 742 the Berbers controlled all of Algeria and threatened al-Qayrawan. For the next two decades, fighting continued and power frequently changed hands. Finally, in 761, the Abbasids, the new rulers of the caliphate, sent an army to the Maghrib to restore order and authority. Eventually the region was divided into four separate Muslim states ruled by dynasties, only one of which accepted the authority of the caliphate.

Almoravids and Almohads. During the 1000s, Abd Allah Ibn Yasin, a Berber religious scholar from southern Morocco initiated a militant* Islamic movement among a group of tribes in Mauritania. He and his followers, known as Almoravids, invaded Morocco in 1056. Within the next 30 years, the Almoravids conquered most of the Maghrib, creating the first empire to unify the region under Berber Islamic rule. But their supremacy did not endure. In 1147 the Almohads, another group of Berber tribes, toppled the Almoravids. By the mid-1200s, however, the Almohad empire had begun to

* **militant** aggressively active in a cause

205

disintegrate and other Berber tribes seized power. The region remained politically unstable for the next several centuries. The Ottoman Turks extended their authority over Tripolitania, Cyrenaica, and Fezzan (the three historic regions that comprise modern-day Libya), the northern part of Algeria, and Tunisia. In the 1600s, the Alawi gained control in Morocco

Facing the Challenges. Like other parts of the Islamic world, North Africa was profoundly affected by European imperialism*. France invaded Algeria in 1830, and after several decades of warfare, French forces gained control of the country. Tunisia fell to the French during the 1880s. In the early 1900s, France and Spain divided Morocco into protectorates*. Italy conquered Tripolitania, Cyrenaica, and Fezzan in 1912. Resistance to colonial rule strengthened the Muslim identity of these regions but also led to conflict between traditionalists and those who called for liberal* reforms.

Since achieving independence in the 1950s and 1960s, the countries of North Africa have faced significant political and social challenges, including poverty, corruption, ethnic* conflicts, and civil war. Particularly in Algeria, civil war has been associated with the struggle for Islamic revival*. As North Africa enters the twenty-first century, it will forge increasingly important ties with the global Muslim community as well as the non-Muslim societies of the developing continent. (*See also* **Algeria; Egypt; Libya; Morocco; Tunisia.**)

Numerology

* **imperialism** extension of power and influence over another country or region

* **protectorate** country under the protection and control of a stronger nation

* **liberal** supporting greater participation in government for individuals; not bound by tradition

* **ethnic** relating to groups of people who share a common racial, national, tribal, religious, linguistic, or cultural background

* **revival** return to traditional values or beliefs

* **Qur'an** book of the holy scriptures of Islam

* **hadith** reports of the words and deeds of Muhammad (not in the Qur'an, but accepted as guides for Muslim behavior)

* **caliph** religious and political leader of an Islamic state

* **Sunni** refers to the largest branch of the Muslim community; the name derives from sunnah, the exemplary behavior of the Prophet Muhammad

The mystical science of interpreting numbers was immensely popular during the early Muslim period. Islamic numerology involves assigning each letter of the Arabic alphabet a number (*alif* = 1, and so forth), and either creating words based on certain numbers, or adding the values of the letters of key phrases. Muslim scholars also find significance in numbers that appear multiple times in the Qur'an*, the hadith*, and other sources of Islamic tradition. Numerology continues in the Muslim world in the present day, as evidenced by the recent attempt of a scholar to prove that the entire Qur'an is based on the number 19.

Early Islamic numerologists composed chronograms, or phrases in which certain letters spell out a date. After the death of Stalin in 1953, for example, a Turkish theologian formed the chronogram "Satan was cast into Hell," which contains the date of his death according to the Islamic calendar. In Iran, ancient buildings display lines of poetry or Qur'anic verses that spell out their dates of completion. Some books in the Muslim world received similar treatment. The title of the story *Bagh va bahar* (Garden and Spring), for example, shows that it was completed in 1803.

Islamic numerologists have noted that certain numbers occur frequently in divine texts and religious rituals. Muslims sometimes repeat actions and formulas three times in imitation of Muhammad, who often practiced threefold repetitions. Four serves as the number of universal order, and appears in the four righteous caliphs*, the four schools of Sunni* law, and the four wives that a Muslim man may legally marry. The number five marks the five Pillars of Islam, the five daily prayers, and in the *Panjtan*—the group composed of the holy persons Muhammad, Fatimah, Ali, Hasan, and Husayn. Muslims often write the names of these figures on hand-shaped amulets as a protective charm.

The number seven has special significance in the Muslim world. It occurs in many ceremonies that take place during the pilgrimage to Mecca, such as the *tawaf*, in which Muslims circle the Kaaba* seven times; the ritual of running seven times between the hills of Safa and Marwa; and the act of stoning Satan three times seven. The Islamic mystical path leads through seven steps or valleys. In Sufi* mythology, saints appear in groups of seven. Seven also plays an important role in the Ismaili* community, where the prophets, the prophetic cycles, and most aspects of life manifest themselves in sevens.

The numbers 14 and 28 also have significance, as does 40, which indicates patience, trial, and maturity. Dervishes* embark on 40-day seclusions, groups of 40 saints often appear in Islamic traditions, and some feasts continue for 40 days. After childbirth, women remain impure for 40 days, and the first memorial after a death occurs on the 40th day. In folktales, one might read about the 40 thieves, or women who give birth to 40 children at once. Proverbs depict 40 as the age at which one reaches maturity.

Muslims use specific number patterns in the recitation of certain phrases and formulas. According to Islamic tradition, God loves odd numbers, being a single entity himself. Muslim prayer beads therefore come in odd numbers, and the repetition of formulas 33 or 99 times is considered beneficial. Dervishes sometimes utter divine names for as many times as the number they represent. Allah, for example, requires 66 repetitions. (*See also* **Magic and Sorcery; Mathematics.**)

* **Kaaba** literally "House of God;" Islamic shrine in Mecca

* **Sufi** refers to Sufism, which seeks to develop spirituality through discipline of the mind and body

* **Ismaili** refers to a major branch of Shi'i Islam

* **dervish** Sufi mystic; member of an order that uses music and dance to enter a trancelike state

Ottoman Empire

Calling themselves Osmanlis, after tribal chieftain Osman I, the Ottomans were Turks from Central Asia. They created a vast empire that encompassed southeastern Europe to northern Hungary, the Middle East to Iran, and most of the North African coast. They rivaled European nations, established a formidable army, and had a religious diversity greater than that of previous Islamic empires.

Conquering Lands in Europe and the Middle East

From the 1300s to around 1600, Ottoman rulers expanded their territory through a series of conquests. Osman I and his followers started out as nomadic *ghazis* (raiders) fighting on behalf of Islam against the Byzantine* Empire. They gained control of the Christian lands (such as Greece, Romania, Bulgaria, and Bosnia) and encouraged large numbers of Turkish warriors to populate their new empire. The Ottomans left Christian rulers in control as long as they accepted the dominance of the Ottomans and provided them with funding and troops. Alarmed by the success of the Turkish warriors, the Europeans launched a series of failed Crusades against them.

* **Byzantine** refers to the Eastern Christian empire that was based in Constantinople

Ottoman Empire

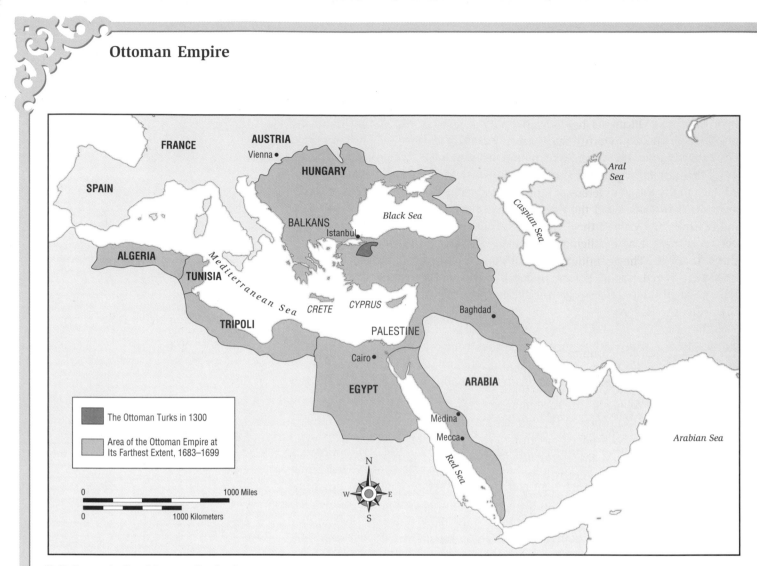

At its peak, the Ottoman Empire included large areas of the Middle East and extended into Europe and Africa. Its expansion came to an end in 1683 when the Ottomans failed to take the Austro-Hungarian capital of Vienna. They soon lost lands in Hungary and southeastern Europe.

* **Spanish Inquisition** investigation carried out by the Catholic Church during the Middle Ages to discover and punish heresy

* **dynasty** succession of rulers from the same family or group

The Ottomans, however, turned their attention to Islamic territories in the late 1300s. Influenced by Christian princesses and court advisers, the sultan Bayezid I began a new policy of seizing Muslim lands. Turkish soldiers refused to participate in these attacks, leaving armies of Christians to conquer new regions. The Mongol conqueror Tamerlane (Timur Lang) viewed Bayezid's aggression as a threat and captured the sultan, ravaging his lands before resuming his invasion of India. Bayezid's son Mehmed I restored the empire in the early 1400s, establishing more centralized Ottoman rule in conquered lands.

In 1453 Mehmed II completed the major task of conquering Constantinople, the former Byzantine capital. Seeking to restore the city to its former splendor, Mehmed rebuilt it and forced his subjects to move there to help the city prosper. He then repopulated the capital with people of all religions. Mehmed appealed to European Jews, who had suffered religious persecution under the Christians. He urged them to immigrate to the Ottoman lands, promising peace and economic prosperity. Thousands of Jews flooded into the Ottoman Empire, many arriving before the Spanish Inquisition*.

During the 1500s, various sultans expanded the empire. They pushed into the Middle East, conquering Syria, Egypt, and the Arabian Peninsula. They also conquered Hungary and laid siege to Vienna, which they did not win, although border *ghazis* carried out raids against the Europeans during the next two centuries. The Ottomans formed an alliance with France against the Hapsburgs, the Viennese dynasty* that controlled much of Europe. By the 1600s, the Ottomans had seized Romania and Transylvania. They had also established a powerful navy, gaining control of key shipping routes.

Ottoman success depended on many factors—the use of sophisticated weapons, a highly organized army staffed with slaves, a religious tolerance that enabled them to rule different groups without provoking discontent, and a government that encouraged the development of agriculture, trade, and the arts. Many Christians viewed their defeat as a sign from God and converted to Islam, accepting it as a religion that values Jesus as a prophet and promotes Christian ideals. They continued to observe certain aspects of Christianity, however, such as celebrating Easter, performing baptism, and venerating saints.

Life Under Ottoman Rule

The Ottomans had a complex society with a lavish court and a strong army. In Istanbul (the former Constantinople), the Topkapi Palace held chambers for the sultan, harem*, and staff members; schools for pages and slaves; military, civil, and religious offices; kitchens; and gardens. The Ottoman military had no rival in Europe or the Middle East, with an elite corps of ground troops (Janissaries) composed of Christians drafted from the Balkans. Under what became known as the *devsirme* system of recruitment, the most promising young men received a palace education and joined the ruling class, serving as pages or officers in the army. The others worked as apprentices to Turkish officers, learning military techniques that surpassed those used by any army in the Middle East or Europe.

Social Structure. Like other empires in the Middle East, the Ottomans maintained a small ruling class and a large subject population organized into self-governing communities according to religion (*millets*) or guilds (*esnaf*). People could join the ruling class only if they demonstrated exceptional loyalty to the sultan, accepted Islam, and practiced the Ottoman way, a complex system of behavior that included the use of the Ottoman language (a dialect derived from Turkish, Arabic, and Persian). Those who failed to meet these requirements served as subjects, even if of royal lineage.

The ruling class consisted of two groups—those of Turkish or Muslim heritage and the *devsirme* class of Christian converts. Christians tended to favor expansion into Muslim territories, while Turks and Muslims urged the sultans to invade Europe. Sultans typically tried to establish a balance between the two groups, giving them equal positions and pay. Members of the ruling class fulfilled specific functions. Some served as advisers to sultans. Others oversaw the treasury, collected taxes, maintained security, led prayers, and served as judges. All members practiced a form of Sunni* Islam that contained elements of Sufism* and Christianity.

Sultans received their authority through their family line, but Turkish custom did not specify who would assume power if more than one male heir survived the sultan. This led to conflicts between brothers, often resolved by tests of military strength, though sometimes by murder. Some sultans favored one son over the others, preparing him for the position by giving him an important administrative or military post. After 1595, however, all of the sultan's male relatives had to live inside the harem, and conspiracies often played a role in the selection of successors.

* **harem** room in a Muslim household where the women live; also, female members of a Muslim household

See color plate 3, vol. 3.

* **Sunni** refers to the largest branch of the Muslim community; the name derives from sunnah, the exemplary behavior of the Prophet Muhammad

* **Sufism** Islamic mysticism, which seeks to develop spirituality through discipline of the mind and body

Sufis and the Empire

Various Sufi orders flourished in the Ottoman Empire. The most influential was the Bektashi brotherhood, which spread over Anatolia and the Balkans in the 1400s. The Bektashiyah performed ritual dancing and wine drinking and adopted certain Christian practices, such as confession of sins.

The Mevlevi (Mawlawiyah in Arabic) thrived in urban areas. The order is often referred to as the Whirling Dervishes, after the rigorous dancing they perform as a meditation ritual.

Wandering Sufi teachers helped the ruling class by spreading Islam, settling disputes, and protecting travelers. Some, however, led revolts against the state. Viewing the Sufis as a threat, sultans worked to integrate them into Ottoman society. The hired them to provide protection for soldiers and sultans and gave them funding for their schools and communities.

* **illuminate** refers to the art of decorating the pages of a manuscript

* **calligraphy** artistic, stylized handwriting or lettering

Ottoman rulers referred to the subject class as the *reaya* (protected flock). Christian, Jewish, and Muslim groups organized themselves into *millets*, each with its own customs and language. Villages consisted entirely of members of one *millet*, while larger towns and cities had different *millet* quarters—gated communities surrounded by walls. *Millet* communities typically centered around a mosque or temple, and religious leaders supervised the administration of schools, homes for the aged, courts, kitchens for the poor, maintenance of public facilities, and police. Leaders of different *millets* gathered together in times of emergency or to prepare for certain festivities but typically worked independently of one another. The sultans had introduced the *millet* system in the hope of preventing the religious conflict that plagued other societies. They achieved a high degree of success but could not always suppress local conflicts between religious communities.

Guilds mainly existed in urban areas, where merchants, craftspeople, entertainers, and even prostitutes banded with their colleagues to manage financial and administrative matters. Guilds settled disputes, collected money for charity, sent members on military campaigns, and organized holiday celebrations. Some had initiation ceremonies involving pilgrimages, prayers, and lectures on sobriety and other virtues. Like *millets*, guilds typically operated along religious lines.

Arts and Culture. Literature, visual arts, and music thrived under Ottoman rule, influenced by Turkish, Arab, Persian, Byzantine, and European culture. In the mid-1400s, Mehmed II supported poets and painters from all over the empire. Later sultans concentrated especially on Arabic and Persian poetry. Poets wrote of military battles, love, and their personal observations and emotions. Prose writers composed histories praising the Ottoman dynasty and recording daily life in the court and the military. World histories, travelogues, and geographical treatises also gained popularity during the Ottoman Empire.

Illumination* became a highly developed art form under Ottoman rule. Mehmed II opened a studio in the royal court, where calligraphers*, painters, illuminators, and bookbinders worked to create illustrated texts and designs for ceramics, carpets, and wood and metalwork. Persian fables and love stories served as the earliest illustrated works, and Persian styles dominated in the 1400s. By the end of the 1500s, however, Ottoman artists had become known for their distinctive illuminations of histories exalting the Ottoman state and the sultan.

In rural areas, wandering poet-musicians were the primary entertainers. In Anatolia (central Turkey), for example, minstrels spread Turkish folk culture with their songs. They entertained people at fairs, participated in contests, sang to soldiers, and celebrated Turkish battles and virtues. Shadow puppet plays were a popular form of entertainment in the countryside.

Decline of the Ottomans

During the 1600s, power slowly slipped from the central government to the provinces of the Ottoman Empire. The Ottoman sultans were less effective as rulers. Their harem upbringing had deprived them of experience in military or state affairs, and rendered them unfit for the task of maintaining the empire. Because it had ceased to expand, the Ottoman Empire lost a major source of revenue—the wealth of other nations. To boost the faltering economy, the ruling class imposed heavy taxes on the population. The army began to break down as poorly paid soldiers seized lands and kept the taxes for themselves. Work shortages led to widespread hunger and poverty, and masses of people moved to the cities to find jobs.

Efforts at Reform. Members of the ruling class made little effort to improve conditions, some even profiting from the chaos among their subjects. Sensing Ottoman weakness, Europeans moved to conquer Ottoman lands in Hungary and southeastern Europe. The Ottomans scrambled to strengthen their empire, hoping to restore it to its former power. They executed corrupt officials and instituted reforms in education and the military. Some wanted to modernize the state, looking to the gains that Europe had made during the Industrial Revolution. Others believed in the superiority of Ottoman practices and did not seek change until Russia and Austria took over some Ottoman lands in the 1700s. Alarmed by these developments, the ruling class invited Europeans to help them train a new army. But the military reforms were resisted by the old military establishment and had little impact.

During the 1800s, Europeans became more powerful and began to intervene in Ottoman affairs. They encouraged Christians to rise up against the Ottoman Turks and secure their independence. Alarmed by these developments, the Ottomans began the task of replacing old institutions with new ones, largely based on Western models. The Ottomans centralized their government, weakening the *millets* and guilds but not entirely replacing them. They organized the government into executive, legislative, and judicial branches, with a prime minister and an elected parliament. They also reformed their legal codes, adopting European models and court systems while retaining *shari'ah** principles.

New political groups also arose within the empire. A group called the Young Ottomans pushed for reforms within the ruling class, including the use of a simpler official language that would create a sense of equality between Ottoman rulers and their subjects. They believed in citizens' rights and held that Islam and modernization could work together compatibly. The Young Ottomans took over the government briefly during the 1870s, but the sultan they placed in power turned against them and implemented strict policies favoring the ruling class. Other groups formed, among them the Young Turks, organized by Young Ottomans living in exile in Paris, and the Fatherland Society, headed by Mustafa Kemal (later Atatürk), the future president of Turkey. These groups both promoted European-style reforms and a stronger central government.

Clashes with Europe. Reforms transformed the Ottoman Empire from a disorganized series of states into a relatively efficient, modern regime whose government treated its subjects far more humanely than those of many Western nations. Europeans, however, continued to threaten Ottoman authority, labeling the Ottoman Empire the "sick man of Europe." Backed by Russia and Austria, Christian nationalist* groups created movements and new states that fragmented the Ottoman Empire. The Ottomans tried to win them over by officially recognizing the equality of all religious groups but reacted with violence when the Christians failed to end their attacks. Such clashes continued throughout the last 50 years of the empire. At the same time, thousands of

* ***shari'ah*** Islamic law as established in the Qur'an and sunnah, the exemplary behavior of the Prophet Muhammad

* **nationalist** one who advocates loyalty and devotion to his or her country and its independence

* **liberal** supporting greater participation in government for individuals; not bound by tradition

* **secularize** to separate religion from other aspects of human life and society

* **mandate** order issued by the League of Nations authorizing a member nation to establish a responsible government in a conquered territory

* **protectorate** country under the protection and control of a stronger nation

Jews fleeing persecution in Russia and central Europe settled in Ottoman lands, where they made significant contributions to agriculture, industry, and trade.

During the early 1900s, the Ottomans continued to make reforms. They could not eliminate Christian opposition, however, and the Ottoman states in southeastern Europe rose up in the First Balkan War (1912), gaining their independence. Muslims and Jews from these regions flooded into Istanbul. The Young Turks seized control over the government, making liberal* reforms and regaining Balkan lands a part of their program. The Young Turks helped secularize* the legal system and provided for the education of women. They also allied the Ottoman Empire with Germany and Austria during World War I (1914–1918). When the Germans lost the war, the empire disintegrated and disbanded completely in 1922. Britain, France, Italy, and Russia carved the Ottoman state up into mandates* and protectorates* to divide amongst themselves.

Mustafa Kemal, however, refused to let the Europeans have all of the Ottoman territories. In 1918 he led the Turkish War for Independence, chasing the Europeans from the former seat of the Ottoman Empire. He took the name Atatürk (meaning "father of the Turks") and created the Turkish Republic, of which he became president until his death in 1938. Out of all the countries in the Middle East, Turkey alone emerged as an independent nation at the end of World War I. (*See also* **Atatürk, Mustafa Kemal; Mawlawiyah; Sufism; Turkey.**)

Glossary

ablution ritual washing that Muslims must perform before prayer

adhan Muslim call to prayer that occurs five times daily

Allah God

Allahu akbar "God is most great," beginning of Muslim call to prayer

amir military commander, governor, or prince; **amirate** office or realm of authority of an amir

aqidah Islamic creed, which consists of the five articles of faith: belief in God, angels, prophets, scriptures, and the Last Day (or Day of Judgment)

arabesque artistic style that uses foliage, fruit, or figural outlines to produce an intricate pattern of interlaced lines

ayatollah highest-ranking legal scholar among some Shi'i Muslims

burqa traditional garment worn by some Muslim women that covers the whole body, leaving only the eyes visible

caliph religious and political leader of an Islamic state; **caliphate** office and government of the caliph

chador veil worn by Muslim women in public that covers the whole body except the face, hands, and feet

Crusades during the Middle Ages, the holy wars declared by the pope against non-Christians, mostly Muslims

dar al-harb "Land of War;" place where inhabitants do not practice Islam

dar al-Islam "Land of Islam;" place where Islamic law is observed

da'wah call to Islam; refers to efforts to convert people to Islam or to draw Muslim individuals and communities back to God

dawlah Arabic for "state"

dhikr Sufi chant for the remembrance of God

dhimmi non-Muslims under the protection of Muslim law; typically applied to People of the Book, particularly Christians and Jews

Dhu al-Hijjah last month of the Islamic calendar and month of pilgrimage to Mecca

Eid al-Adha Feast of the Sacrifice, celebration commemorating Abraham's willingness to sacrifice his son to God; comes at the end of the pilgrimage to Mecca

Eid al-Fitr Feast of the Breaking of the Fast of Ramadan; celebration that ends the holy month of Ramadan

fatwa opinion issued by an Islamic legal scholar in response to a question posed by an individual or a court of law

fiqh human efforts to understand and codify divine law

Five Pillars of Islam five acts required of all Muslims: pledging one's faith, praying five times daily, putting aside a portion of one's wealth for the poor, fasting during the month of Ramadan, and making a pilgrimage to the holy city of Mecca

hadith reports of the words and deeds of Muhammad (not in the Qur'an, but accepted as guides for Muslim behavior)

hajj pilgrimage to Mecca that Muslims who are physically and financially able are required to make once in their lifetime

halal permissible; acceptable under Islamic law

haram illegal; prohibited by Islamic law

harem room in a Muslim household where the women live; also, female members of a Muslim household

heresy belief that is contrary to established religious doctrine or practice

hijab refers to the traditional head, face, or body covering worn by Muslim women

Hijrah celebrated emigration of Muhammad from Mecca in 622, which marks the first year of the Islamic calendar

hudud punishments prescribed by the Qur'an for specific crimes

ijma consensus of scholars on issues of law

ijtihad use of independent reasoning, rather than precedent, to interpret Islamic law

imam spiritual-political leader in Shi'i Islam, one who is regarded as directly descended from Muhammad; also, one who leads prayers

iman in Arabic, "faith"

213

Glossary

insha'a Allah Arabic phrase meaning "if God wills"

intifadah Arabic word for "uprising"

jami congregational mosque used specifically for Friday prayers

jihad literally "striving"; war in defense of Islam

jinn spirit beings

jizyah tax imposed by Muslims on non-Muslims

kaffiyah head cloth worn by some Muslim men

kalam in Arabic, "speech"; refers to the field of theology

kalam Allah in Arabic, "God's speech"; refers to the Qur'an

khan honorific title used for leaders in certain Islamic societies

khutbah sermon delivered at Friday prayers

kohl black powder applied to the edge of the eyelids

Kufic angular style of Arabic calligraphy

kuttab Islamic elementary school

loya jirga tribal council in Afghanistan

madhhab school of legal thought

madrasah religious college or university; also religious school for young students

Mahdi "divinely guided" imam who Muslims believe will return to earth to restore the faith and establish a just government

marabout African term for Sufi leader

mashhad gravesite of a martyr

masjid mosque; place for Muslim communal affairs

Mawlid an-Nabi Muhammad's birthday

mihrab niche, or recess, in a mosque indicating the direction of Mecca

minaret tall, slender tower of a Muslim mosque from which the faithful are called to prayer

minbar mosque platform used for the Friday sermon

monotheism belief that there is only one God

mosque Muslim place of worship

muezzin person who calls the faithful to prayer

mufti scholar who interprets Islamic law and issues fatwas

Muharram first month of the Islamic calendar

mujahidin literally "warriors of God"; refers to Muslim fighters in proclaimed jihads, such as the war against the Soviet invasion of Afghanistan

mujtahid legal scholar who interprets law according to independent reasoning (ijtihad)

mullah Muslim cleric or learned man

musalla informal areas and open air spaces for prayer

mutah a type of marriage contract allowing temporary marriage; prohibited in Sunni Islam.

mystic one who seeks to experience spiritual enlightenment and truth through various physical and spiritual disciplines

nabi "one who announces"; Arabic term for prophet

Pan-Islamic refers to the movement to unify all Islamic peoples

People of the Book for Muslims, religious group with written scriptures, mainly Christians and Jews

polygyny practice of having more than one wife at the same time

polytheism belief in more than one god

pre-Islamic refers to the Arabian peninsula or to the Arabic language before the founding of Islam in the early 600s

prophet one who announces divinely inspired revelations

qadi judge who administers Islamic law

qibla direction of prayer indicated by the mihrab (niche) in the wall of a mosque

qiyas type of reasoning that involves the use of analogy, or comparison based on resemblance

Qur'an book of the holy scriptures of Islam

Ramadan ninth month of the Islamic calendar and holy month during which Muslim adults fast and abstain from sex from sunrise to sunset

revelation message from God to humans transmitted through a prophet

sadaqah voluntary charitable offering of an amount beyond what is required; may enable a Muslim to atone for sins or other offenses

salat prayer; one of the five Pillars of Islam

sawm fasting; one of the five Pillars of Islam

sayyid honorific title equivalent to lord or sir; descendant of Muhammad

scripture sacred writings believed to contain revelations from God

shah king (Persian); ruler of Iran

shahadah profession of faith: "There is no God but God (Allah), and Muhammad is the messenger of God"

shahid martyr, or one who dies for his or her religious beliefs

shari'ah Islamic law as established in the Qur'an and sunnah, the exemplary behavior of the Prophet Muhammad

sharif nobleman; descendant of Muhammad

shaykh tribal elder; also, title of honor given to those who are considered especially learned and pious

Shi'ism branch of Islam that believes that Muhammad chose Ali ibn Abi Talib and his descendants as the spiritual-political leaders of the Muslim community

shura consultation; advisory council to the head of state

Sufism Islamic mysticism, which seeks to develop spirituality through discipline of the mind and body

sultan political and military ruler of a Muslim dynasty or state

sunnah literally "the trodden path"; Islamic customs based on the exemplary behavior of Muhammad

Sunni refers to the largest branch of the Muslim community; the name derives from sunnah, the exemplary behavior of the Prophet Muhammad

surah chapter of the Qur'an

talaq type of divorce in which a husband repeats the words "I divorce you" three times

taqiyah act of concealing one's true religious beliefs in order to prevent death or injury to oneself or other Muslims

taqwa piety, virtue, and awareness or reverence of God

tariqah path followed by Sufis to attain oneness with God; Sufi brotherhood

tawhid refers to the oneness or unity of God; monotheism

tazir punishments not required in the Qur'an but administered by an Islamic judge

ta'ziyah Shi'i religious drama about the martyrdom of Husayn ibn Ali, Muhammad's grandson

ulama religious scholars

ummah Muslim community

vizier Muslim minister of state

waqf donation of property for charitable causes

zakat charity; one of the five Pillars of Islam

zawiyah Sufi center that serves as a place of worship and a welfare institution

ziyadah in a mosque, the wall that holds the facilities for ablution, or ritual cleansing

People and Places

Abbas I (ruled 1588–1629) Shah of Safavid empire of Iran

Abbasids (750–1258) Dynasty that controlled the caliphate after the Umayyads; established capital in Baghdad in 762

Abd al-Qadir (1808–1883) Sufi poet; led uprising in Algeria against French 1832–1847

Abduh, Muhammad (1849–1905) Egyptian scholar and architect of Islamic modernism

Abraham Patriarch of Judaism, Christianity, and Islam; father of Ismail

Abu Bakr (ca. 573–634) Companion and follower of Muhammad; served as the first caliph from 632 to 634

Abu Hanifah (699–767) Legal scholar who founded the Hanafi, one of the four Sunni schools of law

Afghani, Jamal al-Din al- (1838–1897) Political activist and writer, best known for his role in the Pan-Islamic movement

Ahmad Khan, Sayyid (1817–1898) Islamic writer and reformer in British India who sought to modernize the interpretation of Islam

A'ishah (614–678) Muhammad's third and youngest wife; daughter of Abu Bakr, one of the Prophet's most important supporters

Akbar, Jalaludin Muhammad (1542–1605) Mughal emperor who expanded the realm and improved the efficiency of government

Alawi Minority Shi'i sect in Syria and Turkey

Ali ibn Abi Talib (ca. 597–661) Cousin and son-in-law of Muhammad who became the fourth caliph; conflicts over succession and Ali's assassination ultimately led to the division of Muslims into Shi'is and Sunnis

Andalusia Southernmost region of Spain controlled by Muslims from 711 to 1492

Arafat, Yasir (1929–) Founder and leader of Palestinian Liberation Organization

Ash'ari, Abu al-Hasan al- (ca. 873–935) Theologian who founded the Ash'ari school of Islamic thought

Assad, Hafiz al- (1928–2000) President of Syria from 1971 to 2000

Atatürk, Mustafa Kemal (1881–1938) Revolutionary leader and founder of modern Turkish state

Banna, Hasan al- (1906–1949) Founder of Muslim Brotherhood and Egyptian reformer

Bedouins Desert nomads, especially in North Africa, Syria, and Arabia

Beg, Toghril (died 1063) Early Seljuk leader who conquered Iran and Iraq

Berbers North-African ethnic group, primarily Muslim

Bin Laden, Osama (1957–) Islamic militant from Saudi Arabia; head of the al-Qaeda network

Byzantine Empire (330–1453) Eastern Christian Empire based in Constantinople

Caucacus Region of southern Europe between Black and Caspian Seas

Cordoba Caliphate in Muslim Spain from 756 to 1016; also important city and cultural center

Dan Fodio, Usuman (ca. 1754–1817) Founder and ruler of Sokoto caliphate in Nigeria

Druze Offshoot of Shi'i Islam, found mainly in Lebanon and Syria

Elijah Muhammad (1897–1975) Longtime leader of the Nation of Islam, militant religious group promoting the development of African American society

Farabi, Abu Nasr al- (870–950) Arab scholar, regarded as father of Islamic political science

Farrakhan, Louis (1933–) Leader of Nation of Islam, militant religious group promoting the development of African American society

Fatimah (ca. 605–633) Daughter of Muhammad and wife of Ali ibn Abi Talib

Fatimid Dynasty (909–1171) Family claiming descent from Fatimah that established caliphate that controlled North Africa; extended rule as far as Syria

Gasprinskii, Ismail Bey (1851–1914) Reformer who worked to help Turkish Muslims living under Russian rule in Crimea

Ghazali, Abu Hamid al- (1058–1111) Influential Muslim thinker who studied many areas of religion and science

People and Places

Ghazali, Zaynab al- (1917–) Founder of Muslim Women's Association

Gulf States Refers to four nations on the Persian Gulf—Bahrain, Kuwait, Qatar, and the United Arab Emirates

Hagar In Bible, wife of Abraham and mother of Ismail; revered by Muslims

Harun al-Rashid (764–809) Fifth and most famous Abbasid caliph; ruled from 786 to 809

Holy Land Refers to ancient Palestine, land containing sacred sites of Muslims, Jews, and Christians

Husayn ibn Ali (626–680) Grandson of Muhammad and third Shi'i imam; led unsuccessful revolt against caliphs and died in battle; revered as a martyr by Shi'is

Hussein, Saddam (1937–) President of Iraq from 1979 to 2003

Ibn Abd al-Wahhab, Muhammad (1703–1791) Saudi Arabian reformer who founded Wahhabi movement

Ibn al-Arabi (1165–1240) Sufi mystic and poet in Muslim Spain

Ibn Battutah (died ca. 1368) Arab who traveled widely throughout the Muslim world, including West Africa and Southeast Asia

Ibn Hanbal (died 855) Muslim jurist and theologian; founded the Hanbali school, one of the major Sunni schools of law

Ibn Khaldun (1332–1406) Scholar who wrote on society and politics in the Arab world; regarded by some as the founder of sociology

Ibn Rushd (1126–1198) Philosopher and physician in Muslim Spain, known as Averroës in West; gained recognition for his writings on Aristotle

Ibn Sina (980–1037) Philosopher and physician, known as Avicenna in West; wrote the influential *Canon of Medicine*

Ibn Taymiyah (1263–1328) Hanbali jurist and reformer who advocated *ijtihad*; still influential among Islamic reformers

Iqbal, Muhammad (1876–1938) Poet and philosopher from India who advocated the creation of a separate state for Muslims

Ismail Son of Abraham and Hagar, called Ishmael in the Bible; considered the father of the Arab nation

Jafar al-Sadiq (died ca. 756) Shi'i imam who founded the Jafari school of Islamic law

Jinnah, Mohammad Ali (1876–1948) Indian who led Muslim League at time of partition; revered as a founder of Pakistan

Kaaba Shrine in Mecca considered the most sacred place in the Muslim world

Karbala Iraqi city containing the tomb of Husayn ibn Ali; important shrine and pilgrimage site for Shi'i Muslims

Kashmir Contested territory between India and Pakistan

Khadija (565–ca. 623) Muhammad's first wife and supporter

Khayyam, Umar (1038–1131) Persian mathematician and poet

Khomeini, Ruhollah al-Musavi (1902–1989) Leader of Iran's Islamic Revolution in 1979 and the country's political and religious leader during the 1980s

Maghrib, al- coastal region of North African countries of Tunisia, Algeria, Morocco, and Libya

Malcolm X (1925–1965) Controversial African American leader, assassinated by opponents in the Nation of Islam

Malik ibn Anas (ca. 713–795) Scholar who founded the Maliki school, one of the main Sunni schools of Islamic law

Mamluk State (1250–1517) Islamic state based in Egypt, ruled by slave soldiers; controlled Syria and parts of Asia Minor and Arabia

Maryam Jameelah (1934–) American convert to Islam who became a prominent critic of Western society

Mawdudi, Sayyid Abu al-Ala (1903–1979) Founder of Jamaat-i Islami revivalist movement calling for return to traditional Islamic values

Mecca Birthplace of Muhammad and site of Kaaba; most important pilgrimage destination for Muslims

Mehmed II (1432–1461) Ottoman sultan who conquered Byzantine Constantinople in 1453

Mongols Nomadic people from Central Asia who established an empire in the early 1200s that lasted about 200 years; at its peak the empire included much of Asia, Russia, eastern Europe and Middle East

Mughal Empire (1520s–1857) Muslim empire on subcontinent of India founded by Babur; British deposed the last emperor

Moors North African Muslims who conquered Spain

Muhammad (ca. 570–632) The Prophet of Islam, viewed by Muslims as God's messenger

Mulla Sadra (1571–ca. 1640) Influential Persian philosopher

Nasser, Gamal Abdel(1918–1970) Nationalist leader who seized control of Egypt in 1952 and became its president in 1956

Ottoman Empire Large Turkish empire established in the early 1300s that eventually controlled much of the Balkans and the Middle East; disintegrated after World War I (1914–1918)

Pahlavi, Muhammad Reza Shah (1919–1980) Last monarch of Iran, overthrown by Islamic Revolution in 1979

Palestine Historic region on the eastern Mediterranean that includes modern Israel and western Jordan, as well as the city of Jerusalem

Persia name foreigners used for Iran until 1935

Qaddafi, Mu'ammar al- (1942–) Ruler of Libya since 1969

Qom Site of the tomb of Fatimah and major Shi'i pilgrimage site in Iran

Qutb, Sayyid (1906–1966) Influential thinker associated with Muslim Brotherhood; regarded by many as founder of militant Islamic politics

Rashid Rida, Muhammad (1865–1935) Syrian reformer who advocated the establishment of a modern Islamic state based on a reinterpretation of Islamic law

Rumi (died 1273) Persian religious poet; his followers founded the Sufi order known as Mawlawiyah (also known as Mevlevis and Whirling Dervishes) that incorporates dance in its rituals

Rushdie, Salman (1947–) British-Indian author who wrote The Satanic Verses (1988), considered by many Muslims to be blasphemous

Sadat, Anwar el- (1918–1981) President of Egypt 1970–1981; assassinated by Islamic extremists

Sadr, Musa al- (1928–ca. 1978) Iranian cleric who led Shi'i movement in Lebanon; disappeared in 1978

Safavid Dynasty (1501–1722) Ruled Iran and parts of present-day Iraq; converted country to Shi'ism and founded the city of Isfahan

Saladin (1137–1193) Muslim leader who defeated the Fatimids in Egypt in 1171 and founded the Ayyubid dynasty; defeated the Crusaders, ending Christian occupation of Jerusalem

Seljuks (1038–1193) Turkic dynasty that ruled Iran and Iraq and parts of Central Asia; established a sultanate in Turkey that lasted until the Mongols invaded in 1243

Shafi'i, Muhammad (767–820) Jurist who founded the Shafi'i school, one of the major Sunni schools of Islamic law

Sokoto Caliphate Islamic state in Nigeria, founded in the 1800s by Usuman Dan Fodio

Suleyman (1520–1566) Sultan during the peak of the Ottoman Empire; called the Lawgiver in the East and the Magnificent in the West

Tamerlane (Timur Lang) (1336–1405) Mongol chieftain who came to power in Iran and conquered large areas of the Islamic world, including Anatolia and parts of Syria and India

Turabi, Hasan al- (1932–) Sudanese political leader who led efforts to form an Islamic state in Sudan

Umar ibn al-Khattab (ruled 634–644) Close friend of Muhammad and the second caliph; began expansion of Islamic empire

Umayyad Dynasty (661–750) Ruled Islamic caliphate; expanded the empire westward through North Africa and into Spain

Warith Deen Muhammad (1933–) Son of Nation of Islam leader Elijah Muhammad; assumed leadership of the organization in 1975

Zaynab (627–684) Granddaughter of Muhammad and daughter of Ali and Fatimah